ENGLAND UNDER GEORGE I

ENGLAND UNDER GEORGE I

THE BEGINNINGS

OF THE

HANOVERIAN DYNASTY

BY

WOLFGANG MICHAEL

PH.D. (BERLIN); HON. LL.D. (EDIN.); PROFESSOR EMERITUS OF WEST
EUROPEAN HISTORY, UNIVERSITY OF FREIBURG (BREISGAU)

★

TRANSLATED AND ADAPTED FROM THE GERMAN

GREENWOOD PRESS, PUBLISHERS
WESTPORT, CONNECTICUT

Library of Congress Cataloging in Publication Data

Michael, Wolfgang, 1862-1945.
    The beginnings of the Hanoverian dynasty.

    (England under George I ; [1])
    Abridged translation of v. 1 of: Englische Geschichte
im achtzhnten Jahrhundert.
    Reprint. Originally published: London : Macmillan,
1936. (Studies in modern history)
    Includes bibliographical references and index.
    1. Great Britain--History--George I, 1714-1727.
I. Title. II. Series: Michael, Wolfgang, 1862-1945.
Englische Geschichte im achtzehnten Jahrhundert. Band
1-2. English ; [1] III. Series: Studies in modern
history (Macmillan & Co.)
[DA499.M513 1981]   941.07'1   81-6495

ISBN 0-313-23040-4 (lib. bdg.)   AACR2

Copyright

Reprinted with the permission of The Macmillan Press Ltd.

Reprinted in 1981 by Greenwood Press
A division of Congressional Information Service, Inc.
88 Post Road West, Westport, Connecticut 06881

Printed in the United States of America

10 9 8 7 6 5 4 3 2 1

PREFATORY NOTE

THE first volume of Professor Michael's work on George I appeared in German in 1896, and reached its second edition in 1921. It deals with the relations between the Electoral Court and Queen Anne during the last years of her reign, with the establishment of the Hanoverian dynasty, the Jacobite Rising of 1715, and with British foreign policy 1714-18. The second volume, published in 1920, and the third, published in 1934, carry on the narrative till the death of George I. All the three volumes will be translated into English, and each will be published as a self-contained book.

L. B. N.

CONTENTS

ERRATA

P. 67, line 11 from the bottom. *For* " Lord Powlett" *read* " Lord Poulett ".

P. 108, line 7 from the bottom. *For* " the Earls of Dorset and Middlesex " *read* " the Earl of Dorset and Middlesex ". .

P. 192, line 12 from the bottom. *For* " 1707 " *read* " 1708 ".

P. 247, line 5 from the bottom. *For* " King of Savoy " *read* " Duke of Savoy ".

CHAPTER I

THE FOUNDATIONS OF THE HANOVERIAN SUCCESSION

IT was clear, even in the lifetime of William III, that the Protestant branch of the Stuarts was approaching extinction, and that, to secure the Protestant Succession, a choice would have to be made between several foreign dynasties, connected by marriage with the Stuarts; when in 1714 George Lewis, Elector of Hanover and head of the House of Brunswick-Lüneburg, succeeded to the British throne, it was to the exclusion of some fifty-seven relatives with better hereditary titles.[1]

His claim was derived from the marriage of Elizabeth, daughter of James I, with the Elector Palatine, Frederick V; and the aim of that marriage, to link up England with the German Reformation and the Protestant cause, had never been forgotten, either in England or among their descendants. In 1642, Elizabeth's husband, the "Winter King", was dead, while her eldest son, Elector Karl Ludwig, had not yet recovered his paternal dominions; his younger brothers were engaged in the English Civil War on the side of their uncle, Charles I, but Karl Ludwig, when he came to London in 1644, was respectfully received by Parliament, accepted the Covenant, and openly declared against the King. The question of offering him the Crown was canvassed, but nothing was done. Doubts were expressed at that time concerning the parentage of the children of Charles I, just as in 1688 concerning that of the Old Pretender.

Thirteen children were born from the marriage of Frederick V with Elizabeth, and the twelfth, Princess Sophia, married to Ernest Augustus, Elector of Hanover, came in time to be looked upon as the

---

[1] A table of the fifty-seven persons besides James Stuart, who in 1714 had a better hereditary claim than the Electress Sophia and her son, is given in Macpherson, *Original Papers*, vol. i. p. 617, and reproduced with corrections in A. and H. Tayler, *The Old Chevalier* (1934) Appendix.

next in succession to the daughters of James II. The problem of the various hereditary claims to the English throne was extremely involved, and it was never publicly discussed in England before the accession of Sophia's son, who, if the Roman Catholic Stuarts were to be excluded, could alone be taken into serious consideration. But while Whigs and Tories had been united in opposition to the political and religious tyranny of James II, they were not equally unanimous or steady in their support of the Hanoverian Succession, which had friends and opponents in both camps. Nor did the House of Hanover itself always evince the same desire to realize its English prospects, however brilliant they might appear.

The Declaration of Rights in 1689 had laid down that no Roman Catholic could rule in England. But were the son of James II to conform, was he still to be excluded? Though even then, could he, born and bred a Catholic, be trusted sincerely to uphold the Protestant cause? Henri-Quâtre having become a Catholic, followed up his conversion by the Edict of Nantes. When the Declaration was introduced as a Bill in Parliament, the question was considered of fixing the succession in the House of Hanover, a measure favoured by the Lords but opposed in the Commons. While it was still under discussion, the birth of a son to Princess Anne, William Duke of Gloucester, reduced the prospects of a Hanoverian Succession; these, however, came again to the fore on the death of the Prince at the age of eleven, at a time when the Queen could no longer expect to bear children.

The Succession had now to be settled in an unambiguous manner, especially as William III, a widower since 1694, did not think of remarriage.[1] Moreover, in view of the problem of the Spanish Succession and the threat of French preponderance in Europe, it seemed advisable to remove all danger of internal conflict in Great Britain. The Speech at the opening of Parliament in 1701, dwelt on the necessity of securing the Protestant Succession. The Tories had a majority in Parliament, but the Revolution, of which the results had now to be secured, was the work of both parties, and both acknowledged the right of the nation to settle the Succession. In 1701 the Act of Settlement was passed, under the significant title of "An Act for the further Limitation of the Crown and better securing the Rights and

[1] In 1696, however, the idea of a re-marriage had been discussed; cf. Gallus Koch, *Die Friedensbestrebungen Wilhelms III. von England in den Jahren 1694–1697*. Exkurs: "Die Brautschau in Kleve" (pp. 100-105).

Liberties of the Subject"; [1] and the friends of the Protestant Succession asked themselves whether in fact it was not meant "to offer such extravagant limitations, as should quite change the form of our government, and render the Crown titular and precarious". [2] Still, as no Act of Succession could be had except on these terms, they acquiesced, hoping that in future they would be able to repeal some of its extreme provisions.

The Act laid down that in default of issue of William III or of Anne, the Electress Sophia was to be the next in succession, and "the heirs of her body being Protestants"; and it confirmed once more that no person holding communion with the Church of Rome, or married to a Roman Catholic, could succeed to the Crown of England. The Act was to come into force from and after the death of William III and Anne, and in default of their leaving issue, *i.e.* at the accession of the House of Hanover; and the primary aim of the regulations that followed, and which amounted to a considerable limitation on the powers of the Crown, was not to transfer these powers to Parliament, but to guard against the possible abuse of the Royal prerogative by a foreign-born king, especially one who was accustomed to absolutism at home.

In the first place, it was laid down "that whosoever shall hereafter come to the possession of this Crown shall joyn in communion with the Church of England as by law established". This was a cardinal point with the Tory party. The King was the head of the Church, Sophia's sons were Lutherans, and Lutheranism was thought even further removed from Anglicanism than Calvinism, the religion of William III and Sophia; in fact, at one time William III had thought of fixing the succession in Sophia's grandson, Frederick William, Electoral Prince of Brandenburg, who was a Calvinist.

Next, it was laid down that "this nation be not obliged to engage in any war for the defence of any dominions or territory which do not belong to the Crown of England without the consent of Parliament". Two Maritime Powers with parallel interests had been united under William III; under the Hanoverians, England would be tied to a German inland State of secondary importance. Further articles concerned even the movements of a foreign successor to the throne, and his disposal of favours—"no person who shall hereafter come to the possession of this Crown shall go out of the dominions of England

---

[1] 12 & 13 William III, c. 2; *Statutes*, vol. vii. pp. 636-8.
[2] Burnet, *The History of my Own Time*, vol. ii. p. 217.

Scotland or Ireland without consent of Parliament"; and no one foreign-born "shall be capable to be of the Privy Council or a Member of either House of Parliament or to enjoy any office or place of trust either civil or military", or receive any grant of land from the Crown.

Two further clauses were aimed at the nascent Cabinet, a suspicious knot of "courtiers" encroaching on the functions of the Privy Council, and at placemen in Parliament—clauses which, if maintained, would have rendered impossible the growth of representative and responsible government: all matters "relating to the well-governing of this Kingdom which are properly cognizable in the Privy Council . . . shall be transacted there", and all resolutions taken thereupon shall be signed by those who advised them; and "no person who has an office or place of profit under the King or receives a pension from the Crown shall be capable of serving as a Member of the House of Commons".

The independence of the Judges was safeguarded—their commissions were made "*quamdiu se bene gesserint*", and their salaries fixed; "but upon the Address of both Houses of Parliament it may be lawful to remove them". Lastly, it was laid down that no Royal pardon "be pleadable to an impeachment by the Commons in Parliament".

The Act of Settlement is a milestone in English constitutional history; it marked England's determination to preserve and consolidate the results of the Glorious Revolution.

The same Parliament, in its next session, passed an Act of Attainder (13 & 14 William III, c. 3) which adjudged the Pretender and all persons entertaining any connexions with him guilty of high treason.[1] Further, all persons bearing office, civil or military, or ecclesiastical, were to renounce and abjure all allegiance to him, and swear it, in due order, to Princess Sophia Electress of Hanover, "and the heirs of her body being Protestants".[2] Thus the part of the nation most active in public life was sworn to maintain the Hanoverian Succession.

In 1706 another Act, 4 & 5 Anne, c. 20,[3] made provision for the change of Government at the death of the Queen. If the next Protestant successor was abroad, a Regency was to act until his arrival, consisting of seven great Officers of State named in the Act, to whom the heir-apparent had power to add such persons as "she or he shall think fit"; they were to be named by a secret Instrument, which was

---

[1] *Statutes*, vol. vii. p. 739.   [2] *Ibid.* p. 747.
[3] *Ibid.* vol. viii. pp. 498-503.

to be transmitted to England in three copies, and placed in the hands of the Hanoverian Resident, the Archbishop of Canterbury, and the Lord Chancellor. The Act confirmed the provisions of 7 & 8 William III, c. 15, whereby the existing Parliament was to continue notwithstanding the death of the Sovereign "for and during the term of six months and no longer unless the same be sooner prorogued or dissolved by such person to whom the Crown of this realm of Great Britain shall come".

Lastly, the two clauses of the Act of Settlement relating to the Privy Council and to placemen in the House of Commons were repealed, and thus the way was reopened for the development of the Cabinet and of parliamentary government. Still, to prevent a further increase in the number of placemen in the House of Commons, holders of new offices or places of profit under the Crown were debarred from sitting in the House, while acceptance of any other office or place of profit was to vacate the seat of the Member, though leaving him capable of re-election.

Thus by the Acts of 1701 and 1706 the foundations were laid for a peaceful succession of the House of Hanover, which the English nation had come to look upon as best calculated to secure its peace, liberty, and well-being.

CHAPTER II

QUEEN ANNE AND HER SUCCESSORS

THE prospect of inheriting the Crown of Great Britain was alluring for the Guelph dynasty, whose present position was not equal to their ancient glories; and the indifference which at times they showed towards it, was never genuine. But the attitude of the Hanoverian dynasty towards their prospective inheritance had no real influence on the course of events in England—neither did the endeavours of Sophia much good, nor the reputed indifference of her son much harm. Altogether their attitude gained importance only in the last years of Queen Anne, when she and her Ministers seemed to favour the claims of the Pretender. Still, at the decisive moment it was the law, and not measures taken by the Electoral House, which secured their succession.

Princess Sophia was born in 1630 at The Hague, where her father, the exiled "Winter King", died two years later. When at the age of fifty she wrote her memoirs,[1] she still remembered with bitterness the rigour with which, separated from her mother, she was brought up at Leyden. Subsequently at her mother's Court, she met her cousin, the young Charles Stuart, who, after his father's execution, was *de jure* King of England. At that time a marriage was planned between them. From Holland Sophia removed to Heidelberg; there her elder brother, Karl Ludwig, who at the Peace of Westphalia had recovered his patrimony, treated her with paternal care. She grew up a remarkable woman and aimed high; a Portuguese prince, who wished to marry her, was deemed as of insufficient rank. Finally, she became engaged to Duke Georg Wilhelm of Calenberg-Göttingen, the second

---

[1] Edited by Köcher, *Publ. aus preuss. Staatsarchiven*, vol. iv. See also her correspondence with Karl Ludwig, ed. by Bodemann, *ibid.* vol. xxvi.; Bodemann's article about her in the *Historisches Taschenbuch*, 6th Series, vol. vii.; and Köcher, *Geschichte von Hannover und Braunschweig*, vol. i. p. 381.

of four brothers of the younger Guelph line; he, however, preferred to retain his freedom, and effected his retreat by persuading his younger brother, Ernst August, to step into his place, while he solemnly pledged himself to remain unmarried so that their male descendants should be heirs to one or both of his Duchies. Thus the marriage was concluded whereby the hereditary claims of James I's daughter were transmitted to the Guelphs.

The young couple lived a few years at Hanover with Duke Georg Wilhelm, who, too late, came to appreciate the woman he had given up. In 1661 Ernst August succeeded, in accordance with the Treaty of Westphalia, to the Bishopric of Osnabrück, and in 1680 inherited from his brother Johann Friedrich the Duchy of Calenberg-Göttingen, which Georg Wilhelm had exchanged in 1665 against Lüneburg-Celle. Ernst August and his wife now returned to Hanover, and it was he who prepared the reunion of the long separated dominions of the House of Brunswick-Lüneburg, and who obtained for his House the Electoral dignity with a considerable increase of their position in the Empire. He was skilful and tenacious, and intent on renewing the ancient glories of his family.

Ernst August, first Elector of Hanover, died in 1698, and was succeeded by his son Georg Ludwig, the later King George I. The Dowager-Electress Sophia was approaching seventy, and was older than either William III or Princess Anne; but she was full of vitality and young in spirit. As ambitious as her mother, she showed more political insight and a sounder judgment. She had a real understanding of the intellectual developments and political activities of her time, and was a close friend of Leibniz, with whom she kept up a lively correspondence; his influence helped to form her conceptions of the universe and mankind, of the origin and purpose of things. An excess of religious exercises in her youth had left her with little regard for positive religion, wherein she was confirmed by the teachings of Leibniz; and she, designated successor to the English Crown because a Protestant, cared little for confessional differences, seeing the best part of piety in good deeds and in a sincere love of God and of one's neighbours.

Sophia would not have mounted the English throne as a stranger, having from her youth spoken English (whereas her son, even as King, never mastered the language). At the Dutch Court, which was visited by numerous Englishmen, she had acquired a knowledge of English conditions, and throughout her later life she entertained relations with English politicians. She understood and judged correctly the position of parties in England; and she realized the difference between herself and her son who, as she knew, would be looked upon in England as an alien.

After 1689 she hoped some day to enter upon her English inheritance, though in her letters, *e.g.* in 1700, on the death of the Duke of Gloucester, she professed herself too old to aspire to any Kingdom other than that of Heaven. Her son, the Elector, caused a Committee of his Calenberg Estates to vote him secretly 300,000 thalers, which he used to further his interests in England.[1] In 1701, when the Earl of Macclesfield, with a numerous retinue, arrived to present the Act of Settlement to Sophia in the name of the English people, he was given a magnificent reception in Hanover; an account of it has been left by one of the embassy, the writer Toland, who was deeply impressed by the old Electress—he described her as English in nature and outlook, a view which was shared by many others. She herself wished in the inscription on her tomb to figure as Queen. At times she consoled herself with the thought that her health was better than that of the much younger Queen Anne; but at other times she would quote the Dutch proverb, *Krakende wagens gaan lang* (creaking cars last long).

Louis XIV having recognized the Pretender as King of England, the problem of the Protestant Succession was linked up with that of the Spanish Succession; and it became the lever for establishing the Union between England and Scotland. After the Act of Succession had been passed, the question was publicly discussed, even in the press, whether the Electress Sophia, or at least her grandson, the eldest son of the Elector, should not be invited to England with a view to securing a peaceful succession. In 1705 a resolution was moved by the Tories in the House of Lords that an Address be presented to the Queen to invite the heir-presumptive to the Crown, *i.e.* the Electress, "into this Kingdom, to reside here".

It appeared, throughout our whole history, that whosoever came first into England, had always carried it: the pretending Successor might be in England within three days, whereas it might be three weeks before the declared Successor could come.[2]

The motion, which was repugnant to the Queen, was rejected, though

---

[1] See Dahlmann, *Politik*, 3rd edition, vol. i. p. 128, *n.* 3.
[2] See summary of the debate in Burnet, *The History of my Own Time*, vol. ii. p. 407; and in *Parl. Hist.* vi. 469.

her wish that such invitation should be prohibited for her lifetime was not carried out. The debates, however, led to the passing of the Regency Act and of the amendments to the Act of Settlement mentioned above.

The old Electress, in the meantime, applied to Bishop Burnet for a memorial on the constitutional position in England. In that Memorial[1] the position of the Sovereign was magnified. He was represented as "in the Legislature . . . the most essential part; for *from the Royal Assent* our lawes receive their sanction" (whereas that assent, though required, could no longer be withheld under the Hanoverians); and the maxim that "the King can do no wrong", which throws all the responsibility on the Ministers, was quoted to show that the position of the King of England was really preferable to that of an "absolute unlimited Monarch". In short, an attempt was made to present the limitations on the Royal prerogative in the most favourable light—these were thought to render the Elector indifferent to the British Succession, and the Memorial was probably meant as much for him as for his mother.

Queen Anne was unfavourably disposed to the Hanoverians and would not listen to any proposal of inviting them. Not even the promised annuity was paid to the Electress, and the relations of the two women were confined to an exchange of formal letters on joyful or sad occasions. But ultimately the attitude of the Queen mattered less than that of the two parties, and no fundamental difference existed between them on that point; Tories and Whigs had been agreed in excluding the Roman Catholic Stuarts, and the Act of Settlement was the necessary complement to, and commentary on, the Bill of Rights of 1689. There were Jacobites in both camps, but the great majority saw in the Protestant Succession the necessary basis of the Constitution.

But in time a change supervened in the attitude of the two parties towards the House of Hanover. For England war against Louis XIV meant, among other things, a fight for the Protestant Succession, and the greater the victory, the better it was secured. At first Whigs and Tories were equally keen on the prosecution of the war, but as years went by, a cleavage arose between them, the Whigs favouring war

---

[1] "A Memorial, humbly offered to Her Royal Highness the Princess Sophia, Electoress and Dutchess Dowager of Hanover." The original is among Leibniz' correspondence in the Royal Library at Hanover; see Bodemann, No. 131. The Memorial was printed in London in 1815.

and the Tories peace. The House of Hanover, both because of its British interests and as faithful allies of the Emperor, favoured a continuation of the war till the Bourbons were driven out of Spain. If there was now a war and a peace party in England, it was clear with which side the sympathies of Hanover were bound to lie. The *rapprochement* between them and the Whigs was such that the Tories, even though they were not against the Protestant Succession, were forced into opposition to the Hanoverian Court.

So long as the Whigs were in office, the cause of the Elector was safe. Many distinguished Englishmen came to Hanover and were given a good reception. In 1706, one of the leading Whigs, Lord Halifax, brought over, as Envoy of the Queen, a copy of the Regency Act. The Electoral Prince, George Augustus, like his father in 1701, was given the Garter and was summoned to the House of Lords by the style of Duke of Cambridge. When, in 1709, the Barrier Treaty with Holland was concluded, the States General were made to guarantee the Protestant Succession. But when, in 1710, a Tory Administration took office, it was viewed with much distrust by the Electoral Court. Lord Rivers was sent by the Queen to Hanover with a courteous letter to the Elector and his mother, and it was the primary aim of his mission to reconcile the Electoral Court to the turn which things had taken in England. Further, it was rumoured that the Queen thought of depriving Marlborough of his command and of replacing him by the Elector. Others thought that George Lewis would be invited to London; but nothing was said by Rivers about it.

The confused state of British politics and the uncertain attitude of the new Administration with regard to the Succession, rendered it advisable for the Electoral family to have a reliable representative in London who should watch over their interests, and advise them concerning the line they themselves were to adopt. The Hanoverian Resident at the Court of St. James's seemed unequal to the task, and Hans Caspar Baron von Bothmer, the ablest and most experienced diplomat in the Elector's service, was sent to London. He had been Minister at Vienna, had represented his master at the Ryswick Conference, and since 1702 had been Minister at The Hague, a most important diplomatic centre. Bothmer had personal connexions with several leading English statesmen, and was a man of pleasant and conciliatory manners; indeed, some of his friends complained that he was too conciliatory to cut much ice. But at that moment no better choice could have been made, for he knew how to move tactfully in a difficult situation, and did his work with proper regard to men and circumstances.

In January 1711 Bothmer went across to England in the company of the Duke of Marlborough. The Duke was anxious what reception he would be accorded by the Queen, as his wife, once so powerful at Court, had fallen into disgrace, and it was rumoured that only at the price of her resigning all her places could her husband retain his military command, a concession to which neither of them found it easy to agree. And although Marlborough was graciously received by the Queen, the concession had to be made, if, as was much desired at Hanover, he was to remain at the head of the army. Bothmer was instrumental in securing his continuance in the supreme command. He had a talk with the Duchess, who brought herself voluntarily to resign her Court offices; and her husband returned to the army, though no longer with his former, very extensive, powers.

In London Bothmer made contacts with the Ministers, was received in audience by the Queen who graciously enquired after the health of the Elector and his aged mother, and was warmly welcomed by the Whig leaders. While accredited to the Court of St. James's, he saw in the Opposition his natural allies and supporters; for the House of Hanover believed that their rights were in danger from the British Government, in which view they were eagerly confirmed by the Whigs.

Again and again Bothmer had to consider the problem whether to encourage the Elector to come over to England, as the Whigs urged him to do, even without official invitation. But Bothmer knew how much the Queen loathed the idea of seeing her heir in London, and he repeatedly declared that, as his master certainly would not come against her wish, he dared not transmit the suggestion to Hanover; though it was, in fact, carefully reported by him. Faithfully obeying his instructions he made a show of non-interference, but secretly managed to keep Lord Jersey, a notorious Jacobite, out of one of the great offices of State which, on the death of the Queen, would have placed him on the Regency Council.

At first George Lewis was intent on preserving a good understanding with Her Majesty's Government; but the prospect of a peace which would leave Spain to the Bourbons, brought him out in opposition to them. After the preliminaries had been signed, Lord Rivers was sent once more to Hanover to inform the Elector and his mother about the impending Peace Conference, and, as Lord Oxford wrote, "to give your Royal Highness the greatest proofs of Her

Majesty's amitie in the care she has taken of your interest".[1] The
Elector now no longer disguised his annoyance; he wrote to Lord
Oxford that all the fruits of the glorious war would be lost if Spain and
the Indies were abandoned to the Duke of Anjou,[2] and in a memorandum transmitted to England through Lord Rivers, expostulated
against separate negotiations.[3]

In November 1711 Bothmer was sent back to London as Envoy
Extraordinary. But his position was now radically changed: he was
to work against the Peace and to emphasize publicly the divergence
of views between the Queen and the Elector. A few days before the
opening of Parliament, he presented a memorandum to the Ministers
which in strong terms criticized the proposed treaty; while with
regard to the Succession, he added of his own initiative[4] that Louis
XIV having established his grandson in Spain, would certainly try to
restore the Pretender whose claim he had acknowledged. However
displeasing such a declaration from the heir-apparent must have
been for the Ministers, worse was to follow: Bothmer communicated
the document to his Whig friends, and it was undoubtedly through
one of them that it got into print. Bothmer emphatically disclaimed
all responsibility for the publication, which was hardly in the
Hanoverian interests; but the alliance between the Elector and the
Whig party, based on common opposition to the policy of the Administration, was now patent; and seemed to offer a further induce-
ment to the Tory Ministers for amending the Act of Settlement—
their general position, their peace policy, and their understanding
with Louis XIV seemed anyhow to suggest inclinations towards the
Pretender.

The support of the Electoral Envoy gave the Whigs strength for
the attack which on the opening of Parliament they launched against
the Government. Meantime the Administration had, on the one hand,
sought to strengthen their position by creating new peers and by
removing Marlborough from the army command, and, on the other
hand, Lord Oxford tried to remove the painful impression created by
Bothmer's memorandum and to cover up the serious differences
between the Courts of St. James's and Hanover by resorting to an
idea previously canvassed by the Whigs. He had an Act of Precedence
passed through the two Houses which declared that Princess Sophia,
her son the Elector, and his son the Duke of Cambridge, "shall have

---

[1] See Macpherson, *Original Papers*, ii. p. 256.   [2] *Ibid.* p. 263.
[3] See Klopp, *Der Fall des Hauses Stuart*, xiv. p. 208.   [4] *Ibid.* p. 215.

rank and precedence and take place before the Archbishop of Canterbury and all Great Officers", and all the peers "of these Realms".[1]
The measure was of small value, and Sophia was not particularly
pleased when Thomas Harley, a cousin of the Lord Treasurer,
appeared with the Act of Precedence at Hanover, and had to be dismissed with the customary rich rewards.[2]

International politics engrossed the mind of the Elector. He
followed closely developments in England—the struggle over Lord
Nottingham's amendment to the Address (pledging the House
against the peace proposals), the victory of the Whigs and their dis-
comfiture by the counter-offensive of the Government; he sincerely
regretted the dismissal of Marlborough,[3] and did all he could to foil
the Tory plans for peace. After the British troops had been withdrawn under the "restraining orders" in July 1712, the Hanoverian
contingent remained with the army which, under Prince Eugene,
continued the war against France.

In the meantime Bothmer had left London for Utrecht, to represent Hanover at the Peace Conference. But as it was necessary to
have someone to cultivate relations with the British Administration
and to continue unobtrusively the understanding with the Opposition, the Hanoverian Minister, Baron von Grote, was sent to London.[4]
He was to assist the Whigs in their struggle against the Government,
and to pursue the common aim of securing the Protestant Succession,
which was to receive a formal guarantee in the Peace Treaty. But all
open conflict with the British Court was to be avoided; and while
putting forward certain requests, Grote was to give the assurance
that no member of the Electoral family would come to England,
except at the Queen's desire.[5] Still, there was the consciousness of
mutual distrust; and the Envoy, when leaving Holland, was advised
to mind whether the captain of the yacht which was to carry him
over to England, had not secret orders to delay his departure.[6]

Besides the ordinary cypher given to every Minister, Grote

---

[1] 10 Anne, c. 8, *Statutes*, ix. pp. 556-7.

[2] *Publ. aus preuss. Staatsarchiven*, vol. 37, p. 335.

[3] Salomon, *Geschichte des letzten Ministeriums Königin Annas von England
(1710–1714) und der englischen Thronfolgefrage*, p. 162.

[4] For his instructions from the Elector and the Electress Sophia see Klopp,
vol. xiv. p. 423 ff.

[5] Robethon to Grote, Nov. 26, 1712; see Macpherson, *Original Papers*, vol. ii.
pp. 355-60.

[6] *Ibid.* p. 361.

received a curious "small cypher",[1] which was to enable him at critical moments to transmit news with dispatch and additional secrecy. It consisted of 22 signs and letters; one sign meant "the Queen is well", another "she is ill", while a horizontal line crossed three times was to announce her death. All the letters of the alphabet from A to Q referred to the chances of the Jacobites or of the Hanoverians; A: "the Pretender is coming"; F: "the Queen will not have any member of the Electoral family come to England"; J: "the Lord Treasurer is hostile to the Hanoverian Succession"; and lastly, Q: "the Pretender is in hiding in England".

Grote achieved little with the British Government.[2] The memoranda which, following his instructions, he addressed to them, demanding payment of an annuity to the Electress Sophia and of arrears due to Hanover from the late war, or trying to secure the removal of the Pretender from Lorraine, remained unheeded. None the less, Lord Oxford tried to impress on the Elector that he was a faithful guardian of his interests. On February 9, 1713, he gave Grote a paper in which he declared: "I put this as a fundament, that the securing the succession to these crowns in the House of Hanover is our interest and our security".[3] Remarks followed about "the bulk of the clergy and laity" being "zealous for the Succession"—"those who are cool . . . will be quickly made zealous when they see an undoubted friendship between the Queen" and the House of Hanover; but no concrete proposals were made. Although the document was perfectly innocent and even meaningless—"*lequel ne veut rien dire*" the Secretary of the Elector said of it[4]—Oxford was anxious that it should not fall into strange hands, and a year later, after Grote's death, asked his successor, Baron Schütz, for the return of the original, but was told that it could not be found, and had presumably been destroyed by Grote, with other documents, before his death.[5] This seems to have been a genuine mistake on the part of Schütz, as the original is among Grote's papers in the Hanover Archives.[6]

[1] There is a cypher in the Hanover State Archives which, I believe, is that given to Grote, as all the other documents accompanying it ("London 45 IV") are connected with Grote's mission.

[2] Salomon, *op. cit.* pp. 171 ff.

[3] Han. Arch.; published by Pauli, *Zeitschr. d. hist. Ver. f. Niedersachsen* (1883), p. 18.

[4] See Klopp, xiv. p. 450.

[5] See dispatch from Schütz Feb. 5/16, 1714; Han. Arch.

[6] The document in "England 47", f. 36, Han. Arch., is apparently that original.

Grote thought the Government was in close touch with France and the Pretender, and the Whig leaders tried to confirm him in the belief that the Ministers meant to restore the Pretender, and that the failing health of the Queen and financial difficulties would induce them to hasten measures for summoning him to England. They urged that in case of imminent danger, the Elector should proceed to Holland, or at least send the Electoral Prince—an obvious harking back to 1688; they further asked for money with which to encourage their friends and gain new ones. It was presumably at that time that a list of impoverished peers was sent to Hanover, some to be confirmed in their adherence, and others, who as a rule voted with the Court, to be engaged in the interest of the Elector by pensions of £300—£1000 a year.[1] But George Lewis refused to put his hand to his pocket. In consequence Sunderland wrote to Bothmer:

Since it is so difficult for the Elector to contribute to the expence of the ensuing elections, all friends agree to make another proposal to him, which is of greater consequence, and which appears to them to be absolutely necessary. It is to send over the Electoral Prince. It is true, an invitation by a vote of Parliament was formerly spoke of; but all friends are unanimously of opinion, that such an invitation, in the present situation of affairs, in such a Parliament and under the influence of such a Ministry, is impracticable.

They are of opinion, that the Electoral Prince, being a peer of the realm, and his precedency as a Prince of the Blood having been regulated by Act of Parliament, has so many just pretexts and reasons for coming, that those who should oppose him, would thereby do themselves the greatest injury which their greatest enemies could wish them. . . . This is the unanimous opinion of all friends, and they have charged me to write it to you.[2]

George Lewis again refused:

The Elector has been so often amused these two years, with false intelligence of the Queen's health, that he does not know but her death may be still very distant; and it would be imprudent in him, upon an uncertainty, to expose his only son and the only hope of his family.[3]

This was not a mere excuse; his chance of succeeding to the British Crown seemed to him too uncertain to be worth sacrifices—he did not even learn the language of the people whose King he was to be, and

---

[1] Hanover Archives.
[2] Macpherson, *Original Papers*, vol. ii. p. 482.
[3] *Ibid.* p. 498; cf. also Klopp, vol. xiv. pp. 477-9.

he refused to spend large sums of money on preparing for himself the ground in England.

None the less, the friends of the Hanoverian Succession continued to urge on him their idea: the Electoral Prince in London could at least help to counter effectively the plans of the Ministers. If the Prince "could come over this winter", declared Lord Halifax in 1713, "he would answer for it, that the Ministry would be overturned, and all things put out of danger".[1] Yet in fact his coming would probably have done more harm to the cause than did the anxious reserve maintained by the Elector—undertaken without invitation, it would have struck the Queen and the public as a bid for power in her lifetime.

In the Treaty of Utrecht, the Protestant Succession in the House of Hanover was specifically acknowledged by France. Although the Tory Ministers entertained occasional relations with the Stuart Court at St. Germain,[2] and the Jacobites therefore thought it advisable to support them in critical moments, during the peace negotiations their official attitude towards the problem of the Succession was perfectly correct and loyal.

In August 1713 the Electoral Court decided to send a successor to Grote, who had died in April—in the interval the Hanover Resident in London, Kreyenberg, had been in charge. Baron von Schütz, the son of a former Minister in London, was chosen—he had lived many years in England in his father's time, and was personally known to the Queen. But he was young and inexperienced and not equal to the task; the Elector, as his British friends were saying, should have sent over his ablest minister.[3] Schütz received instructions both from the Elector and from the Electress Sophia.[4] He was enjoined to exercise the greatest caution, and not to assume at first an official character, but merely inform a few friends of his mission. Only about the time Parliament met was he to present his credentials to the Ministers and ask for an audience with the Queen.

The instructions from the Elector bid him not to undertake anything without consulting the friends of the Electoral House, an order to which he adhered perhaps too strictly. In the first place he was to consult Lord Halifax, a prudent and moderate man, of proved attach-

---

[1] Macpherson, *Original Papers*, vol. ii. p. 498.
[2] Cf. Salomon, ch. x.   [3] Klopp, vol. xiv. p. 496.
[4] His instructions are dated Aug. 28, 1713, and in most parts are identical with those of Grote; they are preserved in the Hanover Archives.

ment to the House of Hanover; the Duke of Somerset and Lord Sunderland, Marlborough's son-in-law; influential Whig peers, such as Townshend, Somers, Cowper, and Wharton; and Whig leaders in the Commons, such as Cadogan and Stanhope. He was not, however, to act on suggestions from the rash and impetuous Sunderland without the advice of the other friends. In general he was told to be discreet in his relations with the Whigs; important decisions were to be arrived at in secret meetings or through trusted intermediaries. The future King of England had come to look upon the British Ministers as his natural enemies, and upon their opponents as his friends; while the men who stood for the Succession as settled by law, had to act like conspirators, an attempt against it being expected from the Government.

The instructions of the Electress showed less distrust of the Administration, and enjoined complete impartiality. Schütz was to avoid open intercourse with the Whigs, and not give grounds for suspicion to the Ministers. He was much rather to keep on good terms with them, and tell the Lord Treasurer that if he and his friends were prepared to work in the interest of the Electoral House, such behaviour would meet with proper appreciation. The Electress differed from her son in thinking that their purpose could ultimately be best secured through the Ministers themselves. It was left to the Envoy to decide how to reconcile the two sets of instructions. Incidentally it appears from them how much Sophia longed for the British Crown—this was the concern and hope of her widowhood; while to George Lewis, even after his accession, his German Electorate was dearer than his British Kingdom.

Sophia, with an understanding for the religious divisions in England, tried to allay the misgivings of the Anglican clergy with regard to the Lutheran dynasty. Schütz was to explain that the Superintendents of the Lutheran Church closely corresponded to the Anglican Bishops.[1] Should the Pretender change his religion with a view to the British Succession, Schütz was still to press the claims of the House of Hanover: the strict rules of direct succession no longer obtained in Great Britain, and the accession of a Papist Prince, even if he outwardly conformed, was incompatible with the principles of the Revolution of 1688.

[1] On one occasion Grote referred to the doubtful attitude of the clergy; cf. Pauli, "Konfessionelle Bedenken etc.", *Aufsätez zur englischen Geschichte*, N.S., p. 381.

The Elector in his instructions dealt at length with the Whig request for sending the Duke of Cambridge to England, and gave a number of reasons for his refusal. He instructed Schütz to contradict the assertions publicly made by the Lord Treasurer that complete harmony existed between the Courts of London and Hanover; he was to show that the interests of the Electorate had been neglected by the British Ministers in the peace negotiations, and that Grote's memoranda had been left unanswered. Further, he was to counter rumours spread by opponents of the Protestant Succession that the Elector was indifferent to it. His adherents were to be encouraged by assurances that on the death of the Queen the Elector would do whatever could be expected from him.

If he does, will the friends of the succession, who . . . have the nation and the laws on their side, lose courage and submit immediately, when their religion, their laws, their property, and their liberties are at stake? . . . The nation must exert itself, for the Elector cannot save them against their will.[1]

Schütz arrived in England in September 1713. But no one believed the story that private business had brought him to London. Diplomatic circles soon discovered the true purpose of his journey, and in these circumstances he feared that he would be suspected of plotting against the Government; the fact that he avoided the presence of the Queen, although he was personally known to her, would be commented upon. After a month he asked, therefore, the Elector's permission to assume the character of an Envoy, and present his credentials; and he received it immediately.[2] Meantime Schütz had entered into touch with the chief leaders of the Hanover party, and had learnt from them about the chances and still more about the dangers of the situation. The Queen, as "the Tories, who are our friends, as well as the Whigs, acknowledge . . . is totally prejudiced against us; and . . . failing the Pretender, in whose favour, besides her own inclinations, the recommendations of a dying father engage her to act, her hatred against us is so strong, that she will endeavour to leave the Crown to the greatest stranger rather than allow it to fall to the Electoral Family".[3] On another occasion he reported that the

---

[1] Macpherson, *Original Papers*, vol. ii. p. 497.

[2] Schütz to George Lewis, Oct. 9/30, 1713; George Lewis to Schütz, Göhrde, Nov. 6, 1713. Han. Arch., Schütz to Robethon, Nov. 3, 1713. Macpherson, vol. ii. p. 511.

[3] Macpherson, vol. ii. p. 512.

Jacobites spoke with assurance of the Pretender's return,[1] but were divided in their opinion whether he should come alone or with a considerable body of troops from France. The Court was said to be favourable, and the Prince was to land in Scotland, where a great deal of money was reported to have been given to the Highlanders to have them when there was occasion for them.[2] These rumours, even though there was little substance in them, were believed by the friends of the Brunswick Family, who feared that ultimately the Elector would have to fight for his Crown; and they were all agreed about the need of sending over the Duke of Cambridge, or that it should at least be given out publicly that this was intended.[3] Even Marlborough, who was at Antwerp, strongly supported this request. But the Elector and his advisers persisted in their refusal.[4]

In November 1713 Baron Schütz, as Electoral Envoy, entered into official relations with the British Court, and on the 29th was presented to the Queen by the Secretary of State, William Bromley. Schütz, who had not seen her for four years, did not think her much changed, in spite of her illness. Her complexion was fresh and healthy, and less red than before. Her corpulence which, he was told, hindered her from walking or standing, was masked by her robes when she was seated. The Queen enquired about the health of the Elector, and assured Schütz that she would ever wish to guard his interests and to give him proof of her friendship and affection.[5] But she did not say a word about his rights to the British Succession.

During the following weeks Schütz made contacts with the Ministers and Court officers, and was assured by them all that they would do everything in their power to secure the Succession in the House of Hanover. Bolingbroke and Bromley assured him of their friendship, while Lord Oxford began to play the foremost champion of the Protestant Succession.[6] But when Schütz asked Bolingbroke for British support with a view to gaining for the Elector certain advantages in the Empire, he was told that this was impossible.[7] Oxford was inscrutable, as usual, and would reply in vague terms. If Schütz raised the question of the arrears of pay due to the Hanoverian troops for service in the late war, Oxford would ask

[1] *Ibid.* p. 504.   [2] *Ibid.* p. 514.
[3] *Ibid.* p. 521.   [4] *Ibid.* p. 516.
[5] Schütz to George Lewis, Dec. 1/12, 1713, Han. Arch.
[6] Macpherson, vol. ii. p. 509.
[7] Schütz to George Lewis, Dec. 18/29, 1713, Han. Arch.

about the health of the Elector, and if Schütz reverted to the subject, Oxford would make excuses for not having come to see him. Occasionally he himself threw out suggestions for the better securing of the Succession, but if Schütz took them up another time, Oxford would not wish to hear anything more about them.[1]

On December 24, 1713, the illness of the Queen took so serious a turn that her end seemed imminent. There was universal excitement, but after a few days an improvement set in. Her death would have been a serious blow for the Ministers, who, whatever their intentions may have been, had taken no steps to carry them out. The restoration of the Pretender would not have been possible without the support of a French army, while these Ministers could not hope to be continued in office under a Hanoverian King. They did not know which way to turn; Bolingbroke complained about the indolence of Lord Oxford, but hoped that he would take the necessary steps, should the Queen die, to make stipulations for his friends and the country—presumably with the House of Hanover. Otherwise he thought there was no safety except in flight or surrender:[2] to the Ministers the lawful successor was an enemy from whom they had everything to fear, and nothing to hope.

The Whigs, on the other hand, knew exactly what to do on a demise. Those who were Privy Councillors, although for a long time they had not attended the meetings, would immediately go to Council and take the oath to the Protestant Successor. One of the three copies of the Instrument whereby the Electress Sophia designated certain members of the Regency Council, would be opened; they could guess that it was mainly members of their party who were named. This would place Government in their hands, Sophia would be proclaimed Queen, and the Succession would be secured.[3]

The Queen having recovered, the fears of the Hanoverian party increased lest the Ministers should employ their new lease of life for measures in favour of the Pretender. Towards the end of January 1714, it was rumoured that France was arming a fleet of 14 vessels which was to carry 12,000 to 14,000 men; and that the Chevalier of St. George had left Bar-le-Duc for an unknown destination. Con-

---

[1] Schütz to George Lewis, Feb. 2/13, 1713, Han. Arch.; cf. also Macpherson, vol. ii. pp. 503, 505, 518.

[2] See Klopp, vol. xiv. pp. 511-13 and 695.

[3] Bonet's reports of Jan. 1/12, 1714, Feb. 19, and Mar. 2, Prussian State Archives.

siderable excitement prevailed in London. The stocks dropped sharply and a run on the Bank ensued, similar to that caused in 1708 by the rumour of the Pretender having landed in Scotland. Once more the danger of bankruptcy was stayed by the intervention of the Government. A letter from the Queen to the Lord Mayor was published, announcing an improvement in her condition—"We continue determined to open our Parliament on Tuesday, 16th inst. February according to the notice given by Proclamation".[1] Confidence was immediately restored, prices on the Stock Exchange recovered, and the run on the Bank ceased.[2]

The forthcoming session of Parliament was bound to settle the problem of the Succession, and therefore the fate of England. Many friends of the Protestant Succession feared that the Ministers would dissolve Parliament, or adjourn it for a long term, so that it should not be in session at the death of the Queen. It was generally admitted that a majority for the overthrow of the Protestant Succession could not be found in Parliament; but in the past, Parliament had proved amenable to usurpations—a Stuart King in possession of the Crown might be expected to obtain an *ex post* recognition from Parliament. The Government's attitude to the meeting of Parliament was therefore a test of their future intentions.

Even so, the meeting of Parliament on February 16 did not placate the Whigs, who were determined to secure the Protestant Succession by further legislation. The Court had been unable or unwilling to obtain the removal of the Pretender from Lorraine; this was to be made the ground for demanding that the Electoral Prince should be invited to England. The strength of the Whigs lay in the law regulating the Succession, that of the Tories in the fact that they held office; the Whigs could fight in the open, while the Tories had to work underhand.[3]

On February 16 the choice of Speaker fell on Sir Thomas Hanmer, a Tory zealously attached to the Protestant Succession; a Jacobite writer alleges that Oxford and Bolingbroke, not being on such terms as to agree jointly on a candidate equally acceptable to them, "Sir Thomas was pitched upon as alike ill-affected towards both".[4] But

---

[1] Stowe MSS. 226, f. 90.

[2] Schütz to George Lewis, Jan. 26/Feb. 6., Jan. 29/Feb. 9, 1714, Han. Arch.; Bonet's report of Jan. 29/Feb. 9, Feb. 2/13, 5/16, 1714, Prussian State Archives.

[3] Bonet's reports of Feb. 12/23, 16/27; Tindal, Feb. 19/Mar. 2, 1714, Prussian State Archives.   [4] *Lockhart Papers*, i. p. 441.

even assuming that they both wished for the return of the Pretender, the choice of a declared Jacobite for Speaker would have been excessively provocative. The attitude of Sir Thomas was that of a majority in the House; they were Tories, but adherents of the Protestant Succession.

On March 2, O.S., Parliament was opened by the Queen, who went to the House of Lords in a chair. In the Speech which she addressed to the two Houses of Parliament[1] she expressed satisfaction at the ratifications of the Treaty of Peace and Commerce with Spain having been exchanged. "My . . . subjects . . . are delivered from a consuming land-war and entered on a peace, the good effects whereof nothing but intestine divisions can obstruct." She had proceeded on the principle of the wisest and greatest of her predecessors, "to hold the balance of Europe, and to keep it equal, by casting in their weight as necessity required".

Our situation points out to us our true interest; for this country can flourish only by trade, and will be most formidable by the right application of our naval force.

When dealing with the problem of the Succession, her Speech assumed a well-nigh passionate character.

I wish that effectual care had been taken . . . to suppress those seditious papers and factious rumours, by which designing men have been able to sink credit, and the innocent have suffered. There are some, who are arrived to that height of malice, as to insinuate that the Protestant Succession in the House of Hanover is in danger under my Government. Those who go about thus to distract the minds of men with imaginary dangers, can only mean to disturb the present tranquillity, and bring real mischief upon us. After all I have done to secure our religion and your liberties, and to transmit both safe to posterity, I cannot mention these proceedings without some degree of warmth; and I must hope you will all agree with me, that attempts to weaken my authority or to render the possession of the Crown uneasy to me, can never be proper means to strengthen the Protestant Succession.

Union at home was necessary to repair the damages of the war:

I had the concurrence of the last Parliament in making the Peace. Let it be the honour of this to assist me in obtaining such fruits from it, as may not only derive blessings on the present age, but even down to the latest posterity.

[1] *Parl. Hist.* vol. vi. 1256-8.

The Speech caused astonishment and dissatisfaction among the Whigs,[1] and its style and wording were thought inappropriate; Schütz wrote to the Elector that it contained "various coarse expressions". The Queen still harped on the "land-war", concluded two years ago; while her reference to the Hanoverian Succession sounded cold and unfriendly. On previous occasions she used to assure her subjects that she had the Protestant Succession much at heart, and that a good understanding was maintained with the Electoral Court; though it was reported that even in April 1713, "there was the greatest difficulty imaginable in determining the Queen to mention the Serene Family at all in her Speech; and that she did not consent to it, but after the strongest representations, that it was absolutely necessary. . . ."[2] Still, she had spoken of "the perfect friendship" between the two Courts, which may "convince such who wish well to both, and desire the quiet and safety of their country";[3] now, instead of promising her support for the better securing the Protestant Succession, she merely complained of attempts to weaken her own authority.

The Whigs saw in the Speech another proof of Ministerial intentions to prepare the way for the Pretender, and were further confirmed in that belief by an incident which occurred a few days later. An Address was presented to the Queen on behalf of the Convocation of Canterbury voicing their "great and inexpressible joy" at her recovery from her late indisposition and at her happy return to London, and the wish

that after a long and happy reign, you may be able to transmit the protection of this Church and State to a Protestant Successor in the illustrious House of Hanover, which your Majesty, to the great satisfaction and comfort of all your faithful and good subjects, has so often declared to be at your Royal Heart.

The Queen, in a short and dry reply, refrained from mentioning the Succession, and merely thanked the Clergy for the concern they had expressed for her health, and desired them as "servants of the God of Peace" to promote "peace, and the true interest of our most holy religion".[4] This reply, according to Schütz, suggested that Lord

---

[1] Schütz to George Lewis, Mar. 12/23, 1714, Han. Arch.
[2] Bothmer to Robethon, Macpherson, vol. ii. p. 494.
[3] *Parl. Hist.* vol. vi. 1172.
[4] Stowe MSS. 226, f. 241; Boyer, *The Political State,* vol. vii. (1714) pp. 214-15.

Oxford felt sure of his cause, and thought all further disguise superfluous.[1]

The debates in the two Houses took a course favourable to the Government. The Addresses were in the same key as the Speech, and, in the customary manner, restated its main points.[2] They, too, welcomed the Treaty with Spain, condemned those who alleged that the Protestant Succession was in danger, and promised their support against all attempts to weaken her authority. Next, the House of Lords proceeded against the publishers and printers of a seditious pamphlet, directed against the Union with Scotland.[3] But the Royal Proclamation setting a reward for their discovery, produced no result; the author was Jonathan Swift. On a similar occasion, when Richard Steele was arraigned before the House of Commons because "of several scandalous papers lately published", and expelled the House, Robert Walpole had defended him in a long and most eloquent speech. He asked

why the author was answerable in Parliament for the things which he wrote in his private capacity? And if he is punishable by law, why is he not left to the law? By this mode of proceeding, Parliament, which used to be the scourge only of evil Ministers, is made by Ministers the scourge of the subject. . . . In the reign of James, it was criminal to say, that the King was a Papist; but the severity of the law . . . could not eradicate from the mind of a single individual, the confirmed belief of the fact. Steele is only attacked, because he is the advocate for the Protestant Succession; . . . through his sides the Succession is to be wounded; his punishment to be a symptom, that the Succession is in danger. . . .[4]

The attack against Administration was opened in the House of Lords on March 17, O.S.[5] The Opposition moved that an Address be presented to the Queen asking for an account "of what steps had been taken for removing the Pretender from the dominions of the Duke of Lorrain, and what answers had been given by that Duke". The question had been widely discussed, as some time before Parliament met, a letter to the Queen, said to be written by the Duke of Lorraine, had appeared in print, full of praise for the Pretender "the most accomplished, the most virtuous, and most amiable of human race" —the Duke could not comply with a demand for his removal "so inconsistent with our own honour, and the laws of hospitality". The

---

[1] Schütz to George Lewis, Mar. 12/23, 1714, Han. Arch.
[2] *Parl. Hist.* vi. 1258-9.   [3] *Parl. Hist.* vi. 1265.
[4] Coxe, *Walpole*, vol. i. p. 44.   [5] *Parl. Hist.* vi. 1330-2.

language suggested connivance on the part of the British Government, which the Whigs hoped to prove by their demand for papers. The papers were to be laid before Parliament on April 5, O.S. That day [1] Lord Sunderland declared that

he was assured by Baron Fostner, the Duke of Lorrain's minister . . . that, to his certain knowledge, no instances had yet been made to his master for that purpose.

Bolingbroke replied that "he himself had made those instances to the Baron in the Queen's name". Lord Wharton demanded the promised account. Three documents were then laid before the House purporting to prove that the Queen had endeavoured to have the Pretender removed from Lorraine. Wharton, however, wondered at the small number of letters exchanged on so important a subject, and at their lukewarm style, and at no representations having been made to the French Court. The King of France had reason to be grateful to the Queen who had raised him after his defeats; and yet he did nothing to meet her just demands. It was no doubt at the desire of France that the Pretender was suffered to reside in Lorraine; and it was obvious why the King wished to have him near at hand. On Wharton declaring that the Protestant Succession was in greater danger than ever, a question was proposed, "Whether the Protestant Succession was in danger under the present Administration?" The Whigs wished to delete the words "under the present Administration" so that the question should not appear to turn against the Queen; this, however, was what the Court party desired, and they urged that the Queen having

in her Speech from the Throne, taken notice of the insinuations, that the Protestant Succession was in danger under her Government; the question ought to be taken in her Majesty's expressions about the same subject.[2]

In this pointed form it was warmly debated for seven hours, and a number of Tory Lords spoke and voted against the Government— among them the Archbishop of York (followed into the lobby by almost all the Bishops), and several influential peers, such as Lord Anglesea, whose speech made a deep impression on the House.

[1] *Parl. Hist.* vi. 1334-5; Schütz's dispatch to the Elector of April 6/17, Han. Arch. Schütz assisted at the sitting with a view to reporting to his master, and was allowed to remain even after all strangers had been obliged to withdraw.
[2] *Parl. Hist.* vi. 1335.

"I own", said he, "I gave my assent to the cessation of arms, for which I take shame to myself, and ask God, my country, and my conscience pardon. But, however, this fault I did not commit till that noble Lord [turning towards the Lord Treasurer] had assured the Council, that the Peace would be glorious and advantageous both to her Majesty and to her allies." Adding, that . . . if he found himself imposed upon, he durst pursue an evil Minister, from the Queen's closet to the Tower, and from the Tower to the scaffold.

The Lord Treasurer . . . said, "That the Peace was as glorious and advantageous, as could be expected. . . ."

The Duke of Argyle . . . added, that he had lately crossed the kingdom of France . . . indeed one of the finest countries in the universe, but that there were marks of a general desolation in all the places through which he passed. That he had rid 40 miles together without meeting a man fit to carry arms: that the rest of the people were in the utmost misery and want; and therefore he did not apprehend what necessity there was to conclude a peace so precipitately with a Prince whose dominions were so exhausted of men, money and provisions. As to the question now under debate he said, he firmly believed the succession in the Electoral House of Hanover to be in danger from the present Ministers, whom he durst charge with mal-administration, both within those walls, and without.[1]

Though in the division the Protestant Succession was voted out of danger by 76 votes to 64, it was remarked that this majority corresponded exactly to the number of recent creations, who, together with the 16 Scottish peers, had voted with the Government. Thus there was ground for considering the division a defeat of the Government.

The Whigs now thought themselves sufficiently strong to go one step further, and many of the Tories having left the House tired out by the debate,[2] several anti-Jacobite resolutions were brought forward. Lord Halifax moved "that an Address be presented to the Queen, that she would renew her instances for the speedy removing the Pretender out of Lorrain", and that she would enter into new international guarantees of the Protestant Succession; Lord Wharton, that "her Majesty might be desired to issue out a Proclamation, promising a reward to any person who should apprehend the Pretender, dead or alive"—an incitement to murder, irrespective of whether or not he attempted a restoration. It was late, and some Tories proposed to adjourn; "but the other side calling for the question, it was unanimously resolved, that the Address should be

---

[1] *Parl. Hist.* vi. 1335-6.   [2] *Lockhart Papers*, vol. i. p. 471.

presented".[1] When three days later the Address against the Pretender was reported by the Committee appointed to draft it, several lords endeavoured to show the barbarity of encouraging assassination. The Whigs appealed to precedents from English history, but could only quote the example of James II setting a price on the head of the Duke of Monmouth. Finally a milder and more dignified Address was voted,[2] leaving moreover the Queen the choice of time—

that whenever your Majesty, in your great wisdom, shall judge it necessary, you will be graciously pleased to issue your Royal Proclamation, promising a reward to any person, who shall apprehend and bring the Pretender to justice, in case he shall land, or attempt to land, either in Great Britain or Ireland. . . .

None the less, the Queen's answer amounted to a reprimand:

My Lords: It would be a real strengthening to the Succession in the House of Hanover, as well as a support to my Government, that an end were put to those groundless fears and jealousies, which have been so industriously promoted. I do not, at this time, see any occasion for such a Proclamation. Whenever I judge it to be necessary, I shall give my orders for having one issued. . . .

This reply confirmed the Whigs in the conviction that everything was lost "if matters were allowed to continue in that condition".[3]

A few days later the question whether the Protestant Succession was in danger was discussed in the Commons. In the Committee of the whole House Walpole insisted that the Queen might not be mentioned in the question as this would restrain many from voting for it; the Government for the same reason wished it done. The Speaker, Sir Thomas Hanmer, though a Tory, gave it as his opinion that "so much had been said to prove the Succession to be in danger, and so little to make out the contrary, that he could not but believe the first", and that this was the time for patriots to speak. Although his speech made many Tories vote with the Opposition, a resolution that the Protestant Succession was in no danger, was carried by 256 against 208 votes; and similarly on the Report, next day, the Government carried the question in spite of weighty speeches by Walpole and General Stanhope.[4]

None the less the Ministers had no cause for rejoicing; had it not been for the influence which office gave them in Parliament—there

[1] *Parl. Hist.* vi. 1337.   [2] *Ibid.* vi. 1340.
[3] Schütz in his dispatch of April 13/24, 1714, Han. Arch.
[4] *Parl. Hist.* vi. 1346-8.

were about a hundred placemen in the House of Commons—they
would have been defeated. Still, it was clear that there was danger,
should they wish to restore the Pretender. "All honest men . . .
acknowledge", wrote Schütz in February 1714, "that although of
every ten men in the nation nine should be for us, it is certain, that
of fifteen Tories there are fourteen who would not oppose the
Pretender, in case he came with a French army".[1] And rumours were
spread by the Whigs of great French preparations made with a
view to intervention on the demise of the Queen, which, though
unfounded, kept up an opposition ferment in the country.

Meantime the Hanoverian Envoy in London continued his reserve
in relation with the Ministers. When on one occasion Lord Oxford
suggested casually an amendment which would give the Electress
greater latitude in the nomination of Regents, the Whigs suspected
him of a design "to give a blow to the Succession by altering the
Regency Bill" and introducing a few Jacobites among the Lords
Justices;[2] and Schütz was instructed from Hanover to declare to all
and sundry that the Elector was satisfied with the Act as it stood,[3]
while his Whig friends advised him not to say even so much, unless
he was asked again. As the Lord Treasurer never returned to the
subject, nothing more was said about it.

The extreme restraint of George Lewis did not please his English
adherents, and they continued to press for the coming over of the
Electoral Prince, a topic which takes the foremost place in Schütz's
dispatches. The dislike of the Queen for this idea was comprehensible
—she was ill and feared that the presence of the heir would divert
the attention of her people from her, and act as a check on her. The
example of Queen Elizabeth was quoted "who would not so much as
suffer her successor to be declared, expressing herself, that she would
not live with her grave-stone always in her sight".[4] Swift claims to
have advised the Ministers that

the young grandson[5] . . . should be invited over to be educated in
England; by which . . . the Queen might be secure from the influence of

[1] Macpherson, vol. ii. p. 556.
[2] *Ibid.* vol. ii. p. 563.
[3] Schütz's dispatches of Jan. 1/12, Feb. 2/13, March 16/27, 1714; instructions
to him of Jan. 30 and March 16, 1714, in the Han. Arch. See further Macpherson, vol. ii. pp. 544-5.
[4] Swift, "An Inquiry into the Behaviour of the Queen's Last Ministry".
Works, ed. Scott (Edinburgh, 1814), vol. vi. p. 68.
[5] Frederick, son of George II, and father of George III.

cabals and factions; the zealots, who affected to believe the succession in danger, could have no pretences to complain; and the nation might one day hope to be governed by a Prince of English manners and language, as well as acquainted with the true constitution of Church and State.[1]

This idea did not appeal to the Whigs who wished to use the Electoral Prince against the Ministers. In view of George Lewis's attitude, they suggested another, in appearance less objectionable, form: as the Duke of Cambridge was entitled to take his seat in the House of Lords, a writ of summons for him should be applied for. Schütz and Kreyenberg reported that Nottingham had talked of demanding such a writ of the Lord Chancellor, and that Lord Cowper had employed the clerk "who gives out the writs, . . . to inquire at the Lord Chancellor, whether he should bring the Electoral Prince's writ to the Envoy of the Elector's Court". But the Chancellor received the suggestion "in a very angry manner, . . . and ordered that the writ should not be delivered out of the office, even though inquired for";[2] and Schütz himself was in doubt how far he should go without orders, especially as he did not know whether, if the writ was received, the Prince would come over.

While this new proposal failed to change the attitude of George Lewis, it made a considerable impression on the Electress Sophia. In 1705, when the summoning of the heir was proposed by the Tories, she had declared that she would act immediately on such an invitation.[3] At the age of eighty-three, she could no longer think of undertaking the journey, and even when, in January 1714, the death of Queen Anne was expected, she would not have wished to go to England without her son, the Elector, however little this was his intention.[4] But she wrote to Leibniz that her death would be more beautiful if her bones were buried in Westminster Abbey.[5]

On receiving the dispatch about the writ, she wrote to Schütz on April 12, 1714, without informing the Elector of the contents of her letter, and instructed him to tell the Chancellor that surprise was felt at Hanover at the writ not having been sent, though it was owing to the Duke of Cambridge in accordance with the Queen's patent— "*je crois qu'il ne trouvera pas mauvais que vous le luy demandiés et la*

---

[1] Swift, *op. cit.* vol. vi. pp. 68-9.
[2] Macpherson, vol. ii. p. 567.
[3] See von Noorden, *Europ Gesch.* vol. ii. p. 254, and Salomon, *op. cit.* p. 276.
[4] Klopp, *Leibniz' Werke,* vol. ix. p. lxxv.
[5] *Ibid.* p. 429.

raison. . . . ." [1] It is not clear from this whether Schütz was to demand the writ or merely inquire why it had not been issued—a distinction which, though slight in itself, acquired importance when a controversy arose over the request.

Schütz was delighted, and never doubted that he was meant to ask for the writ; but he consulted his friends, Lords Somers and Wharton, also Townshend who had risen to a high position among the Whigs, and Nottingham who had left the Tories. They, and everyone consulted, pressed that it should be done, declaring that this was the last opportunity of saving the Protestant Succession from the treasonable dealings of the Ministers; it being universally held that on the Queen's death the throne would go to the man on the spot— *"primo occupanti"*.

The visit of the Hanoverian Envoy to the Lord Chancellor started with an exchange of civilities; but when Schütz declared that the Electress had ordered him to ask that his Lordship would be pleased to make out a writ for her grandson, Harcourt changed colour and said, much disturbed, that he could not do so without first acquainting the Queen therewith. After being silent for some time, he added that he could not recollect that a writ was ever demanded or sent beyond the sea; to which Schütz replied that if delivered to him, it would not be sent out of the Kingdom. On Schütz taking leave, Harcourt desired him to observe that he did not refuse the writ, but only wanted to know the Queen's orders first.[2] That night Schütz waited in vain for a reply. The Cabinet Council, which met in the presence of the Queen, sat till after midnight; it is reported that the Queen, seconded by Bolingbroke, wished to have the writ refused, but as the majority of the Ministers feared that this might be construed into a breach of privilege, it was resolved that the Lord Chancellor should make out the writ. Schütz, however, was told that the Queen, "not having

---

[1] The text of this letter, published by Pauli in the *Zeitschrift des hist. Vereins f. Niedersachsen* (1883), p. 47, is more complete than that published by Salomon, p. 281, but it seems that both have failed to decipher correctly a few passages in the difficult handwriting of the Electress. I read the passage as follows:

"A Hanover le 12 d'avril 1714. Je vous prie de dire a Mr. le chancelier my Lord Harcourt qu'on est fort estonne icy qu'on n'a point envoyé un Writ a mon petit fils le Prince Electoral pour pouvoir entrer au Parlament comme Duc de Cambrige comme cela luy est due par la patente que la Reine luy a donne comme il a toujours este (été) de mes amis aussi bien que son Cousin je crois qu'il ne trouvera pas mauvais que vous le luy demandiés et la raison. . . ."

[2] Schütz to Robethon, Macpherson, vol. ii. pp. 590-91.

received the least intimation of this demand" from Hanover, could hardly persuade herself that he had acted by direction from thence;[1] and that she considered it contempt and an affront to her person, that she should not have been acquainted with the matter first, as it concerned a Prince of the Blood whom she had made a peer. He was further blamed for having addressed himself to the Chancellor, without consulting Lord Oxford or Bromley. His excuses were brushed aside, and Oxford advised him, as a friend, not to appear any more at Court; and the day after he had actually claimed the writ from the Lord Chancellor, the Master of the Ceremonies, Sir Charles Cotterell, came and read him a letter from Bromley, with an order of the Queen, forbidding him the Court. He was further told that the British Minister at Hanover had been instructed to demand his immediate recall. At the same time, the Hanoverian Resident, Kreyenberg, was informed by Bromley "that any other Minister whom the Elector would please to send over would be well received by Her Majesty".[2] Schütz did not wait for his recall, but in a letter, presumably to Bromley,[3] declared that having had the misfortune to incur Her Majesty's displeasure, and being thereby rendered incapable of serving his master any longer in this Court, he thought it his duty to return home in order to report the manner in which he had carried out his orders. Two days after Cotterell's visit Schütz left London.

The incident was not yet closed. Excitement ran high. The Court party dwelt on the indecent and ill-bred behaviour of the Envoy, or of the Electoral House, and on the evil designs of those who desired the coming over of the Duke of Cambridge;[4] though they could not allege the request to have been irregular, seeing that the Lord Chancellor had issued the writ.[5] On the other hand, those well-affected to the Hanoverian cause rejoiced at the Electoral House having at last discarded their reserve, which had bordered on indifference; and they wished for the Prince's immediate coming. The day after having claimed the writ, Schütz in a letter to George Augustus, urged him to come without delay, to save the Protestant Succession which would otherwise be lost; while Leibniz wrote to the Electress that if Schütz

[1] Lord Harcourt to Schütz, Stowe MSS. 226, f. 422.
[2] Whitehall, April 17/28, 1714, Han. Arch.
[3] Han. Arch.
[4] Bonet's report of April 20/May 4, 1714, Prussian State Archives.
[5] Cf. *Leibniz' Urteil* in Klopp, vol. ix. p. 479.

had acted without orders, he resembled a General who won a battle without awaiting orders, and that if the Electress could not make up her mind to send her grandson across, it should be made clear to the nation that the refusal was due to the hostile attitude of the Administration.[1]

The Electoral Prince was not sent over. Thomas Harley, a cousin of Lord Oxford, had recently gone to the Court of Hanover with instructions "to inquire what further securities the Elector thought necessary for the succession of his family to the throne".[2] In reply he was given a memorandum[3] containing three requests: that the British Government should compel the Pretender to remove to Italy, the more so as "the Pretender's adherents publish, with the utmost assurance, that he is preparing to make a descent in the North of Great Britain, while the Kingdom is unfurnished with a fleet and troops; . . . and that he depends upon a powerful foreign assistance". Next, the hope was expressed "that Her Majesty will own with them, that it is necessary for the security of her Royal Person, and for that of her Kingdoms, and of the Protestant religion, to settle in Great Britain some one of the Electoral Family, who would be attentive to such important concerns", and cultivate reciprocal confidence and a perfect concert between the two Courts (subsequently George Lewis was able to point to this memorandum as evidence of his honest intentions to act in this matter in an understanding with the Queen). Lastly, it was asked that, now that the nation was no longer burdened with the expenses of the war, "a pension and establishment should be settled by Act of Parliament on Her Highness the Electress, as the nearest heir to the Crown usually enjoyed". Sophia, well acquainted with English conditions, had refused a private pension offered to her by the Queen, just as Anne had done when it was offered to her by William III.

It was only after the memorandum had been given to Harley that the news about the affair of the writ reached Hanover. Some were now in favour of sending the Electoral Prince, but George Lewis persisted in his refusal, and a complaint by Harley supplied him with further evidence of the attitude of the British Court. Shortly afterwards Harley left Hanover. If Marlborough's statement is correct, that in sending Harley it was the view of the Administration to obtain some declaration from the Elector which might impose upon

---

[1] Klopp, vol. ix. pp. 449-51.   [2] Macpherson, vol. ii. p. 537.
          [3] *Ibid.* pp. 608-10.

the nation and make it believe that Hanover was satisfied with them, they failed of their purpose.[1] But the Elector disclaimed all responsibility for what Schütz had done, while the Electress, when discreetly sounded about it by Strafford,[2] claimed to have been the innocent cause of the incident—"she says . . . Schütz mistook her orders, which was not to ask, but only to inquire, if the Duke of C. should not have his writ as well as other Dukes, &c".[3] But George Lewis, who was never a tender son, himself did not seem altogether satisfied with her explanation, and in a pointed manner admonished Schütz that where he and his son were concerned, Schütz had to follow his orders only, and act on them alone.

The Whigs had set hopes on the report which Schütz would make on his return, but when he arrived at Hanover, he was not received by the Elector, and all hopes and fears entertained in London concerning a possible revival of the idea to send the Electoral Prince to England proved groundless. The Prince himself and his ambitious wife pressed the Elector to give in to the demands. But on June 5 letters arrived from the Queen to Sophia, George Lewis, and George Augustus, so hostile in tone that the Prince himself could no longer entertain the idea of going to England.

Bolingbroke had suggested the writing of these letters; and whatever their ultimate aim, their immediate and obvious purpose, to prevent the coming of the Prince, was achieved. The Queen told the Elector that the coming of his son would be an infringement of her sovereignty "which you would not choose should be made on your own".[4] Even sharper were her letters to the main culprits, Sophia and George Augustus. She wrote to the Electress:[5]

It is of importance, with respect to the succession of your family, that I should tell you such a proceeding will infallibly draw along with it some consequences, that will be dangerous to that succession itself, which is not secure any other ways, than as the Prince, who actually wears the Crown, maintains her authority and prerogative.

The old Electress was deeply moved—"This affair will certainly

---

[1] Coxe, *Marlborough*, vol. iii. p. 566.

[2] Strafford to the Electress, The Hague, May 4, 1714; the original is in Stowe MSS. 226, ff. 452-60. The letter is printed in Macpherson, vol. ii. pp. 600-603.

[3] Lord Strafford to Mrs. Arundell, May 25, 1714, *Wentworth Papers*, p. 32.

[4] Macpherson, ii. p. 621.

[5] See Tindal, *Continuation of Rapin's History of England* (1768), vol. xviii. (vi. of continuation), p. 197.

make me ill", she wrote on receipt of the letter; "I shall never get over it". At night she sat down to cards, but her mind continued to dwell on the slight put on her. She attached far greater importance to the incident than it deserved, and seemed to think that all prospect of succession in her house was lost: "I shall have this gracious letter printed so that all the world may see that it will not have been by my fault, if my children lose the three Kingdoms." And yet, did she feel altogether innocent in the matter?

Sophia spent the last years of her life in the Castle of Herrenhausen, her dower house. She was much attached to its magnificent gardens, laid out in the French style by the gardener of Louis XIV. The day after having received the Queen's letter, she was taken ill, but two days later, on June 8, she felt sufficiently recovered to take her customary evening walk in the park. Walking along the tall box hedges, between the Electoral Princess Caroline and her lady-in-waiting, Countess Bückeburg, she talked at ease; but when she reached the first fountain, her gait became uncertain, and she only managed to make a few more steps. "I feel very unwell", she said; "give me your hand". After that she sank into the arms of the two women, who laid her down on the ground. Her death was sudden and painless—without a doctor, as she had wished it.[1] She was deeply mourned by all who had been close to her in her lifetime.

As for the probable political consequences of her death, the British friends of Hanover thought a man in his best age preferable as heir-apparent to a woman of eighty-four; but Sophia would hardly have voluntarily renounced her rights in favour of her son. On her death, the name of the Elector of Brunswick was substituted for hers in the liturgy of the Church of England, his title being mentioned. But his name was given as George, the name of England's patron saint, while that of Lewis, borne by England's greatest enemy, the King of France, was omitted. He was to be George I, and not George Lewis I.[2]

The death of the Electress had to be officially notified to the Court of St. James's, and thus offered an occasion for sending once more an Envoy to London, capable of watching over, and working for, the interests of the Hanoverian Family. Various men were considered, among others the Hanoverian Minister, Bernstorff. Lord Oxford seems

[1] Klopp, *Leibniz' Werke*, vol. ix. pp. 457 ff.
[2] Bothmer to Robethon, The Hague, June 16 and 19, 1714, Stowe MSS. 227, ff. 117-20 and 125-6.

to have wished for General Schulenburg who at that time was at Hanover.[1] Finally the Elector decided in favour of Bothmer,[2] although he was known to be intensely disliked by the Queen and the British Ministers, since in 1711 he had openly supported the Opposition in its struggle against the peace. The Palatine Resident, Steingens, who entertained relations both with Lord Oxford and the Hanover Court, thought it a mistake which could only be rectified by Bothmer's recall as soon as he had carried out his official mission. Still, there were good reasons for sending him. He was well acquainted with England, its Court, the political parties, and with the chances and dangers of the situation. At The Hague he had been nearby, and able to watch developments closely and to send many valuable hints to Hanover; had he come to London a few months earlier, the affair of the writ, so offensive to the Queen, might have been avoided. Anyhow, George Lewis thought Bothmer the best man for the post —in March 1713,[3] when Grote was dying, Bothmer had been ordered to go to England immediately, should the Queen's illness take a serious turn. Eventually the Elector had no reason to regret his choice.

About the same time, a British Envoy was sent once more to Hanover. Originally Lord Paget had been chosen, but after the affair of the writ he declined, and Lord Clarendon, a grandson of the famous historian of the Rebellion, and a cousin of the Queen, was appointed in his place. He was a man, to say the least, of mediocre abilities, and ridiculous stories were told about him—e.g. that when appointed Governor in America, he thought it necessary for him, in order to represent the Queen, to dress himself as a woman.[4] Clarendon was to deliver the Queen's reply to the memorandum sent by the Elector through Harley; it amounted to a refusal couched in rather stiff terms. The Queen declared that she looked upon it

to be very unnecessary, that one of the Electoral Family should reside in Great Britain to take care of the security of her Royal Person, and her Kingdoms, and of the Protestant Succession, as is expressed in the memorial. This, God and the laws have entrusted to her Majesty alone, and to admit any person into a share in these cares with her Majesty

[1] Klopp, *Leibniz' Werke*, vol. ix. p. 474.
[2] Cf. Bothmer's letter to Robethon, June 16, 1714, Macpherson, vol. ii. p. 625.
[3] George Lewis to Bothmer, Hanover, March 14, 1713, Han. Arch.
[4] Macpherson, vol. ii. p. 626.

would be as dangerous to the public tranquility, as it is inconsistent with the constitution of the monarchy.[1]

It seems likely that the reply was written by Bolingbroke.

Clarendon and Bothmer crossed in the Thames. Bothmer had not found it easy to accept the mission—he had recently declared that he could be of little service to his master in England,[2] and now, too, he did not underrate the difficulties awaiting him.[3] The Queen was not well disposed towards the Elector, the Ministers were pursuing their secret plans, Oxford was quarrelling with Bolingbroke, which seemed to render it impossible to keep on good terms with both. On the other hand the Whigs desired to appear even now as those who would be called upon to assume office under the future King, and expected his representative openly to take sides with them.

Bothmer's instructions[4] followed those of previous Electoral Envoys. He was to explain that there had been no reason to view the idea of the coming of the Hanoverian Prince to England in "an invidious light". He was to keep on proper terms with the Government and exercise sufficient restraint in his relations with the Opposition to prevent his being taxed with "fomenting factions". Ultimately it depended on his own tact and sense to thread his way through this highly delicate situation.

The British Government was passing through a serious crisis. Next to Lord Oxford, who in 1710 had formed the new system, Henry St. John,[5] now Viscount Bolingbroke, a man of uncommon ability and restless ambition, was the leading figure in the Cabinet. A conflict had arisen between the two, which though originally of a personal nature, had gradually assumed a political character, and affected, among other things, their attitude towards the problem of the Succession.

[1] Coxe, *Walpole*, vol. ii. p. 46.
[2] Klopp, *Leibniz' Werke*, vol. ix. p. 496.
[3] Bothmer to George Lewis, The Hague, June 19, 1714, Han. Arch. For his letters to Robethon see Macpherson and Stowe MSS. in the British Museum.
[4] The instructions are dated Herrenhausen, June 19, 1714, Han. Arch.
[5] See Salomon, *op. cit.*, chs. x., xii., and xiii.

CHAPTER III

THE LAST MONTHS OF THE QUEEN

Dɪᴅ the Tory Ministers in fact plan a restoration of the Stuart Pretender? It is necessary to distinguish between their activities abroad calculated to influence the Pretender, and possibly also France which was bound to play a part in the matter, and those at home, aimed at influencing public opinion, assisting the Jacobites, and ultimately altering the Act of Succession.

That the Ministers entertained relations with the Jacobites and, by raising their hopes, secured their allegiance, does not prove that their aims were identical. Politicians will sometimes make use of parties which can serve them, without any real desire to serve those parties; and after the death of the Queen, in a pamphlet inspired, or possibly even drawn up, by Lord Oxford,[1] the relation of the Ministers to the Jacobites was compared to that of Charles I to the Roman Catholics, and of Charles II to the Presbyterians.

Although Oxford and Bolingbroke would naturally have wished to keep two strings to their bow, and although the continuance of their party in office—no matter who succeeded, the Pretender or the Elector—was their principal aim, circumstances were driving them towards the Pretender. Their peace policy had resulted in a conflict with the Elector, which was aggravated by subsequent developments; while at home the Queen, towards the end of her life, inclined to the Pretender, and the Whigs by identifying themselves with the Hanoverian cause and by insisting that the Tory Administration was opposed to the Protestant Succession, finished by driving them into such an opposition. Bolingbroke complained that the Elector had become the head of a party; and once it was obvious that Hanoverian rule would mean Whig dominion, the Ministers came to incline towards the Pretender.

[1] *The Secret History of the White Staff*, Part II (London, 1714).

Bolingbroke was most active in his cause. In 1712, in personal negotiations with Torcy, he agreed that the Pretender, who was to be forced to remove from France, should be suffered to reside in Lorraine. The time might come, said Bolingbroke, when the well-disposed would wish to have him near.[1] The Queen was privy to the arrangement. Indeed, Bolingbroke himself suggested the arguments with which the Duke of Lorraine should meet the demands, or even threats, which would have to be addressed to him from England.[2] But no decisive step had yet been taken in favour of the Pretender when, at the end of 1713, the Queen was taken dangerously ill. In January 1714 Oxford entered into negotiations with him through Abbé Gaultier, Torcy's secret agent in England, and Bolingbroke through the French Ambassador, d'Iberville.[3] Both demanded that the Pretender should join the Church of England, without which there could be no restoration; whereas once James Edward had become a Protestant, at least according to the Jacobites, he was no longer excluded by the Act of Settlement. Oxford suggested that the Pretender should tell the Pope that his change of religion was made under duress, while he might add that at heart he remained a Roman Catholic; but that publicly he should announce that his conversion was not of an interested nature, and that he would renounce his claims, if his restoration was not desired by the nation. Bolingbroke similarly insisted on the change of religion and did not think that a marriage with a Protestant Princess would alone suffice, but did not favour such a declaration. Both warned the Pretender against the advice of over-zealous Jacobites who wished him to attempt a landing in Scotland, which the Ministers themselves would have to resist; he had much better leave them time to do his work.

Bolingbroke's reasoning was most ingenious. He considered that by the endeavours of the Ministers the public would, in time, be brought back to its allegiance to the old dynasty, and that the entire Tory party would be gained for the cause of the Pretender. He thought this, however, as yet a distant aim which could be attained but gradually. But what if the Queen died before the work was done? Most Jacobites were at a loss what to do in that case and could think of nothing but the proclaiming of the Pretender on the demise of the

---

[1] Weber, *The Peace of Utrecht*, p. 313. [2] F. Salomon, p. 248.

[3] Important light has been thrown on these negotiations by the researches of Mr. F. Salomon, who in chapter xi. of his book *Geschichte des letzten Ministeriums* gives an account of them based on material from the French Archives.

Queen. Bolingbroke thought differently. The accession of a Hanoverian King would certainly not mean the ruin of their chances. The Elector would govern England through his Hanoverian advisers; he would try to rule in an absolute manner as accustomed at home, which would either lose him his throne or lead to such a reduction of the Royal powers as to produce anarchy from which there would be no escape except a Stuart restoration. In short he considered that a Hanoverian King could not last more than a year and that then the time would come for the Pretender.

The rising of 1715 bears out Bolingbroke's calculations, but to succeed, the Pretender had not fulfilled Bolingbroke's cardinal demand. He refused with horror the suggestion of changing his religion; for him, the son of James II and the devout Maria of Modena, religion came before all other considerations. His father had been King for several years, and later on could not understand that all honest men on both sides of the Channel did not sacrifice their lives and property to restore him to his throne. The son grew up an exile, and the greater the sacrifice, the stronger he adhered to his religion; this was his mother's consolation. Meantime an Act had been passed in England excluding Roman Catholics from the throne; and while his refusal of an interested conversion does him honour, he should have gone a step further, and, being unwilling to conform with the wishes of the nation, he should have accepted the consequences, and renounced all attempts at a restoration.

But he had none of the statesmanship of Henri IV, and while refusing to conform, he obstinately asserted his claims. He tried to persuade the British Ministers that his religion was no bar, and his letters to them and to the Queen, his sister, are filled with the desire to regain his ancestral throne. "I should sooner depart from my life, than from my just right to any other" (than his sister).[1] He wrote to Cardinal Gualterio, at Rome,[2] that he knew that his refusal would upset all his friends, but hoped that their zeal would revive, and that

they will prefer to take me such as I am than persevere in the demand that I should dishonour myself in order to regain my rights. Such is my position. My best hope rests on the friendship of my sister, which I cannot doubt, especially since I have let her know that I would not give her any disturbance during her life provided she will secure to me the Crown after her death.

[1] Printed by F. Salomon, *op. cit.* pp. 337-41.
[2] April 23, 1714; Add. MSS. 31255, f. 8. The letter is written in code terms, which are not reproduced above.

In these circumstances the British Ministers could not form any definite scheme for his restoration, though they did not altogether renounce the idea, least of all Bolingbroke, who knew that he had nothing to hope for from the Elector. The difference between the two leading Ministers was marked: Bolingbroke hardly cared to hide his hostility to Hanover, while Oxford imagined that his position towards the Electoral Family was not such as to preclude him from gaining their confidence, and from remaining Lord Treasurer even under a Hanoverian King.

When Baron Bothmer arrived in London on June 24, O.S., the conflict between the two Ministers had reached the breaking point. There was talk of which of the Ministers favoured the one and which the other, the reputed Jacobites, especially Harcourt and Bromley, being considered adherents of Bolingbroke. If he won, reported Bothmer to Hanover on June 29/July 10, 1714, he would certainly plunge into action, being rash, violent, and conceited. He, who because of his daring plans was nicknamed Phaëton, had already won the Queen's favour as against the Lord Treasurer.

Oxford, in view of the visible decline in the Queen's favour towards him, and feeling his position threatened by Bolingbroke, was intent on gaining that of the Elector. In his first conversation with Bothmer on June 28, Oxford promised him to work for a good correspondence between the Queen and the Elector, though this could not be established in a day. Further, in reply to a letter brought to him from the Elector, he assured Bothmer, that he would work for the Hanoverian Succession, and said that he wished shortly to talk to Bothmer about the measures to be taken. On this occasion Oxford was sincere; but neither Bothmer nor the Elector trusted him any longer. "One has always to count with his unscrutable duplicity and perfidy", wrote the Envoy; the Elector would gain nothing by Oxford's victory over Bolingbroke; for both favoured the Pretender, except where Bolingbroke was rash, Oxford was astute—their aims were identical.

On June 29 Bothmer was received by the Queen. She was pale, but there was nothing to suggest that she had only one more month to live. Bothmer proceeded to notify her of the death of the Electress Sophia, presented her the letters from the Elector and the Electoral Prince, and assured her of the friendly feelings of the Hanoverian Court. The Queen answered graciously, and said how much she mourned the death of Sophia, sympathized with anything which concerned the Electoral House, and welcomed every opportunity to show her friendship for the Elector. As usual, the audience was of a strictly official character, and not a word was said about the Succession. Her true feelings for the Electoral House cannot have been cordial, and Bothmer himself was not in her favour. He had no further audience with her, and saw her only once more, at the opening of Parliament.

With the Ministers too his intercourse was reduced to a minimum; but he was in close touch with the friends of the Elector, and discussed with them the measures to be taken. He served the interests of the Elector better than the Prince could have done, but at the same time tried to prove to the Ministers how harmless the Prince's coming would be. He thought he had convinced some of them, but in the end the answer was always the same—that the Queen would not admit it. When, in 1705, the summoning of the Electress Sophia was first mooted, the Queen is said to have cried three days and nights, until her fears were removed. The Ministers told Bothmer that a different way would have to be found to safeguard the Protestant Succession, e.g. by removing the Pretender from Lorraine; though this too was known to be impossible. Altogether, Bothmer received a poor impression of his master's prospects, and in his letters repeatedly commented on the fact that in the end, on the death of the Queen, the Pretender would reach England before the Elector.

In reality the attitude of the British Government with regard to the Succession seemed at that very moment to have taken a turn for the better. The conflict within the Administration contributed to it. Bolingbroke undoubtedly tried to pave the way for the Pretender, though it seems doubtful whether a restoration was the sole aim of his policy. Lord Oxford, on the other hand, with finer discernment, realized that in the short time which the Queen had still to live, it would not be possible by secret means to secure the success of James Stuart, especially in view of his refusal to change his religion. Hence his turning towards Hanover.

During the last few years attempts had been made to enlist recruits for the service of the Pretender. In Ireland a movement in his favour was on foot; and it was reported that considerable numbers of recruits were landing in the ports of Northern France. In July 1714 an affair occurred which made a great noise; two Irish officers were arrested for enlisting men for the Pretender in London and West-

D

minster, and on one of them a passport was found from the Earl of Middleton, Secretary of State to the Pretender.[1] Oxford now urged on the Cabinet Council the need for issuing a proclamation against the Pretender, for which the Queen had recently professed to see no occasion. He suggested a reward of £100,000 for anyone who would apprehend the Pretender whenever he should land or attempt to land, in Great Britain. This measure was contrary to the intentions of Bolingbroke who, however, did not dare to oppose it openly; he subsequently explained to his Jacobite friends, and also to the French Ambassador, that "he was obliged to agree to it, lest he had too soon and too much discovered himself and his designs".[2] But he tried to weaken the proposal, and while he did not deny the need for it, described the sum as excessive and pointed to the precedent in the reign of James II when a reward of £5000 was promised in the Attainder of the Duke of Monmouth. The next day, June 23, 1714, a proclamation was published in the Queen's name that "whereas . . . the person pretended to be Prince of Wales . . . and taking upon himself the style and title of King of England", and who "stands attainted of high treason", continued in Lorraine, notwithstanding the renewed and pressing instances of the Queen for having him removed; anyone who shall apprehend the said Pretender and bring him before the Justices of the Peace, should he land or attempt to land in Great Britain or Ireland, "shall have and receive as a reward the sum of five thousand pounds".[3]

The proclamation marked a turn in the attitude of the Government, and Parliament readily joined in it, feeling apparently that the new policy was more in accordance with public opinion. The next day Lord Nottingham moved in the House of Lords an address of thanks to the Queen for the proclamation, and was seconded by Lord Halifax.

The Earl of Wharton, who likewise supported the motion, holding the Queen's Proclamation in his hand, most pathetically lamented her Majesty's owning that her endeavours to remove the Pretender from Lorrain had been ineffectual. "Unhappy Princess," said he, "how much is her condition altered! Will posterity believe, that so great a Queen, who had reduced the exorbitant power of France, giving a king to Spain, and whose very ministers have made the Emperor and the States-General to

---

[1] Bonet's report of June 18/29, June 22/July 2, 1714. *Parl. Hist.* vi. 1358.
[2] *Lockhart Papers*, vol. i. p. 472.
[3] See Boyer, *Political State of Great Britain*, vol. vii. (1714), pp. 525-7.

tremble, should yet want power to make so petty, so inconsiderable a prince as the Duke of Lorrain, comply with her just request, of removing out of his dominions the Pretender to her crown?''

Bolingbroke was not present, and not one voice was raised against Nottingham's proposal. The Address suggested further measures against the Pretender:

. . . we take this occasion to repeat our humble request and advice to Your Majesty, to endeavour, in the most proper and speediest manner, not only to renew the alliances Your Majesty had with the princes of Europe, but also to invite them, and particularly the Emperor and the King of Prussia, into the guaranty of the Protestant Succession as by law established, in the most serene House of Brunswick, and to desire them to join with Your Majesty, in pressing the Duke of Lorrain, not to suffer the Pretender to remain in any part of his dominions. And . . . we most humbly beseech Your Majesty to issue out your Royal Proclamation, promising a reward to all such persons as shall discover to any of your magistrates, and cause to be apprehended any person who hath already listed any person, or hath been listed in Great Britain or Ireland, into the service of the Pretender. . . .

It is further reported that Lord Bolingbroke

being come into the House of Peers, just after the above Address was voted, appeared a little surprised at that resolution, and said, "There was a more effectual way to secure the Succession in the House of Hanover". Some members expressing their desire that he would offer it to the House, he proposed a Bill, to make it high-treason to list or to be inlisted into the Pretender's service.

The Whigs naturally assented and

the Bill was accordingly brought in, and, in a Committee of the whole House, of which the Lord Bolingbroke was chairman, the Lords Halifax, Townshend, Cowper, Somers, and Wharton, made it their business to shew, "That the Pretender was inconsiderable of himself, and not to be feared, but so far forth, as he was countenanced and protected by the French king, whose interest and constant design was to impose him upon these realms" . . . The Bill was sent to the Commons, who gave it their concurrence.[1]

In the Commons the Royal Proclamation against the Pretender was received with no less enthusiasm than in the Lords. Here too, an Address of thanks was proposed, receiving universal support; it was

---

[1] *Parl. Hist.* vi. 1359-61.

further urged "that the £5000 mentioned in the Queen's proclamation was too small a recompence for so important a service" as apprehending the Pretender. It was apparently known that Lord Oxford had originally proposed a much larger sum in the Cabinet and an amendment was moved to the Address "that this House would cheerfully aid and assist her Majesty by granting the sum of £100,000 as a further reward to any, who should perform so great a service to her Majesty and her Kingdoms". This was opposed by Secretary Bromley who suggested "that the promising of a reward so far beyond what was mentioned in the Queen's Proclamation, would be a sort of reflection on her Majesty".[1] None the less the Address thus amended was carried unanimously.

The Queen's answer was colourless; in reply to the Lords she said:[2]

You may be assured I shall continue to do whatever I judge necessary for the securing of our religion, the liberty of my people, and for putting an end to the vain hopes of the Pretender.

Even less was said in the answer to the Commons. None the less, a good impression was produced with the public, and the Protestant Succession was now thought as secure as previously it had been believed in danger.[3]

The last attempt to overthrow Bolingbroke was made in the House of Lords in a debate on the Spanish trade which the Peace Treaty had failed safely to re-establish. Whatever the joy had been over the peace, trade with France, Spain, and the West Indies continued to linger, while the prices of British manufactures declined. To three articles of the Treaty of Commerce signed at Utrecht explanations were added at Madrid, and in the debate of July 27, 1714, Lord Nottingham declared that by reason of the discouragements to which the Spanish trade was subjected by the explanations "it was impossible for our merchants to carry on their trade without certain loss". It was next proposed that the Spanish merchants should be heard; Bolingbroke strenuously opposed this proposal, which Oxford supported and carried.

The merchants being called into the House, unanimously averred, that, unless the explanations of these three articles were rescinded, they could not carry on their commerce without losing twenty or twenty-five

---

[1] *Parl. Hist.* vi. 1358.　　　　　[2] *Ibid.* 1360.
[3] Bonet, June 29/July 10, 1714, Prussian State Archives.

per cent.[1] . . . After a long debate, it was resolved to address the Queen for "All the papers relating to the negociation of the Treaty of Commerce with Spain; with the names of the persons, who advised Her Majesty to that Treaty". The Queen sent an Answer, "That, being given to understand, that the three Explanatory Articles of the Treaty of Commerce with Spain were not detrimental to the trade of her subjects, she had consented to their being ratified with the Treaty". The Queen making no mention of the persons, who had advised her to ratify those Explanatory Articles . . . several members excepted against the Answer as unsatisfactory. And, among the rest, the Earl of Wharton and the Lord Halifax represented, "That, if so little regard was shewn to the addresses and applications of that august Assembly to the Sovereign, they had no business in that House"; and moved . . . That the House should insist on Her Majesty's naming the persons. . . . But the courtiers warded off that blow, which was chiefly levelled at the Lord Bolingbroke. . . .[2]

The dissension between the two leading Ministers had become connected with the problem of the Succession, and the embittered rivalry was now forcing them into more determined partisanships. Oxford, so inscrutable and unreliable, became an outspoken champion of the Hanoverian cause, while Bolingbroke was developing into another General Monk. The Queen at the end of her life seemed to turn towards him as to the only man, able and willing to place her brother on the throne against the Act of Succession and against the will of the nation. The voice of the blood in her became stronger at the approach of death—her duty to the memory of her father seemed to count for more than her duty to her people; and she hated the Elector and his House, and loathed to think of him as her successor.

Bolingbroke could hardly be overturned without the help of Oxford who had promised it to the Whigs, but at the decisive moment remained inactive and mute. To this day it is uncertain whether his attitude was determined by his not wishing to throw in his lot with the Whigs, or whether he thought that he could still retain or regain the confidence of the Queen, or whether he feared that he himself might be involved in Bolingbroke's ruin. Perhaps even more plausible is the assumption that he had promised his help merely with a view to fanning the storm against his rival, without meaning to keep his word—a stratagem compatible with his character.

[1] A slightly different account of the proceedings is given in the pamphlet published a few months later, *An Inquiry into the Miscarriages of the Four Last Years' Reign*, p. 23.

[2] *Parl. Hist.* vi. 1361-2; Bonet's dispatches, Prussian State Archives; Bothmer's letters, Han. Arch.

Excited scenes continued in Parliament. To the Address concerning the Assiento Treaty the Queen replied:

That she always had a great consideration for the advice of the House; and, as to the particulars desired, she would dispose of them, as she should judge best for the service.[1]

This answer was very ill-relished by the Whigs, and after it had been read on July 9, a number of Lords rose—Devonshire, Nottingham, Anglesea, Wharton, and Cowper—and complained of its language; that its concluding part contradicted the first; that it was incompatible with the dignity of the Throne and offensive to the House; and that never had an Address of the Lords received such a reply. It was proposed not to print it, but, so far as possible, to pass it over in silence. Others declared that it was necessary to discover who had advised the Queen to give such a reply. The decisive attack against Bolingbroke seemed imminent.

At that moment the Queen appeared, and put an end to the session. Leaning on two companions, she walked up to the throne. The Commons were summoned to the bar of the House of Lords, and the Speaker delivered an Address in the set terms, expressing the hope that she would be graciously pleased with what the House had done during the session and recalling the most important votes. The Queen gave her Royal assent to several Bills, and next read her Speech in a firm and audible voice:

. . . My chief concern is to preserve to you, and to your posterity, our holy religion, and the liberty of my subjects, and to secure the present and future tranquillity of my Kingdoms. But I must tell you plainly, that these desirable ends can never be attained, unless you bring the same dispositions on your parts; unless all groundless jealousies, which create and foment divisions amongst you, be laid aside; and unless you shew the same regard for my just prerogative, and for the honour of my Government, as I have always expressed for the rights of my people.

With that Speech Parliament was prorogued till August 10, 1714.

Bolingbroke, its presumed author, thus tried to silence the Whig tirades concerning the Protestant Succession. But that the Succession was not touched upon in this Speech, seemed remarkable and was taken for further proof of the Queen and her Minister meaning to overturn it. Bothmer and his friends were persuaded that the last

[1] *Parl. Hist.* vi. 1363.

article reflected "on the Protestant Succession and on the intention of having one of our Princes in this country".[1] By the prorogation, Bolingbroke had eluded the attack, but it was bound to be resumed.

On July 13/24, 1714, Bothmer wrote to Robethon about Bolingbroke:

His lordship, they affirm, will be prosecuted vigorously in the next session; but as he apprehends this himself, it is feared he will bring over the Pretender before that time, to save himself and to finish his grand scheme, from which he expects the completion of the fortune which his ambition promises him.[2]

Bothmer had a difficult and thankless task, and his dealings with the friends of the Elector were almost as difficult as with the Ministers. The Queen's letters of May 19/30, 1714, to the Electress Sophia and the Electoral Prince, and Lord Oxford's letter to the Electress, had been recently published in London. This was highly embarrassing to the British Court which had tried to preserve the appearances of good concert with the Electoral House. It was thought that "the copies can only have been obtained from Hanover",[3] and Bromley complained to Bothmer of the indiscretion. Bothmer could truthfully protest his innocence—how could he have been instrumental in publishing correspondence in which the Queen showed so much aversion to the Electoral House? He declared that he could not consider him a friend who had done it.[4]

But it seems that the matter can, after all, be traced to Hanover. The Electress had said that she would like the whole world to read these letters, and had communicated them to a man connected with Marlborough. When a few weeks later Bothmer arrived in London, he was surprised to find many people in possession of copies of those letters which shortly afterwards appeared in print. The fact that the letter addressed to George Lewis was not among them, further strengthens the case against Sophia; possibly Marlborough had a share in the matter.[5] Bothmer's assurances cannot have found ready acceptance, and his relations to the Ministers became still more unpleasant.

But even more serious for him was the fact that the adherents of

---

[1] Bothmer to Robethon, July 13/24, 1714, Stowe MSS. 227, f. 98; Macpherson, vol. ii. p. 636.
[2] Macpherson, vol. ii. pp. 635-6.
[3] Bromley to Lord Clarendon, July 27, 1714, Macpherson, vol. ii. pp. 638-9.
[4] Bothmer to George Lewis, July 6/17, 1714, Han. Arch.
[5] Cf. Klopp, vol. xiv. pp. 622-3.

the Hanoverian Succession began to waver. In spite of their urgent requests, the Elector had maintained his reserve. They now desired to be clearly told what they could expect from the Elector in the dangerous situation which would arise if the Pretender came to England in the lifetime of the Queen. Should he wait till she was dead, there was not much to be apprehended—for then, according to the law, the Elector would be proclaimed, and pending his arrival the Regency Council would find means to guard against the Pretender. Much more serious would have been for them a resort to arms on the Government declaring for the Pretender in the lifetime of the Queen, or opposing him after he had established himself as the de facto King. This had to be prevented, and they now proposed that the Elector should conclude an agreement with the Emperor and the States General, and if possible with the King of Denmark, to prevent a landing of the Pretender, or to seize London in case of danger, or to send troops to Scotland for an invasion of England. For these purposes money was required, and the Elector was asked to put £100,000 at the disposal of his friends. Lastly, a threat to send the Electoral Prince to England might perhaps be used for securing the removal of the Pretender from Lorraine.

In writing to the Elector Bothmer argued that, whatever his intentions, something had to be done. His friends in England were dissatisfied and dejected, and those recently acquired were wavering. Some even asked to be told if the Elector did not mean to support his cause in England; they were ready to risk their lives and property, but did not wish to do so to no purpose. They hinted that in that case they would offer the Crown to the royal family of Prussia, a prospect most displeasing to the Elector. But before an answer could be received from Hanover, events of first-class importance supervened in London.

Bolingbroke had succeeded in driving Oxford from office. It had been clear for some time past that one of them must go, and before the proclamation against the Pretender was issued, Bolingbroke had brought in a Schism Bill against the Dissenters which could easily have proved fatal for the Lord Treasurer. Oxford, however, maintained himself, but when in turn he had failed to bring down Bolingbroke over the Commercial Treaty with Spain, his fate was settled. The inscrutable intriguer who had kept in with all parties, and thought he could play with them all, finished by ruining himself with everybody. He had estranged the Tories and failed to gain the Whigs, and had lost the Queen's favour without winning that of the Elector. The Jacobites turned from him, and the Court of St. Germain is said to have wished for his removal.

It was said at first that to soften his fall, the Queen designed to bestow on him a pension of £5000 for life,[1] with the title of Duke of Newcastle; but nothing was heard of it subsequently. Bolingbroke, who realized the importance of female influence with the Queen, had come to an understanding with Lady Masham who had a hand in the game. The Lord Treasurer was dismissed with mortifying circumstances. In presence of other members of the Cabinet the Queen gave her reasons for parting with him:

that he neglected all business . . . that he never came to her at the time she appointed . . . that he behaved himself towards her with bad manners, indecency, and disrespect.[2]

On July 26 the two rival Ministers are said to have had a violent altercation in presence of the Queen, concerning their relations to Hanover and the Pretender; but no detailed, reliable report of that conversation seems to exist. On the night of July 27, Lord Oxford surrendered into the hands of the Queen the White Staff, the insignia of his office, but warned her "that those people who pretended to succeed him, would embark Her Majesty in impracticable schemes, which . . . would be her ruin" and "would embroil her, not only with her . . . allies abroad, but with her own subjects at home";[3] the Queen, however, did not listen. Oxford, before his dismissal, is said to have filled with his own men sixty vacant places depending on the Treasury—he did not think his political career was ended. Next he assured Baron Bothmer of his inviolable attachment to the Elector and the Protestant Succession.[4] It was rumoured that Bolingbroke intended to restore the Pretender.

Thus Bolingbroke had gained a free hand; but as the condition of the Queen was becoming precarious, he had to provide against her death. On the day of Oxford's dismissal, he entertained at dinner the foremost leaders of the Whigs, among them General Stanhope; Walpole too was invited, but was out of town. When over the wine restraint was dropped, and the outstanding problem came up for dis-

---

[1] Bothmer to Robethon, July 27/Aug. 7, 1714, Han. Arch.
[2] Lewis to Swift, July 27, 1714.
[3] *A Secret History of the White Staff* (1714), Part I. pp. 53-4.
[4] Bothmer to Robethon, July 27/Aug. 7, 1714, Han. Arch.

cussion, Bolingbroke started by declaring his zealous attachment to the Protestant Succession;[1] but on the Whigs insisting on the removal of the Pretender from Lorraine, he replied that this would never be sanctioned by the Queen. General Stanhope declared in plain words that deeds were required, and not fine words, and that he would not believe Bolingbroke's assurances unless the army command was given to Marlborough, the Admiralty to Lord Orford, and the army filled with reliable officers; Bolingbroke and his friends, of whom, said Stanhope, few were fit for the highest posts, might retain the places of profit. Finally, Stanhope turned to Bolingbroke with brutal frankness:

> Harry! you have only two ways of escaping the gallows. The first is to join the honest party of the Whigs, the other to give yourself up entirely to the French King and seek his help for the Pretender. If you do not choose the first course, we can only imagine that you have decided for the second.

Bolingbroke was taken aback and did not know what to answer; whereupon Stanhope said that he did not need to declare himself immediately, but could do so later on. Bolingbroke now saw that he would not be able to conciliate or deceive the Whigs.

It is difficult to gauge and impossible to assert what were his real intentions, for his power was of short duration. After Oxford's fall he sent assurances to the Pretender that he continued of the same mind *"pourvu qu'il prît les mesures qui conviendraient aux honnêtes gens du pays"*.[2] He was prepared to declare for the Pretender if he changed his religion; not otherwise, as Bolingbroke could not openly come out against the Protestant Succession. In the correspondence of 1714 much is said about measures taken for the Restoration of the Pretender—about the dismissal of Admiral Byng, who in 1708 had defeated the Stuart-French attempt against Scotland; the laying aside of troops in Ireland attached to the Hanoverian cause, and the plans for remodelling the Irish army; about money given by the Government to Highland chiefs inclined to Jacobitism; and the filling of many military commands with Jacobites. Such things had roused intense jealousy even while Oxford was in office, the Hanoverian party being always inclined to put the worst interpretation on the

---

[1] Bothmer to George Lewis, July 30/Aug. 10, 1714. See also Mahon, vol. i. p. 91.

[2] Gaultier to Torcy, Aug. 7, 1714, N.S., Mahon, vol. i. p. 91.

measures of the Government. They were not to be deceived by professions of loyalty; it was Jacob's voice, but the hands were the hands
of Esau.

Bolingbroke now sought to secure his power by a proper choice of
Ministers; a restoration of the Stuarts would have been the logical
complement of his foreign policy. He meant to retain the management
of foreign affairs, but otherwise seemed about to form a purely
Jacobite Administration, consisting of Bromley, Mar, Atterbury,
Ormond, and Wyndham. Even the rumour that the Duke of Marlborough, who was about to return to England, would be of the new
Cabinet had no effect with the Whigs, and merely made them think
that the Duke, whose occasional transactions with the Pretender
were known, had gone over to the Jacobites.

It seemed as if nothing could now prevent Bolingbroke from
carrying out his plans; and the Government would have had the support of French troops in an attempt to coerce the British people.[1]
Bolingbroke's opponents thought him capable of bringing over the
Pretender even against the will of the Queen.[2] The work of a few
months might have sufficed to pave the way for the Pretender, and
Bolingbroke, as a Stuart Minister, in a close understanding with
France, would have been, after Louis XIV, the most powerful man
in Europe. His character and views suggest that he would not have
shrunk from sacrificing the political and religious liberties of his
country to his personal ambitions. But—"what a world is this, and
how does Fortune banter us! "[3]

[1] Salomon, p. 306.
[2] Bothmer to George Lewis, July 30/Aug. 10, 1714, Han. Arch.
[3] Bolingbroke to Swift, Aug. 3, 1714.

CHAPTER IV

THE ACCESSION

THE excitement produced by the conflict between the Ministers and by Oxford's dismissal was more than the frail health of the Queen could stand. The quarrel of the two rivals in her presence centring on the problem of the Succession, must have had a shattering effect on her. She had several sleepless nights and told her clergymen and physicians that "she should not outlive it". Serious symptoms set in; during an audience the pen dropped from her hand, and when, on July 28, in the Cabinet Council, within a quarter of an hour she repeated the same question three times in identical words, the doctors were summoned. They found her pulse irregular, ordered her rest, and forbid her meat or drink, of which she used to partake in excess. The next day, the bad symptoms increased; in the afternoon she fell into a lethargic sleep, was cupped, and recovered consciousness. At night her stomach could not retain a glass of wine, but the vomiting produced relief, and she slept well. At 10 A.M. she was seized with a violent fit, and became unconscious. Having been bled she recovered, but the fit re-occurred and lasted two hours. After that she recovered her senses. The next night she was delirious, but ultimately fell asleep. The day after, her breathing was difficult, her pulse weak, the dozing heaviness increased, while her strength was ebbing. About 11 P.M., the doctors declared that she had only two hours to live. On Sunday, August 1, O.S., about 7.15 A.M., Queen Anne breathed her last.

The news that her life was despaired of produced indescribable excitement. The adherents of the Elector were jubilant, the Jacobites in despair. In a flash it was clear that the rule of Bolingbroke and the Tories was nearing its end; and the Whigs took measures to secure an undisputed accession. In the morning of July 30, the Privy Council met at Kensington. Two of the leading Whigs peers, the Dukes of Somerset and Argyll, who were members of the Council but had been absent from it for a long time past, repaired to Kensington to attend its meeting. But first they had had a conference with Bothmer and promised to inform him immediately of the death of the Queen, and to arrange for a speedy proclamation of the Elector and the opening of the instruments of Regency. The Privy Council were surprised at the unexpected appearance of the two Whigs, but no one could challenge their right to attend. On entering the Council Chamber, they acquainted the Board with the reasons of their coming; and the Duke of Shrewsbury, who held two high offices but was a zealous adherent of the Protestant Succession, returned them thanks for their readiness to give the Council their assistance in that critical juncture. From now onwards the three seem to have guided the deliberations of the Council.[1]

The physicians of the Queen having been examined, orders were given for the militia and the Guards to be kept under arms during the coming night. Next, the choice of a Lord Treasurer seemed the most pressing business. On Oxford's dismissal it had been intended to place the Treasury in commission, but nothing had been done. As by the Act of Succession the chief officers of State were to be of the Regency Council, Oxford flattered himself with yet being one of them—he obtained an opinion from the leading lawyers that his claim to the place was incontestable if at the Queen's death his late post was not filled.[2] Possibly he hoped thus to find himself once more at the head of affairs, first as one of the Lords Justices of the Regency, and next as Minister of George I. But the Whigs hated him almost as much as they did Bolingbroke, who however, as Secretary of State was not of the Regency Council; while Oxford's return to power had to be prevented by the immediate appointment of a successor. The Duke of Shrewsbury was proposed for Lord Treasurer. Bolingbroke, conscious that his time was out, raised no objection. The physicians having assured the Council "that the Queen was sensible"—she had just recovered from a violent fit—the Chancellor, the Duke of Shrewsbury, and some other lords, were ordered to attend her, and laid before her the unanimous opinion of the Council: upon which she expressed her agreement, and giving the Treasurer's Staff to Shrewsbury bid him "use it for good of the people". She further desired him

---

[1] About the meeting of the Privy Council see Lecky, vol. i. p. 164, and the sources indicated by him; the dispatches of Hoffmann and the Diary of Bothmer confirm and supplement the accepted account of the meeting.

[2] Bothmer's Diary, July 30/Aug. 10, 1714, Han. Arch.

to keep the Chamberlain's Staff, so that he now held three of the highest places—he was Lord Treasurer, Lord Chamberlain, and Lord Lieutenant of Ireland.[1]

Shrewsbury's appointment secured the Succession in case of the Queen's death. Upon the motion of Somerset and Argyll, it was agreed that all members of the Privy Council should be summoned to attend, which brought back to it Lord Somers and other Whig friends of the Hanoverian dynasty. They knew what policy to pursue, and the necessary measures were promptly taken. Besides the troops in London, cavalry was brought up, and the necessary orders were sent to Scotland and Ireland; of the troops in Flanders, some were ordered to embark immediately, others to keep in readiness. An embargo was laid on all shipping in the port of London, except when Bothmer wished to send a courier to the Elector.

The Privy Council was at the head of affairs; the Cabinet, out of sympathy with public opinion, had lost credit. The Privy Council had for centuries been the body to advise the Sovereign, had a well-defined position, and was now able to make public opinion prevail. The Cabinet had no acknowledged constitutional existence, and was helpless against a hostile public, once it had lost the support of the monarch.

As the death of the Queen was approaching, the Hanoverian Envoy, Bothmer, acquired authority. To avoid attracting attention, Somerset and Argyll did not call on him a second time after the decisive meeting of the Privy Council on July 30, O.S., but sent him a report of the sitting. The next day Bromley informed him of the condition of the Queen, and assured him that everything would be done to secure the Succession. Next, the Duke of Buckingham, the President of the Council, called on him to inform him of the measures taken. Bothmer was invited to attend the Privy Council; and on going there was informed that a letter would be written to the Elector to acquaint him with the "extreme danger the Queen's life was in . . . and to desire him to repair, with all convenient speed, to Holland, where a British squadron . . . would attend him, and bring him over, in case of the Queen's death".[2] Bothmer was consulted which of the Dutch ports would be most convenient for the Elector. He was further informed that a letter was written to Lord Strafford at The Hague, "to desire the States General to get ready to perform the

---

[1] Bothmer's Diary, July 30/Aug. 10, 1714, Han. Arch.

[2] Tindal, vol. vi. p. 228.

guarantee of the Protestant Succession if need should require".[1]
Lastly, they offered to take any further measures which Bothmer
should advise for the service of his master.

A few hours before the Queen's death, the younger Craggs was sent
to Hanover with a letter from the Privy Council and reports from
Bothmer. The Elector approved of the measures taken by the Privy
Council, and promised to set out immediately on receiving the news
of the Queen's death. When on July 31, O.S., the physicians declared
that the Queen had only a short while to live, the Privy Council sent
orders to the heralds-at-arms to be in readiness to proclaim the new
King.

The Queen died the next morning. The Privy Council immediately
met at Kensington, and proceeded to St. James's. Bothmer and
Kreyenberg were summoned, and the three instruments of the
Elector concerning the Regency Council, which were with the Lord
Chancellor, the Archbishop of Canterbury, and the Hanoverian
Resident, Kreyenberg, having been opened, were found to agree, and
the Regency was set up. To the Lords Justices of the Regency the
Privy Councillors paid quasi-royal honours, rising in their presence
when called upon to give their votes.

After the Privy Council, the Regents, and other high officers of
State, had taken the oath of allegiance, they proceeded to the palace
gate of St. James's, where the King was proclaimed for the first time.
Standing with bared heads, they listened while the herald-at-arms
proclaimed, to the accompaniment of drums and trumpets and amid
the loud and joyful acclamations of the crowd, "that the high and
mighty Prince George, Elector of Brunswick-Lüneburg, is now, by
the death of our late Sovereign, of happy memory, become our only
lawful and rightful liege Lord, George, by the Grace of God, King of
Great Britain, France, and Ireland, Defender of the Faith, etc."[2]
Meanwhile gunshots announced to the population of the capital the
accession of the new King. Custom demanded that the proclamation
should be read at four other places, and the procession proceeded
from St. James's, the heralds in front, followed by the lords in their
coaches—first the Lord Chancellor, and next the Duke of Buckingham as President of the Council, with Baron von Bothmer. The
second time the proclamation was read at Charing Cross, and the

[1] *Ibid.*

[2] The proclamation is printed in full in Boyer, *The Political State of Great
Britain,* vol. viii. (1714), pp. 115-16.

third time at the Temple Bar. From now onwards the coach of the Lord Mayor was at the head of the procession, immediately behind the heralds. The Aldermen tried to take place after the Lord Chancellor, but the Duke of Buckingham and the lords behind him did not suffer them to do so. The fourth time the proclamation was read in front of Bow Church, and the last time in Cheapside, in the square before the Royal Exchange. "The people showed great and sincere joy", wrote the Imperial Resident. The streets were thronged with vast multitudes who made joyful acclamations each time the heralds called out the name of the new King. Oxford and Bolingbroke, who were in the procession, were hissed and insulted, and had to withdraw through back streets. Everywhere the crowds gave expression to their loyal feelings for the new King. A French Papist who drew his sword and rashly declared that he would have preferred to hear the proclamation of the Stuart Prince, was with difficulty saved from the fury of the populace; and even the French Ambassador in his own house feared for his safety, and asked for military protection for his person and property.[1]

After the uncertainty and excitement of the preceding months, the prospect of more settled times was highly welcome. At the first news of the Queen's life being in danger, the public funds rose, but fell whenever it was thought that she would recover. The first day after her death they rose by 3 per cent.[2]

The formation of the new Government was now proceeded with. The name of the King and his family was included in the liturgy. Certain doubts arose in this connexion—should Sophia Dorothea, the divorced wife of George I, be prayed for as Queen? Bothmer knew the King's intentions and asked that, for the present, she should not be mentioned;[3] nor, of course, was it done afterwards. Further, opinions differed as to whether the heir to the throne was to be designated as Prince of Wales without formal creation. It was customary to give that title to the eldest son of the King, and James II at the birth of his son announced that a Prince of Wales had been born. Even Lord Nottingham at first shared this misapprehension,

---

[1] Report from Kreyenberg and copy of d'Iberville's letter in the Hanover Archives. About Atterbury's intention to proclaim the Pretender, see Lecky, vol. i. p. 166.

[2] Hoffmann, Aug. 14, 1714, Vienna Archives; Boyer, *Political State*, viii. (1714), p. 113.

[3] Bonet, Aug. 6/17, 1714, Prussian State Archives.

but it was established by documentary evidence that at birth the eldest son of the King had only the title of Duke of Cornwall, and Nottingham informed Bothmer that he would have to be created Prince of Wales by the King on his arrival in London.

The Regency Council, in accordance with the Act of 1706, included the seven principal officers of State, among them the Duke of Shrewsbury as Lord Treasurer, but also the Lord Chancellor Harcourt, a man of doubtful loyalty; it was considered lucky that neither Oxford nor Bolingbroke was among them. Still, it was not the seven Ministers but the eighteen Members added by the new Sovereign who had the greatest weight. It was with good reason that paramount importance had been attached at Hanover to the three instruments prepared first by Sophia, and next by George Lewis; the rumour that Lord Oxford had tampered with the copy in his safe-keeping had caused there considerable excitement. But when at Bothmer's arrival the old instruments were replaced by those of the Elector, the copy of the Lord Treasurer was found intact, and Oxford laughingly complained about human malice.

The Elector had naturally chosen men of whose devotion he felt assured. The Duke of Shrewsbury who, as Lord Treasurer, was any-how of the Regency, was in his list; most of the other seventeen English and Scottish peers were Whigs: Lord Halifax, who had re-peatedly proved his zeal for the Protestant Succession and was personally known to the King, a man of outstanding ability and conscious of it; the Dukes of Somerset, Bolton, and Devonshire, the Earl of Orford, Lords Cowper and Townshend, and a few other old friends of the Electoral Court; the Earl of Nottingham, who had crossed over from the Tories to the Whigs, and his son-in-law the Duke of Roxburgh, who had been in touch with Hanover for years and ren-dered many services; lastly, the Earl of Anglesea, representing on it the Hanoverian Tories.

But there were some remarkable omissions which must have caused intense resentment: the Duke of Marlborough—a pique which George Lewis is said to have felt against him since the campaign of 1708, is hardly a sufficient explanation of his exclusion; his son-in-law, Lord Sunderland, whose appointment as Secretary of State in 1706 had marked the beginning of the Whig Administration; Lord Wharton (Lord Carlisle openly told Bothmer that he would have preferred if Wharton had been named in his place as much more suitable for the work); and Lord Somers, the author of the Act of

E

Settlement. Marlborough had only just returned from voluntary exile, and when he landed at Dover on the day of the Queen's death, was "hailed with the shouts of exulting crowds". The enthusiasm reached a climax when on August 4 the Duke entered London; he was received with military honours, as if returning from a victory; the crowd shouting "Long live King George" and "Long live the Duke of Marlborough". The news that his own name and that of Lord Sunderland had been omitted from the list of Lords Justices had reached him on the road to London, and he did not disguise his mortification. He said to Baron von Bothmer that the King must have had his reasons, for a measure so calculated to injure them in the estimation of the public. "But it is probable", writes Mahon, "that the real motive for the slight put upon these illustrious men was a jealousy of great party leaders, an impression derived from Tory insinuations that they had attempted to dictate to Queen Anne. . . ."[1] The King's desire to keep the ultimate direction of affairs in his own hands was clearly shown by the position which Bothmer held in London before the King's arrival. Rescripts to the Regents were sent through him, and he was free to deliver or withhold them, as he thought best; and the King acted on Bothmer's advice, both with regard to his journey and the filling of important posts. In consequence Bothmer was besieged by applicants for office or honours, all those who aspired to the favour of the King now turning to him.

On the day of the Queen's death, Bothmer sent a courier to Hanover informing his master that everything went "very well for him here". There was no opposition to the new régime. The King had merely to come, and he could rely upon a most enthusiastic reception from his faithful subjects. Bothmer seconded the request of the Privy Council that the King should repair to England with all speed. George promised to do so, and asked the Regents to hasten the fitting out of the fleet which was to accompany him from Holland to England; but it was only on September 11, 1714, a month after the Queen's death, that he left Hanover.

Meantime preparations were made in London for inaugurating the reign of the Hanoverian King.[2] Lord Berkeley was entrusted with the command of a fleet of forty warships which were to expect the

---

[1] Mahon, *History of England* (1836) vol. i. p. 140.

[2] See letter from Acherley to Leibniz, Aug. 3, 1714, in Kemble's *State Papers*, 579; also *Ztschr. d. hist. Vereins f. Niedersachsen* (1853), p. 133.

King on the Dutch coast. The Regency Council met two and three times a day; and sometimes the entire Privy Council assisted at their meeting. Joseph Addison, the writer, was appointed Secretary of State. All officers, civil and military, had to take the oath to the King. Throughout England he was proclaimed without opposition. At Exeter alone some disturbances were caused by the mob, but these were easily suppressed. At York, where part of the population was Roman Catholic, their arms and horses were seized—as allowed by the law—and the King was proclaimed peacefully, in accordance with the orders of the Archbishop and the Lord Mayor. In some places an effigy of the Pretender was "dragged about the streets and burned".[1] The enemies of the Protestant Succession had been taken by surprise by the Queen's death, and did not dare to resist for fear of incurring the penalties of high treason.

Similarly in Scotland the accession was carried through without any dangerous commotion. Here sympathies for the Stuarts were naturally stronger, but there were neither leaders nor foreign support for a Jacobite rising. France, Scotland's old ally, preserved a waiting attitude. And so nothing happened except for some unimportant disturbances. In a few places the Pretender was proclaimed by the name of James VIII, noisy crowds gathered in the street and drank his health. At Aberdeen, when the accession was celebrated at night by illuminations, a Jacobite rabble threw stones at the windows of the well-affected. In the Western Highlands a few lairds tried to take up arms on behalf of James VIII; old Lord Breadalbane retired to his castle Kailholm, built on an inaccessible rock in the middle of a loch, and defended by some cannon, where the Pretender was to find a safe refuge, should he come to Scotland. But all these attempts ended in complete failure. The armed bands fled at the approach of regular troops, and many a Lowland laird, who at the news of the Queen's death had mounted on horseback and gone with his sons and retainers into the Highlands, returned home disappointed, having found nothing stirring for the service of the Pretender.

In Ireland too the accession was carried through quietly. Soon afterwards, the Regents had to remove the Lord Chancellor of Ireland, Sir Constantine Phipps, a Jacobite, who had refused to obey their

[1] Lady Mary Wortley Montagu, *Letters and Works* (1887), vol. i. p. 86.

orders; a measure which produced a considerable and wholesome impression.[1]

Thus the new régime was secure. When the Queen was dying, General Stanhope had written to his friend, the Emperor Charles VI, that a quiet accession was assured, but that if her illness was protracted even for a few weeks, it might cause serious embarrassment.[2] A French epitaph[3] for the Queen expresses views widely entertained at the time:

> Cy git la Reine Anne Stuart
> Morte trop tôt, morte trop tard.
> Trop tôt pour l'ancien Ministère
> Trop tard pour le party contraire
> Tout calculé, tout rabattu
> Voici ce que j'en ay conclu:
> Trois ans plus tôt le Roy de France
> N'auroit pas vu tourner la chance,
> Six mois plus tard les Protestants
> Auroyent fort mal passé leur temps.
> Qu'on La loue, qu'on La condamne,
> Graces a Dieu cy git la Reine Anne.

After years of passionate argument, few had expected such a peaceful accession. The House of Hanover had been thought in danger from the Ministers who openly favoured the Pretender, practising severity against the Whigs and leniency towards the Jacobites. On one occasion Bolingbroke had hinted to Lockhart, a Jacobite, what would happen after Oxford's fall, "as our interest would increase, and many come over to us when they saw the thing done and the game secured".[4] Jacobite meetings were held in London and its neighbourhood, at which the health of the Chevalier was drunk. "Vast numbers of Popish priests, Jesuits, and the Pretender's friends, came over from France to prepare the way for the intended restoration. . . . The speedy change his Majesty has made in the Government sends them away in despair."[5]

---

[1] Bothmer to the King, Sept. 7/18, 1714, Han. Arch.; Diary, Sept. 2/13, 4/15, 5/16, 15/26, Han. Arch.; Kreyenberg to Robethon, Sept. 3/14, 1714, Brit. Museum.

[2] Klopp, *Leibniz' Werke*, vol. ix. p. 504.

[3] Given in Bonet's report of 1715, Prussian State Archives.

[4] *Lockhart Papers*, vol. i. p. 477.

[5] *An Inquiry into the Miscarriages of the Four Last Years' Reign* (London. 1714), p. 28.

In Scotland the old hatred against England had been fanned
anew by the Union which had abridged or destroyed prescriptive
rights; and a Stuart restoration was to mark its dissolution. North of
the Tweed, Tories and Whigs were synonymous with friends and
opponents of the Pretender.[1]

Throughout Great Britain even the mass of the people had been
affected by the dynastic controversy. Numerous pamphlets argued
the sacred and indefeasible rights of Princes, not to be infringed even
for the sake of religion. In 1713 Defoe wrote in his pamphlet *Reasons
against the Succession of the House of Hanover*:

> Why, the strife is gotten into your kitchens, your parlours, your shops,
> your counting-houses, nay, into your very beds. You gentlefolks, if you
> please to listen to your cook-maids and footmen, in your kitchens, you
> shall hear them scolding, and swearing, and scratching, and fighting,
> among themselves; and when you think that the noise is about the beef
> and the pudding, the dish-water, or the kitchen-stuff, alas you are mis-
> taken, the feud is about the more mighty affairs of the Government, and
> who is for the Protestant Succession, and who for the Pretender. Here the
> poor, despicable scullions learn to cry *High Church, No Dutch King, No
> Hannover*, that they may do it dexteriously when they come into the
> next mob. Here their antagonists of the dripping-pan practise the other
> side clamour, *No French Peace, No Pretender, No Popery.*

And now of a sudden all the noise had stopped: "nothing can go
quieter", wrote Strafford to Robethon from The Hague on September
4, 1714, "than things do in Great Britain and we have prospect of
the gloriousest reign we ever had".[2] A feeling of security replaced the
awful tension of recent years. The Pretender in Lorraine no longer
seemed dangerous, and no one worried any longer about Bar le Duc
being nearer to England than Hanover. And yet there was nothing
miraculous in this sudden change. The law had prevailed.

In the first days after the accession of George I, London society
thronged to Bothmer's house to congratulate him on the success of
his master. Among the foreign diplomats d'Iberville played a pitiful
part; when on August 2/13, he called on Bothmer, he did not know
what line Louis XIV meant to take, but as in the Treaty of Utrecht
France had recognized the Protestant Succession, he could not with-

---

[1] *Observations sur l'état de la nation britannique.* Par un Pair du Royaume.
Translated from the English. London, 1713. It appears from the introduction
by the translator that its author was Lord Nottingham.

[2] Stowe MSS. 227, f. 377.

hold recognition of the new dynasty, though he did not wish to commit himself too far in case his King chose to disregard the Treaty. Accompanied by Gautier, he called on Bothmer, and congratulated him, without saying on what, and refrained from naming King George, though he denied all hostile expressions ascribed to him. He said that pity was felt in France for the Pretender, but that this did not signify an intention to support him. Gautier remained silent.[1] When two days later Bothmer returned the call, the French Ambassador, having heard that his peculiar congratulations had been animadverted upon, tried to remove the bad impression and referred with exaggerated frequency to "His Britannic Majesty" and "*le roi votre maître*".[2]

Bothmer endeavoured to arrange matters which might have embarrassed the King on his arrival in London. In his and Kreyenberg's presence, a search was made among the Queen's papers at Kensington and St. James's, to discover whether she had left any directions for her funeral, and a paper was found at Kensington, bearing neither seal nor signature, but indicating her wish to be buried privately in Henry VII's Chapel, at the side of her husband, George Prince of Denmark.[3] This was done on the night of August 23, and her request for a private interment was carried out all too literally. Few followed her coffin, and the most famous general of her reign, though invited, was not among the mourners. "I could not" wrote the Prussian Minister, "draw up a report on the Queen's funeral."

No formal will was found in the Queen's closet at Kensington, only a mysterious sealed packet, with directions in her own hand and over her signature that on her death it should be burnt unopened. The Regents were unanimous in wishing to carry out the order, but first consulted Bothmer, who thought that the King would certainly want it to be burnt in accordance with her directions, and before his arrival in London. He supposed that the parcel contained letters from the Pretender; but now there was no longer any point in enquiring into the Queen's intentions. A fire was lit in the adjoining room, and in the presence of a few lords, and of Bothmer and Kreyenberg, the Duke of Somerset threw the parcel into the fire; they remained till the last bit of paper was reduced to ashes. But when the fire broke the

[1] Bothmer's Diary, Aug. 2/13, 1714, Han. Arch.; Hoffmann's report of Aug. 14, Vienna Arch.
[2] Bothmer's Diary, Aug. 4/15, Han. Arch.
[3] *Ibid.* Aug. 2/13.

cover and the sheets fell apart, Bothmer thought his supposition confirmed—the letters seemed all written in the same hand, in large, well-shaped characters of a French type.[1]

At first the Regents had meant to settle domestic matters, while leaving foreign affairs for the King's decision; but urgent business calling for immediate action, they had to anticipate the King's foreign policy. They naturally reversed the system of the late Administration, and resumed the previous Whig policy with regard to France and Austria—the conflict between these two Powers dominated the politics of Europe, persisting in spite of the Peace Treaty concluded between them at Baden in 1714.

Much depended upon the action of two Powers. In 1713 the States General had guaranteed the Protestant Succession—were they prepared, in case of danger, to carry out their Treaty obligations? On the other hand, Louis XIV had for a quarter of a century promoted the Stuart interest—would he now take up the cause of the Pretender? When the Queen was dying and the Privy Council reminded the States General of their obligations, the Dutch declared themselves resolved to perform them.[2] They rejoiced at the peaceful accession and were willing to co-operate with London and Hanover. They were probably pleased to help in sending back the British troops from Flanders. The two Hanoverian diplomats at The Hague now gained in importance, and were told that "Their High Mightinesses will be very glad if His Majesty will please to take his journey through their dominions", and stop there on the way. They were prepared to supply Dutch warships if a sufficient number of British warships was not available; though the Pensionary wished that unnecessary *éclat* should be avoided.[3]

No immediate danger threatened from France. Louis XIV was not prepared to plunge into a great war for the sake of the Pretender. He immediately recognized George I, declaring that he would faithfully adhere to the Treaty of Utrecht.[4] James Edward, on the death of his sister, had secretly left Bar le Duc for Paris, but the King, through his Minister Torcy, had asked him not to enter the capital,

---

[1] Bothmer's Diary, Aug. 4/15, Han. Arch.; Bothmer to the King, Aug. 6/17, Han. Arch.

[2] Bromley to Strafford, July 31/Aug. 3, 1714.

[3] See the letters of Klinggraff and Schrader to Robethon, Stowe MSS., 227.

[4] "*Je ne veux en aucune manière altérer les conditions de la paix*". Louis XIV's own words to Prior. Prior to Bolingbroke, Aug. 12/23, 1714, S.P. 78/159.

and warned him insistently not to engage in any undertaking against England; though he offered him a few ships, should he venture on it.[1] The Chevalier returned to Lorraine disappointed, to await a more favourable juncture; while the King saw to it that the incident, which could not be kept secret, was reported to the British Court in a manner showing off the loyalty of France.

The negotiations carried on by Bolingbroke for a defensive alliance with France, Spain, and Sicily, gave the Regents the first occasion to determine their foreign system. The idea had originated with King Victor Amadeus, intent on securing his recent gains, especially Sicily, against the House of Austria. Bolingbroke was favourably disposed, and carried on the negotiations, mainly with Louis XIV; Spanish support had been gained and the accession of other Italian States was expected. The matter advanced so far that a draft of the Treaty was prepared in Paris, and a commission for concluding the alliance was sent to Prior.[2] On the Queen's death, Bolingbroke hastened to instruct him to discontinue negotiations and await the pleasure of the new Sovereign. Although all the Regents were against the alliance, some cautiously wished to draft a report which would seem at least to justify the negotiations; but others, among them Lord Halifax, objected, and a report was drawn up declaring the plan prejudicial to the King's interest.[3] George I concurred in condemning the proposal. Its existence had, in the meantime, become public knowledge and caused considerable commotion. One of the Regents remarked to Hoffmann, that in making their report they had assumed the King would cultivate the friendship of Charles VI, and would not enter into a treaty directed against him. Never was the close connexion between foreign and domestic policy clearer; the Whigs were bent upon resuming their traditional foreign policy, while Bolingbroke had reverted to the Stuart policy of friendship with France.

The Tory Administration had favoured the King of Sicily, that of

---

[1] See Salomon, p. 317.

[2] See Mr. Prior's commission for concluding a defensive alliance, July 21, 1714. It contains the following phrase: "*Cumque dictus Siciliae rex sese plurimum vereri declaraverit, ne controversiae quaedam de iis rebus, praesertim vero de Siciliae regno, exoriantur. . . .*" About the plans of the alliance cf. F. Salomon, pp. 267 and 311-12; also dispatches from Hoffmann, Bonet, and Bothmer.

[3] See Bothmer to Robethon, Aug. 10/21, and Halifax to Robethon, Aug. 24, 1714, Stowe MSS. 227, ff. 292-5 and 381-2.

George I was against him, if only because in succession to James Edward he was the next Roman Catholic claimant to the British Crown. In negotiating the alliance, the King of Sicily had counted on British naval help against Austria; and in fact, the British Mediterranean fleet under Admiral Wishart, a Tory suspected of Jacobitism, was meant to serve the alliance. Three of his ships had recently acted as convoy to the Spanish fleet, while five had been placed at the disposal of the King of Sicily to secure the connexion between the island and his Continental possessions. Wishart was now instructed to recall all his ships and with his entire fleet to await at Port Mahon orders from the King. The Sicilian Minister in London tried in vain with the Regents to have the order rescinded, while Bothmer bade him wait for the arrival of the King. George I, however, adopted an unfriendly attitude towards Sicily. With the order to Wishart the position of Victor Amadeus in Sicily became practically untenable— he had won the island with the help of British naval power, and it was lost the moment England withdrew her support.

The news that the plans for an alliance with France, Spain, and Sicily had been scotched by the King and the Regents, reassured the public. They trusted the new Government to deal effectively with international problems. In a heroic poem, "Britannia rediviva, or Britain's Recovery", an anonymous author celebrated the restoration of her European position. The great Louis XIV, recently the scourge of Europe, watches thunderstruck the transformation, disclaims the Chevalier, and greets the true monarch, fearing his wrath:

> No insults now we dread from France, Lorrain;
> No sep'rate leagues with Sicily or Spain.
> Not Dunkirk undemolished, nor Mardike
> Can England now with the least terror strike.

In spite of the favourable position the Regents took precautionary measures. Lord Orford told Bothmer that as far back as he could remember the condition of the fleet had never been so bad; this could not be remedied immediately, but necessitated additional caution. The news had been received from Portsmouth of an embargo imposed at Le Havre and other French ports with a view to the secret embarkation of an expeditionary force of 6000 men against England. Although this did not sound credible, a squadron of five warships under Admiral Baker was sent to cruise in front of Le Havre and the French Channel ports. The Governor of Portsmouth, Lord North and

Grey, suspected of Jacobitism, was not dismissed, but carefully watched.[1]

The negotiations with France aroused the Regents' suspicions against Prior and Bolingbroke. There was something wrong about their correspondence—either Prior failed to send regular reports, or his correspondence was intercepted; for there were references to previous letters of which Bolingbroke denied receipt. Prior would send even unimportant communications in cypher, which in those days was not much used. With a view to clearing up the matter, the Regents sent a messenger to him, ordering him to transmit copies of all his reports of recent weeks; moreover in future he was to send his dispatches not to the Secretary of State, Lord Bolingbroke, but to the Lords Justices of the Regency.[2]

Bolingbroke, the man in whom the previous system seemed embodied, was removed before the arrival of the King. He could not expect to play the same part under George I as under Queen Anne, and yet he was not prepared for so sudden a fall. The Regents were directed by the King, perhaps at Bothmer's suggestion, to demand from him the surrender of the Seals. They held a meeting at which Bothmer was asked to assist, and placed the other Secretary of State, Bromley, in charge of both Departments. But as he also seemed suspect, the Post Office was soon afterwards ordered to send letters addressed to Bolingbroke and his office to the Regency Council, who decided to transact themselves the business of the Southern Department.

Possibly the main purpose of the Regents in the sudden dismissal of Bolingbroke was to gain an insight into the policy of the late Government; for he could hardly have done much harm had he remained in office a little longer. But there was already the intention of prosecuting him and his friends, and it was of importance to seize his papers with a view to such a prosecution. The explanation, however, was given that this was to stop the abuse recently practised by Secretaries of State of removing official correspondence on leaving their post.

Three members of the Regency Council were instructed to inform

[1] Bothmer's Diary, Aug. 8/19; and Bothmer to the King, Aug. 10/21, 1714, Han. Arch.

[2] Bothmer to the King, Aug. 13/24 and 17/28, 1714; Diary, Aug. 11/22 and 14/25, 1714, Han. Arch.; Prior's reports after Aug. 18/29, 1714, S.P. 78/159; Hoffmann's dispatch Aug. 21, 1714, Vienna Arch.

Bolingbroke of his dismissal, to demand the surrender of the Seals, and to lock up his office. He broke down completely when, in the waiting room of the Regency Council, he learned his fate. He had no choice but to submit. The three Regents went immediately with him to the Cockpit and placed seals on the doors of his office, professing to him that this was merely to guard against possible abuse, not from suspicion against him. Bolingbroke understood the real intention and resented the unprecedented insult. But even then it was rumoured that he had made use of the last few weeks to remove all incriminating documents.[1] From now onwards he skilfully played the part of one gratuitously insulted. The next day he declared, in a conversation with Bothmer, that he had intended to resign in his first audience with the King, but that he could only ascribe this unjust treatment to misrepresentation. He denied having favoured the Pretender, and claimed that this would be borne out by his correspondence; but should he be attacked because of the Peace Treaty, it would be found on enquiry that he had merely obeyed orders.

Oxford, whom Bolingbroke suspected of working against him, had, since his own dismissal, posed as the foremost champion of the Protestant Succession. He now claimed to enjoy the King's favour and a decisive influence in the distribution of places—whoever wished for office should apply to him in time. He tried the game even on some of the Regents; thus he urged the Duke of Devonshire to ask for the Presidency of the Council, or otherwise he, Oxford, would have to recommend Lord Powlett (in reality it was practically settled that Lord Nottingham was to have it).[2] In these troubled days, Oxford, usually dignified and inscrutable, cut a comic figure—no one heeded his mysterious hints, no one trusted him, and no one, except himself, believed in his future power. When the King arrived in London, Oxford found himself as completely excluded from Government as his rival Bolingbroke.

Pursuant to the Act of Succession, Parliament met the day after the Queen's death; but as the Speaker, Sir Thomas Hanmer, was in the country, a few days elapsed before the session started. On August 5, O.S., Parliament was opened by the Regents, who went to the

[1] Bothmer to the King, Aug. 31/Sept. 11; Diary, Aug. 31/Sept. 11, Han. Arch.; Pauli, *op. cit.* pp. 61-3; Hoffmann's reports, Sept. 11 and 14, Vienna Arch.; Bonet's reports, Sept. 11/14, Prussian State Archives.
[2] Bothmer to Robethon, Sept. 3/14, 1714, Stowe MSS. 227, ff. 413-4; to the King of the same date, Pauli, *op. cit.* p. 65.

House of Lords in a body. Below the throne a bench was drawn across the hall, three steps above its floor. The most prominent members of the Regency were seated on it, the others stood behind. After the Commons had entered, with the Speaker at their head, the Lord Chancellor Harcourt read the Speech on behalf of the Regency Council:

It having pleased Almighty God to take to himself our late most gracious Queen, of blessed memory, we hope that nothing has been omitted, which might contribute to the safety of these realms, to the preservation of our religion, laws, and liberties, in this great conjuncture. . . .

It was recounted how, in accordance with the Act of Succession, the three instruments concerning the Regency were opened in a meeting of the Privy Council, and how the Regency Council assumed office and immediately proceeded "to the proclaiming of our lawful and rightful·Sovereign King George". Turning to the Commons, the Speech recommended "the making such provisions . . . as may be requisite to support the honour and dignity of the Crown". And lastly the two Houses were exhorted "to a perfect unanimity, and a firm adherence, to our Sovereign's interest. . . ."[1]

After the reading of the Speech the Lords adjourned, while the Commons returned to their own chamber. Mr. Secretary Bromley moved for an Address of condolence and congratulation, "insisting much on the great loss the nation had sustained by the death of the late Queen". In reply Mr. Thomas Onslow (afterwards Lord Onslow) observed

that the stress of the Address ought not to lie upon condoling, but upon congratulating and giving the King assurances of their maintaining both His Majesty's undoubted title to the Crown, and public credit.[2]

Robert Walpole moved for something more substantial "to give the King assurances of their making good all parliamentary funds".

The Address was drafted in this sense, and was unanimously agreed to the next day. From the condolences it passed to congratulations on the accession of the King,

whose princely virtues give us a certain prospect of future happiness in the security of our religion, laws, and liberties, and engage us to assure Your Majesty, that we will, to our utmost, support your undoubted right

[1] *Parl. Hist.* vii. 4.   [2] *Ibid.* vii. 5-6.

to the Imperial Crown of this Realm, against the Pretender and all other
persons whatsoever.—Your faithful Commons cannot but express their
impatient desire for Your Majesty's safe arrival and presence in Great
Britain.—In the mean time, we humbly lay before Your Majesty the
unanimous resolution of this House, to maintain the public credit of the
nation, and effectually to make good all funds which have been granted
by Parliament, for the security of any money which has been, or shall be
advanced for the public service, and to endeavour, by every thing in our
power, to make Your Majesty's reign happy and glorious.

Similarly the House of Lords voted a dutiful and loyal Address to
which the King made an answer, concluding as follows: "I am hastening to you according to your earnest desire, and the just expectations
of my people".

It was hoped that the show of loyalty on the part of the Tory
majority in the Commons would incline the King towards close co-
operation with Parliament. The Act of Succession had been an important step towards establishing the Parliamentary system. Now the
Tory majority, who had little to expect from the King, tried to
entrench themselves behind the Parliamentary institutions. The
suggestion was made in the Commons, possibly also in the Lords,
that a deputation should be sent to the King, as was done before the
return of Charles II. Bothmer immediately understood the purpose,
and rightly compared the proposed delegation to the Field Deputies
whom the States General used to join to their military commanders,
to keep them under constant control and direction. The King was
to settle every step with this Parliamentary deputation—a highly
troublesome control which would have deprived both him and the
Regents in London of their freedom of action. King George, on the
other hand, in settling his British Government, wished to be advised
not by Englishmen, but by his faithful Bothmer, who was well
acquainted with conditions both in Hanover and England, and with
the wishes of his master. Bothmer knew that he was acting in the
sense of the King when he tried to prevent the sending of the Parliamentary deputation. He said he could not see its purpose; the King
was hastening his departure, and required all his time in Hanover to
settle the Government for the period of his absence; while England
was, in the meantime, governed by the Lords Justices of the Regency.
When on August 12, O.S., the proposal was actually made by two
menbers, the Speaker managed to suppress it.

One of the first matters which came before the House was the Civil

List of the new ruler. The Speaker and Robert Walpole succeeded in having Mr. Conyers at the head of the Grand Committee of Subsidy, and not the Jacobite Sir William Wyndham. A Civil List of £700,000 had been voted to the late Queen for life, but now, to render the King dependent on Parliament, some favoured a yearly vote. It was, however, decided that the King should not be treated worse than his predecessor, and the Tories, trying to curry favour with him, moved to give him £1,000,000 a year; but as the Whigs did not support the motion, it was dropped—they suspected the Tories of acting insidiously, with a view to reproaching the King afterwards as oppressing the nation by a higher revenue than his predecessor had enjoyed. The Whigs were thought to have acted with extraordinary prudence, though it is doubtful whether they had done a real service to the King. Bothmer rejoiced to report that there were at least hopes of a higher Civil List in future, since the King had children for whom he had to provide.[1]

Next, the payment of £65,000 was moved, "being the arrear due to the troops of Hanover, for their service in the Low Countries in the year 1712"[2] which the Electoral Envoys had so far failed to obtain. Now Bothmer was enabled to inform the King that he would have the money ready for him on his arrival.[3] Further, the vote of £100,000 was renewed for apprehending the Pretender, should he attempt to land.[4] Still, the tone of these debates was deteriorating, the section of the Tories, which had recently seemed to adhere to the new Government, once more drawing closer to those who were in formed opposition to the Hanoverian King. Bolingbroke's influence was suspected, and a wish on his part to show his power which would make the King reconsider his dismissal.[5] This alone should have hastened the King's departure; moreover, the most important decisions were, if at all possible, deferred until his arrival. Even the carrying out of some of his orders was delayed by Bothmer. Thus, e.g. he arranged with the Duke of Marlborough that his reinstatement as Commander-in-Chief of the British Army should remain secret for the present.[6]

[1] *Parl. Hist.*; Coxe, *Walpole*, vol. i, p. 59; Bothmer to the King, Aug. 6/17, 10/21; Diary, Aug. 7/18, 11/22, 1714, Han. Arch.

[2] *Parl. Hist.* vii. 7.

[3] Bothmer to the King, Aug. 10/21, 1714, Han. Arch.

[4] *Parl. Hist.* vii. 7-8.

[5] Bothmer to Robethon, Aug. 17/28, 1714, Stowe MSS. 227, ff. 339-40; letter to the King, same date, Han. Arch.

[6] Bothmer to the King, Aug. 24/Sept. 4, 1714, Han. Arch.

Lord Clarendon, the Queen's Envoy, had recently arrived in Hanover, where, however, little importance was attached to his coming. He was considered an adherent of Bolingbroke and a mediocrity. George Lewis was in no hurry to receive him. Clarendon arrived on July 31, but as the King of Prussia was staying at Herrenhausen, he was not received by the Elector till August 4.[1] Clarendon argued that the Queen had "done all that could be done to secure the Succession of her Crowns" to the Electoral Family, but that if the Elector suspected any design, she wished "he should speak plainly upon that subject". George Lewis referred to the Memorial which he had given to Harley; Clarendon replied that he had just "had the honour to deliver to him an answer to that Memorial". On Schütz being mentioned, George Lewis once more asserted that he had had nothing to do with the matter, and that even his mother had merely instructed Schütz to enquire about the writ, and not to demand it.[2] Every time they met, the Elector assured Clarendon of his wish to maintain good correspondence with London, and "that he has, nor will have, no dependence upon anybody but the Queen".[3] Other members of the Electoral family gave similar assurances. At dinner the Elector asked Clarendon several questions about England: "it is very plain to me", wrote Clarendon, "he knows very little of our Constitution".

Clarendon was still in Hanover when the Queen died. He is said to have gone to Herrenhausen late at night, obtained an audience with George Lewis, and thus been the first to do homage to the new King.[4] Messengers and reports soon arrived from London with the news of the King's undisturbed accession in the three Kingdoms. George Lewis could now take his time in preparing for his journey. For a while the Hanover Court was still full of bustle. No such festivities had been witnessed since the day when, some twenty-two years ago, the ruler of Hanover had obtained the rank of Elector.[5] Now he was a King.

A few weeks passed before King George Lewis—he retained the full name while still in Hanover—started for England. The delay in

---

[1] Coxe, *Walpole*, ii. 41.

[2] Clarendon to Bromley, Hanover, Aug. 7, 1714, N.S.; Stowe MSS. 242, f. 161.

[3] Same to same, Aug. 15, 1714, N.S.; *ibid*. f. 163.

[4] Cf. Klopp, xiv. 646, No. 3; there is, however, nothing about it in Clarendon's letters from Hanover.

[5] Letter from Hanover, dated Aug. 23, 1714, in Bonet's reports, Prussian State Archives.

his departure has been ascribed to profound policy, and to the prudent wish of obtaining some further intelligence from England before settling the new Administration.[1] But all this is too subtle. Parliament and the public, and even his own representatives in England, pressed him to hasten his departure; and when he promised to do so, it was his intention. But he had many matters to settle in his Electorate for the time of his absence; a way had to be found to guard the sovereign rights of the ruler and yet to secure for the Government in Hanover the necessary freedom of action.

The arrangements laid down by Ernest Augustus in 1680[2] served for precedent, and were quoted as such in the order which, on August 29, 1714, George Lewis published for his German dominions.[3] The Privy Council, the supreme Board in the country, received wider powers, extending even to various matters on which the decision had hitherto lain with the Elector; on such occasions, however, all the Privy Councillors had to sign the document. In urgent cases, when there was no time to refer to London, the Government could act, even in questions of first-rate political importance. If a foreign army invaded the country or demanded the right of passage, the Privy Council was to consider with the military commanders, appointed by the King, whether to resist or to yield; and in such matters Hanover was to act in an understanding with Wolfenbüttel, and other neighbouring States. The possibility of Swedish troops engaged in the Northern War demanding a passage was specially considered. Their intentions could only be hostile, declared George I, and their passage should therefore be resisted, be it by force.

The most important decisions were reserved for the King, especially as his chief Hanoverian Ministers were with him in London. The Electoral Ministers at foreign Courts had to send their dispatches in two copies, one to London for the King and his German Ministers, and the other for the Privy Councillors at Hanover. Juxtaposition of business was by itself bound to entwine British and Hanoverian interests; Hanoverian Ministers frequently intervened in British affairs, while Hanover was now to some extent governed from a British angle. The Hanover Privy Council were proud of being associated with the King of Great Britain, and the Hanoverians felt half-English, and considered themselves superior to the other Germans.

---

[1] Coxe, *Walpole*, i. 60; and Mahon, i. 106.
[2] Printed by Spittler, *Sämmtliche Werke*, vol. vii. pp. 426 *seq.*
[3] *Ibid.* p. 438 *seq.*

On September 11 George I set out from Hanover with a considerable retinue. His departure was watched with grief by the population.[1] With him went the Electoral Prince, who was to be created Prince of Wales on his arrival in England; his wife and daughters were to follow soon, but the King's grandson, Prince Frederick, remained at Hanover. The Ministers Bernstorff and Goertz, Count Platen, Baron von Kielmansegge, and other Hanoverian nobles, accompanied the King; they all hoped to reap honours and riches in England. Clerks, servants, cooks, etc., more than a hundred in all, followed the Court.[2]

The King took the usual route through Holland. At the frontier he was received and complimented by Deputies of the States-General.[3] In the Dutch cities he was greeted by salvoes of cannon. The Mayor of Amersfoort, in an elaborate address, expressed the wish that the King should be the defender of the Protestant religion and establish relations between England and Holland on a basis as intimate as under William III. At Leyden, fifty-four gunshots were fired to mark his age. On September 16 he entered The Hague.

Here the King and his German advisers had the first opportunity of embarking on the new system of British foreign policy. For eleven days unfavourable winds delayed their departure, which allowed them time for a series of conferences with the Grand Pensionary and other Dutch statesmen. Of all the foreign Powers Holland was the sincerest, perhaps the only sincere, adherent of the Protestant Succession, which to her was a safeguard for both countries. A return to the system of William III, an alliance of the Maritime Powers with the House of Austria, was desired. But in the Peace negotiations the Emperor had been deserted by England, and unconvinced of the stability of the new dynasty, he waited before entering into closer relations with George I. The greatest reserve was prescribed to Baron von Heems, the Imperial Minister at The Hague. When the King's Ministers expressed their desire for a good understanding with the Emperor and for an alliance of the Maritime

[1] *Europäische Fama.*

[2] See Malortie, *Beiträge zur Geschichte des Braunschw.-Lüneb. Hauses und Hofes*, vol. i. pp. 58-60.

[3] *Theatrum Europaeum*, 1714, p. 270. Further see *Umständliche Relation der Reise*, etc. (Hamburg, 1714); "Reisejournal S. Königl. M. von Engeland, etc.", *Zeitschrift d. hist. Vereins f. Niedersachsen* (1883), p. 69 *seq.*; the descriptions in Tindal and Lamberty; Bothmer's Diary, Han. Arch., Hoffmann's reports, Vienna Arch.; etc.

Powers with Austria, he replied that he would report to his master. Nor was an alliance between Austria and Holland possible until a Barrier Treaty had placed the Emperor in possession of the Habsburg Netherlands. So far the contending claims were irreconcilable. The English assumed that the Treaty would have to come about through their mediation, though the Emperor as yet seemed hardly inclined to accept it. Bernstorff, in his first talk with Heems, enquired about the matter. Next, he pleaded that the Emperor should, for the sake of the cause, forget the past and renew the old friendship with Holland; a few disaffected people had previously made the policy of the States General, but now the well-intentioned party was in power. He claimed that alone the Emperor could hardly hold the Netherlands against France, and that he could not altogether dispense with the Dutch garrisons. The King, declared Bernstorff, would try his best to reduce the demands of the States General, to meet the wishes of the Emperor. Heems replied in generalities, and promised to report to Vienna.[1]

The future line of British policy can be traced in these conversations: a Barrier Treaty is to reconcile the Emperor with the States General and render possible an alliance of the Maritime Powers and Austria. The old system of the wars against Louis XIV was to be reconstituted—was it with a view to a renewal of the war? Possibly this was considered at The Hague, for a few months later British policy distinctly took that turn. It seemed natural that the Whigs who had been violently opposed to the Peace Treaty and had attacked it at every opportunity, should, having returned to power, restart the war and try to attain what they considered an honourable peace.

In these dealings with Dutch statesmen and foreign ambassadors, Bernstorff was the moving spirit; at The Hague he acted the part of a British Minister, and, though a complete alien, cheerfully meddled in British affairs. Transplanted to London, he hoped to exercise the same sway on an infinitely wider stage. In future, British affairs were often to suffer by being considered and decided from the Hanoverian point of view.

The foreign diplomats at The Hague were received by the King and the Prince, and offered their congratulations, Chateauneuf no less than Baron Heems and the Portuguese and Russian Ambassadors. On September 22, a reception was given by the British Ambassador, Lord Strafford, who, hitherto known as a Jacobite, now

[1] Instructions for Heems, Aug. 25 and Sept. 1, 1714. Heems' reports of Sept. 14 and 28, 1714, Vienna Arch.

evinced the greatest devotion to George I. Political negotiations, receptions, and bad weather detained the King in Holland; but on September 27, favourable winds at last enabled him to set out for England. The next day, the Royal yachts, accompanied by British and Dutch warships, sailed along the English coast, greeted at various places by salvoes from the land, and at night entered the Thames. A programme for the King's landing and entry into London had been drawn up on Bothmer's advice, based on that of 1697, when William III returned after a victorious war with France. William had spent the first night at Greenwich, and the joy was still remembered which had accompanied his triumphant entry. The populace now looked forward to the festivities, and the Regents were alarmed when Bothmer mentioned that the King might land at Harwich—"which would disconcert their plans, and disappoint the people, who had assembled to receive His Majesty at Greenwich"; and Bothmer had to desire Robethon "to soften the expressions in their letter to the King, when he translates it".[1]

The night of September 29 was still spent on board the ship. The next morning there was a thick fog on the river. It cleared after a few hours, but the wind being contrary, the King entered a barge, and the Prince another, and, with a small retinue, they were rowed up the Thames. Boats with people desirous to see the King quickly covered the river. It was dark when he arrived at Greenwich. The Prince happened to land first, and was by many taken for the King. The guard was about to withdraw when they realized their mistake. Most of the nobility had assembled to compliment the new sovereign. He was received by the Archbishop of Canterbury, and the Lord Chancellor, at the head of the Regency Council. The King proceeded to the Palace through streets blocked by dense crowds. Soon his arrival was signalled by rockets and the guns of the Tower "and nothing was seen at Greenwich but fireworks and illuminations". The same evening the King received the principal officers of State. No one was invited to dinner, to avoid distinguishing between those present, and there was not room for all. The King and the Prince dined in their own apartments. The next day, which was a Sunday, and was still spent at Greenwich, they dined in public, but without summoning anyone to their table. Many prominent men who, the previous night, had failed to reach the King, were allowed to kiss his hand. George I showed himself repeatedly to the people, and more than 50,000 had

[1] Macpherson, *Original Papers*, vol. ii. p. 653.

come from London to see him. With the Duke of Marlborough he had an hour's private conversation, in which he appointed the Duke Captain-General of the British armies. The same day the Duke of Ormond was notified through Lord Townshend of his dismissal. He had been about to ask an audience from the King; in his anger he now returned immediately to London, although the King had sent him word that he would be glad to see him at Court. He similarly kept away from the celebrations on the King's entry. Among those admitted to kiss the King's hand was Lord Oxford; he had made some people believe, and perhaps even himself, that under the Hanoverian King he would regain rank and position—the first meeting showed how little he could expect. Lord Dorset as Chamberlain, announced: "Here is the Earl of Oxford, of whom your Majesty must have heard". The King allowed Oxford to kiss his hand, but gave him a glance of contempt, and turned away without a word.

The next day, Monday, September 20/October 1, 1714,

the King and Prince of Wales made their entry (in London) with great pomp and magnificence. There were in the King's coach the Prince and the Duke of Northumberland, Captain of the Life-Guard in waiting. Above two hundred coaches of the nobility and gentry, all with six horses, preceded the King's. When he came to St. Margaret's hill in Southwark, he was met by the Lord-Mayor, aldermen, recorder, sheriffs, and officers of the City of London; in whose name Sir Peter King, recorder, made a congratulatory speech. The Lord-Mayor delivered the sword to the King, who returned it to him, and he bore it in the procession bare-headed. The royal pomp continued till his arrival at his palace of St. James's, and was favoured by as fair a day as was ever known in that season of the year.[1]

The streets were richly decorated, in many places stands had been erected, and from the country people had come in to watch the display of uniforms and state coaches—the crowd was estimated at one and a half million. They cheered whenever the inane face of George I appeared at the window. The procession had left Greenwich at noon and only long after dark did the royal coach reach St. James's. A foreigner now entered where the Tudors and Stuarts had resided, a King unacquainted with the manners, language, and laws of the country. And yet, George I had the best title to the Throne which, to the English mind, a King could possess—he was called to it by the people.

---

[1] Tindal, *The Continuation of Mr. Rapin's History of England* (5th edition, London), vol. xviii. (vi. of Continuation), p. 312.

CHAPTER V

"THE happy day is come: His Highness the Elector has arrived in his Kingdom", wrote a devoted servant of the House of Hanover on the landing of George I, which seemed to signify more than the union of the King with his nation; it was compared to the triumphal progress of a liberator, and a medal was struck in England representing him as ruler of the seas, a Neptune cutting the waves.[1] Hardly a discordant note marred the rejoicings. This was more than the joyful intoxication which attends the appearance of a new ruler—it was the relief felt after a prolonged anxiety, and the hope of a lasting settlement. The Court acquired new life, and society hurried to St. James's, into the presence of the King. The Crown seemed about to regain its old splendour. The frantic joy was not a tribute to the personal qualities of the King, for he was unknown to the nation. In him the Protestant Succession was peacefully and securely established; the principles of the Glorious Revolution were preserved.

George I was fifty-four at his accession. In his youth he had gained experience of international affairs. His family had been faithful allies to the Emperor in the wars against France and the Turks. He distinguished himself at the relief of Vienna in 1683, and in the subsequent campaign in Hungary. At Neervinden, where the French under Marshal Luxembourg were victorious, he was in personal danger, and but for the self-sacrifice of his aide-de-camp would have been taken prisoner by the enemy. In 1698 he succeeded his father, Ernst August, as Elector of Hanover, and on the death of his uncle, Georg Wilhelm, inherited the dominions of the younger line of the Guelph dynasty. In his reign the long quarrel with his Wolfenbüttel

---

[1] *Ztschr. d. hist. V. f. Niedersachsen* (1853), p. 133; Bonet, Sept. 21/Oct. 2, 1714, Prussian State Archives; *The Metallick History of the Reigns of King William III and Queen Mary, Queen Anne and King George I* (London, 1747).

cousins, concerning the Electoral dignity, was settled: Ernst August had been made Elector in 1692, but it was not till 1708 that Hanover was formally received into the Federal College of Electors. Thus George Lewis held a foremost place among the German princes, and his position was enhanced by his English prospects. In the War of the Spanish Succession, he commanded for a time the German Federal troops against the French, and, if the success did not answer expectations, the fault lay with the poor military organization of the Empire. In international politics he was a determined adherent of the Emperor, and as such had come into conflict with the Tory Cabinet.

George Lewis married his cousin, Princess Sophia Dorothy of Celle, the daughter of Duke Georg Wilhelm of Celle. He was the man who had married off his fiancée, Princess Sophia, to his youngest brother, Ernst August, promising to make their children his heirs, while he himself was to remain unmarried. Anxiously watching over the rights of the children, Sophia herself had a hand in arranging a life-community between Georg Wilhelm and Eleanor d'Olbreuze,[1] as a safeguard against his marrying; and it was with pain and indignation that she saw in after-years the Frenchwoman raised to the status of his lawful wife. In her memoirs and letters, Sophia expressed hatred and contempt for the upstart who now occupied the place once assigned to her, and whose offspring might deprive hers of their inheritance. Although the rights of Ernst August and his heirs were repeatedly confirmed, her hatred extended to Sophia Dorothy, the only child of Georg Wilhelm; and when she grew up and suitors came forward, the previous guarantees seemed no longer sufficient. Although the idea of a *mésalliance* with the daughter of Madame d'Olbreuze was repugnant to Sophia and her son, George Lewis, dynastic interests and a rich dowry overcame their aversion. At the age of sixteen, Sophia Dorothy became the wife of George Lewis.[2]

Love played no part in the conclusion of this marriage, and the tragic fate of Sophia Dorothy was determined by its nature. She was young, lively, and beautiful like her French mother, from whom she

[1] Cp. Köcher, *Die letzte Herzogin von Celle* (Preuss. Jahrb. 64, p. 430), and "Denkwürdigkeiten der cellischen Herzogin Eleonore geb. d'Olbreuse" (*Ztschr. des hist. V. f. Niedersachsen*, 1878, p. 25).

[2] For the following cp. Schaumann, *Sophie Dorothea, Prinzessin von Ahlden, u. Kurfürstin Sophie von Hannover* (Hanover, 1879); Köcher, "Die Prinzessin von Ahlden", *Historische Zeitschrift*, vol. 48, pp. 1-44, 193-235.

had inherited a passionate nature and easy manners, or at least a disregard of Court etiquette; while her husband was cold, stiff, and formal, and, having married her for reasons of State, despised her without taking much care to conceal from her his contempt. The Court of Louis XIV was at that time copied all over Europe, and a small Versailles with its system of royal mistresses was reproduced at Herrenhausen. The Electress Sophia had suffered early in her own married life from her husband's infidelity, nor was George Lewis faithful to his young wife; at Court his mistresses counted for more than she. Moreover, Sophia Dorothy must have suffered severely from her mother-in-law, who, though largely instrumental in arranging the marriage, now treated Sophia Dorothy as an inferior and an intruder in her house.

The easy style of the Princess seems to have given frequent offence. George Lewis wrote to his mother about the intimacy which he alleged his wife to have allowed to the Grand Duke at Florence in 1686. During that journey she had further made friends with a French *galant*, who, many years later, published a number of love letters which he claimed to have written to her.[1] There was gossip about her at that time, and, when the catastrophe occurred, Elizabeth-Charlotte of Orleans expressed her surprise at Sophia Dorothy's not having been imprisoned on her return from Italy—"for she deserved it fully even then, having lived such a mad life, but I don't want to talk about her any more".[2] Still, there is no evidence of actual misconduct on her part, and even her relations with Count Königsmarck, which proved fatal to her, surely lacked that character. In 1694 when, owing to the hatred of her mother-in-law, her position in Hanover had become intolerable, she started an intrigue with this notorious Swedish adventurer, who was to assist her in her flight. The plan was discovered, Königsmarck disappeared in a mysterious manner, and the Princess was imprisoned. The trial resulted in the dissolution of her marriage, the Court explicitly allowing the Elector to re-marry, while this was forbidden to the divorced wife, as the guilty party; the real reason being that her re-marriage might have endangered the reunion of all the Lüneburg possessions prepared by Ernst August.

[1] Bodemann in *Zeitschrift des Hist. Ver. für Niedersachsen* (1890), p. 111 *seq.*

[2] "*Den sie hatt es ja damahlen schon genug verdint, so ein doll leben geführt zu haben, aber ich will nicht mehr von ihr reden.*" See Köcher, "Auslassungen der Herzogin Elis. Charl. v. Orl. üb. d. Prinzessin von Ahlden", *Ztschr. d. h. V. f. Nieders.* (1882), S. 221.

The Court of Hanover was most anxious to keep the circumstances secret, and even from official documents everything was removed which could ultimately have served to elucidate the case. Mysterious happenings in ruling houses intrigue the public, and the person and story of the Princess came to be treated like a novel; indeed, later narratives were based on a novel, *The Roman Octavia* by Anton Ulrich, Duke of Wolfenbüttel. Only recent researches have succeeded in separating fact from fiction. In spite of the extensive destruction of documentary evidence, it can be seen that the very nature of her position rather than her last indiscretion was the cause of the catastrophe. George Lewis had talked to her about divorce before the affair with Königsmarck; now the time seemed ripe for it. The Court of Hanover displayed the same repulsive callousness as it had in the conclusion of the marriage, which had served its purpose: two children had been born—the future George II and Sophia-Dorothy, subsequently the wife of Frederick William I of Prussia. The father of the Princess, Georg-Wilhelm, yielding to his Hanover relations, imprisoned her for life in the Council House of Ahlden; there the visits of her mother, who was unable to alter her fate, were her only comfort. Her husband refused her all share in his honours. Her name was deleted from the liturgy in Hanover and never included in that of Great Britain.

King George was of medium height, and without real dignity in his appearance; his countenance, as seen in portraits, was heavy, broad, and lifeless, with a vacant look in his large eyes; he had a big and broad nose, an ugly mouth, and no trace of a moustache. His face, framed in a dark wig, might almost have been that of a woman, except for its selfish hardness. His parts were neither remarkable nor altogether insignificant; he had inherited none of his mother's gifts, but had a solid understanding and a certain stock of ideas. He was slow in thought and action, and never rash in his decisions. He receded behind Ministers with whom he knew himself in fundamental agreement, and let them act in details according to their lights. He was not jealous of his power and its exercise, and realized his own limitations. He was reluctant to speak in public, even where he could have used French, of which he had a fair command; for he lacked the gift of ready address and accurate expression. Only in his familiar circle, where he could be merry in his own fashion, he would occasionally make a shrewd and apposite remark. He never refused to receive a foreign Minister, but would not commit himself in such talks.

Although for thirteen years he was heir-apparent to the British Crown, he failed to acquire even an elementary knowledge of the English language.

He had not the habit of hard work, and circumstances in England still further estranged him from business. The morning hours he had to himself; after that the Ministers used to report to him till dinner, to which he sat down alone at two o'clock. Rarely were they allowed to see him on business in the afternoon.

The King was as poor in heart as in intellect. His mother had often complained of his coldness. He never lived on good terms with his own son, and when defied by him, punished both him and his family with extreme severity. At no time was intercourse with him easy, but when he was in bad humour no one dared address him. His coldness, said Elizabeth Charlotte, was fit to chill his *entourage*. Still, he was not devoid of qualities; he had a reputation for justice and fairness, and was known to be methodical and economical. He had a certain *bonhomie*, and could be a friend to those near him; their deaths pained him deeply. Even as ruler of Great Britain he adhered with all his heart to his own home and never forgot that he was a German; indeed he can be justly reproached with having allowed Hanoverian interests to influence his policy in Great Britain. "His views and affections" wrote Lord Chesterfield, "were singly confined to the narrow compass of the Electorate; England was too big for him."

George I transplanted his Hanover Court, such as it was, to England; his German counsellors went with him, his mistresses followed him. The English public had long been accustomed to take a lenient view of marital infidelity in kings. Under Charles II royal mistresses had played a more important part than under the Hanoverians, but grace and spirit atoned, at least outwardly, for vice. Other princely debauchees, contemporaries of George I, such as Augustus the Strong, or Frederick IV of Denmark, showed taste and artistic predilections. George I's *entourage* was lifeless and tedious, and vice, as represented by the clumsy ugliness of a Frau von Kielmannsegge or a Fräulein von Schulenburg, was devoid of charm. The latter, previously a Maid of Honour to the Electress Sophia, had the oldest claim on the King, whose favour she had enjoyed for many years. It was alleged, though without foundation, that there had been a morganatic marriage with her, and of two girls whom she had brought to England as her nieces, the younger was generally reputed to be a daughter of George I; the fact that she was created Countess of Walsingham, and most of all, her striking likeness to the King, seemed to bear out this belief. The lean Mlle. Schulenburg was of a mature age when she came to England.

> She . . . refused coming hither at first, fearing that the people of England, who, she thought, were accustomed to use their Kings barbarously, might chop off his head in the first fortnight; and had not love or gratitude enough to venture being involved in his ruin.[1]

But she came over on hearing that her most dangerous rival meant to steal a march on her. A few years later she was naturalized in England, but there was resentment when she was created Duchess of Munster in Ireland, though no rights or revenues were attached to the title. In 1719 she was even raised to the British peerage as Duchess of Kendal.

At Hanover she had never interfered in politics, unequal as she was to play a part in them. In England the temptation was much stronger, and though she had no ideas of her own, she was able to use her influence with the King on behalf of other people; nor was she averse from selling it. Ministers did not spurn her friendship, and in time she became for them a useful counterweight to German influence at Court. In 1720 Walpole declared that the Duchess of Kendal "was, in effect as much Queen of England as ever any was; that he did everything by her".[2]

Very different was George I's other mistress. Horace Walpole as a boy was terrified at Mme. Kielmannsegge's enormous figure.

> Two fierce black eyes, large and rolling, . . . two acres of cheek spread with crimson, an ocean of neck that overflowed . . .—no wonder that a child dreaded such an ogress, and that the mob of London were highly diverted at the importation of so uncommon a seraglio![3]

She was a daughter of Countess Platen, who had been the mistress of Elector Ernst August, and who had from the outset intended her for mistress to his son; and though at first this was hindered by a necessary marriage with Kielmannsegge, son of a Hamburg merchant, it came about later on. George I gladly agreed to Mme. Kielmannsegge accompanying him to England, though he did not offer to

---

[1] Lady Mary Wortley Montagu, "Account of the Court of George I" published in *Letters and Works* (1887), vol. i. pp. 1-14.

[2] *Diary of Lady Cowper*, p. 132.

[3] Horace Walpole, *Reminiscences*.

facilitate her journey by paying her debts. Having squandered a large fortune, she now had to get out of Hanover in disguise, made her way in a postchaise to Holland, and embarking with the King, "arrived at the same time with him in England".[1]

Mlle. Schulenburg and Mme. Kielmannsegge were rivals for position and influence at the English Court. After her husband's death in 1721, Mme. Kielmannsegge was created Countess of Leinster and, a year later, Countess of Darlington. She was clever at retaining her hold on the King and her position at Court, though sometimes her behaviour was ridiculous; when on one occasion the Prince of Wales had reflected upon her morals, she produced "a certificate under her husband's hand, in which he certified, in all due forms, that she had always been a faithful wife to him".[2] Intellectually she was much superior to her rival; she had vivacity, loved reading, and was amusing in company; besides being an expert at Court intrigue. The Princess of Wales said about her that "she never stuck a pin into her gown without a design".[3] But like Mlle. Schulenburg, she was not fit to take a hand at politics. Little credence attaches to the rumour, current in 1715, that Mme. Kielmannsegge favoured the Tories, so that the Ministers had to resort to Mlle. Schulenburg. Mme. Kielmannsegge took an eminently practical view of her position at Court, and had to be paid in cash by those whom she obliged: one man for whom she secured a profitable post, gave her 500 guineas down, besides an annuity of £200 as long as he had the place; "and I have since learnt", wrote Lady Cowper, ". . . that he gave her also the fine brilliant ear-rings which she wears, it being certain she never had any such jewels abroad".[4] Services of that kind are said to have earned her £20,000 to £25,000.

The King had eyes also for other ladies at Court.[5] Soon after his arrival, the Duchess of Shrewsbury was seen trying to win his favour. She was a clever Italian, had once been beautiful, but now had merely the art of entertaining people, though exceeding sometimes the bounds of decency. Amusing in her conversation, she spoke several languages to perfection, and presumed towards the King a familiarity which gave offence to others, but was tolerated by him. He even

---

[1] Lady Mary Wortley Montagu, "The Court of George I."
[2] *Diary of Lady Cowper*, p. 68.
[3] *Ibid.* p. 13.   [4] *Ibid.* p. 31.
[5] *"La médisance va jusqu'à préférer les moeurs de Charles II à celles de George"*, Bonet, Jan. 7/18, 1715, Prussian State Archives.

prevailed upon the Princess of Wales to include the Duchess among her Ladies of the Bedchamber, saying that "it would be an obligation to him".[1] The Duchess of Bolton was similarly said to have captivated the King; Lady Cowper too, was much admired by him—charming and clever, she had preserved her reputation in a frivolous Court and society. She, too, was of the family of the Princess of Wales, but kept aloof from its intrigues. Refined and sensible, she watched the ways of the fashionable world, and has left in her Diary a vivid picture of Court life during the early years of the Hanoverian dynasty. George I liked her and one day, when he paid her exceptional attention, the Princess told her that she could do what she pleased, and that it was her fault if she did not rule them all. Lady Cowper replied that she did not believe it, and that "supposing it were true, power was too dear bought when one was to do such dishonourable work for it".[2] Lady Mary Wortley Montagu, equally unresponsive to such advances, also enjoyed the sincere admiration of the King. When in 1716, during his stay in the Electorate, Lady Mary, whose husband was appointed British Ambassador to Constantinople, passed through Hanover, "the King . . . took but little notice of any other lady, not even of Madam Kielmansegg".[3]

George I was an elderly gentleman of comfortable habits, and even as King of England, naturally wished to continue in the style he had been used to as Elector. He would not endure the levees, customary at the English and French Courts. No one was refused access to the King, but the Royal Bedchamber was closed to strangers. On Bothmer's advice, the office of Groom of the Stole was left vacant for the present. If absolutely necessary the King held his levee fully dressed, in his so-called "Bedchamber". He lived a retired life in the bare Palace of St. James's, and, in the first years, never spent any length of time either at Kensington, or Hampton Court (of which the surroundings resembled his native Herrenhausen), or even at Windsor. At St James's he inhabited two rooms only, sleeping and eating in one, and giving audiences in the other. In former reigns the "Gentlemen of the Bedchamber" and the "Gentlemen of the Table" waited upon the King; now the places were filled, but their services were dispensed with. George I was attended by his German servants, and by Mohamed and Mustapha, prisoners from his Turkish campaign. Their sight was repugnant to the populace; it was rumoured

---

[1] *Diary of Lady Cowper*, p. 8.   [2] *Ibid.* p. 172.
[3] *Ibid.* App. E, p. 195.

that they were still Mohammedans—fit servants indeed to attend the person of His Protestant Majesty!

George spent his evenings with Mlle. Schulenburg, Mme. Kielmannsegge, or at the Princess of Wales'. He often went to the Opera, but, being shy, preferred not to appear in the royal box. He usually sat "like another gentleman" in a private box, behind Mlle. Schulenburg and his daughter, Lady Walsingham. Since the King knew no English, and the Prince and Princess of Wales but imperfectly, elaborate shows, ballets, and pantomimes were in favour. The wife was lacking in the King's household; and had it not been for the Prince and Princess of Wales, social life at Court would have been exceedingly poor.

The Prince of Wales was popular as such—as heir to the Crown, whose issue guaranteed the continuance of the dynasty. Since 1649 there had been no Prince of Wales; when James II announced the birth of a male heir to the Throne, people refused to believe him, and both were driven into exile.

George Augustus, Prince of Wales, was over thirty at his father's accession. He had fought in the War of the Spanish Succession, and a song by Congreve praised the behaviour of "Young Hanover brave" in the battle of Oudenarde:

> In this bloody field, I assure ye,
> When his war-horse was shot
> He valued it not,
> But fought still on foot like a fury.

Otherwise he was in no way distinguished, except by his zeal for the British claims of his family. In England his name was much canvassed in connexion with the affair of the writ. His face as seen in portraits was more expressive than that of his father. He had a high forehead, lively blue eyes, and a big, well-shaped nose. But the small, alert figure lacked dignity, and the loud, gesticulating manner of the foreigner impressed Englishmen unpleasantly. In fact, the Prince did not exceed his father in ability, and there was less difference in character between the two than was thought in the lifetime of George I, because of the conflict between them. The Prince, too, was a stranger to England and her Constitution, though he, at least, acquired in time a certain knowledge of the language. Both father and son were indifferent to intellectual pursuits. The Prince was perhaps more obstinate than the King, but not so devoid of feeling. It is said that he meant to bring Sophia-Dorothy over to England and declare her Queen Dowager after his father's death, had she survived her husband; but during his life, he did not even dare to hang up her picture.[1] He attached no more importance to marital fidelity than George I; still, he felt love and tenderness for his wife, and the influence which he allowed her became a subject of ridicule with his critics.

Caroline, Princess of Wales, *née* of Ansbach-Bayreuth, was handsome and clever, and intellectually superior to her husband. She was popular because of her strict Protestantism, and was proud of having refused the Imperial Crown at the price of conversion to Rome; which was not altogether correct, because when the marriage with the Archduke Charles was discussed, he was hardly expected to become Emperor. An adulatory account of her person is given by the Dutch diplomat Duvenvoirde, who met her at The Hague in October 1714, on her way to England. He describes her as being dignified and unassuming, gentle, friendly, and kind, charming in her natural distinction, and in her easy and pleasant conversation. "She discusses the most important problems with accurate knowledge, in a judicious manner such as is rarely found in women."[2] This letter, full of further extravagant praise, was, it is true, written to the private secretary of the King. But so much is certain that Princess Caroline was the most attractive figure in the new Court, and even the King's pompous manner did not awe her. When a few years later George I had resigned the conduct of affairs to his Ministers,

she chid the King . . . and told him he was grown lazy. He laughed, and said he was busy from morning to night. She said, "Sir, I tell you they say the Ministry does everything, and you nothing".[3]

The King to his confidants termed her *"cette diablesse Madame la Princesse"*.[4]

Fashionable society gathered round her. Besides ladies of the nobility, the King insisted on her receiving the wives of Members of Parliament. At her evening parties *l'hombre* and *piquet* were played a great deal, and not for low stakes. There were also formal receptions; in the first year, before Lent, the Prince and Princess gave a ball at

---

[1] Horace Walpole, *Reminiscences.*

[2] Duvenvoirde to Robethon, The Hague, Oct. 23, 1714, Stowe MSS. 227, f. 488.

[3] *Diary of Lady Cowper,* p. 79.   [4] Horace Walpole, *Reminiscences.*

Somerset House every week; the Court seemed to recover the splendour of Charles II's days.

The Court society consisted of English and Germans, jealous of each other. The respective merits of the two nations formed a favourite subject of conversation; but as the Royal family was German, the English could not speak their minds as freely as the other side. Baron Schütz once said in the presence of English women nothing could make him believe "that there was one handsome woman in England". The Prince on the contrary used to say of the English

that he thought them the best, the handsomest, the best shaped, the best natured, and lovingest people in the world, and if anybody would make their court to him, it must be by telling him he was like an Englishman.[1]

No one, of course, would have ventured to do so. George II remained a German all his life, like his father; only in the fourth generation did the Guelphs strike root in England.

The King had allowed the three daughters of the Princess to come to England with their mother; the eldest, Princess Anne, not quite five, seemed highly gifted; she "speaks, reads, and writes both German and French to perfection," writes Lady Cowper,[2] "knows a great deal of history and geography, speaks English very prettily, and dances very well". The eldest son, Prince Frederick (who predeceased his father), had, by the King's order, been left behind to be educated at Hanover,[3] almost as if with the intention to prevent his acquiring a more intimate knowledge of England than was possessed by his father and grandfather; only in 1716, when he was nine, was a tutor sent across to teach him English. The prospect of a succession of foreigners, unfamiliar with the language and Constitution of the country, was naturally displeasing to the English.

The King's prerogative in the State was limited, but his authority in his family was absolute. The Prince was debarred from any business of State, except some which related to the Principality of Wales. At the opening of Parliament in 1715, he took his seat in the House

---

[1] *Diary of Lady Cowper*, p. 99.

[2] *Ibid.* p. 38.

[3] About him see letter from Lady Mary Wortley Montagu, dated Hanover, Nov. 25, 1716, *Letters and Works* (1887), p. 135; Bonet's report of July 17/28, 1716, Prussian State Archives; Whitworth to Townshend, Hanover, Sept. 28/ Oct. 9, 1716.

of Lords, after having taken the oath of allegiance and abjuration. He did not, however, receive high rank either in the Army or in the Navy. Similarly at Hanover he had been unable to obtain from his father either a regiment or a seat in the Privy Council. Relations between the two were strained, and continued so at St. James's.[1] They were hardly ever seen together, and their mutual dislike and jealousy increased till it produced an open breach.

It was not easy for Germans, surrounded by Germans, to acquire popularity in England, and they did little to earn it.[2] The Court was reproached with a lack of dignity. William III, though also a foreigner, had commanded respect; Queen Anne's majestic bearing was remembered, and one word from her was valued more by the ladies than all the condescending addresses of the Princess of Wales.

The King showed no understanding of his new subjects. Offences heavily scored against him, were often committed from sheer ignorance. He seldom showed himself in public, and his manner was stiff and cold. Ignorant of the language, he was cut off from all contact with the common people. It was not till June 1715, and then probably on the advice of his Ministers, that he appeared on horseback at the review of the troops in Hyde Park, and admitted people to kiss his hand; but by then this was interpreted by the anti-courtiers as a symptom of weakness and fear. The King never visited the provinces. False economy restrained him from spending money, and from impressing the nation by building, as was done by other Kings. When in 1715 a serious fire broke out in London, the worst since 1666, it was taken amiss to George I that neither he nor his son visited the scene, as Charles II and the Duke of York had done, and that the Guards were not sent to help fighting it.

It was in their practice of religion that the Royal family found it hardest to satisfy the nation.[3] Protestantism had been their title to succession, and now their conduct was jealously scrutinized in this light. The King belonged by law to the Church of England, and though bred a Lutheran and ignorant of English, had to attend the Anglican

---

[1] "*J'avoue que le père traite son fils avec trop de rigueur, ne voulant le satisfaire dans la moindre chose qu'il luy demande. . . . Mais d'un autre côté le fils se conduit et se prend d'une manière que le père a raison de s'en plaindre*" (Schulenburg to Leibniz, July 1/12, 1714); Klopp, *Leibniz' Werke*, vol. ix. p. 415.

[2] See reports of Bonet and Hoffmann.

[3] See reports by Bonet; and also Pauli, "Konfessionelle Bedenken", *Aufsätze z. engl. Gesch.*, N.S., pp. 379 *seq.*

service. Lord Nottingham, a leading Churchman, suggested that the King should have the service conducted according to the rites of the English Church, by German or French clergy, ordained by an Anglican Bishop. But the suggestion did not meet with approval, and George I had to go every Sunday morning to the Royal Chapel at St. James's and listen to the liturgy and sermon in English. So did the Prince of Wales, while Princess Caroline, who had a better command of the language, earned praise by daily attendance at prayers in the Chapel.

Further, the King's conduct during service gave rise to criticism; he omitted to say a silent prayer on entering the Church, he did not kneel down with the congregation, nor did he hold the prayer book in his hand, to follow the service and say the prayers. The Prince and Princess of Wales were more careful to conform with these customs. It caused considerable offence when at Christmas 1714 the King and his son failed to attend Chapel and receive the Holy Communion; they did it on Easter Sunday 1715, "and in all respects conformed themselves to the rites and ceremonies of the Church of England; which 'tis to be hoped, will effectively defeat the stale insinuations of a designing faction of 'the Church being in danger' ".[1]

. . . . . .

At the root of politics in 1714 was the problem of the future attitude of the Hanoverian dynasty towards the two great parties in Great Britain. Was the new Government to be composed of both, or was one of them to predominate? The Tories could claim that they, too, had stood by the Protestant Succession; the bulk of the party had no share in the Jacobite intrigues. The poet and diplomat, Mathew Prior, wrote from Paris:

I hope Whig and Tory are eternally buried in the same grave, and that henceforth we shall have no other contention but who shall love with most zeal the person of their Sovereign and the laws and liberties of their country.[2]

These expectations were soon disappointed. The new Administration was composed of Whigs. The Tories were not barred on

[1] A. Boyer, vol. ix. (1715), p. 313.
[2] Mathew Prior to Lord Dorset, Aug. 9/20, 1714, S.P. 78/159; see further Prior to Stanhope, Oct. 1/12, 12/23, 1714, *ibid.*; Stanhope to Prior, Oct. 7/18, 1714; Whitworth to Robethon, Frankfurt, Aug. 18, 1714; and Strafford to Robethon, The Hague, Aug. 27, 1714. Stowe MSS. 227, ff. 336-38.

principle, and at first it was intended to offer places to some of them; but in view of the preponderance given to the Whigs, the Tories preferred to leave the field entirely to their opponents.

It was no easy task for George I, a complete foreigner, to form his Government. His acquaintance was limited to those who of recent years had acted with his Envoys, Grote, Schütz, and Bothmer. In London he had at first no one except Bothmer to advise him on men and measures. Bothmer could afford to be impartial; as a foreigner, he was debarred from office and places of profit, whereas all others who approached the King sought something for themselves, their relatives, their friends, or party. All that Bothmer cared for was to preserve his influence with the King, and this that indispensable man was not likely to forfeit. It had been the source of his power during the Regency—the Lords Justices had acted upon his suggestions.

Bothmer had long been connected with the Whigs and used all his influence in their favour. His fellow-conspirators of yesterday now came forward and claimed their reward for their past adherence to the House of Hanover. "As soon as the Queen was dead", wrote Edward Wortley Montagu, "the Palace of St. James's was filled with the Whigs, who were impatient to see the choice of the Regency."[1] During the next week they remained in constant touch with Bothmer, informing him of their wishes with regard to the new Administration, on which he then reported to the King. His letters to George I and to the King's secretary, Robethon, are preserved in Hanover and London. For every important post he had his candidate. He advised that the Treasury and Admiralty be put into Commission; Halifax should be made First Lord of the Treasury and Orford of the Admiralty. To Robethon he expressed the hope that some consolation would soon be provided for Marlborough; subsequently he advised the King to put him at the head of the Army, in place of Ormonde. Provision should be made for Stanhope and Cadogan; also for Somers, who was less infirm than he was thought to be. A week later Bothmer heard from Cadogan that Sunderland, whom he had previously recommended, wished to be Secretary of State. Even non-political posts (*e.g.* a vacant bishopric) should be filled with the well-affected. Most of these suggestions were made against the King's arrival, and were then acted upon. Meantime Bothmer advised

---

[1] "On the State of Affairs when the King entered", by E. Wortley Montagu, published in Lady Mary Wortley Montagu, *Letters and Works*, vol. i. pp. 15-21.

Robethon to compile a list of those who were to be remembered in the distribution of places.

But Bothmer went even further, and put before the King a complete scheme, "How His Majesty King George, on His arrival in England, could settle His Court and Government". In this memorandum, which is preserved in his own handwriting, he said that everything depended on the appointments made to the great offices of State and in the Royal Household, for of them consisted the Cabinet Council which determined the character of the Government. William III was quoted who, having made a wrong choice of Ministers at the outset, could never afterwards work well with either party. It was necessary to act on firm principles; offices must be filled according to merit and fitness and "without regard to whether a man is a Whig or a Tory". But this seeming impartiality was immediately explained away: no true servant of the King could think of recommending the continuance in office of those who had served under the previous Government. These have disgusted the nation, and "turned everything upside down, and maliciously endangered the whole of Europe", chiefly in order to prejudice the rights of the present King; and now they should much rather think of how to justify their actions in the eyes of the nation. The King, said Bothmer, was entitled to forgive wrongs done to himself, but should not prevent a public enquiry into the insults and damage inflicted. The Whigs, with the power once more in their hands, obviously meant to follow up their indictment of the Tory Administration and of the Peace Treaty by impeachment; and therefore, clearly, no important share could be conceded to the Tories in the new Administration.

Lord Nottingham, too, had considerable influence with Bothmer, and his advice was bound to count when given against the interests of his late party. At a time when candidates to office were besieging Bothmer, Nottingham came to him and put before him a scheme for the new Administration.[1] The King, he said, should stand above parties, but he himself, though a Tory, was bound to admit that now only a Whig Administration was admissible, though a few well-affected Tories might be included. He spoke further of the necessity of an enquiry into the administration of the Queen's Ministers and into the accusations raised against them. In his alliance with the Whigs, Nottingham accepted their foreign policy, while they abandoned their traditional Church policy. The name of Sacheverel still had

[1] Bothmer to the King, Sept. 10/21, 1714, Pauli, *op. cit.* p. 66.

its popular appeal. The Whigs on their return to office, would be well advised to abandon, for the time being, their religious latitudinarianism—this was Nottingham's advice, which King George eagerly accepted. The Church was to feel safe under his rule [1]—he implemented the Church policy of the Tories under a Whig Administration. The restrictive laws against the Dissenters were not repealed, and the Test Act and the Act against Occasional Conformity were continued.

The future system of politics was thus fixed before the King had landed in England; and a few days after his arrival the new Administration was formed. It consisted of the ablest and most experienced statesmen. To the old Whig Junto — Marlborough, Sunderland, Somers, and Wharton—and to Cowper and Halifax, new men were added: Nottingham, Stanhope, Townshend, and Robert Walpole, though the last, to begin with, in a subordinate position. But it soon became obvious that it was these new men who had the real influence in the Administration.

No one Minister at that time, by rank or custom, so much overtowered the others as to be Prime Minister. Nor was such a development desired by the King—Bothmer had advised him in his memorandum not to appoint a Lord High Treasurer who by his power might "become troublesome for the King himself". This could only have been prevented by a Sovereign sufficiently active and well informed to reconcile the divergent views and wishes of his Ministers, and to impart the necessary unity to the Government. This was possible even after 1688; William III had played that part, and Queen Anne, however strong the influence of Marlborough and Godolphin had been at times, or of Oxford and Bolingbroke, was jealous lest any subject should encroach on her prerogative. But George I was a stranger, and a First Minister was needed to establish unity in the Administration. Still, the rise of a First Minister was a matter of time and evolution, and for a few years British policy was without a clear system or a directing hand.

Among the Ministers, custom assigned the first place to the Lord Chancellor, though for a long time past he had not held it in reality. Still, he presided in the House of Lords and in the Court of Equity, was Keeper of the Great Seal, had the disposal of a number of lucrative places, and held a prominent position in the Cabinet Council. The last Chancellor had been Lord Harcourt, a reputed Jacobite. The King had not acceded to the request of the Regents to

[1] Instructions to Bothmer, Sept. 25, 1714, Han. Arch.

have Harcourt deprived of the Great Seal before his arrival;[1] but he delayed signing the patent of the Prince of Wales till Harcourt's successor was appointed, in order to withhold from him the fee of £5000, incident on the appending of the Great Seal to that patent.[2] Lord Cowper, who had been Chancellor in the last Whig Administration of Queen Anne, and had resigned in 1710, was considered the obvious choice. He was distinguished as a lawyer, and of an irreproachable character,[3] a thing rarer in those times than political talent. An able orator and implacable dialectician,[4] in private life he was kind and just; he was in every way superior to his predecessor. At Court he exercised tact in difficult situations, and was one of the few who in the conflict between the King and the Prince managed to remain favourites with both. A few years later George I declared that Cowper and Devonshire were the only two men whom he had found honest and disinterested;[5] and that Cowper alone "had treated him with good manners whilst in his service".[6] His predecessors accepted New Year's gifts from barristers practising in Chancery "which used to come to near £3000 . . . The Earl of Nottingham, when Chancellor, used to receive them . . . and at the same time he took the money . . . he used to cry out, 'Oh tyrant cuthtom!' (for he lisped)".[7] Lord Cowper, though not a rich man, abolished that custom, which looked like bribery. When in 1716, George I was starting for Hanover, he received above fifty people that day—"everybody . . . asked him something but my Lord Cowper".[8]

The first place in the Cabinet had of recent times been held by the Lord High Treasurer. Now, however, a Board was formed consisting of five Lords of the Treasury, an arrangement frequent in the seventeenth century, but which was now made permanent (still, in time the First Lord of the Treasury re-established his superiority not at his Board alone, but in the Cabinet, and became once more the First Minister). Lord Halifax was appointed First Lord of the Treasury in 1714. He was one of the foremost financiers of

[1] Bothmer to the King, Sept. 10/21, 1714, Pauli, *op. cit.* p. 66; advice to Bothmer, The Hague, Sept. 25, 1714, Han. Arch.

[2] Hoffmann's report of Oct. 2, 1714, Vienna Archives.

[3] "*Cowper . . . non seulement l'efface dans les affaires de judicature, mais il est de plus d'une probité, d'une douceur, d'un désintéressement et d'une capacité pour les affaires politiques qu'on n'a pas reconnu dans l'autre*" (Bonet).

[4] Swift, "History of the Four Last Years", *Works*, vol. v. p. 177.

[5] *Diary of Lady Cowper*, p. 115.   [6] *Ibid.* p. 138.

[7] *Ibid.* p. 63.   [8] *Ibid.* p. 111.

his time. Under William III he had established the system, continued by Godolphin, of employing the liquid resources of the public in the service of the State; thus it was possible to finance England's wars and to offer profitable business to the monied interest. Halifax was versatile, far-sighted as a statesman, and eloquent in debate. He was a patron of literature, and at his death left a house full of art treasures. He was the principal promoter of the compilation of State Treaties which, known as Rymer's *Foedera*, covers five centuries of English history. Since 1706, when he brought to Hanover the Regency Act and the Garter for the Electoral Prince, he was personally known to the King as a zealous adherent. When in 1713 George Lewis sent Baron Schütz to London, Lord Halifax was named to him as one "who is invariably concerned for the interests of our House and is a man of eminent ability, wise, and moderate". Halifax had no small idea of his own importance, and did not doubt that a leading place would be assigned to him under the new dynasty. He expected to be appointed Lord High Treasurer immediately on the King's arrival at Greenwich, and was disappointed when he found himself merely First Lord of the Treasury. The Earldom and the Garter conferred on him by George I did not satisfy his ambition; nor did he lose hope of the higher rank and, in the meantime, tried to impose his policy on the King and the other Ministers. But as no such pre-eminence was conceded to him, there was friction. He offended his fellow-Ministers by his "insupportable pride", and was accused of plotting with the Tories, and particularly of "being too much Lord Oxford's friend".[1] Halifax is said to have meddled even in the private affairs of the King.[2] A conflict within the Cabinet seemed unavoidable, when Lord Halifax suddenly died in May 1716.

Among the junior Lords was Edward Wortley Montagu, a near relation of Halifax, who had at first thought it beneath his dignity to accept anything below the Secretary of State.

Lord Nottingham became President of the Council. Disapproval of the Peace policy and hatred of the Lord High Treasurer had

---

[1] Montagu, "State of Affairs"; Hoffmann, May 31, 1715, Vienna Archives; Coxe, *Walpole*, vol. ii. p. 47 ff.

[2] The allusion in Bonet's letter of May 20/31, 1714, is obscure: "*Aussi S.M. est consolée de la perte d'un ministre, habile à la vérité, mais qui le contrôlait en tout, et qui l'exposait ouvertement en Parlement pour favoriser ses propres amourettes. Cette historiette est tenue fort secrète.*"

made him abandon the Tories, and enter into sharp opposition to the Oxford-Bolingbroke Administration. With calm self-assurance he faced the curses and jeering of those whom he had deserted; but he failed "to bring over one single proselyte, to keep himself in countenance".[1] It was of supreme importance for George I that in his Whig Administration he had a wise and experienced man who could interpret the views of the other side. Lady Cowper was right in saying that "Lord Nottingham's heart was never with the Whigs".[2] He resigned two years later because of a conflict with the other Ministers.

With the Whig Ministers, Marlborough re-entered the scene. His political past was not unexceptionable. In 1688 he had abandoned his King, but under William III entertained secret relations with the Stuart Court. Nor was his attitude to the Succession above reproach; though a frequent and welcome guest at Hanover, he made the Pretender believe that in certain circumstances he might espouse the Stuart cause. It may have been this which caused the Elector to omit him from the list of Regents. Deeply chagrined, Marlborough "at the instance of the Duchess, adopted a resolution to hold no official situation under the new Government".[3] But he could not resist the temptation and yielded to the persuasion of his friends. If the Government was to take up the work interrupted in 1710, Marlborough had to resume his place. His reappointment was delayed, by agreement, till the King's arrival.[4] At Greenwich the King appointed him Captain-General, Master of the Ordnance, and Colonel of the First Regiment of Foot Guards; he was restored to all his previous posts, worth £16—£17,000 a year. The popularity of the Duke of Ormonde, a high Tory and possibly Jacobite who in 1712 had replaced Marlborough, was an additional reason for his removal.

But Marlborough had no chance of adding to his military fame. There was no war, and he had no share in crushing the Rising of 1715. Because of his avarice, he was disliked in his regiment. Soon his health broke down, and he lingered on a sick man till his death. But in the beginnings of George I's reign, he played an important part and belonged to that inner circle of Ministers who transacted the most important business of State. Once more he "was making the same figure at Court that he did when he first came into it

---

[1] Swift, "History of the Four Last Years", *Works,* vol. v. p. 179.
[2] *Diary,* p. 18.
[3] Coxe, *Marlborough,* iii. p. 593.   [4] See above, pp. 70 and 76.

. . . bowing and smiling in the antechamber. . . ."[1] But his Duchess had given up the ambitions of her youth and seldom appeared at Court. She wrote to Lady Cowper in September 1716: "I think anyone that has common sense or honesty must needs be very weary of everything one meets with in Courts".[2]

Marlborough knew how to provide for his relations, near or distant. His four sons-in-law received lucrative appointments. The most prominent among them, Sunderland, was made Lord Lieutenant of Ireland, which did not, however, satisfy either him or Marlborough; for though the post carried a seat in the Cabinet, it removed him from the centre of Government and sent him into a kind of honourable exile. The Whigs would have been glad of his services, but George I seems to have remembered Sunderland's behaviour towards Queen Anne, and may have shunned him because of his previous connexions with those republican Whigs who would have wished to abolish the monarchy and nobility—he is reported once to have said to his friends that he "hoped to see the day when there should not be a peer in England".[3] George, when still Elector, had warned his Envoy against Sunderland's violent views, and now as King preferred not to see him daily in his closet, whatever his merits were towards the Hanoverian Succession.

The historical greatness of the Whigs since the Revolution was embodied in Lord Somers. He had made his name in 1688, in the Seven Bishops' case, and from a practising lawyer had been raised to be Chancellor and a peer. He became the leader of the Whigs, and neglect of his advice almost invariably proved fatal—he had, e.g., cautioned his party against prosecuting Sacheverell. Always sickly, by strength of mind he had overcome his infirmities; and though passionate by nature, he appeared invariably calm and easy. Now he was old and weak, and no longer fit to bear the burden of business; he was therefore given a place in the Cabinet without office. He died two years later.

The King while still in Holland had appointed Viscount Townshend Secretary of State, so that Townshend and not Bromley should countersign his orders on his landing in England; but Bromley, Bolingbroke's colleague, was not dismissed till after the King's arrival.

Of the Ministers the most powerful was at first Lord Townshend.

---

[1] Lady Mary Wortley Montagu, "Account of the Court of George I".
[2] Diary of Lady Cowper, App. E, p. 196.
[3] Swift, "Four Last Years", Works, vol. v. p. 176.

He was of an old Norfolk family; on the Restoration his father's zeal was rewarded by a peerage, and afterwards by the further rank of Viscount. Townshend himself had played a part in the negotiations of Gertruydenberg, and still more in the conclusion of the Barrier Treaty of 1709; but the Conference of Gertruydenberg ended in failure, and Townshend's Barrier Treaty was rejected by the Tory Administration and not revived even by the Whigs in 1714. In Holland, Townshend had met Robethon, treated him civilly, and charmed him "with a reception which his birth and education did not entitle him to".[1] He established for himself the reputation of a foremost champion of the Hanoverian Succession, and had been on intimate terms with the Elector's Envoys in London. On the accession of George I, he was recommended by Robethon and Bothmer[2] to the King and his German Ministers. "It was publicly known that Lord Marlborough, Lord Townshend, and Lord Halifax did each of them aim at the whole power."[3] Townshend attained it through the favour of the King's foreign advisers.

Unsullied both in his private and in his public life, honourable, efficient, hard-working, and conscientious, Townshend would have made a useful peace minister, but was not a great statesman. In his foreign policy he followed the lead of his colleague, Stanhope; in home affairs, of his brother-in-law Robert Walpole. Occasionally he was carried away by his temper and by personal resentment, and knowing himself to be "extremely warm"[4] he hesitated to adopt a conduct which he might regret in his cooler moments. In Parliament he spoke to the point, but his speeches were unadorned and uninspired. Towards foreign diplomats he vindicated British policy as best he could, but in times of difficulty he would take cover behind the other Ministers, and especially behind Stanhope. The style of his dispatches was simple and clear. His manner, especially towards his inferiors, was often abrupt, overbearing, and impatient of contradiction; he was not a favourite with his contemporaries.

Lord Townshend was in charge of the Northern Department, comprising Holland, the German Empire, the Scandinavian countries,

---

[1] Lady Mary W. Montagu, *op. cit.*
[2] Bothmer to Robethon, Aug. 31/Sept. 11, 1714, Stowe MSS. 227, ff. 404-5, Sunderland, he writes, wished for Bolingbroke's place. *"Je souhaite par beaucoup de raison qu'on pût le contenter d'une autre manière, pour faire Mylord Townshend Secrétaire d'État."*
[3] E. Wortley Montagu, "State of Affairs."
[4] Coxe, *Walpole*, vol. i. p. 338.

Russia, and Poland; James Stanhope of the Southern Department—
France, Spain, Portugal, Italy, and Turkey. Still, the need for unity
in foreign policy almost invariably resulted in the preponderance of
one of the two Secretaries; in this case it lay with Stanhope.

Stanhope was one of the most eminent and most gifted men of his
time, distinguished as a general, statesman, orator, and diplomat,
and known as a man of wide culture. "This general", wrote Bonet, "is
the only Englishman I know possessed of a universal spirit." [1] He had
commanded the British troops in the Peninsula with varying success,
but it was through no fault of his that the Habsburgs lost the
Spanish throne. Even in those days he had played a part in politics,
and his hostility to the Tory Administration had brought upon him
an enquiry, in which he and Marlborough were accused of financial
irregularities. "It was proved however from Stanhope's account and
explanation, that far from his owing the Government anything, he
left them his debtors." [2]

It is difficult to believe the statement of Horace Walpole (the
younger) [3] that Stanhope was at first surprised, or even unwilling to
accept the place of Secretary of State. He had long been reputed one
of the foremost champions of the Electoral House, had been one of
the chosen advisers of the Hanoverian Envoys, and it was surely not
without his knowledge that Bothmer recommended him to the King
for high employment. Stanhope turned with zeal to the work of his
office. He built up the political system which was to give Great
Britain the leading place among the European Powers and which,
in 1718, culminated in the Quadruple Alliance. He was bold in his
conceptions and untiring in their execution. His fellow-Ministers—
even Sunderland—readily conceded him the first place, and gave
him credit for his achievements. He was skilful in adjusting his plans
to circumstances, and by preference carried on foreign negotiations
personally, or through Envoys blindly following his instructions. He
was not an easy man to negotiate with. Saint-Simon's acquaintance
with him must have been only social when he said that Stanhope
"never lost his equanimity, and seldom forgot his manners". In
reality his temper sometimes "betrayed him into starts of passion
and precipitate decisions". [4] Foreign diplomats feared the harsh voice

[1] Sept. 24/Oct. 5, 1714, Prussian State Archives.
[2] Mahon, *History of England* (1836), vol. i. p. 161.
[3] "Reminiscences", *Works*, (1798), vol. iv. p. 287.
[4] Mahon, *op. cit.* vol. i. p. 161.

in which he refused unreasonable demands. He had common sense and practical understanding. After hours of discussion about detail, he would be the first to recall the big issues and to suggest a solution; he would take the pen, and cut about a disputed draft till a formula was found acceptable to all. If important decisions were pending in a foreign Court and negotiations seemed to drag on, he would go there himself, and try to force a decision. If unsuccessful, he would at least gain a clear view of the situation. In Vienna, Paris, and Madrid, this peripatetic statesman worked for his European ideas.

As an orthodox Whig, Stanhope seriously considered the idea of renewing the war; hostility against France and the Habsburg alliance were the pivots of his policy. Personal connexions influenced him in the same direction; in the war he had served with the Archduke who was now the Emperor Charles VI, and had remained in touch with him ever since. When the Queen was dying, he wrote to the Emperor assuring him that all honest men in England condemned the way in which he had been treated by the Tory Administration, and wished to make amends. Possibly Stanhope meant to secure the Emperor's favour for his party, or even for his own person, and their friendly relations may have had something to do with his appointment as Secretary of State. Stanhope remained Austria's best friend among the British Ministers. Sometimes he was thought by the others to go too far and he then failed to carry them with him; "his great zeal for your Majesty's service", wrote Hoffmann, "makes him occasionally go further than he knows".

Taking the new Administration as a whole, it was inferior in ability and experience to the Tory cabinet of Queen Anne. The eight principal officers of State formed the King's Cabinet, which gained in importance under George I. But membership of the Cabinet did not depend solely on office: Somers was of it without holding any, whilst Wharton and Orford, Lord Privy Seal and First Lord of the Admiralty, were left out. To this day, there is no absolute rule fixing either the size or the membership of the Cabinet.

The Cabinet alone were in the secret of domestic and foreign politics. Hitherto they had met in the King's presence, as his confidential advisers, and only sittings at which he presided were called Cabinet meetings. Already in the previous reign they had frequently met without the Queen, as a Committee to discuss business with a view to reporting the results to her in the Cabinet, for her decision; and it was her presence which determined whether this was a Cabinet

Council, or merely a Committee of the Cabinet Council. George I's accession did not produce any immediate and fundamental change in the relations between King and Cabinet. "To-day His Majesty held his first Cabinet Council", wrote Bothmer in his Diary on October 8, 1714. Nor was it his last. For several years Cabinet Councils continued to be held in the presence of the King. It was the general trend of constitutional development, and not the King's ignorance of the English language, which gradually made the work of Government centre in ministerial meetings held in his absence.[1] With the conduct of Government, they took the very name of Cabinet with them from the Palace. The King still appeared in the Privy Council where, on certain occasions, his presence was indispensable. His absence from the meetings of the Ministers was bound to work a change in the constitutional practice and lead to the rise of a Prime Minister, presiding over the Cabinet; while the Cabinet was bound to gain in independence. But the power which they gained in one direction, they were to lose in another—in the course of the eighteenth century the Cabinet became dependent on Parliament.[2]

In importance the Privy Council could no longer compare with the Cabinet. In law it remained the body from which all Royal communications to the people had to emanate. But it had no longer access to the secrets of State; from these it was precluded even by its numbers[3]—under Queen Anne its membership had risen to eighty. Lord Peterborough once remarked "that the Privy Council were such as were thought to know everything and knew nothing, while the

[1] This subject will be discussed more fully in the third volume.

[2] The Committee of the Cabinet Council, called for short Committee of Council, is not as Lord Morley believed (*Walpole*, p. 145), a body distinct from the Cabinet and the Privy Council. Their relation is clearly defined in Bonet's report of Dec. 24, 1714, O.S. (published in full below in Appendix No. 2, pp. 372-8.): "*Cette ignorance de la langue et des affaires . . . n'a pas permis au Roi d'abolir un Conseil que l'ignorance des affaires dans le chef a introduit sous le règne précédent. Je veux parler du Comité du Conseil du Cabinet, composé des principaux officiers, qui s'assemblent en l'absence du Roi, et qui minutent toutes choses, pour rendre compte ensuite du résultat à S.M. en Conseil. Cette nécessité où S.M. est de continuer ce Conseil le prive d'une infinité de lumières, ne lui fait voir que l'écorce de plusieurs affaires, et confère un grand pouvoir à ses ministres.*" This report confirms that, to begin with, George I did assist at the Cabinet Council as distinct from the Committee of the Cabinet Council.

[3] "The Great Council", which Lord Morley treats as a distinct body, is certainly identical with the Privy Council, which is thus described in contradistinction to the Cabinet.

Cabinet were those who thought that nobody knew anything but themselves."[1] Now an entirely new Privy Council was appointed, from which the inveteracy of the Whigs excluded the Tories; only a few so-called Hanoverian Tories were summoned, such as Lords Anglesea, Pembroke, and Scarborough, who, the previous year, had voted with the Whigs to declare the Protestant Succession in danger.

The chief Ministers having been chosen almost entirely from among the Whigs, the same had to be done with regard to minor posts. It was, however, given out that the Tories would be considered in that matter, so that the King should not appear as father to one-half of his subjects only. The late Speaker, Sir Thomas Hanmer, was offered the post of Chancellor of the Exchequer, and Bromley, of Treasurer of the Chamber; but they, as all the prominent Tories, refused, wishing to be free to serve their party. Nottingham alone accepted office, long disclaimed by all his party.

Thus the Whigs remained in sole possession of the patronage, and friends and dependants could be provided for in places, high and low. Now "all people who had suffered any hardship or disgrace during the late Ministry would have it believed that it was occasioned by their attachment to the House of Hanover".[2] Fitness for office was a minor consideration. Whoever was connected by blood or marriage with one of the new rulers, confidently claimed a place, and in most cases obtained one. According to Lady Cowper, the report of intimacy between Halifax and Oxford had no other foundation "than my Lord Dupplin's not being yet out of his place, which is given to my Lord Nottingham for his son-in-law, Sir Roger Mostyn. . . ."[3] Lady Cowper herself had to suffer a great deal from the importunities and ingratitude of her relations clamouring for Royal favours.[4] A number of posts had to be assigned to the Duke of Argyll and his connexion. Marlborough was so busy in providing for his family that in the end there was a shortage of places, and the King himself was incensed at his claims. One day he asked Marlborough whether the Archbishop of Canterbury had no relations, and being told that he had, remarked: "Queer, he was two hours with me and asked me for nothing".[5]

Robert Walpole, though prominent in the House of Commons, was not as yet of the Cabinet; he merely received the highly lucrative post

[1] Cf. Morley, *Walpole*, p. 144.
[2] Lady Mary Wortley Montagu, "Account of the Court of George I".
[3] *Diary*, p. 29.   [4] *Ibid.* pp. 24-30.
[5] Bonet, Oct. 5/16, Oct. 26/Nov. 6, 1714, Dec. 24, 1714/Jan. 4, 1715.

of Paymaster of the Forces. Still, his influence was considerable; he was the brother-in-law of Townshend, and his financial expert—not primed by him Townshend could hardly have argued in the Cabinet with Halifax, the First Lord of the Treasury.[1]

The Earl of Orford, who had commanded at La Hogue, became First Lord of the Admiralty; he refused a salary higher than that of the other Lords at his Board, but reserved to himself the choosing of them.[2] He thought that thus alone could he reclaim the fleet from the neglect into which it had fallen under the Tory Administration: men had been lately appointed Lords of the Admiralty who had never been to sea. Now experts were chosen, among them Admiral Sir George Byng. The First Lord of the Admiralty was, as a rule, in the Cabinet: Orford was omitted, presumably on personal grounds. Perhaps George I did not want in it a man who had deemed himself insufficiently rewarded by William III, and who had offended Queen Anne by his caustic remarks on the incompetence of her husband, the Prince High Admiral.

Similar reasons may have operated in the case of Lord Wharton, the Privy Seal. He too, had belonged to the Whig junto and was a man of great natural parts, a brilliant orator, "the mainstay of the Whigs, and the terror of the Tories".[3] He served the King a few months only, as he died in April 1715. Pulteney was given the subordinate place of Secretary at War. The Duke of Shrewsbury, who at the death of Queen Anne had been in possession of three high places, willingly parted with two; he had never been keen on office, and was now too ill to stand the strain of a political post. As Lord Chamberlain he played no real part under George I. More important at Court was his Italian wife, whom he had preferred to one of the richest heiresses of England—it was remarked of him that he "had been tricked out of the best marriage (meaning the Duchess of Somerset when Lady Ogle), and into the worst in Christendom".[4] He was not in the Cabinet: he was of a Catholic family, had defended Sacheverell, had joined the Tory Administration, and taken part in the Peace negotiations. Not even his zeal for the Protestant Succession and the services rendered in the decisive crisis could make him acceptable to the Whig Administration.

---

[1] Cf. E. W. Montagu, "State of Affairs", where, however, Walpole's influence in the early years of George I seems to be exaggerated.

[2] Hoffmann, Oct. 12, 1714.

[3] Bonet, April 12/23, 1715.   [4] *Diary of Lady Cowper*, p. 8.

The Duke of Montrose, who had proclaimed George I at Edinburgh, replaced the Earl of Mar as Secretary for Scotland; he, and the Duke of Roxburgh, Nottingham's son-in-law, now Lord Privy Seal of Scotland, and subsequently Montrose's successor, had been Members of the Regency Council. All the chief offices in Scotland and Ireland were filled with trusted adherents.

Other forces were at work, strongly influencing the Government of Great Britain: there were men who were not of the Cabinet, nor even in office, and yet took part in forming the most important decisions. These were the foreign advisers of the King. George I had transplanted his German Court to London. The Act of Settlement barred aliens from places at Court and in the Government; they could establish themselves by underhand methods only. The German Court of George I had the reputation of being corrupt.

You cannot think [Ker of Kersland was told about the Hanoverian Ministers] they are come here only to learn your language; if you resolve to keep your money, depend upon it, you shall never have that Government[a military Governorship] notwithstanding all your pretences which I know are very just and very deserving.[1]

Yet there was a certain measure of exaggeration in this wholesale indictment. The King's own hands can be said to have remained clean. His German Court was paid with German, and not with English, money[2]—the King followed therein Bothmer's advice, who had warned him not to draw on his Civil List for that purpose.[3] Englishmen alone were appointed to his Bedchamber, and the only German who was given a place at Court was Baron Schütz—having been born on English soil, he could claim British nationality. None the less, German influence was considerable. George I consulted by preference his German Ministers, and in the first years of the reign Bernstorff and Bothmer were very nearly the chief figures at Court.

Andreas Gottlieb von Bernstorff was an old man when he came to England with George I. He had served several masters,[4] had passed from the service of the Duke of Mecklenburg into that of Duke Georg-Wilhelm of Celle, after whose death he removed to Hanover.

---

[1] *Memoires of John Ker of Kersland* (1726), p. 103.

[2] Bonet, Dec. 24, 1714/Jan. 4, 1715.

[3] Bothmer to Goertz, Aug. 27/Sept. 7, 1714, Stowe MSS. 227, f. 393. See below, Appendix, No. 1, pp. 371-2.

[4] Bernstorff's *Autobiography* (ed. by Köcher) consists of short entries; see however, sources quoted by the editor, p. 3 *n*.; also Ilten in Bodemann, p. 158.

He had a wide experience of European politics, and a proper appreciation of the Elector's new position, and also of his own. But he did not see why he should not advise the King of England as freely as he had the Elector of Hanover. Lord Halifax knew whom to cultivate, when a few weeks after the accession he wrote to Hanover: "His [Bernstorff's] position with the King, his wisdom and abilities, will be of inestimable service to the nation".[1] Already at The Hague Bernstorff played a foremost part in the discussions of the Barrier Treaty;[2] in London he formed a close connexion with Townshend who seemed to accept him as leader. Bernstorff would discourse on British, no less than on Hanoverian affairs, on problems of foreign and domestic politics, and his opinion was frequently decisive. His power seemed to rest on the respect paid to him at Court; there he was pleased to play the part of the elder statesman, the mediator, the adviser, the teacher, who treated of all problems as if they were his own concern, and discussed the filling or exchanging of offices, of which he himself, as a foreigner, could not claim any. He seemed to know everything, and if not, then only because he did not care to know. Many Englishmen, according to Bonet, considered him "a mentor in wisdom and politics".[3] It was his own master who in the end failed him; and he was a broken man when George I requited his long and faithful service with disgrace.

Behind Bernstorff stood Jean Robethon,[4] in a minor position, but neither insignificant nor without influence in public affairs. He had left France after the Revocation of the Edict of France, and gone to Holland; as William III's private secretary, Robethon had rendered him invaluable services both in Holland and in England. Trained in that school of diplomacy, Robethon became equal to dealing with the most difficult problems. He had good natural parts, a quick understanding, great working powers, remarkable versatility, and a perfect command both of French and English. After the King's death, he joined Georg-Wilhelm of Celle, and there became connected with Bernstorff. Together with him, Robethon entered, in 1705, the

[1] Halifax to Robethon, Aug. 24, 1714, Stowe MSS. 227, f. 381.

[2] See above, p. 74.

[3] Bonet, Feb. 8/19, 1715: *"Le Ministre d'État de Bernstorff continue à être à la tête de la confiance comme des affaires du Roi, et il passe parmi les Anglais pour un Mentor en sagesse et en politique"*.

[4] For Robethon see R. Pauli, *Aufsätze zur engl. Geschichte*, pp. 349 and 381; *Nachrichten von der Gesellschaft der Wissenschaften* (Göttingen, 1881), pp. 265 *seq.* and pp. 409-37; and Klopp, *Leibniz' Werke*, pp. lvi-lvii and 496.

service of the Elector, George-Lewis, and as his private secretary came to England in 1714. Adventurers who changed their masters and countries in pursuit of their own advantage or ambition, were frequent in the seventeenth century, and not rare in the eighteenth; but Robethon, the Huguenot, cannot be classed among them. He worked with single-minded devotion for the establishment of the Protestant Succession in England, and when the Elector was half-hearted about it, Robethon continued his endeavours, maintained connexions, and remained in correspondence with politicians all over Europe, but foremost with the Hanoverian party in England. It has been even said by a student of the period, that without Robethon's untiring labours George-Lewis would never have become King.[1] He was bound to play an important part at the Court of St. James's. Even at Hanover Bernstorff was said to have been governed by Robethon.[2] In England, thoroughly acquainted with conditions, he must have been indispensable to Bernstorff. Robethon certainly used his influence with the King to his own advantage;[3] the bad sides of his nature were notorious, and the Princess of Wales called him a knave.[4] But his merits must not be overlooked.

Baron Bothmer, hitherto Envoy in London, now remained at Court as Hanoverian Minister; and if now, when English and Hanoverian interests had become intertwined, he had a share in settling problems of British policy, his position was hardly more anomalous than it had been at the Court of Queen Anne. He too was accused of taking what money he could,[5] and the accusation sounds credible. Baron Goertz was another of the Hanoverian Ministers in London. A man of pleasant and obliging manners, he had for many years successfully managed the finances of the Electorate.[6] In England, his connexions were with the Tories rather than with the Whigs, and he pleaded at least for a mixed Administration. After circumstances and Bothmer's influence had defeated all such schemes, he still continued his relations with the Tories, and was therefore, in 1715, sent out of England under a suitable pretext.

The King, slow-witted by nature, for a long time found Bernstorff

---

[1] Spittler in Meiners and Spittler, *Gött. hist. Magaz.* i. 546.

[2] Coxe, *Walpole*, vol. ii. p. 44.

[3] See *Diary of Lady Cowper*, p. 42, and *Memoires of John Ker of Kersland*, p. 103. Ker relates having been told that he could not succeed, if he made not Robethon his friend "by a present of 500 guineas, because he had such a prodigious influence with Bernstorff".   [4] *Diary of Lady Cowper*, p. 87.

[5] E. W. Montagu, "State of Affairs".   [6] See Ilten in Bodemann, p. 158.

and Bothmer the most comprehensible among his advisers. "It is still a secret", wrote Bonet in January 1715, "that the Ministers von Bernstorff and von Bothmer are the first to know about all business".[1] These two were joined by certain British Ministers, and the Cabinet was split and overshadowed by a small group of German and British Ministers, among whom the Germans had as yet the greater weight. Under cover of darkness, Marlborough, Townshend, and Bernstorff, met every night at Bothmer's house, and this quadrumvirate, as Bonet called them, decided everything.[2] They were soon joined by Stanhope. The worst that this mode of governing could produce in home politics was a narrowing of the basis and outlook of the administration; but in foreign affairs, Hanoverian interests now came to have a detrimental influence on those of Great Britain. Foreign Ambassadors turned to Bernstorff and Bothmer, rather than to Townshend and Stanhope. In September 1715 Hoffmann reported that he had to transact business with the Hanoverian Ministers, as Townshend and Stanhope were too much engrossed by domestic matters—it was during the Jacobite Rising—and "could give no attention to foreign affairs".[3] The German Prince on the throne, surrounded by aliens, seemed at times to have become King solely with a view to promoting the interests of his Electorate. It is true that in these first years of his reign, in which the Whigs successfully established their rule at home, a great system of European policy was initiated under Stanhope's leadership, which secured for Great Britain the first place among the Powers; at the same time, however, Great Britain was involved in difficult and costly undertakings in which she had no real interest, but which served primarily, or exclusively, Hanoverian interests—this was against the spirit of the Act of Settlement. And while Bernstorff and Bothmer, in advising the King, were careful not to offend against the law, their influence was fundamentally unconstitutional.

George I was helpless in his seat of power; he found himself at the helm of a mighty ship which he was not fit to steer. He could not speak to his people, nor read their laws in the language in which they were written. He could not preside in the Cabinet Council and in

---

[1] Feb. 8/19, 1715.

[2] Similarly Hoffmann in his dispatch of Feb. 22, 1715.

[3] Bonet, in his dispatch of July 24, 1715, at the time of the ministerial impeachments, reports having been told by the British Ministers themselves that they had no time for anything else.

Parliament he assisted as a dumb witness, while the Lord Chancellor read out his Speech. If ever he attempted to say a few English words in public, they sounded awkward in his pronunciation. He received his Ministers singly, and talked to them in French—none of them knew German. He could transact business with the Secretaries of State who required a knowledge of French in their diplomatic intercourse; and this naturally pleased the King, who had more understanding for (and interest in) international affairs than for those of Great Britain. But some of his ablest Ministers, e.g. Somers and Cowper, knew no French. Later on, Robert Walpole tried to overcome the difficulty by speaking Latin to the King,[1] which they both spoke equally badly. Even those who knew French found it difficult to explain to the King specifically English matters for which there was no counterpart on the Continent, and no expressions in Continental languages. Nottingham, in spite of his "facility of utterance" (admitted even by Swift[2]), found great difficulty in reporting the discussions of the Privy Council to the King. On many a document did the King scrawl his heavy *George R*, without well knowing what it was that he signed.[3]

The King's intervention in home affairs was therefore perfunctory; but he had all the more important documents regarding foreign affairs submitted to him in French translations. These were usually made in London, but occasionally the British representatives abroad appended such translations to their dispatches, or wrote their dispatches in French. Early in 1717, on the King's return from Hanover, British diplomats abroad were instructed to write their official dispatches in English, but to append a French text for the King.[4] To make it easier for them, they were told that they were not required to write the best French style.[5]

The Coronation of George I took place on October 20/31, 1714.[6]

---

[1] Horace Walpole, *Reminiscences*.

[2] "Four Last Years", *Works*, vol. v. p. 179.

[3] "*Cela fait, que S.M. donne souvent son consentement à des choses qu'il n'entend pas bien et dont il ne comprend pas toutes les raisons*" (Bonet, Dec. 24, 1714/Jan. 4, 1715, Prussian State Archives).

[4] Also in a letter from Stanhope to Stanyan in Vienna, Jan. 25, 1717 (O.S.). Cf. remarks by Wiesener, *Le Régent, l'Abbé Dubois et les Anglais*, p. 9.

[5] Instructions to Crawford in Paris of March 7, 1717.

[6] For the coronation see A. Boyer, *The Political State of Great Britain* (1714), vol. viii.; *Umständliche Relation*, etc., and *Ausführliche Nachrichten*, both published at Hamburg, 1714; Wickham Legg, *Three Coronations*.

The ceremony was postponed so as to enable the Princess of Wales and her daughters to assist at it. As there was no Queen, ladies did not walk in the procession, which rendered it less gorgeous than the last three, still remembered by contemporaries. A gilded State coach, drawn by six horses, now a show piece at Herrenhausen, conveyed the King, together with the Prince and Princess of Wales, about 8 A.M. from St. James's to Westminster. The King retired to the Court of Wards. The first part of the proceeding being put in order by the Heralds, came down in solemn procession to Westminster Hall, where the King, surrounded by peers and bishops, was seated under his Canopy of State. Meantime the Insignia of the Realm had been taken under strong guard by water from the Tower to Westminster, and "delivered to the Lords appointed to carry them". Thereupon the procession crossed a platform raised between Westminster Hall and the Abbey. It was lined by Foot Guards; behind them were the Horse Guards. The procession started with the Dean's Beadle and the High Constable of Westminster, followed by drums and trumpets; the six clerks in Chancery; the aldermen of London, the law officers, and serjeants; the Judges; the choir-boys of St. Peter, Westminster; Francis Atterbury, Bishop of Rochester (a well-known Jacobite, who could not be omitted as he held the Deanery of Westminster *in commendam*); Privy Councillors not peers. They were followed by the Peers arranged by rank, two abreast; first the Barons in crimson velvet robes, with their coronets in their hands; next the Bishops; the Viscounts; the Earls; Marquesses; Dukes; (for the first time the Scottish Peers took part in the procession). The Lord Privy Seal; the Lord President of the Council; the Archbishop of York; the Lord Chancellor. The Archbishop of Canterbury ought to have come next, but Dr. Tenison, because of his advanced age, was allowed to receive the King at the Abbey door. Medieval English history was commemorated by two men in robes of crimson velvet edged with miniver, representing the Dukes of Aquitaine and Normandy. Next the Lords who bore the Regalia: the Earl of Salisbury, the St. Edward's Staff; the Viscount Longueville, the Spurs; the Earls of Dorset and Middlesex, the Sceptre with the Cross and the Royal Sceptre; the Earls of Sutherland, Pembroke, and Lincoln carrying the three swords, the symbol of the King's justice—the pointless sword of mercy called "curtana", supported to the right and the left by two pointed swords, spiritual and temporal. Then Garters Deputy, with his coronet, between the Usher of the Black Rod and the Lord Mayor of London in a red velvet robe carrying the jewels of the City and the golden staff, the insignia of his office; the Lord Great Chamberlain of England, single; the Prince of Wales "in his robes of estate in crimson velvet, furr'd with ermine, his coronet set with precious stones, and cap born by the Earl of Hertford on a crimson velvet cushion, and wearing a like cap of crimson velvet turned up with ermine, by His Majesty's Royal permission". Then came the Earl of Derby with the Sword of State, the Duke of Grafton with the Crown, the Duke of Argyll bearing the Sceptre with the Dove, and the Duke of Somerset with the Orb; the aged Bishop Burnet of Salisbury, the adviser of William III, carrying the Bible, between the Bishop of Litchfield and Coventry, with the Patten, and the Bishop of Bangor, with the Chalice. And "then the King in his Royal Robes of crimson velvet, furr'd with ermine and border'd with a rich broad, gold lace, wearing the collar of the order of St. George . . . and on his head a cap of estate, turn'd up with ermine, adorned with a circle of gold, enrich'd with diamonds, supported by the Bishops of Durham and Bath and Wells, under a canopy borne by the Barons of the Cinque Ports; his train borne by four noblemen's eldest sons". Soldiers "and the officers and yeoman of the Guard closed the proceeding". Enormous crowds watched it.

In the Abbey there happened a dispute between the Sicilian and Venetian Ambassadors, "touching the manner of placing themselves in the gallery appointed for the foreign Ministers". [1] After the King had entered the Abbey, the service started with hymns, then the King rose, and the Archbishop of Canterbury addressed four times the question, to the East, South, West, and North, whether the people would accept the new King; each time the shout was raised from each side: "God save the King". The so-called Recognition stood for the old English idea that the King had to be chosen by the people.

Next, the religious service was celebrated in the usual manner; the King, kneeling, offered his first oblation, a pall of cloth of gold, and an ingot of a pound-weight. After that a sermon was preached by the Bishop of Oxford on a text from Psalm cxviii: "This is the day which the Lord hath made; we will rejoice and be glad in it". The Psalm was interpreted as written by David when he was anointed King over Israel. The further analogy was obvious; only after Ishbosheth had been killed, could David begin to reign over Israel. Great Britain, too, had been threatened by the rule of an Ish-bosheth,

[1] A. Boyer, *Political State of Great Britain* (1714), vol. viii. p. 361.

the Pretender. But God in His mercy had ordained King George's peaceful accession; and, plunging into politics, the Bishop indicated that thanks should be given to the Almighty for having appointed the day of the Queen's death when

the unsettled posture of affairs abroad, would not permit the Pretender's foreign friends to send any forces to encourage an insurrection, and the unreadiness of his surprised abettors here, would not permit them to appear in such a manner, as to invite an invasion.

Thus England had been mercifully preserved from a King "educated in the maxims of French tyranny, and in the principles of Popish superstition", under whom

we should have been ruled not by law, but by will, and have held our lives and fortunes at pleasure only. . . . We have had woeful experience of two Popish reigns . . . but . . . if those Princes chastised us with whips, this would have done it with scorpions, who would have come with a spirit, not only of popery and bigotry, but also of resentment and revenge. . . .

The nation would have been oppressed by financial exactions, and finally been given up "as a province to his great patron", Louis XIV. No less eloquent was the Bishop about the blessings which the new dynasty would bring on Great Britain; and the children and children's children of the King were described as "pledges of the lasting happiness of these Kingdoms".

After the sermon the King repeated and signed the Declaration or Test, and took the Coronation oath to govern according to the laws and customs of the British nation, cause justice to be done, maintain the Protestant religion, and preserve the rights and privileges of the Church. Now for the first time, because of the Union, the Scottish Church was mentioned. The King took the oath kneeling, with the Bible in his hand. After he was anointed, presented with the regalia, vested with his purple robes, amid the enthusiastic acclamations of the crowd, he was solemnly crowned; whereupon His Royal Highness the Prince of Wales and the Peers put on their coronets, the Bishops their caps, the Dukes of Aquitain and Normandy their hats, and the Kings of Arms their coronets. A banner was raised from the roof of the Abbey, and soon after the guns in the Tower and Hyde Park were discharged to announce that the King had been crowned.

In the Abbey the *Te Deum* was sung and the homage was done. The first to offer it was the Prince of Wales; the Lords Spiritual and

Temporal followed him, approaching the throne, and seemingly kissed His Majesty's left cheek, and afterwards touched the Crown; while the Treasurer of the Household threw about among the people Coronation medals, which represented Britannia crowning King George. After the King had received Communion and the service had been concluded, the procession returned in the previous order to Westminster Hall, the King wearing the Crown of State, set with precious stones valued at £200,000. He carried the sceptre and orb. The Prince of Wales and the peers now wore their coronets. In Westminster Hall, where since Norman days the English kings used to dine on the day of their Coronation, the King and the Prince of Wales sat down at a table at the upper end of the Hall; the nobility and Court were seated at other tables. Hundreds and thousands of dishes were brought in, and when the feast was over, these were given to the crowd, the Princess of Wales watching with amusement from her box how the dishes disappeared in no time. While the King was at table the royal champion entered the hall preceded by trumpets and heralds, himself on a white horse in complete armour, between two mounted companions. He threw down his gauntlet, challenging anyone who "shall deny or gainsay" the King to be the right heir to the Crown— he would say "that he lieth, and is a false traitor". The King then drank to the champion out of a silver-gilt cup, and gave it to him as his fee.

The Coronation was thus celebrated with traditional splendour: it was interpreted by some as a sign of God's mercy that the sun shone brightly that day, while before and after the weather had been dull as is frequent at that time of the year. "There scarce was ever such an appearance of Lords Spiritual and Temporal, as on this occasion."[1] Even Oxford and Bolingbroke, though they could not hope for the King's favour, walked in the procession and kissed his cheek in homage.

There was the usual distribution of Coronation honours. Eight new peers were created, which incidentally served the purpose of strengthening the influence of the Crown in the House of Lords and supplying a counterweight to the Tory creations of 1712. There was difficulty in finding titles for some of the new peers, and in a few cases the names of places were taken, distant from the seats of the new peers. Care was had to raise to the peerage none but such as possessed a sufficient fortune; it was customary for the Crown to pay impoverished peers pensions of £500 a year, and there was no desire to

[1] A. Boyer, *Political State of Great Britain*, vol. viii. p. 360.

add to these burdens.[1] A few refused promotion, *e.g.* the Secretary of State, Viscount Townshend, who was offered an earldom; and Lord Orford refused the Garter, as the King had to provide for so many other claimants.

"His Majesty's auspicious coronation was celebrated with great rejoycings throughout his Majesty's dominions, but in several great cities of England the enraged Jacobites endeavoured to raise commotions among the mobb"; thus, *e.g.*, at Bristol. In some places there was bloodshed, but order was soon re-established. Even in Scotland and Ireland the Coronation Day passed without any serious disorders. In Edinburgh there were demonstrations in honour of the new dynasty.

Whatever difficulties the advent of the foreign dynasty was to cause, they were insignificant when compared with the blessings of the Protestant Succession. This has laid the foundations for all that has since constituted the greatness of Great Britain. The ideas of 1688 were victorious, and their power was now proved with even greater cogency. William III had raised and organized European resistance to French domination, and his policy was endorsed by the British nation; while his wife was the next heir to the British Throne, if James II renounced it and his son was not legitimate. George I was called to the throne merely because he was a Protestant, and not because of his person or his policy; while his hereditary title was exceedingly slender. Thus Monarchy and the Constitution in Great Britain were bound up for all time with the principles of the Glorious Revolution. The accusation of the anti-Hanoverians, that the dynasty meant to introduce an absolutist Government in Great Britain, such as they were accustomed to at home, was absurd. The popular element in the Constitution was victorious in 1714, and it was only under the Hanoverians that the British Parliamentary system attained its classical form. Britain's power on the Continent was established, and her rule of the seas was secured. Outside Europe she outstripped all her European rivals. Liberty at home was joined to power abroad. The shortcomings of the Hanoverian Monarchy could not interfere with the rise of a strong nation. The Protestant Succession became the corner-stone of Britain's greatness.

[1] See enclosure in Bonet's dispatch of Oct. 19/30, 1714, Prussian State Arch.

CHAPTER VI

MINISTERIAL IMPEACHMENTS

GROUND gained in historic progress has to be defended, and achievements have to stand the test of counter-attacks before they are proved valid and permanent. The Protestant Succession was established in Great Britain without difficulty, its opponents having been taken by surprise; but they soon reverted to their aims and recovered their strength, and even looked forward to improving it.

The most serious crisis of George I's reign occurred a year after his accession; provoked not by the alien character of the Hanoverian rule, but by the violence of the victorious Whigs who, intoxicated with their initial success, branded the past policy of their opponents as criminal and proceeded to impeach them. For a while a chance seemed to offer to the Pretender; but his attempt failed, and the new order became consolidated, at home and abroad.

From the outset the problem of Parliament occupied the minds of the Whig Administration; for, representing one party only, they could not have maintained themselves against an unfavourable majority in the House of Commons, as was proved under Queen Anne. George I, absolute master in his German dominions, was soon to learn the limitations set to his authority in Great Britain. "The King" wrote the Imperial Envoy, Hoffmann, in October 1714, "has started his reign without encountering the least difficulty or obstacle, but as divisions in this country cannot be healed, nor the nation be satisfied, it would seem that his best and most peaceful days have been spent and left behind on the other side of the water."

The six months during which the existing Parliament could be continued,[1] were the time allowed to the Government for preparing the new elections. Parliament was not summoned after the landing of the King, and was dissolved on January 5, 1715. The Proclamation

---

[1] See above, p. 5.

calling a new Parliament contained strictures on the late Administration: the country had been found by the King "under the greatest difficulties" with regard to trade and navigation, and the National Debt was much increased since the end of the War; in conclusion, the King, while "firmly resolved to maintain" the freedom of elections, expressed the hope that his subjects would return the fittest persons to Parliament, and "have a particular regard to such as shewed a firmness to the Protestant Succession, when it was in danger". The King's desire that Whigs should be chosen was thus clearly stated.[1]

In November 1714, a Declaration was issued by the Pretender[2] under the style of James III, in which he addressed himself to "all Kings, Princes, and Potentates", and to his "loving subjects". In a highly compromising manner, he alluded to the plans of the late Tory Administration, and claimed "that for some time past he could not well doubt of his sister's good intentions towards him . . . which were unfortunately prevented by her deplorable death". He had left his ordinary residence to put himself at the head of his loyal subjects, but France had refused him "succour and assistance" and even "debarr'd passage" across her territory. He solemnly protested against the injustice he had suffered, and reserved his "rights, claims, and pretentions"; nor would he hold himself "answerable before God and men for the pernicious consequences which this new usurpation of our Crown, may draw on our subjects and all Christendom."

In Great Britain the Declaration was received "by almost all the lords in office" and other persons of distinction. At first many doubted its being genuine, and the Tories, in their embarrassment, described it as a Whig contrivance;[3] but its authenticity was confirmed by Mr. Prior, British Minister at Paris. The Court now became still further estranged from the Tories, giving little credit to their assurances of passive obedience; and even more harm was done to them by the Declaration among the common people, confirming them in the belief that all Tories were Jacobites, which seriously impaired their chances at the general election.

[1] Hoffmann, Jan. 29, 1715. Edward Wortley Montagu, in his "State of Affairs", asserts that it was Sir Robert Walpole who had this passage inserted in the Proclamation.

[2] Published in French translation in Lamberty, viii. p. 675. An English copy of the Declaration is in the P.R.O., S.P. 35/1, No. 30.

[3] See *Diary of Lady Cowper*, p. 20.

That election was of decisive importance, and France and Spain protracted negotiations to see how the British Government would stand its test. The Tories started their campaign even before the arrival of the King, enjoying still for a while the advantages of office; and they retained throughout a strong position in the country as "the Church Party". Nor did they spare expense. England, they said, should be governed by Parliament, but they, "the landed interest", should have the greatest share in it; and the utmost exertions must be made to avert disaster. It was given out that Oxford and Boling-broke had become reconciled, and Dr. Sacheverell once more travelled in the provinces preaching that the Church of England was in danger from Lutheranism. Even more telling was the allegation that Whig rule meant a renewal of the war.

Government at first showed great restraint. The King was said to have refused money for elections, to avoid the accusation of having started his reign by corruption. The principle could not, however, be adhered to without endangering the Whig majority in Parliament; for there were voters who insisted on being paid. Attempts were made to hamper the Tory campaign; a Royal Proclamation recalled the Acts against Roman Catholics and Non-Jurors, and the clergy were directed not to discuss politics and party in their sermons, but to preach unity.

The new writs were issued in January 1715, and the election campaign was carried on with even more violence than in 1710. A Whig victory was universally expected; the greater were the exertions made by the Tories, and the outrages committed by mobs roaring "The Church" and "No Roundhead".[1] Sacheverell preached on the text Matthew xxiii. 34-36, with bold allusions to conditions at Court and in the Administration; while the Government remembered the events of 1710 too well to take action against that favourite of the people.

A pamphlet published under the title *English Advice to the Free-holders of England* represented the Tories as standing for "the preservation of our religion and laws as now settled", and the Whigs as hostile to the Constitution—"they design to repeal or explain away" the limitations on the Royal power, and to increase the standing army and taxation, they "are resolved upon an immediate war", etc. A parallel was drawn between the King's Lutheranism and Popery, and the case of Poland was cited, who had placed a German Elector

---

[1] See Wright, *Caricature History of the Georges*, p. 16.

on her throne and lost her freedom. The Government promised high rewards for the discovery of the author and the printer of that seditious libel, but to no purpose. More effective was the counter-campaign by Whig pamphleteers. As early as 1714, a pamphlet had appeared called *An Inquiry into the Miscarriages of the Four Last Years' Reign*, which went into many editions, and which in a register of sixty-five articles enumerated the ill-deeds of the Tories, from the first appearance of Sacheverell to the final attempts of the Ministers in favour of the Pretender. With this the writer contrasts the new Government which

will bring glory and honour to the Crown, and liberty and plenty to the people. Then the farmers' wool will come to a good market, the weavers' looms set to work, the cloathiers will have demands for cloath from the factors, the merchants will have calls from abroad, the poor will be every where employ'd, tradesmen and artificers will find business and work come in, and money circulate in every county, city and town. This will be the issue of a good Parliament. . . .

The election results even exceeded the expectations of the Government; the Whigs had a safe majority of 150 in the House. The position of George I seemed assured. Stanhope wrote exultantly to Lord Stair, the British representative at Paris, that the reports "industriously spread" (largely from France), which charged England with an intention to break the peace, had been defeated.[1] "So many Whiggs have never been return'd since the Revolution."[2] Foreign Powers could no longer doubt the stability of the Hanoverian dynasty. In March two new Envoys from the States-General, MM. de Duvenvoirde and van Borsselen, presented their credentials at the Court of St. James's; their speeches were printed[3] and the intention of their High Mightinesses was proclaimed to give permanency to the ancient alliance between the two Powers, formed under Elizabeth and strengthened under William III; while Austria preferred not to wait any longer for the Barrier Treaty, on which the rest depended, but asked for an immediate conclusion of the intended alliance.[4]

The new Parliament met on March 28. The King, seated on his

---

[1] Stanhope to Stair, Feb. 17/28, 1715, F.O. 90/14. Strictly speaking, Lord Stair was in Paris as yet in an unofficial character.

[2] Same to same, Feb. 2/13, 1715, *ibid.*

[3] Lamberty, vol. ix. p. 161.

[4] Cobham to Townshend, Vienna, May 1, 1715, S.P. 80/32.

throne in the House of Lords, through the Lord Chancellor directed
the Commons, who had been ordered to attend, to proceed immediately to the election of a Speaker. Spencer Compton, a Whig who was
Treasurer to the Prince of Wales, was the choice of the Court, and
the election took its customary course. A leading member proposed
him, another seconded, the candidate declared his own insufficiency,
but the House acclaiming him, he was led up to the Chair by the two
proposers; where, upon the steps, he turned once more to the House,
appealing to them to "desist from so improper a choice" as "the
errors he might commit . . . might be prejudicial to the whole Kingdom". But the House crying "No! no!" Compton took the Chair and,
the mace being laid upon the table, stood up to say that he would
appeal for the intercession of the King. The same cries were repeated
by the House, and four days later, again in the House of Lords, the
Speaker-elect was presented to the King, who refused his excuses and
graciously confirmed his election. The Speaker thereupon laid before
the King the claim of the Commons "to all their ancient rights and
privileges", particularly privilege from arrests and disturbance for
their persons and estates, liberty of speech, and free access to his
Royal Person; and these received the customary confirmation.[1]

The difficult moment for George came at the proper opening of
Parliament—he had to say a few words in English, though it was
merely that the Chancellor would read the Speech in his name.[2] In
claiming that he had been called by Almighty God to the throne of
his ancestors, the Speech emphasized his hereditary rights as against
those derived from the Parliamentary settlement, so dear to the
Whigs. The Treaty of Utrecht, it was said, did not answer the
justified expectations; moreover, its essential conditions were not
duly executed, its performance remaining necessarily precarious until
defensive alliances were formed to guarantee the Treaties. There was
a reference to the Pretender "who still resides in Lorrain . . . and
boasts of the assistance which he still expects here". Trade was described as languishing, and the public debt as "surprisingly increased,
even since the fatal cessation of arms". Turning to the Commons for
supplies, the Speech dwelt on the insufficiency of the Civil List from
which provision had to be made for a Prince of Wales—"an expence,
to which the nation has not of many years been accustomed, but such
as surely no man will grudge". It concluded:

[1] *Parl. Hist.* vii. 39-42.
[2] For the Speech see *ibid.* vii. 42-44.

The eyes of all Europe are upon you, waiting the issue of this first session. Let no unhappy divisions of parties here at home, divert you from pursuing the common interest of your country. Let no wicked insinuations disquiet the minds of my subjects. The established Constitution, in Church and State, shall be the rule of my government; the happiness, ease, and prosperity of my people, shall be the chief care of my life. Those who assist me, in carrying on these measures, I shall always esteem my best friends; and I doubt not but that I shall be able, with your assistance, to disappoint the designs of those who would deprive me of that blessing which I most value, the affection of my people.

The Speech was drawn up by Nottingham, but some significant alterations were made in his draft: [1] the "Throne of this Kingdom", in its opening sentence, changed in the final text into "the Throne of my ancestors", and a few important sentences were omitted. Naturally it was widely feared that the King, accustomed to absolute rule, would dislike the fetters imposed on him in Great Britain, and possibly wish to throw them off; and his ignorance of English conditions was animadverted upon. Nottingham proposed to meet such criticisms by the King declaring himself convinced of "the wisdom and happiness of our Constitution, which, while it makes the Sovereign great and glorious, renders the people happy and free"; [2] and further:

It has not been my fortune to live among you, but the more shall I now apply myself to a thorough study of your interests, for I consider that I have none, nor do I wish to have any, which would differ from yours.

But had George I spoken these words, his deeds would soon have given them the lie.

The draft of the Address in the Lords, while, in the customary way, gratefully restating the main points of the Speech, added some sharp reflections on the late Tory Administration. The King would no doubt

recover the reputation of this Kingdom in foreign parts; the loss of which, we hope to convince the world by our actions, is by no means to be imputed to the nation in general.

Several speakers took exception to this clause as "injurious to the

---

[1] This seems to have been preserved in a French translation only: "20/9 Mars 1714/5. Project de Harangue fait par Mylord Nottingam" ; Stowe MSS. 228, f. 23.

[2] These passages are necessarily a re-translation from the French.

late Queen's memory," and clashing with the part of the King's Speech which recommended unity to Parliament. That day Bolingbroke, who as Secretary of State in the Tory Government was immediately concerned, spoke for the last time in the House of Lords, protesting that it was "very hard to be censured without being heard"; he felt sure that the King, in his "great wisdom, equity, and justice", would not do so. The Earl of Strafford, one of the signatories to the Treaty of Utrecht, defiantly declared that the reputation of England never stood higher than at the death of the Queen.[1] And even the Duke of Shrewsbury, although a member of the Government, spoke against the clause; the House of Lords "ought, on all occasions, to be most tender of the honour and dignity of the Crown, from which they derive their own honour and lustre".[2] Of members of the Cabinet, Cowper and Nottingham defended the clause; they expressed reverence for the memory of the Queen, but distinguished between her and her Ministry. The Address was carried by 66 votes against 33. "I saw at that time", wrote Bolingbroke in his *Letter to Sir William Windham* in 1717, "several lords concur to condemn, in one general vote, all that they had approved of in a former Parliament by many particular resolutions."[3]

Things hinted at in the Lords' Address, were declared with ominous clearness in that moved in the Commons by Robert Walpole. It spoke of "the many open and secret practices that have of late years been used to defeat the Protestant Succession", and of the reproach brought on the nation by the unsuitable conclusion of the War—its reputation will now be restored through the King's "great wisdom, and the faithful endeavours of your Commons". They promised support for his foreign policy and expressed their resentment at the Pretender still residing in Lorraine and building hopes on "the measures that had been taken for some time past in Great Britain". "It shall be our business to trace out those measures whereon he placed his hopes, and to bring the authors of them to condign punishment."

Again objections were raised to the Address as reflecting on the memory of the late Queen, and were countered by the argument that it was rather designed "to vindicate her memory, by exposing and punishing those evil counsellors who deluded her into pernicious measures".[4] The intended impeachments were thus openly avowed,

[1] Hoffmann, April 5, 1715.
[2] *Parl. Hist.* vii. 46.
[3] Edn. of 1753, p. 90.
[4] *Parl. Hist.* vii. 47-50.

and Stanhope declared that, in spite of the conveying away of papers from the Secretaries' offices,

the Government had sufficient evidence left to prove the late Ministry the most corrupt that ever sate at the helm . . . and that it would appear, that a certain English general [the Duke of Ormond] had acted in concert with, if not received orders from, Marshal Villars.[1]

He asserted that the Peace Treaty had supplied France with allies and deprived England of her friends, and that her isolation would be even more marked, were it not for the confidence which foreign Powers placed in the King; [2] and he alleged that the Emperor had accepted British mediation between Spain and the Island of Majorca, thus adhering to the inaccurate official version of that story.[3]

The Address, which settled the question of the impeachments, was carried in the Commons by 244 against 178. Lord Nottingham had spoken of them to Bothmer while the King was still abroad, and though they remained in doubt until the Government had assured itself of a great majority in Parliament, attempts were made to secure the necessary material. Bolingbroke's papers, in so far as they had not been destroyed or removed, were seized; and even before Parliament met, similar action was taken against Matthew Prior and Lord Strafford, who had taken a foremost part in the Peace negotiations.

Prior's recall had long been settled, and his successor, Lord Stair, was instructed by Stanhope to demand from him delivery of all the papers relating to the negotiations in which he had been employed since 1711. In those days Ministers, when leaving their posts, used to treat official correspondence as their property; and as that practice was hardly ever objected to, such a step signified serious distrust; but Prior readily complied, and his papers were found in very fair order.[4] The seizing of papers, wrote Hoffmann on January 29, 1715,

further proves that nothing is left undone in the way of enquiry into the activities of the previous Administration and with a view to discovering material against them.

Lord Strafford, as Minister at Hanover and Berlin, had become acquainted with the Electress Sophia, and they kept up a corres-

[1] *Parl. Hist.* vii. 49. [2] Hoffmann, April 5, 1615.
[3] See below, p. 271.
[4] Stair to Stanhope, Paris, Feb. 2, 1715, S.P. 78/160.

pondence even while he was engaged on the Peace negotiations. These, however, had rendered him odious in Holland, and he could hardly show himself in the streets of Amsterdam for fear of insults.[1] To George I he was suspect because of his close connexion with Oxford and Bolingbroke, and when in December 1714, General Cadogan was sent to Antwerp to negotiate the Barrier Treaty, Strafford was recalled. On January 21, to his great surprise, Townshend came to him by order of the King to demand the delivery of his papers— among Bolingbroke's correspondence letters from Strafford are said to have been found, disrespectful to the King. Strafford refused, and the next day he was summoned to a meeting of the Privy Council in the presence of the King. Having previously asked to be sworn of the Council, he may have thought that he was summoned for that end; but the President, Lord Nottingham, demanded that he should deliver all documents and correspondence relating to the Peace negotiations. Strafford demurred: that he had been but second plenipotentiary, that his baggage had not yet come, that this was the first instance of anyone so treated, that he had not merited such suspicions, and that a new precedent should not be set in his case. He spoke with warmth though in the presence of the King, who resented an attempt by the Duke of Shrewsbury, after Strafford had retired, to shelve the matter, and demanded that his papers should be seized. It was resolved that he should deliver them to the two Secretaries of State for submission to the Privy Council.[2]

On April 16, in the House of Commons, old Sir William Whitelock, Member for Oxford University, incidentally described the King's Proclamation for the new Parliament as "unwarrantable" (because it had favoured one part); but when called upon by some Members, made an excuse and the matter was dropped, as it was not desired to send to the Tower a man of Whitelock's high character at the age of eighty. But Sir William Wyndham, who was still under thirty, provoked by the Whigs, declared that he had on a previous occasion described the Proclamation as dangerous, and that he would repeat the charge; and he demanded that a day be appointed for considering

---

[1] See letter from Duvenvoirde to Robethon, The Hague, Dec. 28, 1714: ". . . la canaille ne le laisserait pas passer sans l'insulter, tant on l'abhorre dans cette ville parmi le peuple"; Stowe MSS. 227, f. 545.

[2] See "Minutes of Privy Council Proceedings", Jan. 11, 1714/15, in Wharton's handwriting, Hist. MSS. Comm., Portland MSS., v. 503-4; Bonet, Jan. 14/25, 1715; Hoffmann, Jan. 18/25, 1715.

I

the Proclamation. The motion was in order as the Proclamation was counter-signed by Lord Townshend, who was thus responsible for it; none the less such a discussion would have reflected on the King. The Proclamation was read, and Wyndham being called upon to justify his charge, declined, claiming freedom of speech; and he renewed his motion for a day. A long debate ensued, in which Wyndham was threatened with punishment, though Robert Walpole declared against sending him to the Tower, which "would make him too considerable". William Pulteney, Secretary at War, moved the adjournment, which, opposed by Wyndham himself, was carried in the negative. Finally, by 208 votes against 129, Wyndham was ordered to withdraw, but those who had voted in the minority, to a man, rose and went out along with him; while according to a Tory report, a Member of note who had "as few rash words to answer for as any man . . . could not forbear declaring that the liberties of England withdrew with them".[1] Their opponents, though masters of the field, were afraid to go to extremes and merely resolved that Sir William Wyndham be reprimanded by the Speaker, which was done the next morning. Wyndham thanked the Speaker for performing that duty, but asserted that he was not conscious of having deserved the reprimand. The incident showed the degree party feeling had reached, and the length to which the Whigs would go—they refused to discuss the Proclamation which, in the circumstances, was a Whig document.

It was rumoured that Oxford, Bolingbroke, and the late Lord Chancellor Harcourt, were to be impeached, and possibly also Strafford, Prior, and the Duke of Ormonde. For four years Bolingbroke had been in charge of foreign policy, and from the hundreds of dispatches in the hands of the Government, it should not have been difficult to trump up a case against him, especially when the very principles of the Peace Treaty were condemned. Bolingbroke's courage failed him; he appeared several times in the House of Lords, showing signs of uneasiness, and on April 6, having gone to the Playhouse, left before the end, and went off to Dover in disguise, landing at Calais the next night. The captain who had carried him across, was arrested and examined by the Privy Council.[2]

---

[1] See anonymous pamphlet *The Honour and the Impartiality of the House of Commons, set forth in the Case of Sir William Wyndham*; it gives the fullest account of that incident.

[2] The Protocol is enclosed in a dispatch to Bonet, Prussian State Archives; see also Tindal.

His flight was not really displeasing either to the King or to the Ministers, who at bottom did not relish the idea of opening the reign with executions. If only Lord Oxford would follow his example! But he remained. Meantime, a letter from Bolingbroke appeared in which he claimed that the resolution had been taken to pursue him to the scaffold, and that his blood was to have been "the cement of the new Alliance". In reality such atonement was desired by the Whigs alone, who, having bitterly arraigned the authors of the Treaty, now felt bound to act. On April 20 Stanhope presented the House of Commons with the powers, instructions, memorials, and other papers relating to the Peace negotiations, and moved that they be referred to a Select Committee. Another Member added that while the King could do no wrong, Ministers were accountable for their maladministration. Next, Edward Harley stood up and assured the House that his brother, Lord Oxford,

would neither fly his country nor conceal himself, but be forthcoming whenever he should be called upon to justify his conduct. He would make his innocence appear to all the world; but if he should be so unhappy as to have been guilty of the crimes that were laid to his charge, he would think all his blood too small a sacrifice to atone for them.

The motion for a Select Committee passed unopposed; but not a single Tory was among its twenty-one Members, who included Walpole, Stanhope, and Pulteney. The Committee were given powers to send for persons, papers, and records; their proceedings were to be secret. Robert Walpole was chosen Chairman; but for a short time, while he was ill, Stanhope supplied his place.

In May the question of an increase in the Civil List was brought into the House of Commons, the Court wishing to have the matter settled before the impeachments. Long and warm debates ensued, hardly fit to raise the prestige of the King, but finally the £700,000 which had been asked for, were voted by the Whig majority. The Tory motion to give a separate revenue to the Prince of Wales was rejected, as clearly intended to lessen the dependence of the Prince on the King, and still further to divide the Royal Family. The heir-apparent was to receive £100,000 from the Civil List of the King, subject to his pleasure.

On June 13 Walpole acquainted the House that the Secret Committee had prepared their Report, and desired the House to appoint a day for receiving it. Its reading, on June 20, took up five hours.

Impartiality can hardly be expected in political cases, in which measures based on different principles, are liable to be distorted into crimes. The Report claims to give a history of the Treaty of Utrecht based on documents, of which a selection is reproduced in an Appendix; but it is a story warped by prejudice, and incomplete because of gaps in the material before the Committee—the fact most compromising for the Tory Administration remained unknown to its authors. Document No. 1 in the Appendix is "the first propositions of France, dated April 22, 1711":

> To whom these Propositions were directed, what previous steps had been made on the part of France, or what encouragement had been given on the part of England; does not appear.

These "Propositions" had not come from France, but had, in fact, been suggested from England.[1]

But even in the documents before the Committee, they thought they found sufficient evidence to warrant their charging the Ministry with the "little concern they had to make good the repeated assurances that had been given to the Allies in the Queen's name" and with a "manifest violation" of The Hague Treaty of Alliance which precluded separate peace negotiations with the enemy. Nor was it the particular advantage of Great Britain which they had pursued in the negotiations: the most material points were given up against nothing better than vague assurances that the Crowns of France and Spain should never be united. The Report deals at length with the suspension of arms declared through the Duke of Ormonde—the "Restricting Orders"—whereby the French alone could profit; and when the separation of armies resulted in the defeat of Prince Eugene at Denain, this was announced by Torcy to Bolingbroke as if that victory "obtained by the Queen's enemies over her good allies" was expected to be " a pleasure or satisfaction to Her Majesty". The tone of the Report becomes increasingly severe:

> It is almost incredible that the English Ministry, however determined they were to give up the honour of the Queen, and the interest of their country, in following the dictates of France, should venture to do it in this open manner.[2]

It would serve no purpose to discuss the distortions and exaggera-

---

[1] See Weber, *Der Friede von Utrecht* (1891).
[2] *Parl. Hist.* vii. App. col. xlvi.

tions of the Report which represented the Ministers of the Queen, her Commander-in-Chief, and her Plenipotentiaries at the Congress, as a set of rogues bent on betraying the honour and interest of their country. The makers of the Treaty of 1713, whatever their personal ambitions, were serious statesmen, no less patriotic than their vindictive adversaries; and behind them stood the nation, desirous of peace and applauding their policy. Even if the Whigs now had the King on their side, and a majority in Parliament, an attempt to brand their opponents as traitors could not meet with the approval of the public, and was bound to reflect on its authors.

The news of the impending impeachments produced considerable excitement, and as a precaution against riots, the Government thought it necessary to move some regiments towards London. The Bishop of London addressed a Pastoral Letter to the clergy of his diocese enjoining them to exercise a pacifying influence. Meantime, the Whigs were pressing on with the prosecutions. On June 22 the second reading of the Report was concluded, and though the House had not had time to peruse and digest it, the Tory motion that its consideration be adjourned, was rejected by 280 votes against 160. Robert Walpole, in a long and impressive speech,[1] moved the impeachment of Bolingbroke, the chief culprit. He was accused of having signed the Preliminaries without authority from the Queen, of having issued contrary instructions to Strafford, and having the next day, in a letter to Torcy, disclosed to the enemy intelligence of her Majesty's counsels; and of having directed the Duke of Ormonde to concert his operations with Marshal Villars. Incidentally Walpole pointed to Ormonde's responsibility in having acted on secret orders from Bolingbroke, in neglect of his official instructions—it was Walpole's intention to frighten him into flight, and save the Government the awkward and dangerous task of executing a popular general. Least conclusive was Walpole's evidence for Bolingbroke's relations with the Pretender, as Bolingbroke had succeeded in covering up his tracks.

When Walpole finished his speech, there was a great silence. Little was said against the impeachment, and the motion, supported by Stanhope, was carried. Bolingbroke was impeached under Statute 25 Edward III, which forbids comforting the enemy, giving him intelligence, or corresponding with him.

---

[1] Bonet's Report of June 14/25, 1715, forms a valuable supplement to that in the *Parliamentary History*.

Bolingbroke's impeachment was followed by that of the Earl of Oxford—a much more difficult task, because, as Lord Treasurer, he was not directly responsible for foreign policy. Moreover, in this case punishment could be inflicted, for Oxford was determined to stay his trial; he assured his friends in the House of Lords, which he regularly attended, that he would rather die than fly the country. Lord Coningsby moved his impeachment in an almost flippant manner:

The worthy Chairman of the Committee has impeached the hand, but I do impeach the head; he has impeached the clerk, and I the justice; he has impeached the scholar, and I the master.

Edward Harley endeavoured to justify his brother, but did it in a feeble manner, declaring in conclusion "that the facts mentioned in the Report, and which were charged on the Earl, could not be construed to amount to high treason, but only in strict rigour, to misdemeanours". The doubts expressed by Sir Joseph Jekyll, a member of the Secret Committee, whether there was sufficient matter or evidence to impeach Lord Oxford of treason, carried greater weight. But the Whig zealots had their way. Stanhope denied there having been any necessity for peace, and argued that in the three years which followed its conclusion the Government had obtained larger supplies from Parliament than the Whigs in three years of the glorious War. When a Tory Member again dragged in the memory of the Queen, the Speaker intervened and asked him to choose other arguments. After a long debate the Committee of Secrecy was instructed to draw up articles of impeachment against Lord Oxford.

Meantime the Government tried to influence public opinion, which was less compliant than Parliament; they moved regiments towards London, and gave time to Oxford and Ormonde to leave the country, as they feared resistance from the populace against the arrest of Ormonde, who was their favourite. In many places his name was a signal for tumults against the Court. His zeal for the Church earned him the support of the Tory party. Moreover, at an awkward moment, Marlborough, Ormonde's predecessor and successor in the supreme command, caused dissatisfaction in the Army by ill-judged economy in the clothing of his own regiment. Samples cut out of the coats and shirts were sent about and paraded as Hanover cloth and linen, and hundreds of soldiers burnt their new shirts in front of Whitehall, crying out "Ormonde for ever". Still more indignation was caused by the rumour that men had been hired to murder

Ormonde. He, while boasting of his noble birth and his services, "took a great deal of pride to be the idol of the rabble"; and in a printed piece, which was widely read, he justified his conduct in the campaign of 1712.[1] His ostentatious behaviour was a challenge to the Court.

But at first the Government tried leniency; they were prepared to drop proceedings against him provided that, in a submissive letter to the King, he disowned the mobs who used his name in committing outrages. For a while Ormonde seemed inclined to make his peace with the King, by whom he is alleged to have been received in private audience; but as he made no further steps towards reconciliation, the impeachment was proceeded with. It was carefully prepared. General Cadogan was brought over as a witness from Holland, where he was negotiating the Barrier Treaty, and on July 2 the impeachment was moved by Stanhope, himself a general of high rank.

A long debate ensued[2] of which the issue was uncertain, as some Whigs, and among them a member of the Secret Committee, pleaded for Ormonde, or at least demanded that he should not be charged with high treason, but merely with high crimes and misdemeanours. Archibald Hutcheson, a Tory, urged that Ormonde had merely obeyed the Queen's commands, disobedience to which would have earned him the penalty of death. Walpole declared that no order from the Sovereign could cover high treason, and Aislabie added that the law, and not the will of the Sovereign, must determine the actions of ministers. There were precedents of prosecutions against those who had acted differently—an allusion to Strafford. It was the Ministers themselves who now, under the Hanoverians, stressed the constitutional principle of ministerial responsibility.

The resolution to impeach Ormonde passed by 234 votes against 187; and the next day the impeachment of Strafford was voted, not for high treason, but for high crimes and misdemeanours. In the course of July and August the Articles of Impeachment were drawn up, and on July 20 Lord Coningsby, attended by about a hundred Commoners, went up to the House of Lords, and at their bar impeached Robert, Earl of Oxford and Mortimer, of high treason, and

---

[1] See Tindal, *Continuation*, vi. pp. 373 and 380.

[2] There is no full report of this debate in Bonet's dispatches but some important details are mentioned which he learned from Members of Parliament: "*De sorte que je me trouve réduit à quelques observations, dont ils m'ont fait part, et qui ne sont qu'un échantillon de ce qui s'est passé dans ces deux grandes journées*".

other high crimes and misdemeanours. Article XVI accused him of
having tried "to destroy the freedom and independency of the House
of Lords" by creating a batch of new peers. A motion for adjournment was rejected, and similarly one that the Judges be consulted
whether the charge contained in the Articles amounted to high
treason. Lord Chancellor Cowper, "showed the contrary" and
challenged all the lawyers in England to disprove his arguments. A
debate ensued and a resolution was carried to commit Lord Oxford
"to safe custody in the Tower". Lord Oxford rose and answered
in a short and dignified speech which did not, however, change
the issue. He argued that the nation had wanted peace and that it
had been France, and not Great Britain, which made the first steps
towards a negotiation.

I am justified in my own conscience, and unconcerned for the life of an
insignificant old man. But I cannot, without the highest ingratitude, be
unconcerned for the best of Queens; a Queen who heaped upon me
honours and preferments, though I never asked for them; and therefore
I think myself under an obligation to vindicate her memory, and the
measures she pursued, with my dying breath.

My Lords, if Ministers of State, acting by the immediate commands
of their Sovereign, are afterwards to be made accountable for their proceedings, it may, one day or other, be the case of all the members of this
august assembly . . .

He concluded by saying that he would acquiesce in the verdict of his
peers. "And, my Lords, God's will be done."

After Lord Oxford had withdrawn, the question of committing
him to the Tower was discussed and carried in the affirmative, the
Prince of Wales voting in the majority. As, however, Oxford was very
much indisposed, he was suffered to remain at his own house. Three
days later he appeared at the bar of the House of Lords, receiving a
copy of the Articles of Impeachment against him, and was allowed a
further three days' reprieve. Sympathy was felt for him standing there
at the bar, in danger of life, but refusing to evade it by flight. On July
27, Oxford, accompanied by his family, went in his own chariot from
his house near St. James's Palace to the Tower; to avoid a crowd, he
did not take the shortest route through the Strand, but went through
Piccadilly and Holborn. None the less he was accompanied by a great
and growing concourse of the common people; cries of "Down with
the Pretender" and "Down with the Traitors" were heard, but the
counter-cries prevailed—"High Church" and "Ormonde and Oxford

for ever". It seemed as if the times of the Sacheverell case had returned.

Next, the Articles of Impeachment against Bolingbroke and Ormonde were drawn up and brought into the House of Lords. Bolingbroke had fled the country four months ago, and now, at the beginning of August, the Duke of Ormonde, too, suddenly disappeared. This was not due to cowardice—he had remained hoping to lead a rising against the Hanoverian dynasty, and fled when the immediate chances of such a rising had vanished; though even now he believed that he would soon return to England at the head of a Stuart army. The fugitives, who could not be tried before the House of Lords, were, by an Act of Attainder, declared guilty of high treason, though a few peers entered the usual formal protest. Further, Lord Strafford was impeached of high crimes and misdemeanours; the Articles against him having been read in the House of Lords he "stood up and complained of the hardship that had been put upon him, by seizing his papers in an unprecedented manner". He was not imprisoned, but the case against him took the same course as that against Oxford. Oxford replied to the Articles of Impeachment in a long and elaborate Answer, to which a Replication was drawn up by the Commons before Parliament was prorogued, after a long Session and at a time full of imminent danger.

CHAPTER VII

THE JACOBITE RISING

ON July 23, 1715, during the debate on the sending of Lord Oxford to the Tower, Lord Anglesea, a Hanoverian Tory, said "that it was to be feared that these violent measures would make the sceptre shake in the King's hands". The speech aroused indignation and Anglesea was forced to apologize. But the words had gone forth— even more obnoxious because they were felt to be true. Unrest was spreading throughout the country and finding vent on every occasion. The excitement of the mob was growing, street disturbances were becoming frequent in London, and the news from the provinces became threatening. In one place, Lord Oxford, previously most unpopular, was acclaimed together with Ormonde, in another the health of the Pretender was drunk; here the mob attacked the meetinghouse of the Dissenters, there it proclaimed James III. In July 1715, travellers were stopped by Jacobite mobs in Lancashire and, to escape ill-treatment, had to join in the cry dating back to the Commonwealth: "Down with the Rump".[1] On the anniversary of the Restoration a mob gathered before the statue of Queen Anne, in front of St. Paul's, and shouted "Down with the House of Hanover" and "God bless King James III". Bonet wrote in 1715 that the Jacobite cause had made more progress in the eight months of George I's reign than in the preceding four years of the Tory Administration.

The movement had the solid support of the Tory party,[2] embittered by George I having so completely committed himself to the Whigs. The Hanoverian Tories had counted on the King's fairness and moderation, after they had in difficult times shown their zeal for the Protestant Succession; but they, too, saw themselves debarred

[1] See "Letter from Preston, July 3/14, 1715" (in French translation), Stowe MSS. 228, ff. 61, 62.
[2] See Bolingbroke, *Letter to Sir W. Windham.*

130

from office. Moreover, the un-English character of the Government and the prominence of foreigners at Court were resented. A lampoon, circulated in London in January 1715, described Bothmer as "Father Petre in disguise", the Irish and Scotch as "both . . . counsellors grown", and threatened the King with the fate of James II:

> Remember, George, when this set led the dance
> They sent a greater King than you to France.

These feelings were further exacerbated by the impeachments, perhaps the most important single factor in the coming revolt; the Tories, taught to apprehend the worst from the virulence of their opponents, would take any risk rather than meekly suffer destruction.

The moment seemed not unfavourable for an attack against the Whigs who, through death, had lost several of their most distinguished leaders: the Marquess of Wharton, Lord Privy Seal; the Earl of Halifax, not always an asset as First Lord of the Treasury, but an effective opponent of the Tories; and Bishop Burnet of Salisbury, not a first-rate leader, but possessed of wide historical and political knowledge which he placed at all times at the service of the party in the House of Lords. Lord Somers, though still alive, was much weakened in mind and body, while the rising men among the Whigs, Townshend and Stanhope, and even Robert Walpole, could not as yet adequately fill the places of those who had just left the stage.

The strongest ally of the Tories against the Government was the clergy. The Protestant Successor, summoned to protect the Church of England, as a Lutheran encountered the distrust of the High Church; though he had by his very accession joined the Church of England, attended her services, and tried, not very convincingly, to appear her dutiful son. The cry of *"The Church in danger"*, so fatal to the Whigs, exercised its old sway over the masses.

The Tories, in their party zeal, had not envisaged at first the ultimate aims and consequences of the movement. They did not plan the overthrow of George I, but merely meant to force a change of system, to get the King away from the Whigs, and secure a due share in Government for themselves who, as representatives of the landed interest, were the natural exponents of conservatism, and by far outnumbered the Whigs. In the summer of 1715, it was estimated that two-thirds of the nation were hostile to the new dynasty.[1]

[1] Hoffmann, Aug. 2, 1715.

The masses, however, could not grasp refinements of policy. Even irrelevant occurrences served to swell the rising tide of disaffection,[1] dislike of the Government was widespread, the people inveighed against the King, against Marlborough and his connexions, against the Dissenters and the entire Whig party. Disaffection began to assume a Jacobite colouring. The movement, which originally was not directed against the dynasty, at least not in England, finished in an attack on the throne of George I.

Without foreign support, success was, however, impossible, for the Whigs and the monied interest, and, once the Protestant Succession was at issue, even the greater part of the Tories, were with the King. Most important of all, Parliament was behind the Government, and was in session with a view to giving them effective support. Hoffmann wrote on August 2, 1715: "No King of England who had the support of Parliament had ever been defeated while Parliament was in session, and should the Chevalier dare to come here, he will find things different from what he has been made to imagine, especially if he comes without an army". Moreover, Government had taken counter-measures to allay the discontent. The King had announced his intention to promote the building of a number of churches.[2] Persons who flaunted their Jacobite views received corporal punishment, and the military were summoned in to deal with serious riots. In the City the Lord Mayor called out the militia on the Pretender's birthday, and a few rioters were killed and many arrested. In July similar encounters occurred at Manchester and other places. Many of the Justices of the Peace in the provinces were Tories, and had so far been left on the bench, in order not to alienate the landed gentry. They had, however, frequently shown undue leniency towards the rioters, and an Address was voted by the House of Commons asking the King "that such justices, who shall appear . . . to have neglected their duty, be forthwith put out of the commissions of the peace"; and that the sufferers in the riots "may have full compensation made them for their damages". The King replied that he would "give immediate directions for putting in execution the several matters" recommended to him by the Commons.[3] The Government was fully equal to deal with the move-

---

[1] Thus, e.g., early in 1714, there was a serious outbreak of cattle plague in the home counties, and when, with the spreading of the distemper, the payments from the Civil List to the owners of the slaughtered cattle could not be continued, this became a serious grievance with the farmers.

[2] Bonet, July 9, 1815, N.S.   [3] Parl. Hist. vii. 108-11.

ment at home, and everything depended on whether foreign powers
would support the Pretender and whether he would consider the
time ripe for a new attempt.

After the Queen's death, James Edward showed little skill in the
conduct of his affairs. His Proclamation had only done him harm,
and whereas previously the British Government had disregarded him,
now they would no longer tolerate his stay in Lorraine but desired
to remove him to a distance of many hundred miles from England.
In November 1714 the Envoy of Duke Leopold of Lorraine was
refused an audience with George I on the ground that the King
could not receive him so long as the Pretender continued to reside
in Lorraine.[1] The Duke answered in an ostensible letter to his Envoy
pointing to the position of his State, surrounded by France; the
Chevalier of St. George had not been invited by him, nor could he
be sent out of the country; he came and went, like a traveller in an
open country.[2] Meantime, Prior had been instructed[3] to present a
note to the French Court asking them to urge the expulsion of the
Pretender on the Duke of Lorraine. Marquis de Torcy, the Minister
for Foreign Affairs, gave Prior the verbal reply that the King of
France was not concerned with the Chevalier of St. George, and had
satisfied his obligations under the Treaty of Utrecht when, on the
death of Queen Anne, he had turned him back from French soil;
but he refused to interfere with the Duke of Lorraine.[4] Thus the
burden fell once more on the Duke, and the Marquis Lamberti was
about to leave London when Townshend informed him of the French
reply. It was obvious, however, that the influence of a greater Power
must have determined Lorraine to grant hospitality to the Pretender.
The Marquis d'Iberville hastened to ascribe the responsibility for it
to Charles VI, which was, of course, indignantly repudiated by
Hoffmann.[5] Anyhow, James Edward continued to reside in Lorraine.

The Pretender was a man of mediocre abilities and little judgment. He was tall and slender, "the upper part of his face very much
like Charles II, the lower part very much like the late Queen Mother",[6]
Maria of Modena, who now, separated from her son, had her Court

---

[1] Marquis Lamberti (to Townshend?), Nov. 16/27, 1714, S.P.

[2] Duke Leopold to Marquis Lamberti, Dec. 6, 1714, S.P.

[3] Townshend to Prior, Nov. 15/26, 1714, F.O. 90/14.

[4] Prior to Townshend, Dec. 7, 1714, S.P. 78/159.

[5] Reports of Bonet and Hoffmann of Dec. 10/21, 14/25, 1714.

[6] See letter published in *Eng. Hist. Rev.* vol. i. p. 776, and Thornton, *The Brunswick Accession*, p. 217.

at St. Germain. The Prince remained of the same mind as when he indignantly refused to change his religion. Imbued with a belief in his divine right, he firmly counted on his restoration, and expected at any moment to be called to the British throne. He showed for news favourable to his cause the credulity peculiar to princes in exile.

Had he been restored, he would probably have followed in the footsteps of his father. For his religion was everything to him and to suffer for it was his consolation. He expected all Roman Catholic Princes, and in the first place the Emperor, to support him for the sake of religion, and the Church to give freely of her treasure—for what better purpose could it serve than to help the faithful in oppression? "It is not so much a devoted son, oppressed by the injustices of his enemies", he wrote to the Pope, "as a persecuted Church threatened with destruction, which appeals for the protection and help of its worthy pontiff." [1] But France alone could have given effective help to the Pretender by supporting him with ships and troops, as she had done in 1708; Louis XIV, whose powerful personality still dominated the European stage, immediately recognized George I when he saw his accession so easily effected, and relations between England and France in the first months of George I's reign were no worse than was to be expected, as either side was aware that it had little to hope for from the other. Negotiations for an alliance between Britain and France, and of the two with the King of Sicily, could not be seriously continued; though the King of France wished to make a show of friendly intentions. How could he otherwise? According to Prior—and others shared the view—France was not in a position to renew the war either on land or by sea. Still, did not the same opinion prevail after the Peace of Ryswick?

At first Matthew Prior remained British Ambassador in Paris. He was devoted to Bolingbroke and wrote to him on the death of the Queen: "Whilst you continue to act as you have done for the safety and honour of your country, I will abandon you and life at the same time. . . ." [2] George I, while still in Hanover, had authorized the Regency Council to recall Prior if they thought necessary; but they merely kept a watch on his correspondence, and he was left in Paris till the beginning of 1715.

Among the subjects of negotiation none was of greater weight than the French harbour works at Mardyke near Dunkirk. By an article

[1] Chevalier of St. George to Pope Clement XI, March 14, 1715, Add. MSS. 20292, f. 71.   [2] Paris, Aug. 6/17, 1714, S.P. 78/159.

of the Treaty of Utrecht, Louis XIV had engaged to demolish the
fortifications of Dunkirk, to fill up the harbour, and to destroy the
sluices; with the express condition that they should never be restored.
In the last two wars Dunkirk had proved a deadly danger to English
commerce; it was a refuge for whole fleets of French privateers,
always ready to emerge from it and prey on British merchantmen—
the East wind which carried ships from the Thames into the Channel,
also favoured privateers starting from Dunkirk. The Tory Administration had ventured to conclude a treaty which left Spain to the
House of Bourbon, but would not have dared to leave Dunkirk un-
touched. This seemed to remove the chief danger to British trade,
as the other great harbour of Northern France, Brest, was much
farther removed from the English coast than Dunkirk.

It was therefore with dismay that the Regents heard in September
1714 that Louis XIV, while adhering to the letter of this article,
tried to evade its purport. Dunkirk was not yet choked up when
men were actually at work on a new, much larger, harbour in the
adjoining Mardyke. Lieutenant Armstrong, one of the British Commissioners who were to supervise the demolition of Dunkirk, made
a verbal report about it to the Regents. The pilots sent out by
the Commissioners to sound the depth of the new canal were
imprisoned by the Governor of the fortress; and when the Commissioners complained, he referred them to the Governor of the harbour.
Nor was any satisfactory answer given when the Commissioners expressed their astonishment at there being a Governor of the harbour
of Dunkirk when there was to be no harbour.[1] They soon realized
that the new harbour was capable of receiving whole fleets of great
ships.

The Regents were helpless, and even after the arrival of George I
no progress was made in the matter. Prior was directed to present
a note to the French Court and warn them against building the harbour in open contravention of the Treaty of Utrecht. The French
persistently replied that the new canal was merely intended to drain
off the water and save the country from floods. Naturally no one
gave any credence to this excuse; for why had this innocuous canal
to be so wide and deep as to be capable of receiving a fleet of warships? An equally fruitless argument was carried on between d'Iberville and the Ministers in London. The King himself took the greatest
interest in the question, and Lieutenant Armstrong had to report to

[1] Bothmer's Diary, September 13/24, 1714.

him on it; Dunkirk, he said, had been a pirates' nest, but Mardyke will be a naval base. On one occasion the King was talking about the matter at Court, without noticing that d'Iberville was standing behind him. On his attention being drawn to it, he turned straight to the French Ambassador who immediately rattled off the story about making a passage for the land floods with a view to saving the country. He was contradicted by Admiral Berkeley; and the King concluded the conversation by remarking that before it had been a round, and now it was a long, harbour.

The British Government was in an embarrassing position. Obviously Louis XIV thought them weak, and therefore ventured to infringe the Peace Treaty. England could try either to enforce the Treaty by war, or to come to a friendly understanding with France; and while the latter was hardly possible for George I in the lifetime of Louis XIV, war, though contemplated at one time, was delayed in expectation of Louis XIV's death. Meantime the French could continue building the harbour of Mardyke without fear of anything worse than empty threats from Great Britain.

Such was the position when in January 1715 Lord Stair was sent to Paris, at first in an unofficial character, but in reality to replace Prior, who was disliked by the new Government as one of the negotiators of the late Treaty, a Tory, and a friend of Bolingbroke's. Stair's instructions [1] naturally dealt with the removal of the Pretender from Lorraine, with the demolition of Dunkirk, and "the new canal or port which is making near Mardyke". With regard to Mardyke, he was given a memorial which at the first opportunity he was to present to the French Court.

John Dalrymple, Earl of Stair, had served under Marlborough, and on the accession of George I was appointed Commander-in-Chief in North Britain. He was a soldier by nature rather than a diplomat, and at first gave offence at the Court of Louis XIV by his rough manner. Torcy declared that he did not wish to continue negotiating with him, and the King himself was unwilling to receive him again.[2] If at that time the British Government thought of restarting the war, Stair's behaviour was a suitable preparation for it. A little later things took a different turn, but the five years of his embassy in Paris form a most important chapter in the relations between the two Powers.

Lord Stair was received in a cool and almost unfriendly manner.

---

[1] F.O. 90/14.
[2] *Mémoires de Saint Simon* (Paris, 1843), vol. xxii. p. 208.

The King paid him the customary compliments and said that he desired to do all he could to maintain friendly relations with England, and that this was surely attainable, as both sides alike needed peace. But the talks with Torcy soon assumed an irritated tone. The two charged each other with desiring war. On the part of France this was a manoeuvre intended to influence the general election in Great Britain against the Government of George I. Stair now presented his Note concerning the harbour of Mardyke. Torcy replied curtly that it contained nothing new, but that they were prepared to repeat their previous answers. Even so the reply was delayed for months, and then reiterated once more that Louis XIV had conscientiously observed the article of the Treaty of Utrecht concerning Dunkirk, and that the canal of Mardyke was merely meant to preserve the district from floods. The treatment accorded to Stair was caused by doubts concerning the stability of the Hanoverian dynasty. But when the general election produced a Whig majority, the French attitude changed immediately, and Torcy now patiently listened to what the British Ambassador had to say about the locks at Dunkirk and the canal of Mardyke.

Meantime Lord Stair did not limit himself to intercourse with the Court.[1] From the very outset he considered it his task to study the condition of the country and, most of all, the state of its resources, to watch public opinion and form a judgment concerning the danger which always, and now more than ever, threatened England from France. Stair kept open house, frequented fashionable society, and even made contacts with the middle classes; he watched and listened, and thus closes his account of French conditions: "This is the reasoning of some of the first people of Paris that I have talk'd with".[2] The picture he gives is unfavourable. "The provinces are exhausted, the people discontented, and finances in a hopeless condition. At the beginning of the War, the King had a hundred millions clear of revenue, whereas now it takes very near that sum to pay the interest of the debt at four per cent." Stocks were falling, and this mainly owing to the action of the French Government which was at pains to give out that Lord Stair's business "in this country was only to seek a quarrel". "But I keep myselfe retired, and seeing very few people and speaking with reserve, they take all that to be misterious and that I am to leave this place very soon."[3] Everyone dreaded a

---

[1] See Wiesener, p. 16.   [2] Stair to Stanhope, S.P. 78/160.
[3] Stair to Stanhope, Feb. 9 and Feb. 20, 1715, *ibid.*

K

break, as France was not in a position to renew the war. Indeed, some Frenchmen thought the Treaty of Utrecht bad, not because its conditions were hard, but because it would have been much better for France if they had been less favourable. Her having come out of the war unscathed, keeps up the jealousies of the other Princes; France maintains a great force on foot and cannot pay off her debts. At the head stands a senile King; the Ministers fear his death and try to keep from him anything which might cause him worry and shorten his life. This is the chief concern of Madame de Maintenon who counts for more than the entire *Conseil*. It was obvious that the death of Louis XIV was bound to work a very considerable change—according to Stair it was his senile vanity alone which prevented Great Britain from obtaining satisfaction.

It seems as if the aim of Stair's reports had been to encourage a renewal of war with a view to the final defeat of France; and in fact Stanhope seemed decided to restart it, in alliance with the Emperor, on the death of Louis XIV. Nor did the negotiation conducted in Paris by Stair with a view to mediating between Charles VI and Philip V with regard to Majorca, improve Anglo-French relations; it was cut short by the King of Spain seizing the island with the silent connivance of his grandfather, the King of France. Over this matter a violent scene occurred between the Marquis Torcy and Lord Stair, which, if England had been so inclined, could easily have constituted a serious incident. Stair had complained of lack of good faith on the other side, meaning thereby Spain. When Torcy, in whose house the conversation took place, denied it, Stair replied that obviously their ideas of good faith differed. Torcy flew into a rage and, foaming at the mouth, said that he would teach Stair not to insult him, and, opening the door, exclaimed *"Sortez, Monsieur"*. The talk was not immediately broken off, and Torcy admitted that there had been no ground for such an outburst; but they parted in anger, Stair declaring that Torcy would still have reason for regret if he estranged the King of France from his two powerful neighbours, England and the Emperor, who wished nothing better than to preserve peace and friendship.[1]

The conversation took place on July 11, at a time when the British Government had already to count with the Jacobite danger. Stair was therefore careful not to produce a complete break with France,

[1] See Stair's own account in Hardwicke, *Miscellaneous State Papers*, vol. ii. pp. 530-32 (in French); also Wiesener, i. p. 25.

and remained in Paris, however unpleasant his position had become now that the Court was forbidden to entertain any relations with him. But he could find compensation in the approval which he received from London. The King praised his moderation and wished him also in future to avoid any further provocation. To Stair's enquiry whether to present a further note concerning the Pretender, Stanhope replied that this was not considered advisable; "whatever incouragement or assistance that Court has thought fit to give for promoting the design which now seems to be on foot in his favour, . . . the surest way to defeat it, is to shew spirit and vigour here".[1] If it was no longer possible for Stair to entertain friendly relations with the French Court he could still be of infinite service to his Government; he watched carefully the movements of the Pretender and of his followers on the Continent, and was able to supply exact information concerning the steps taken in his favour in France. Stair's reports and advice had for some time a decisive influence in London.

Special importance attached to them since Lord Bolingbroke's arrival in France. The British Government was glad not to have to seize his person; and yet followed his further movements with concern. Stair was instructed to observe his behaviour and "likewise what kind of countenance or reception he shall find there from the Court".[2] The impeachment against him not having been started, the French Court could not be reproached for entertaining relations with one who was well known to them from previous times. Stair reported that Torcy had shown remarkable *empressement* to meet Bolingbroke and even to hold secret conferences with him. Possibly the conditions were discussed between them under which an attempt could be made in favour of the Pretender. Of a similar character was Bolingbroke's meeting with the half-brother of James Edward, the Duke of Berwick. Stair thought necessary to enter a complaint at Court concerning the relations with Bolingbroke, the effect of which he thought to feel in the heightened pride and coldness of Torcy.

At that time Bolingbroke was still anxious to appear as a loyal subject of George I, and was averse to any engagements with the Pretender and his adherents. He managed to enter into personal touch with Lord Stair to whom he made profuse assurances, repeated in a letter which he sent through Stair to Stanhope. He stayed in Paris a few days only; and retired into the Dauphiné, where he

---

[1] Stanhope to Stair, July 20/31, 1715, F.O. 90/14.
[2] Same to same, March 31/April 11, 1715, *ibid.*

awaited further developments. In reality he was determined to seek his interest in promoting the Stuart cause; but knowing that he was constantly spied upon by Lord Stair, he naturally avoided any step which would disclose his connexion with the Pretender. James Edward had impatiently asked for a meeting; Bolingbroke as yet refused it, but circumstances forced his hand.

The Prince had learned with great satisfaction that Lord Bolingbroke had come to France as a refugee—for what was now left to that ambitious man but actively to join the Stuart Prince, who had the less reason to doubt his friendly sentiments as he had proved them in the lifetime of the Queen? The Pretender wrote to Bolingbroke that he would altogether "depend extremely" on his advice.[1] Most of all he hoped that Bolingbroke's solicitations with the French Court would prove effectual; he was to act in an understanding with the Duke of Berwick, who was one of the best generals of Louis XIV, was highly esteemed, and was expected to become the military chief of the undertaking. At first Bolingbroke was too cautious to enter fully into the schemes of the Pretender. But in the South of France an emissary reached him with news from England: he was informed [2] "that the whole Tory Party was become avowedly Jacobite", that the principal men among them were in a concert with the Duke of Ormonde, and that "the others were so disposed, that there remained no doubt of their joining as soon as the first blow should be struck"; that in England the people were exasperated against the Government, and that Scotland was ready to take to arms. Moreover, he received a letter from the Pretender conjuring him not to lose a moment's time in setting out—"my impatience to see and discourse with you is equal to the esteem and confidence I have for you, and to the importance of the present conjuncture, in which I should be loath to make some certain steps, or determine any material point without your previous advice." [3]

Bolingbroke was at the crisis of his career. He imagined that in the service of the Pretender he would yet realize his ambitions. Looking across the Channel, he saw his inveterate enemies the Whigs about to brand him as a traitor and to exclude him for ever from power—no honours were to be won by him under George I. It was

[1] The Chevalier to Bolingbroke, May 1, 1715. P. M. Thornton, *Stuart Dynasty*, p. 356.

[2] *Letter to Sir William Windham* (1753), pp. 105-6.

[3] Commercy, July 2, 1715. Thornton, *Stuart Dynasty* (1890), p. 365.

then, and not as he says only when "the smart of a Bill of Attainder
tingled in every vein", that he decided to proceed to Lorraine. In
July 1715 Bolingbroke joined his King James III at Commercy. "If
we saw one another I am sure we should part very well satisfyd
with one another",[1] the Pretender had written about Bolingbroke
to Berwick on May 3, 1715. Bolingbroke felt otherwise—he began
to repent of his rashness in joining James Edward, who talked
like a man convinced that nothing was wanting for success [2] but
his own presence in England; though he was unable to name to
Bolingbroke any reasonable grounds for such expectations. They
were based on assurances received from English friends, who believed
in success because they desired it. With the empty title of Secretary
of State Bolingbroke left the Lorraine residence of his new master.

He proceeded to Paris, to solicit the French Court on behalf of the
Pretender. James Edward was impatient to start for England, at
Havre a few ships were fitted out to carry him across, with all the
arms and ammunition that could be collected; these were "hardly sufficient to begin the work even in Scotland" and yet "had exhausted
the treasury of St. Germain". The preparations, as well as messages
from across the Channel, were not treated with the necessary secrecy.
Bolingbroke "was not a little concerned to hear, in two or three places,
and among women over their tea that . . . arms were provided and
ships got ready" [3] for the impending rebellion. "A Minister less alert
and less capable than the Earl of Stair would easily have been at the
bottom of the secret." [4]

Measures were taken in Great Britain to meet the danger of a
hostile landing, for so long as this was prevented the Government
could keep the enemies at home in check. On July 1, 1715, a British
squadron was ordered to cruise along the French coast between Calais
and Cherbourg; they were to show themselves off Boulogne, Dieppe,
Havre, and Cherbourg, and inform themselves in the best manner
"what preparations are making there, either of men or war, or transport ships or vessels, and whether any considerable number of troops
are drawn. . . ." [5] A few weeks later Sir George Byng, the Admiral

---

[1] Thornton, *Stuart Dynasty*, p. 360.

[2] Cf. letter from the Chevalier to the Duke of Berwick, July 9, 1715. Thornton, *Stuart Dynasty*, p. 360.

[3] Bolingbroke to James Edward, Paris, July 23, 1715. Mahon, vol. i. App.

[4] *Letter to Sir William Windham*, p. 128.

[5] Instructions of the Lords of the Admiralty to Capt. Dore-Windsor, July 1,
1715, O.S., Adm. Records.

who had defeated the Pretender's attempt to land in Scotland in 1708, was again ordered to pursue any ships which he encountered carrying troops, and to sink and destroy them.[1] He was to cruise along the northern coast of France, to show himself off Havre, and watch what preparations were making; similarly the British coasts, and especially those of Scotland and Ireland, were carefully watched to prevent the landing of troops, officers, or war munitions for the service of the Pretender.[2] News reached England alleging that in the Elbe and Weser troops and munitions were being embarked for Scotland to support the Stuart rising; and the Privy Council of Hanover was directed in the name of George I to request the Cities of Hamburg and Bremen, and the Governments of Glückstadt and Oldenburg, to search all ships passing their shores, and in the case of empty ships to make certain that they were not intended as troop transports for the Pretender.[3] Lastly, Admiral Baker, who commanded the Mediterranean fleet stationed at Port Mahon, was instructed closely to watch the movements of the French and Spanish squadrons, and to ascertain whether they were not bound for the North; if so, he was immediately to sail for home so as to forestall them, and be ready to defend the British coast. But most of these apprehensions were devoid of foundation; and everything was quiet in the Mediterranean.

The news which reached James Edward from England made him write to Bolingbroke on July 18: ". . . you will see the necessity of losing no time, so I shall part the 28th and the 30th at Diepe, where I desire you will be by that time, that we may embark together".[4] But Bolingbroke managed to restrain him; he argued that

in England things are not ripe; that at least you cannot tell with certainty whether they are so or not; that the secret is divulged; that Harry [the King of France] has not yet spoken clearly, whether he will not, in some manner or other, give a private assistance now, and perhaps a public one hereafter.[5]

James Edward, however impatient, had to admit the "solid reason"

---

[1] Townshend to the Lords of the Admiralty, July 25, 1715, O.S.; to Sir George Byng, July 25, 29, Aug. 10, 22, 1715, Adm. Records.

[2] According to the Admiralty Records in P.R.O.

[3] George I's instructions to the Privy Council in Hanover, Aug. 2/13, 1715, Hanover Arch.

[4] Thornton, *Stuart Dynasty*, pp. 366-7.

[5] Bolingbroke to James Edward, Paris, July 23, 1715. Mahon, vol. i. App.

of Bolingbroke's argument,[1] who did not expect to be able to restrain him for more than a month; but then when the entire British nation was roused, the person of the Stuart Prince would be of greater value than an entire army which it would take a few months to raise.

Meantime a memorial was sent across from England, first to the Chevalier and next to Bolingbroke, containing a complete programme for a rising in England, and for the part which James Edward was to play in it. It contained "the unanimous sense of the principal persons engaged . . . and . . . had been delivered . . . by the Duke of Ormonde"

> This memorial asserted, that there were no hopes of succeeding in a present undertaking, . . . without an immediate and universal rising of the people in all parts of England upon the Chevalier's arrival; and that this insurrection was in no degree probable unless he brought a body of regular troops along with him: that, if this attempt miscarried, his cause and his friends, the English liberty and government, would be utterly ruined: but, if by coming without troops he resolved to risque these and every thing else, he must set out so as not to arrive before the end of September, O.S. . . . In this case twenty thousand arms, a train of artillery, five hundred officers with their servants, and a considerable sum of money were demanded.[2]

But where was the Pretender to find the means? His own were wholly insufficient. Without pensions from the King of France, neither Queen Maria at St. Germain nor James Edward at Bar-le-Duc could have kept up their courts. Even in the matter of making provision for his family, James II had failed to learn from the history of his own house, and had prepared no reserve abroad for the case of exile.

James Edward and Bolingbroke were agreed that without ample succour from France the venture could not succeed. It was essential to impress the French Court with the urgency of the situation; Bolingbroke tried to do so in a conversation with Torcy, and also in a letter [3] written at Torcy's request, presumably to enable him to plead the cause of James Edward to the King. Should the undertaking fail, Bolingbroke wrote, all the friends of France in Great Britain were irretrievably lost. The issue of the venture lay in the King's hand— according to Bolingbroke, he would find it easier now to restore the son than it had been for the States General to dethrone the father;

[1] James Edward to Bolingbroke, Bar, July 26, 1716. Thornton, *op. cit.* p. 368.

[2] *Letter to Sir William Windham*, pp. 131-2.

[3] The letter (in French), dated merely August 1715, is printed in Mahon, vol. i. App.

never had the position been so favourable. But the Pretender was in financial straits: without French subsidies he could not even cover the daily cost of the ships at Havre; and to retain these seemed necessary, if only to divert English attention from another port at which the Pretender would meantime embark.

Louis XIV and his Court would undoubtedly have welcomed a Stuart restoration, but "they would not hear of a direct and open engagement". First the Tories had to prove themselves a match for the Hanoverian Government—"the people here endeavour to feel Margaret's [1] pulse", wrote Bolingbroke to the Chevalier on August 3, 1715, "and determine to guide themselves as that rises and falls".[2] But while Louis XIV would not risk a war with England, nor grant all the supplies which were asked for, he did not mean to drop the Pretender altogether:

> They granted us some succours, and the very ship in which the Pretender was to transport himself was fitted out . . . at the King of France's expence. They would have concealed these appearances as much as they could; but the heat of the Whigs and the resentment of the Court of England might have drawn them in. We should have been glad indirectly to concur in fixing these things upon them: and in a word, if the late King had lived six months longer, I verily believe there had been war again between England and France. This was the only point of time when these affairs had, to my apprehension, the least reasonable appearance even of possibility: all that preceded was wild and uncertain: all that followed was mad and desperate.[3]

A dispatch from Lord Stair, dated July 28, put the British Government on its guard. The Pretender was reported to have gone secretly to Paris and there to have held counsel with his friends and Bolingbroke; and they were alleged to have resolved that officers were to be sent in small batches across the Channel, that the Duke of Berwick was to proceed to England and organize the rising, and that eventually James Edward himself should land in Great Britain with an army.[4] This time, however, Stair's spies had misinformed him: the

---

[1] "Margaret" and "Maryland" were code names used for England in the correspondence between Bolingbroke and the Chevalier.

[2] Mahon, vol. i. App.

[3] *Letter to Sir William Windham*, pp. 134-5.

[4] On this point the dispatches from Bonet and Hoffmann, dated Aug. 2, 1715, roughly agree. Stair's report of July 28 is not in the Record Office, and he remarks in his Diary (Hardwicke, *Miscellaneous State Papers*, ii. p. 534) under the same date that he has kept no copy—"I had reason for so doing". In

Pretender could hardly have been in Paris in July 1715, as his correspondence with Bolingbroke and Berwick places him in Lorraine during that month; and also the other statements were, to say the least,
greatly exaggerated. But in British Government circles, which were
accustomed to rely on Stair's information, the report produced a
great impression.

Stair's dispatch reached London early on July 31, and the Cabinet
Council immediately met to concert emergency measures. It was
decided that the King should go to Parliament the same day and
apprise them of the danger of invasion. His Speech and the Addresses
from both Houses were drafted. At 3 P.M. George I appeared in the
House of Lords, the Commons were summoned, and the King gave
his assent to several bills, including the Mutiny Bill. The Lord Chancellor read out the King's Speech. It started with a reference to an
Address voted by the Commons two days earlier "to prevent all
riotous and tumultuous proceedings";—"but I am sorry to find",
proceeded the Speech, "that such a spirit of rebellion has discovered
itself, as leaves no room to doubt that these disorders are set on foot
and encouraged by persons disaffected to my Government, in expectation of being supported from abroad". Advices had been received
of attempts preparing by the Pretender against "our excellent Constitution and the security of our holy Religion". Next he turned to the
Commons, confident that they would not "leave the nation, under a
rebellion actually begun at home, and threatened with an invasion
from abroad, in a defenceless condition: And I shall look upon the
provision you shall make for the safety of my people as the best
mark of your affection to me." [1]

In the Lords great indignation was expressed at the schemes of the
Pretender, the Tories evincing not less zeal for the House of Hanover
than the Whigs; they seemed intent on showing that, although in
opposition to the Government, they were loyal to the dynasty. Lord
Anglesea, who had spoken of the sceptre shaking in the hands of the
King, now declared that he would be the first to draw the sword
against the Pretender. The Duke of Shrewsbury, who had been
recently forced to resign, spoke in a similar strain. Lord Strafford,
though actually impeached, Lord Peterborough, who so far had been
left unmolested, and even open adherents of Lord Oxford, such as the

fact there seems to be none among the Stair Papers at Oxenfoord Castle, or
otherwise Wiesener would undoubtedly have used it in his work.

[1] *Parl. Hist.* vii. 111.

Archbishop of York and the Bishop of Bristol, emphatically affirmed their loyal sentiments. The Address, wherein the House declared that they would stand by and assist the King at the hazard of their lives and fortunes, was cheerfully agreed to.

The same day the Commons went with the Speaker to lay before the King their unanimous Address in which he was asked immediately to give "directions for fitting out such a number of ships as may effectually guard the coasts, and to issue out commissions for augmenting his forces by land"; and assured him that the House would, without loss of time, enable him to do so.

On the night of July 31, in a sitting of the Privy Council which the Lord Mayor of London and the Magistrates of Westminster attended, certain measures were decided upon. In the night the arms and horses of Papists and non-jurors in the metropolis were seized, and the same was ordered to be done in other towns. The militia in London and the provinces was called up. The standing army of 8000 men appearing insufficient, it was decided to raise ten new regiments of dragoons consisting of 3000 men, and eight regiments of foot consisting of 4000 men. A few generals of suspect loyalty were removed, while officers reduced since the conclusion of peace were once more placed on full pay. The Commons, at the request of the Government, willingly voted to supply such extraordinary expense as the King "should be at on this account". Of the 1800 officers concerned, 500 were gazetted to the new regiments, while the others, for fear that they might join the Pretender, were to be embodied in the militia or otherwise employed in the provinces. As news was received from Scotland about an imminent rising in the Highlands, three regiments were sent across from Ireland. The question of recalling the remaining British troops from Flanders was considered. The Act promising £100,000 to anyone who would seize the Pretender, dead or alive, in case he attempted to land, was still in force. The Government acted with vigour; and every day new proclamations were issued prescribing measures of defence or calling upon the authorities to do their duty in the crisis.

Meantime public opinion was rallying to the Government. On August 2 the Anglican clergy, met in convocation, presented the King with a Loyal Address. On the 9th, the same was done by the Common Council of the City of London, whose example was widely followed. From all parts of England and Ireland addresses were sent by counties and boroughs expressing abhorrence of the threatening invasion by the Pretender.[1] In Northern Ireland the Presbyterian clergy read out an exhortation to the people to remain loyal to the King. The Commons could hardly have given stronger proof of their confidence than by suspending the Habeas Corpus in this time of danger. The City and the Bank offered their financial support as soon as the threatening news became public.

The measures taken by the Government produced the most favourable impression. The position of the King and his Government seemed strengthened, and a landing by the Pretender, should he venture upon it, was calmly awaited. But nothing happened, and the enemies of the Government were already spreading rumours that it had all been a vain alarm, and that the story of an impending invasion had been invented to supply a pretext for increasing the standing army and curtailing liberty. Hoffmann himself became doubtful and asked Bothmer whether a landing of the Pretender was in fact expected, or whether the preparations were made by the Government merely in order to strengthen themselves against new disturbances at home. Bothmer replied that even the place was known where James Edward would land. Once the Government had shown its strength, popular commotions immediately stopped. When on August 12 the first anniversary of George I's accession was celebrated with gunshots and illuminations, no excesses were committed by the London mob, as had been feared. Also the customary public burning of an effigy representing the Stuart Prince passed without disturbance. The Speech and the Addresses were communicated to foreign Powers, and helped to raise British prestige. Prince Eugene confided to the British *chargé d'affaires* in Vienna, that he, too, had received news from Paris that the Chevalier intended a landing, that Berwick would accompany him, and Ormonde command his army; and, referring to the increase in the British army, the Prince remarked that in fact nothing better for the King could have happened than these Jacobite attempts.[2]

The British Ministers, however, thought it advisable to assure themselves beforehand of foreign assistance. When the King reminded the Dutch Ambassador of the help promised by the States General as guarantors of the Protestant Succession, they left no doubt concerning their readiness to fulfil their obligations. With the Emperor also, relations had so much improved that in an emergency

---

[1] An enumeration of these addresses will be found in the *London Gazette* of Aug. 27, 1715, O.S.

[2] Schaub to Townshend, Aug. 21, 1715, S.P. 80/32.

he could have been appealed to for help; George I himself expressed to the Imperial Resident the hope that in such a case the friendship of Charles VI "would not fail him".

Party divisions seemed suddenly forgotten and, faced with the danger of a Stuart restoration, the Tories rallied to the Protestant King. It was this re-awakening of national feeling which defeated all prospects of a Jacobite attempt. But Bolingbroke, at a distance, gave different reasons for the change; he writes in his *Letter to Sir William Windham*: "Two events . . . happened, one of which cast a damp on all we were doing, and the other rendered vain and fruitless all we had done. The first was the arrival of the Duke of Ormonde in France, the other was the death of the King."

In any undertaking a great deal depends on the name of the man at its head. The Duke of Ormonde possessed all the qualities which the Jacobites could look for in their leader. He was a brave soldier, and an experienced general; popular with the army and with the masses, the bearer of an old and famous name, he seemed worthy to restore the direct heir to the throne. He was impeached and had nothing to hope for from George I, whom he hated since the day when the King, on his arrival, had replaced him by his worst enemy, Marlborough. Ormonde had hitherto defied the danger, and, residing in splendour at Richmond, had maintained connexions with the Jacobites in the West and North of England, as well as in Paris. It was he who, in July 1715, had urged the Chevalier to embark for England and appeal to the British nation; at that time he would undoubtedly have received considerable support. But everything was left vague, and not even the place at which the landing was to be attempted was indicated.[1] James Edward therefore let himself be persuaded by Bolingbroke to defer action. Ormonde proposed to stay at Richmond so long as he could safely do so, and afterwards to raise the revolt in the West and North. He was in touch with people at Bristol, Plymouth, and Exeter, whom he expected to deliver these towns to him. But the proceedings in Parliament on July 31 destroyed his hopes, and he could no longer remain at Richmond. He disappeared early in August; the Government feared that he might have gone to Portsmouth to seize the harbour, and were relieved to learn that he had crossed to France.[2] Ormonde had obviously despaired of raising a rebellion in England, and did not even warn his friends in various parts

---

[1] *Mémoires de Berwick*, p. 232.
[2] *Ibid.* p. 233. Hoffmann's dispatches of Aug. 2 and 6, 1715, Vienna Arch.

of the country, who had counted on him, of his leaving. Now that he felt his freedom and life to be in danger, he thought that he could work better for the Jacobite cause on the other side of the Channel. Bolingbroke describes the painful impression which Ormonde's arrival produced in Paris:

We had sounded the duke's name high. His reputation and the opinion of his power were great. The French began to believe that he was able to form and to head a party; that the troops would join him; that the nation would follow the signal whenever he drew his sword: and the voice of the people, the echo of which was continually in their ears, confirmed them in this belief. But when, in the midst of all these bright ideas, they saw him arrive, almost literally alone . . . they sunk at once from their hopes: . . . they had had too good an opinion of the cause, they began to form too bad an one. Before this time, if they had no friend-ship for the Tories, they had at least some consideration and esteem. After this, I saw nothing but compassion in the best of them, and con-tempt in the others.[1]

Louis XIV was dying. Few were alive who remembered his begin-nings. For seventy-two years he had ruled France, the longest reign in history. In him and his Court was centred the political, economic, and intellectual life of France, and in him was embodied, to a supreme degree, the system of absolute monarchy. It was seriously asserted that something akin to divine insight was inherent in a crowned King. The example of Louis XIV, his conception of the Royal dignity, his system of Government, his Court, were copied throughout Europe. In England alone a Parliamentary monarchy was growing up in the age of absolutism.

Louis XIV had sinned against the nations of Europe, worst of all against his own subjects, but he was royal in good and in evil days, and preserved his dignity even in death. He stood before the world as the King whose word decided about the fate of millions and whose will for half a century had been a power in European politics. It remained to be seen what France would be without him; some looked to his death with fear, others with hope, but all alike felt that it would produce a considerable change.

His death was bound to acquire additional importance owing to the international situation and to the peculiar circumstances of the French

---

[1] *Letter to Sir William Windham*, pp. 136-7, Stair writes in his Diary under Aug. 10 (Hardwicke, *Miscellaneous State Papers*, ii. p. 538): "I wrote by the post to give Mr. Secretary an account of the Duke of Ormonde's arrival and his behaviour here, and that the spirits of the Jacobites seemed to be quite down".

royal family. His immediate successors had died in his lifetime—
three heirs to the throne within a single year. Now his heir-apparent
was a child of five. The title of his great-grandson to the succession
was incontestable, but for years to come there would have to be a
Regency. In direct succession this would have gone to Philip V of Spain,
the younger grandson of Louis XIV; but he had renounced his rights
to the throne of France. Next to him came the King's nephew,
Philip, Duke of Orleans, a clever and ambitious man, in whom the
King had no confidence and to whom he was reluctant to entrust
the fate of France and of her infant ruler. The situation would have
become even more perplexing if the small Louis XV, a delicate child,
had died young. The succession would have lain between Philip V
and the Duke of Orleans; but a European war had been waged for
ten years to prevent a union of the Crowns of France and Spain.

To the British Government, faced by an attack from the Pretender,
the change in France could only be welcome and the news that
Louis XIV was sinking was received with satisfaction. "In short,"
wrote Stair in a private letter on August 15, "everything here goes
as well as can be wished; the old monarch declines, and fast." [1]

Louis XIV calmly faced his end, took leave of his *entourage*, blessed
his great-grandson, and died. The Duke of Orleans assumed the Regency with the full powers of kingship, although this was contrary
to the will of the dead monarch, who had not meant to concede to
him such a position. In the famous sitting of the Paris Parliament
on September 2, 1715, one day after the death of Louis XIV, his
last will was practically overturned. By determined action Philip of
Orleans had checked the schemes of his opponents at home and
the ambitions of his cousin at Madrid.

In the history of the Jacobite Rebellion of 1715, the rise of the
Regent is an event of first-rate importance. "My hopes sank as he
declined," wrote Bolingbroke about Louis XIV, "and died when he
expired." [2] The foreign policy of France was now determined by the
personal interests of the Regent who had constantly to bear in mind
that Philip V was a rival for his position. The so-called Spanish Party
at the French Court was working against him. Spain and France, in
a compact under Louis XIV and Philip V, were now divided by the
jealousy of the two Bourbon Princes, which for many years had a
decisive influence on European history. The position of the Duke of

---

[1] Stair to Robethon, Stowe MSS. 228, f. 79.
[2] *Letter to Sir William Windham*, p. 139.

Orleans was not sufficiently assured for him to engage in a great war. He was pleased to be left in peace and in an undisturbed possession of his power; and because of the Jacobite danger, this wish for peace was reciprocated by England.

In these circumstances it was natural for the two Powers to try to maintain good relations. For Great Britain the Regency of the Duke of Orleans was a further safeguard against the union of the two Bourbon Crowns. Moreover the Duke's mother, Elizabeth Charlotte, daughter of the Elector-Palatine Karl Ludwig, was a niece of the Electress Sophia and a first cousin of George I—she remained German in feeling and "howled" when in October 1681, as sister-in-law of Louis XIV, she entered with the French Court the newly conquered Strasbourg. George I, since his accession, had sought the friendship of the Duke of Orleans, and found response. In a courteous letter the Duke congratulated him on his accession; and Stair, when sent to Paris, was instructed to seek a close understanding with the Duke. He was to assure Orleans that the British Government "were ready to concert measures with him for securing for him the Regency, and, in case of other accidents, the Crown",[1] and to give him whatever assistance he should want; and Stair was instructed to take no step without consulting the Duke. In return information was expected from the Duke concerning the schemes and movements of the Jacobites. A month later Stair complained that he had not been given the least notice by the Duke of the designs of the Pretender, for which the Duke felt it necessary to make his excuses.[2] Appealed to by Stair, he repeatedly promised that he would do justice as to Mardyke, as soon as ever he was in possession of the Regency, and inquired of the Ambassador what it was that the British specially desired. Stair was justified in attaching a certain importance to these promises made as late as the last days of August when Louis XIV was dying. The Duke of Orleans knew then positively "that there was no thoughts of the King of Spain [in the King's testament]; that he was to have the Regency; but . . . he believed there were some conditions in the will to hamper him by a Council of Regency;" still, "he was little in pain about that, being sure of the Parliament and the troops".[3] On August 27 the British Ambassador when giving him "the strongest assurances of the King's firm friendship . . . and his readiness to use all the power of his Kingdom to serve him," added "that

---

[1] Hardwicke, ii. 533.   [2] *Ibid.* p. 541.
[3] Stair's Diary, Monday, Aug. 26, 1715; *ibid.* ii. p. 544.

the true way to establish a perfect good correspondence between the two nations, and with the King, was to send the Pretender out of Lorrain, and his adherents, naming Ormonde and Bolingbroke, out of France; which he heard very well".[1]

It would be of the greatest interest to know whether, and in what manner, Stair had, at the decisive moment, helped the Duke to establish himself as Regent. Unfortunately no dispatches from Stair are available for that time. The testament of Louis XIV, about which there were guesses and rumours, received a measure of prominence in his previous dispatches—it would almost seem credible that the Ambassador had his share in its being laid aside. It is known that he was present in the gallery during the memorable sitting of the Paris Parliament; though it is not possible to tell whether by his presence he meant to support Orleans, or even whether he could, in his place, be seen by the assembly. It is anyhow remarkable that in one of the most powerful States of Europe the attitude of a foreign diplomat should have been supposed to carry so much weight in domestic affairs.

On August 19, 1715, Bolingbroke had written to the Pretender:

Things are hastening to that point, that either you, Sir, at the head of the Tories, must save the Church and Constitution of England or both must be irretrievably lost for ever.[2]

And again on August 20:

Your affairs hasten to their crisis; and I hope that, with prudence and fortitude, for they must go hand in hand, your Majesty's restoration will be soon accomplished.[3]

In those days, when naming the principal men expected to join James Edward, Bolingbroke would mention Marlborough among them, beside Shrewsbury and Peterborough. Although Marlborough certainly would not have come out on the side of the Pretender until he could count on his being victorious, he gave promises, raised hopes, and even contributed money; [4] and James Edward fondly imagined that on his landing in Scotland the greatest living British general would join him, or openly declare for him in England. He wrote to the Duke of Berwick on August 23, 1715, "I think it is now more than ever *Now or Never*".[5] As the King was sinking, the Pretender and his

---

[1] Hardwicke, *State Papers*, ii. p. 546.
[2] Mahon, vol. i. App.
[3] *Ibid.*
[4] Thornton, pp. 377-8.
[5] Mahon, vol. i. App.

friends had naturally to seek to establish "a tie of union" with the Duke of Orleans. In a letter, on August 15, Bolingbroke suggested to James Edward the idea of a marriage between him and one of the Duke's daughters, and hinted that the Duke himself was not altogether a stranger to the suggestion;[1] but nothing came of it. On August 26, Bolingbroke wrote to the Pretender that the King's death was now a question of a few hours and all would then centre in the Duke of Orleans—"for God sake let me know whether I should not, or rather Charles [Ormonde] ask to see him and speak to him in your name; he is left Regent".[2] The previous day James Edward had written to Bolingbroke that "nothing ought to be neglected for to court his nephew" [the King's nephew, *i.e.* the Duke of Orleans].[3]

Thus the Government of George I and the House of Stuart, Stair and Bolingbroke, were competing for the favour of the Regent. Bolingbroke realized that the Regent, if pressed in France, could expect support from the British Government, while the Pretender had nothing to offer. He therefore rejoiced, no less than Stair, when he saw that no serious difficulties were to be expected, and wrote to the Chevalier on August 30, 1715:

The great danger I was apprehensive of is over; all will certainly submit without the least struggle to Overbury [Duke of Orleans], and he will by consequence be under no want of assistance from his neighbours, but remain att liberty to pursue the general interest of his own and his neighbour's estate.[4]

Indeed, until the Rebellion was crushed in Great Britain, the Regent retained a measure of freedom in shaping his policy. His own position did not allow him to come out openly against George I, as Louis XIV might have done; but in the interest of France he favoured, to some extent, the Jacobites. Still, they did not receive the succour which they had expected from Louis XIV, and the fighting remained localized in Great Britain, where forces were too unequal to admit of any doubt concerning the issue.

The Scottish Rising[5] actually broke out before Louis XIV had died, but without French support having been secured and any plans having been fixed with the advisers of the Pretender. At its head stood a prominent Scotsman, well acquainted with local conditions but

---

[1] Mahon, vol. i. App.   [2] Thornton, p. 376.
[3] *Ibid.* p. 375.   [4] *Ibid.* p. 379.
[5] For the following account the chief source is R. Chambers, *History of the Rebellions in Scotland in* 1689 *and* 1715.

inexperienced in war—John Erskine, 11th Earl of Mar, of a family which had played an important part in 1688. He himself, shrewd but unreliable, had at times sided with the Whigs, at other times with the Tories, till he came to be known as "Bobbing John". He had taken office under Queen Anne, and when in 1710 the Tories came into power, Mar, who as Whig had been instrumental in bringing about the Union, suddenly turned Tory and was appointed Secretary of State for Scotland. In 1714 he was ready to serve the Hanoverians, and wrote from London about the accession of George I "that it is a great happiness all has been done here with so much unanimity and quietness. It will, I hope, make our country follow the same example, and keep any from makeing disturbance."[1] He tried to curry favour with George I and hoped to retain his office; but the Whigs would have nothing to do with him, and the King showed him disfavour. Now Mar became a zealous Jacobite, and when in 1715 a revolutionary movement started in the Highlands, he vanished from England, and placed himself at the head of the Rising.

Lord Mar is said still to have attended the *levée* of George I on August 1. On the 2nd, "in the dress of a private person" he embarked with Major-General Hamilton, Colonel Hay, and two servants at Gravesend. He landed in Fifeshire and went on his way to the Highlands, and from there he sent letters to all the leading Jacobites round the country inviting them to a hunt at his seat Kildrummy in Aberdeenshire; under similar cover some Scottish noblemen had met the previous year and proclaimed the Chevalier. This time everybody understood the meaning of the summons and a great number of gentlemen of the best quality and interest attended. The Dukes of Gordon and Athol were represented by their eldest sons; nor did the old Earl of Breadalbane appear in person. The Earls Nithisdale, Marischal, Traquair, Errol, Southesk, Carnwath, Seaforth, Linlithgow, and many others of the nobility and gentry obeyed the call.

Having thus got his friends together, Mar addressed them in a public speech, inciting them to take arms for the Pretender. He inveighed against the Union and deplored having been instrumental in forwarding it. He spoke of the evil which the Elector of Hanover had brought on the country, pursuing a plan to deprive the nation of its ancient liberties. The revocation of the Union and the overthrow of George I were the aims put before them. He claimed to have been appointed by the rightful King, James VIII, commander of his forces

[1] *Hist. MSS. Comm.* Report III, App. p. 379.

in Scotland, and showed them a commission which he alleged to have received from the Chevalier to raise all his friends to arms. He claimed that the Chevalier was assured of French help, and would come over himself once the movement was started and entrust his person to the fidelity and valour of the Scottish nation. Mar having declared that he would arm his tenants and friends, all present took an oath to take part in the enterprise and be faithful to one another; as they returned each to his estate to gather their servants and dependents, they took with them copies of the Pretender's manifesto to distribute it throughout the country. Under the clan system the landlord was both the chief of his people and their commander; and a man would much rather refuse service to the King than to his feudal superior. A letter is preserved in which Mar threatened his tenants that, if they did not come forth "with their best arms", he would "send a party immediately to burn what they shall miss taking from them".[1]

The Jacobites were coming in slowly, and only about sixty men were present when on September 6, in the village of Kirkmichael in Braemar, the Earl raised the standard of the Pretender. The Highlanders looked upon it as a bad omen that as the pole was planted in the ground the gilt ball fell down from its summit (there had been a similar omen when the banner of Charles I was upset by a gale at Nottingham). While the preparations for the Rising were making, the news of Louis XIV's death produced serious dismay; some of the Jacobite chiefs advised Mar to abandon the enterprise, but he persisted and did his best to compose their fears. Shortly afterwards he professed to have accounts of the Duke of Orleans having "declair'd that he'll assist the King more than ever his unckle did".[2] It was with much difficulty that Mar succeeded in making them come out.[3]

In reality they could not go back on what they had done: the Government had learnt to distinguish its opponents. In England, after the Habeas Corpus had been suspended, the prisons were soon over-crowded. An Act was passed at that time "for Encouraging Loyalty in Scotland" which enabled the King to cite suspects to Edinburgh, where they had to give sureties for their good behaviour;

---

[1] Lord Mar to John Forbes of Inverawe, Bailie of Kildrummy, Invercauld, Sept. 9, at night, 1715. See Chambers, p. 188.

[2] See Mar's letter of Sept. 11, 1715, O.S., Thornton, p. xvi.

[3] Chambers, pp. 185-6.

but only those obeyed whose loyalty could anyhow have been trusted, while the waverers were driven by fear into rebellion. More effective was another Act which gave tenants who refused to follow their superiors into rebellion, the land they held; even some tenants on Mar's estates,[1] attracted by the offer, repaired to Edinburgh in order to prove their loyalty and acquire the title to their land.

On the death of Louis XIV, the British Government, thinking that the main danger was over, had stopped a few regiments which were on their way to Scotland. Soon, however, they found that these would still be required, and had them resume their march.[2] Still, the time was ill-chosen for the rising. There was no assurance of foreign help— even Louis XIV had not promised any ample succours—nor was there any proper understanding and collaboration with the English Jacobites. Roughly speaking, the Rebellion was restricted to Scotland, and therefore doomed to failure. Had Mar started it on his own or in an understanding with the Pretender? The Duke of Berwick relates [3] that Mar acted under a secret order received from the Chevalier in September 1715, and that it was given without his or Bolingbroke's knowledge. As Mar had gone to Scotland early in August, the date is certainly wrong, while James Edward in a letter to Bolingbroke on September 23, 1715,[4] professed sentiments and hopes which would seem to contradict Berwick's statement. But then could he be expected to confess to Bolingbroke his secret transactions with the Scottish Jacobites? Probably Berwick's information is accurate, except that the order was given in July and not in September. Otherwise it would be necessary to assume that Mar, when claiming to act by order of James VIII, practised gross deceit on his Scottish associates, and that these let themselves be deceived; probably there was good ground for their believing his statement.

In 1715 the British Government obtained information of a plot to murder the King and the Prince of Wales. A letter is preserved in which the writer alleges that rewards were promised to him and his associates by "His Majesty" (the Pretender), while they were still in Lorraine, should they carry out their promise and "expedite both the Georges". The discovery must have obviated the danger,

---

[1] Bonet, Sept. 13/24, 1715. [2] Hoffmann, Sept. 17, 1715.
[3] *Mémoires*, ii. p. 246.
[4] ". . . I still hope our Scotch friends will, at least, wait for my answer, if they cannot stay so long as to expect a concert with England, which I begin to flatter myself they may" (Mahon, i. App.).

but, if true, the story is certainly discreditable to the Pretender.[1] Again Bolingbroke and Berwick knew nothing about it.

The leaders of the Rebellion now tried to raise the entire Scottish nation, most of all the Lowlanders, against the Hanoverian King. A "Manifesto by the Noblemen, Gentlemen, and others" pointed to the dissolution of the Union and the restoration of the Stuarts as their principal aims.

> They have empowered a foreign prince . . . to make an absolute conquest . . . of the three Kingdoms, by investing himself with an unlimited power not only of raising unnecessary forces at home, but also of calling in foreign troops ready to promote his uncontroulable designs.

Under "the auspicious Government of our native-born rightful sovereign" Scotland will regain the direction of her "own domestic councils" and the protection of her "native forces and troops", and the laws, liberties, and properties of Scotsmen will be secured "by the Parliaments of both Kingdoms". Lastly:

> We will endeavour to have such laws enacted as shall give absolute security for the Protestant religion against all efforts of arbitrary power, Popery, and all its enemies.

To counter the obvious objection that James Edward himself was a Papist, the proclamation explained that it could be expected from

---

[1] That letter is the only evidence for its own story, of which the sense, however, is quite clear; and as it is among other contemporary documents in the Record Office (*State Papers, Domestic*, George I, Bundle 3, No. 62) the letter probably never reached the addressee, but was intercepted by the Government. It is in French, is addressed to "Sieur Daille à Londres", is dated Lime, June 13, 1715, and is signed Jacques Jones. He writes: "*J'ai reçu votre lettre par votre messager, et je suis bien aise d'apprendre que vous avez eu une lettre de notre roi, et que S.M. nous dit qu'on est convenu de toutes choses, si vous et moi voulons tenir notre parole d'expédier les deux Georges, comme nous promîmes à S.M., lorsque nous étions en Lorraine, et que S.M. nous donnera présentement 20,000£ entre nous, si nous les dépêchons dans deux mois de temps, et 500£ en main avant que nous le fassions, outre qu'on nous donnera de bons emplois s'il est couronné roi d'Angleterre*". It is further stated that shots are to be fired at the two Georges from a window, and next, preparations for a rising in Scotland are mentioned. Judging by the date, this plot probably produced the rumour mentioned in Rapin-Tindale (The Hague, 1749) xiii. p. 68, of a wide conspiracy for destroying the entire Royal Family. An even more extensive conspiracy, of which the details can hardly be ascertained any more, is hinted at in a letter dated Sept. 29, 1715, *Hist. MSS. Comm.* Rep. XIII. App. 3, p. 52.

God, from the truth of the Protestant Religion, and from the sound judgment of His Majesty, that the good example of, and intercourse with, the Scottish clergy would wean him from the superstitions which, in spite of his having been educated in a Catholic country, could not have struck deep root.

In the Highlands the rebels were eminently successful. The Clan of Macintosh rose, and marched five hundred strong against Inverness, which had no garrison and surrendered without resistance. One place after another was captured by them. At Castle Gordon the Pretender was proclaimed by the Marquis of Huntly; he was also proclaimed at Aberdeen and Dundee. Thus, within a short time, Central Scotland fell without fighting into the hands of the Jacobites; but the success was unimportant—wherever the rebels met Royal troops, they were checked. Without siege-train they were helpless against Fort William, at the mouth of the Lochy river, of which the garrison was in good time reinforced by the Government; only some outworks were taken. With Fort William holding out they were unable to establish connexions with the Western Highlands, and even if most of the country between the Tay and Moray Firth was under Jacobite control, they had not conquered Scotland so long as the Lowlands were held by the Royal forces. But for an attack against these the rebels had not the necessary resources. "It may take a long time," wrote Bonet in October, "before the rebellion is defeated, but I do not think that much is to be apprehended from people who are strong in their hills, but weak in the plain, who have no cavalry and stand greatly in fear of it, men without money and stores, without guns, munitions, and generals, without ships and ports; especially once they are faced by regular troops, and have to consider that, if captured, they will be sent to the gallows." [1]

Meantime an attempt had been made by the Jacobites to take Edinburgh Castle by a *coup*. In the Castle there were arms for 10,000 men to equip the Royal army, and a sum of £100,000, paid to Scotland at the time of the Union as compensation for her having assumed a share of the English national debt. Fortunately the preparations for the enterprise and its execution were deficient. Eighty Edinburgh Jacobites under Lord Drummond, a Roman Catholic, tried in the night to capture the Castle, which was considered impregnable, having bribed three of the garrison to pull up an anchor to which a rope-ladder was attached. This done, five hundred men were to enter the

[1] Bonet, Sept. 13/24, 1715.

town and proclaim the Pretender. But the plan was given away by a woman, and the Governor was informed in time. He did not seem to take the matter too seriously, and merely cautioned his men to keep watch. The conspirators, gathered at an inn, missed the right moment. When they proceeded to execute their plan the time had practically come when their friends among the sentinels were about to be relieved by others. Now they started scaling the wall—a few moments of intense expectation. The decision came from Lieutenant Lindsay who came to relieve the guard just as the ladder was being pulled up. The surprise attack was foiled. The guard let the ropes with the ladder fall, the conspirators sought safety in flight, while some of them were injured falling down the scarp; the City Guards went in pursuit after them but only four were captured.

With the failure of the attack against the Castle, the other plans collapsed. Guns from the Castle were to have signalled the news across the Forth to Fife that the attempt had succeeded, and beacons on the hills would have transmitted the news to the Highlands that Lord Mar and his bands could march on Edinburgh from there to subdue the whole of Scotland to the sceptre of James VIII. Now the position remained more or less unchanged. A number of suspect gentlemen were arrested by the Government, and the rebellion was for the present confined to the Highlands, while the Government in the meanwhile seemed satisfied with preventing its extension south of the Forth. All the available troops in Scotland, together only about 1300 men, were gathered in a fortified camp at Stirling under General Whitham, to defend the passage of the Forth against Mar. Besides, it was hoped to hold the Northern Highlands, beyond Glenmore. Lord Sutherland was directed by the Government to embark for the extreme north, where, as the leading nobleman of that district, he was to raise his vassals and other well-affected clans against the rebels.

On the whole the Government, though it rated the danger in Scotland sufficiently high, did little to fight the rebellion. They counted with the possibility of Mar raising in the Highlands an army of 15,000 to 20,000 men, though in fact he mustered not more than one-fifth of that number. But on the other hand they considered that they could not spare any of their anyhow inconsiderable forces from England, fearing lest a dangerous rebellion would meantime break out in the West; and so long as England remained quiet, a certain complacency was admissible concerning the northern movement. In Ireland, before Parliament met in October, the King created five new peers from among the Whigs, which secured to the Government a favourable majority in the Irish House of Lords.[1]

A few days after the failure at Edinburgh, Mar gained a success which consolidated his position in Central Scotland. He learnt that the Earl of Rothes was advancing on Perth at the head of 500 of his Fife vassals and friends; and on September 25, he ordered a small party in the town to forestall Rothes who was forced to retreat.[2] It was now fairly obvious where the decisive battle would be fought; the rebels could not effect a passage across the Forth without displacing the Royal troops from their position near Stirling, while these could not reduce the Highlands without first taking Perth. Thus the issue of the rebellion had to be determined within the country between Stirling and Perth, about thirty miles apart.

Lord Mar had to move his headquarters to Perth. He did not dare to do so immediately, for he had as yet only a small force with him in Aberdeenshire, consisting in the greater part of his own vassals; the clans under their chiefs were coming in but slowly. The first to appear in Mar's camp was the impetuous old Lord Breadalbane who would have liked best to have raised the banner of James VIII immediately on the death of the Queen. Now he was summoned to Edinburgh, to reside there and find bail for his good behaviour. He answered that at eighty the disabilities of age weighed so heavily upon him that he could not travel without endangering his life; and the next day he joined the rebel army. Mar was anxiously awaiting further reinforcements. It was decided to assemble a more considerable body of men in the Highlands and then "to march down togither in a body to be joind by the gentlemen in the low country, when we will be able to protect them and ourselves too, which had we mett in the low country, we would probablie have come in, stragling and separat parties, and so been exposed to some danger . . . .".[3] As yet he had hardly 1000 men, and in London the danger was now rated lower than before; the intention to apply to Holland for 6000 men was very nearly abandoned.[4] Mar was disappointed, yet did not lose courage, and hoped soon to have an army under his command superior to any forces which the enemy could send into the field.

[1] Bonet, Sept. 30/Oct. 11, 1715.
[2] Hoffmann and Bonet, Oct. 1, 1715; cf. also Chambers, p. 203.
[3] Mar to the Laird of Glengarry, Sept. 11/22, 1715. Thornton, p. xvii.
[4] Hoffmann, Oct. 4, 1715.

On October 9 Lord Mar entered Perth. His army, estimated at 3000-5000, certainly outnumbered the Royal army at Stirling, of which the command had been taken over by the Duke of Argyll. The Royal forces had to fight against heavy odds, and it may seem astonishing that the Government did not send Marlborough, who was Captain-General of the Army. The passing over of Marlborough may be ascribed, partly to his age, but also to a certain distrust entertained of him by the Government. What if the Duke chose to declare in Scotland for the Pretender? It may have been known at Court that the Pretender counted on his support.

The Duke of Argyll was Marlborough's foremost opponent at Court; there was an old feud between them, dating back to the War of the Spanish Succession. Some alleged that Marlborough, who hated Argyll, had once placed him in battle where death seemed certain; while others maintained that Argyll had deserted the post assigned to him. As Groom of the Stole Argyll had formed a friendship with the Prince of Wales, and thereby made enemies of all those who, in the constant quarrels between the King and the Prince, sided with the father; they may have thought that Argyll, whom they feared, would earn no triumphs in Scotland at the head of a very few troops. It may therefore be true that it was much against his own inclination and endeavours that he assumed the command.[1] His friends ascribed to secret orders of the Duke of Marlborough that even the small reinforcements which were to be sent to him to Scotland "were so long a coming, that the Earl of Mar had time to strengthen himself".[2]

Such stories were not always without foundation; still, no danger arose from these Court intrigues to the throne of George I. The choice of Argyll as Commander-in-Chief in Scotland seemed good. The Argylls were old enemies of the Stuarts; the eighth Earl (and only Marquis) of Argyll had fought against Charles I, and his son had tried to support Monmouth's Rebellion by a landing in Scotland. Both paid with their lives for taking arms against the Stuarts. The Duke was an experienced soldier, moreover the Government hoped that his influence would secure for them one part of the Highlands.

These expectations were not fully realized; when on September 29 Argyll arrived at the camp near Stirling, he found only 1300 men at

[1] *Hist. MSS. Comm.* Rep. VII, App. p. 239.
[2] *Diary of Lady Cowper*, pp. 58-9. Lady Cowper, who was of the Court of the Prince of Wales, obviously sided with Argyll, and her statements cannot therefore be accepted without reserve.

his disposal, a force wholly insufficient to suppress a rising of that size.[1] His position was unfavourable and it was urged at Court that his forces there "should be immediately augmented"; for "it seems certain that if any disgrace befall your Majesty's troops in Scotland", wrote Lord Cowper to the King, "insurrections will immediately follow in England in many places. . . ." [2] Still, some time had to elapse before the reinforcements which Argyll expected from Scotland, Northern England, and Ireland, could reach him. In the meantime, his opponents might have scored considerable successes. Argyll's own clan did not dare to leave their country for fear of exposing it to raids by hostile neighbouring clans. Mar's force was double the number of Argyll's, and he held the Highlands. Even the neighbouring towns of Glasgow and Dumfries were not secure against the rebels, who seemed very nearly to have a free hand, while Argyll could hardly venture beyond the range of the cannon of Stirling.

The more remarkable is it that Mar undertook practically nothing against the enemy. Recently, while still in the Highlands, he deplored having to lose "so luckie an opportunity" of attacking the weak and ill-paid army at Stirling.[3] Now he faced them with superior forces, but did not carry out the attack—he lacked that ruthless determination which is indispensable in the leader of a rising; whoever wants to overthrow a constituted Government, must be prepared to stake everything. A successful battle would have delivered the whole of Scotland into Mar's hands. His Highlanders thirsted for battle but had little liking for hanging about camp. Mar intended to await the coming in of further clans, and then to attack his opponent with an even greater superiority of numbers and from several directions. But the delay turned to the advantage of Argyll's army, while many of his own people sneaked off home.

Thus a considerable time elapsed without any decisive action. But every week the prospects of the rebellion grew worse and this in turn reacted on England. The Government had good reason to look upon the Scottish rising as an intended prelude to a Stuart rebellion in England. The English Jacobites had their eyes fixed on Scotland; but nothing happened there which could have encouraged them to take up arms, while the caution was fully justified which made the

[1] Argyll to Townshend, Stirling, Nov. 4/15, 1715, S.P. 54, Bundle 10, No. 18.

[2] See *Diary of Lady Cowper*, App. C, p. 181.

[3] Mar to Gordon of Glenbucket, Sept. 9/20, 1715. Thornton, p. xv.

Government retain their slender forces, so as not to lose England while reconquering Scotland.

Most active among the Ministers was Stanhope who was in charge of the now all-important relations with France. He, more than Marlborough, decided even about military measures. At this time Robert Walpole became First Lord of the Treasury, which post, after the death of Lord Halifax, had been held for a few months by the Earl of Carlisle. Walpole had proved one of the foremost supports of the throne. His knowledge, especially of finance, his abilities, and his power in debate, were universally acknowledged. He had previously acted as adviser to his brother-in-law Townshend; now he was Townshend's colleague in the Cabinet, much more clever and practical than he who outwardly retained a more prominent position.

The White Staff of the Lord High Treasurer, which Godolphin and Oxford had held, was not given to Walpole nor to any of his successors, but even the position of the First Lord of the Treasury sufficed to secure for him the leading place in the Cabinet. "Great men have generally been of the Treasury", wrote Edward Wortley Montagu early in the reign of George I; "and when a Commissioner of the Treasury has equal favour with any of the other Ministers, he will be First Minister".[1] For a long time Walpole took second place to Townshend, but in the end, as Walpole himself admitted, the name of the firm changed from Townshend and Walpole to Walpole and Townshend.[2] Robert Walpole was the first to introduce the conception of Prime Minister into English constitutional life.

The task of fighting the rebellion naturally fell in the first place on the Secretaries of State, Stanhope and Townshend. They worked day and night with their eyes still always on England rather than on Scotland. They received news from Stair of a rising planned in the West of England, which would declare for the Church against the Whigs and a standing army, but in reality in favour of James Edward.[3] The de-

---

[1] E. W. Montagu, "State of Affairs".   [2] Coxe, Walpole, i. p. 339.

[3] Stair to Montrose, Oct. 2, 1715; *Hist. MSS. Comm.* Rep. III, App. p. 384; Stanhope to Stair, Oct. 5/16, 1715. Stair writes to Robethon on Oct. 2, 1715 (Stowe MSS. 228, ff. 115-16): "*J'ay raison de croire que leur première tentative sera sur Bristol, il serait bon de les prévenir là, car ils y trouveroient des armes, des munitions de guerre et beaucoup d'autres choses dont ils auront besoin. Ils se proposent dans les différens pays de se saisir des armes de la milice et se flattent que tant des trouppes auront marché de coté de l'Écosse, que l'Angleterre sera dépourvue et que le Parlement n'étant pas assemblé, il y aura moins d'autorité pour s'opposer à leur rébellion.*"

tails of the conspiracy were disclosed when one of those engaged in it, Maclean, turned traitor. The Government proceeded to arrest the leaders and to secure the strategic points. Among the leaders were three peers and six Members of Parliament, who even under the recent legislation could not be arrested without permission from the two Houses. None the less, during the night of October 2, the arrests were made, and the next day Lord Townshend in the Lords, and Stanhope in the Commons, obtained without difficulty votes of indemnity for this measure.

The most dangerous among the arrested leaders was Sir William Wyndham, since Ormonde's flight the head of the English Jacobites. He was at his house in Somerset, but when the officers came to arrest him he managed to elude them and to escape through a back door. A price of £1000 was offered for his discovery, and seeing that he was bound to be caught, he surrendered voluntarily. He had hoped to be protected by the interposition of his father-in-law, the Duke of Somerset, who was a Whig. The Duke tried to speak in his favour at a meeting of the Privy Council, at which the King was present. But Lord Townshend "deemed it necessary that Government should not appear afraid to arrest such an offender, let his rank and connections be what they might, and moved . . . to have him taken into custody", which was resolved accordingly. "As the King retired into his Closet, he took hold of Lord Townshend's hand, and said 'You have done me a great service to-day'." [1] The Duke of Somerset's assisting Sir William Wyndham was made the pretence for depriving him of his place at Court.[2]

Wyndham asserted his complete innocence. It was impossible to extort a confession from him; torture, wrote Bonet, was unknown in England, as in the ancient republic of the Jews. In Wyndham's possession a few treasonable letters were found from Lord Lansdowne, who had also been arrested: Wyndham retorted that he could not prevent anyone from writing to him. In arresting him the Government was less concerned to punish him for something done than to stop him from doing harm in the future. Military measures were taken in the west. Troops were sent to Bristol to secure it against attack. The garrisons from the Channel and the Scilly Islands were sent to Southampton and Plymouth.[3] At Oxford the Jacobites were

---

[1] The story is told by Coxe (i. p. 71) as he had it from the grandson of Lord Townshend.

[2] *Diary of Lady Cowper*, p. 51.   [3] See Admiralty Records in P.R.O.

numerous and the Colleges favoured the Chevalier: on October 17 at daybreak, dragoons, under General Pepper, entered the town. Both the town and the University were cowed and did not dare to remonstrate when a few of the most daring Jacobites were arrested. After that the soldiers again left the town. Such measures sufficed to preserve the peace in England. Wyndham and Lansdowne were, according to Bolingbroke, the only two men he knew who were capable of taking the lead in the western counties.[1] Even if a man as popular as Ormonde ventured on an attempt to raise the Jacobites in the west, he was bound to meet with disappointment. Stanhope wrote to Stair that it would be not at all unfavourable if Ormonde and his new master now attempted a landing in England.[2]

This they could not do without the connivance of the French Government, and the attitude of France under the Duke of Orleans was hardly of less moment than it had been under Louis XIV. Lord Stair had welcomed the rise of the Regent, thinking that he would have to seek English backing; and offered him help in a case where it could easily have embarrassed him. The intention was ascribed to the Spanish Ambassador, Prince Cellamare, to enter a protest on behalf of Philip V in the *"lit de justice"* where the resolution of September 2 was to receive the assent of the infant King. In that case Stair, as he himself told the Regent, proposed to declare that the protest was an infringement of the Treaty of Utrecht.[3] Spain and Great Britain discussing in the Paris Parliament who was the rightful Regent in France would indeed have been a scene humiliating to French pride.

Prince Cellamare did not carry out his intention, but Orleans seemed to place great value on British friendship. On September 4 he gave Stair "great assurances of his observing the Treaty and doing justice as to Mardyke, according to his promise", but as he said nothing positive about the Pretender, Bolingbroke, and Ormonde, this suggested to Stair that he still meant "to keep that game going". "I . . . shewed him how much his interest had been connected with the King's."[4] In view of the personal relations between George I and the Duke of Orleans, argued Stair in a Memorial, dated September 14, 1715, which he presented to the Regent about the middle of September, and of the kinship and amity which united the two princes, it

---

[1] Bolingbroke to the Chevalier, Oct. 24, 1715. Mahon, i. App.
[2] Oct. 31/Nov. 11, 1715, F.O. 90/14.
[3] Cf. Wiesener, i. pp. 106-7.
[4] Hardwicke, *State Papers*, ii. p. 547.

was unthinkable that the Pretender and his adherents should be assisted and encouraged by France. The simplest thing would be to send him across the Alps; this would secure the peace and safety of Great Britain, and rid France of having to pay a pension which could only serve to aggrieve England. As the Regent seemed well-inclined to a connexion with England, he probably concurred in suggesting a Treaty in which George I would guarantee the succession in France as fixed by the Treaty of Utrecht, and the Regent the Hanoverian Succession in England. A treaty was contemplated similar to that concluded with the States General in 1713, when Holland guaranteed the Protestant Succession, and Great Britain the Barrier.

The British obviously aimed at making the Regent assume treaty-obligations concerning the Pretender, while Orleans aimed at strengthening his position by obtaining British support. Besides, he desired to secure important advantages for France. In return for a commercial treaty, he was prepared to destroy Mardyke harbour; but the British Ministers refused and argued that "even during the reigns of Charles II and James II, when there was an entire confidence between the two Courts, there was no Treaty of Commerce." [1] To dissuade the Regent, Stanhope declared that the Treaty should contain nothing but a mutual guarantee, so that King George on his part would renounce Mardyke being mentioned. Nor would the British listen to the wish of the Regent to change the treaty into a defensive alliance; it would have been contrary to the entire system of Whig foreign policy to start with a French alliance, even if it was the France of the Regent. Still, the prospects of the negotiations seemed favourable. In October, Stair assumed the character of an Envoy Extraordinary and Ambassador Plenipotentiary and received the formal authorization to conclude the Treaty.

Thus at first England had reason to be satisfied with the new French Government. "They wish us well," wrote Stair to Robethon on September 21, 1715, "and their new system needs us." [2] The Duke of Orleans stood in a conscious opposition to the policy of Louis XIV. At his Court "cela ressemble trop à l'ancien système," was an answer so often given, that it became a jest, and almost a proverb. [3]

The Pretender and his friends were filled with apprehensions at

---

[1] Stanhope to Stair, Sept. 19/30, Sept. 21/Oct. 2, Oct. 5/16, and Oct. 20/31, 1715; the full-powers are dated Sept. 24/Oct. 5, 1715, F.O. 90/14.

[2] Stowe MSS. 228, f. 105.

[3] *Letter to Sir William Windham*, p. 143.

the untoward change in the situation. "I now most heartily wish
that the King had gone away two months ago" wrote Bolingbroke to
Mar on September 20, 1715. Louis XIV had promised a French ship
for transporting the Pretender, while now he could not cross France
unless he "steals off unknown"; moreover "the whole coast from
Jutland to Spain is against us. . . . The troops we hoped for from
Sweden are refused us. . . . The money we expected from Spain is,
in my opinion, still in the clouds. . . ." [1] James Edward persisted in
his scheme, though he saw things in an equally unfavourable light;
he wrote to Bolingbroke on September 23: "On the whole, I must
confess my affairs have a very melancholly prospect; every post almost brings some ill news or other; all hopes of the least foreign help
are extinguished . . . and all our endeavours and pains are in a manner
lost, and it is all rowing against the tide". [2]

For the present, the attitude of the Regent towards the Jacobites
seemed wholly negative. He refused to receive Bolingbroke and
Ormonde, while the Marshal of Berwick was, from regard for George I,
omitted from the Regency Council. And when in September Admiral
Byng came into Havre and, apprized by Stair's informers, was able
to demand by name the ships on board which were arms and stores
for the Pretender, the Regent, though he did not think fit to give
them up, ordered them to be unloaded into the royal magazines. The
Pretender was in no condition to repair the loss, and had now practically nothing to offer to his friends in Great Britain except his own
person. [3]

However pleased the Ministers in London were with the news from
Havre, warned by Stair they by no means relied on the Regent's
friendship. On September 26, Stanhope told Hoffmann that, while
the attitude of the Regent gave ground for hopes, France remained
France—she could not be easily weaned from the principles of her
policy, and would act with more cunning than sincerity. [4] Soon Bolingbroke thought he perceived a change at the Regent's Court. "I do
verily think", he wrote to James Edward on September 25, "that they
begin to stagger on their Whiggish ground." [5] The Duke of Orleans
had never given a formal refusal to the Jacobites, and had, on the
death of Louis XIV, expressed his friendship for the Chevalier, and

---

[1] Mahon, i. App.   [2] *Ibid.*
[3] See *Mémoires de Berwick*, p. 245.
[4] Hoffmann's dispatch of Sept. 27, 1715, Vienna Arch.
[5] Mahon, i. App.

good-will to his cause. But these assurances, as Bolingbroke remarked to James Edward, seemed "to point to very distant services"; [1] for great weight attached to relations with George I who seemed firmly established on his throne. But now news were received of a successful advance of the rebels in Scotland, which at a distance was judged far more important than it was. It was not understood in France that the British Government was deliberately keeping back its army and refraining from immediately crushing the Scottish Rebellion, which it was in their power to do, in order to avoid provoking a serious Jacobite danger in England. Even Bolingbroke, however critical, had an exaggerated idea of the difficulties confronting the British Government, and thought that nothing but the presence of James Edward was wanting in Great Britain to decide the whole in his favour. [2] Now that the Regent began to think the fall of George I imminent, he drew closer to the Pretender, and the idea, previously entertained, of a marriage between his daughter and the Pretender was once more considered. The Regent's attitude towards Stair cooled off remarkably, [3] and the negotiations for a Treaty of Mutual Guarantees came to a complete stop.

The time for carrying out the plans of the English Jacobites was approaching; Ormonde was to cross over, and James Edward was to follow. Every post brought news to the Jacobites in France about the situation in England. Couriers travelled daily between Paris and Bar-le-Duc. [4] Stair, spying on the Jacobites, had "people on most of the roads"; to watch their movements narrowly was his foremost and, soon, nearly his sole task. Finally Stanhope himself wrote to Stair that the less he appeared at Court, the better. [5] At Havre he kept a reliable agent, to inform him of what was doing. It was Stair who drew the attention of the British Government to the plans for a rising in the West. He was acquainted with the hopes of the Pretender and the intentions of the French Government—he knew where the rising was to start in England, and what Bolingbroke had boastfully divulged over his wine. He realized that people were trying to deceive him, but occasionally they succeeded; thus he believed the story of Bolingbroke having managed to convert the Pretender to

---

[1] Letter of Sept. 3, 1715. Mahon, i. App.
[2] Bolingbroke to James Edward, Sept. 25, 1715, *ibid.*
[3] See Stair's "Diary", Hardwicke, *State Papers*, ii. p. 549.
[4] Stair to Robethon, Oct. 2, 1715, Stowe MSS. 228, f. 115.
[5] November 26, 1715, O.S., F.O. 90/14.

Anglicanism. In view of the uncertain attitude of France, correct information was of capital importance; where Stair could quote facts to the Regent, his justified demands could not be refused without a complete breach. In spite of imminent danger, the Ambassador preserved on the whole a calm and unbiassed judgment; he did not overrate the chances of the Jacobites because Ormonde was at their head, for he knew that Ormonde lacked initiative, and he did not think the English Jacobites keen to engage in open rebellion. "There are very few among them", he wrote to Robethon on October 30, 1715, "whose love for the Pretender goes so far as to make them lie three nights under a hedge in November." [1] And similarly in a letter to Montrose: [2] "By the time they have layn a week under a hedge in the end of October or the beginning of November, it will be easie dealling with them".

Before Ormonde left Paris, he was granted a secret audience by the Regent, who made many excuses for not having done so sooner and gave as reason "the great measures they were obliged to keep with the people on the other side of the water, but att the same time made great professions of his concern and friendship" for the Pretender and promised him "a great number of arms and ammunition"; [3] also to help him to embark at Dunkirk. But even while he was giving these assurances, he feared their consequences and made Ormonde promise that he should keep them secret even from Bolingbroke. He feared to be driven into war with England by Bolingbroke, who saw in it the only chance of success. James Edward and Ormonde lent themselves to the intrigues of the Regent. The entourage of the Pretender delighted in the mysteries of backstairs diplomacy; instead of sensible co-operation, they practised mutual deceit. How could Bolingbroke successfully conduct the affairs of his master when such important information was withheld from him? Ormonde, in turn, was kept in ignorance of the negotiations with Marlborough, his personal enemy. And they were all deceived by James Edward, who, without their knowledge, was discussing with Lord Mar a rising in Scotland.

In the end the Chevalier got what he deserved, and saw himself abandoned by the generals whom he had expected to fight his battles. His hopes of Marlborough were not realized—in fact, the Duke was

[1] Oct. 30, 1715, Stowe MSS., 228, f. 150.
[2] *Hist. MSS. Comm.* Rep. III, App. p. 384.
[3] Ormonde to the Chevalier, October 21, 1715. See Thornton, p. 401.

M

hardly in a position to do anything for him; similarly, to the relief of the British Government, Berwick refused his co-operation. While relations with the Regent were still tolerably good, Stanhope had privately instructed Stair to express the hope that Berwick, as Marshal of France, would not be permitted "to joyn or act in any attempt against a King and nation which is in amity with France";[1] and the Regent forbade the Marshal to follow the Pretender.[2] Berwick himself seems to have valued the prospects of the Stuart cause too low to sacrifice to it his position in France, and preferred to disobey the phantom King of England rather than the French Regent. He could hardly have been sincere when he wrote to Bolingbroke on October 21, 1715: "I will try what my conscience and honour will allow me, for my inclination, ambition, and personal glory bids me comply with the King's command and the desire of Scotland".[3] The Pretender was dismayed and indignant, and was convinced that nobody could have hindered Berwick if he had resolved to go;[4] and, ungrateful as usual, he declared that Berwick had never done him any good at the French Court, and that he would now put it out of Berwick's power to do him harm. But to Mar he sent a message that he did not regret Berwick's refusal, for this would give Mar an opportunity to conclude the work which he had so auspiciously begun.

While Ormonde was preparing to sail for the West of England, which he thought actually in revolt, Bolingbroke was preparing propaganda material to be dispersed among the people. Numerous proclamations, pamphlets, and circulars were printed, and letters, signed by the Chevalier, were to be addressed to the Army and Navy, to the Universities, and to the City of London. The Whigs had introduced these methods and next, "we have been forced to combat them at their own weapon".[5] By these means the bulk of England had in 1710 been brought "from a fondness of war to be in love with peace"; the same methods must be pursued now. A Declaration was prepared which James III was to publish on his arrival in Great Britain; over this the differences which would have divided his government became apparent. The Pretender refused to make any promise in favour of the Church of Ireland, and even the promise which related to the

[1] Stanhope to Stair, Sept. 21, 1715, O.S., F.O. 90/14.
[2] See correspondence in Thornton, pp. 388-91.
[3] Thornton, p. 393.
[4] James Edward to Bolingbroke, Oct. 10, 1715, *ibid.* p. 391.
[5] Bolingbroke to James Edward, Oct. 18, 1715, *ibid.* pp. 393-7.

Church of England was so ambiguous that it was bound to give offence. Bolingbroke refused to countersign [1] the Declaration—the cleavage between the Catholic Stuarts and the Protestant nation was making itself felt.

In the second half of October Ormonde set out from Normandy for England. He embarked in spite of the news which reached him while still on the coast of France that Maclean, who had been "in the whole secret of the rising of the West", had betrayed them, that Wyndham and his friends had been seized, and that the British Government had taken military counter-measures. "Two gentlemen acquainted with the country," writes Bolingbroke, "and perfectly well known to all our friends in those parts, were dispatched before, that the people of Devonshire and Somersetshire, who were, we concluded, in arms, might be apprised of the signals which were to be made from the ships, and might be ready to receive the Duke." [2] Ormonde sailed with some fifty officers and men of a French regiment stationed on that part of the coast. The ship hovered off Teignmouth, near Exeter, next came to an anchor in Torbay, and fired three guns as a signal to the friends on the coast that the leader of the rebellion had arrived; [3] but there was no reply. Only a few Customs officers came on board, and were refused admission to the cabin and to the hold. The suspect behaviour of the ship spurred the authorities to increased vigilance; and as the signals remained unanswered and no one moved on the coast, Ormonde had to recognize that his hopes of active support from the gentlemen of the district, many of whom were Roman Catholics, were vain. No landing was attempted, and Ormonde does not seem to have set foot in England.[4] It was presumably on board his ship that he met the gentlemen who had been sent ahead, and learnt from them how hopeless the position was. Nothing was left for him but to return. "In a word," writes Bolingbroke, "he was refused a night's lodging in a country which we had been told was in a good posture to receive the Chevalier, and where the Duke expected that multitudes would repair to him." [5] Returned to St. Malo

---

[1] Same to same, Nov. 2, 1715, Mahon, i. App.

[2] *Letter to Sir William Windham*, pp. 168-9.

[3] For the following see besides printed sources (especially Berwick's *Mémoires* and Bolingbroke's *Letter to Sir William Windham*) and dispatches from Bonet and Hoffmann, a letter from Sir J. Elwill to Lord Sunderland, dated Bedford House in Exon. Oct. 22, 1715, P.R.O. Home Office, Admiralty Entry Books 4.

[4] *Letter to Sir William Windham*, p. 170.   [5] *Ibid.*

he met James Edward, who had been waiting to hear from Ormonde before embarking. Now he was ready with a disparaging judgment about Ormonde. "Our good hearty Duke wants a good head with him" he wrote to Bolingbroke on November 15, 1715; [1] and again on November 27: "D.O. (Duke of Ormonde) gott out of the bay last night and sett sail this morning. . . . He will certainly go to Cornwall, which I am sorry for. . . ." [2] This time Ormonde was nearly cast away in a storm, and was forced back to the French coast. The hopes of the Pretender were now set on Lord Mar and his Highlanders.

In Scotland the armies under Mar and Argyll still always faced each other in their positions near Perth and Stirling. But the rising was no longer limited to Scotland; in Northumberland, where Roman Catholics formed a considerable part of the population, a number of country gentlemen with their tenants had risen in arms. At their head was Thomas Forster, M.P., who, hearing that there was a warrant out for his arrest, resorted to open rebellion; he and Lords Derwentwater and Widdrington became the leaders of the movement. Forster found himself in command of a few hundred horse, not because of his superior influence or supposed abilities and military knowledge—"for he had never seen an army in his life", [3] says Lady Cowper—but because he was a Protestant, and it did not seem wise to place a Catholic at the head of the movement. Thus the Jacobites were led not by a Marlborough, Berwick, or Ormonde, but by Mar and Forster, politicians without military experience.

The rebels were disappointed in their hope of procuring possession of Newcastle, which contained many Jacobites among its inhabitants and especially among the coal-miners. At that time it was a walled town and could have served the rebels as an important base for their enterprise in the North; moreover by capturing it they would have been able to cut off the supply of coal for London. But the well-affected citizens, uniting with the Dissenters, contrived to muster 700 volunteers, and when regular troops reached Newcastle on October 20, the place was put out of danger. The Earl of Scarborough, who commanded the troops, strengthened the defences of the town, armed the militia, and ordered the most active Jacobites to be arrested.

Scottish help was required if the Northumbrian rising was to be saved from complete collapse. Forster sent a message to Mar asking him for some foot, as he himself had none. Mar could not easily supply

---

[1] Thornton, p. 413.   [2] *Ibid.* p. 414.   [3] *Diary,* p. 57.

it while Argyll lay near Stirling. But now Mar was preparing, though with excessive caution, a concentric attack against Argyll's position. He sent a strong detachment into the Western Highlands, thence to advance against Stirling; the Jacobites who had recently risen in the southern parts of Scotland, under Lords Kenmure, Carnwath, and Wintoun, were to support the attack from the south; lastly, Mar proposed to throw a strong detachment across the Firth of Forth, to operate against Argyll from the east. It was difficult to effect such a crossing, as some warships kept watch in the Forth; but Brigadier Macintosh, who was in charge of the enterprise, was a skilful and experienced soldier. Mar sent him forth with 2500 men, including the best part of his own clan of Macintosh. Old Borlum, as he was called, succeeded in eluding the warships by a feint attempt to cross with 500 men at Burntisland; meantime, during the night, he started crossing with the main body further down the Forth. By the morning they had only half crossed the wide estuary; the warships came up, but the wind and tides were against them. By setting out boats, the English sailors managed to take forty prisoners while a few rebel boats were forced into the Isle of May in the Firth. The rest, 1600 strong, reached with their leader the southern bank, having effected the crossing which the Government had thought impossible.

A number of ships were now sent to the Firth of Forth and ordered to seize all ships or vessels which could be of service to the rebels, and to co-operate with Argyll.[1] But this did not meet the immediate danger; a considerable force was threatening Edinburgh. The alarm was given, and everybody took to arms. It was the panic produced by Macintosh's approach which suggested to him the idea to start by attacking Edinburgh. He seized the Citadel of Leith, which dated back to Cromwell and was half in ruins, and fortified it against attack. The Edinburgh garrison was reinforced by Argyll, who, at the head of 600 men, "marched, or rather posted", to its relief. The rest of the army was left near Stirling under General Whitham. Argyll's summons to the rebels to lay down their arms and surrender was met with a defiant refusal. But an attack against the city was clearly impracticable, and Borlum left the citadel during the night and took up new positions further east. The Duke planned to attack them there, but on receiving intelligence that Mar was marching against Stirling and had reached Dunblane with 4000 men, while another 4000 followed, Argyll, at Whitham's request, rejoined him; and now Mar,

[1] See Admiralty Records in P.R.O.

too, could think of nothing better than to make a sudden return to his previous position near Perth.

Macintosh meanwhile marched along the coast towards the English border, and on November 2 joined the rebels from the Border and Northumberland at Kelso. Next day being Sunday, a service was held for all, Catholics and Protestants; Forster's chaplain preached the sermon on the text "The right of the firstborn is his" (Deut. xxi. 17). On Monday morning the Pretender was proclaimed. The forces gathered at Kelso consisted of 1400 foot and 600 horse, and General Carpenter was marching against them from the south at the head of 900 regulars; but these were newly raised troops who had never seen active service, and the rebels, superior in number, could have risked a battle. Neither this course nor the proposal of the Scots to march against Stirling was adopted. The rebel army marched to the south-west, along the English border, arguing all the time where to go and what to do. Meanwhile Carpenter had crossed the frontier and was following in their tracks. On one occasion the rebels could have attacked him with good prospects, but they continued their march. When approaching Dumfries, which they intended to capture, they heard that the town was held by so many volunteers as to render an attack hopeless. They therefore decided to invade north-western England. On November 12, they crossed the border; only 500 Scots refused, possibly remembering the fate of the Scottish army after the Battle of Worcester.

The English Jacobites had, from the very outset, urged the advantages of a march into England, hoping that Westmorland, Cumberland, and most of all Lancashire, with its many Catholics, would join the Stuart banner. Wherever they went, they proclaimed James III and seized the public money. There was a clergyman in the rebel army "who went into the churches in their way, and scratched out His Majesty King George's name, and placed the Pretender's so nicely that it resembled print very much, and the alteration could scarce be perceived".[1] In Lancashire they received some reinforcements, and marched by Kendal and Lancaster to Preston. At Manchester, in expectation of their arrival, the mob proclaimed the Pretender. At Liverpool, on the contrary, the citizens were preparing to defend their town.

For a short time the rebels managed to keep off General Carpenter's pursuit, having misled him by a letter which they contrived to get

---

[1] R. Patten, *The History of the late Rebellion*, p. 90.

into his hands and which made him believe that an attack against Newcastle was intended.[1] Having diverted him in that direction, the rebels invaded Lancashire. But meantime another small army was sent against them. Troops were posted in the neighbouring districts which the Government knew to be unreliable, and an able officer, General Wills, who had distinguished himself in Spain, was instructed to form those garrisons into an army and march against the rebels; [2] he left only one regiment at Manchester to keep the disaffected elements in check, and on November 23 advanced from Wigan with six regiments of horse and one of foot to join Carpenter before Preston. A mile from Preston he had to cross the River Ribble, and expected to find the bridge strongly held. In reality there were only some two or three hundred men, who hurriedly retreated before him. Even now he did not believe that he would be able to reach the town without fighting, for he had to pass through a deep, narrow lane of which the slopes lined with hedges offered cover. Here Cromwell was reported to have found himself in a difficult situation in 1648, when the enemy rolled down stones on him and his men. General Wills, finding the scarps deserted, concluded that the rebels had abandoned Preston and retired to Scotland. But he was soon informed that they had retreated to the town only, where they were resolved to meet his attack.

Preston was an open town, and the position was hurriedly fortified by the rebels. Forster concentrated his forces in the inner town, thinking that it offered the greatest security to his troops. The street approaches were barricaded, and troops were posted also in the houses. Wills ordered his dragoons to dismount and to advance against two strong barriers on foot. The attack was made with vigour, but the defenders held a strong position and were able to direct a terrible fire upon the troops from the barricades and windows—the Highlanders were excellent shots. The Royal forces suffered heavy loss, and at both points had to retire without having secured any advantage. Wills now invested the town and laid siege to it.

Next morning, November 24, General Carpenter reached Preston with his army. Forster, quite disheartened, did not think himself equal to the reinforced Royal army. He sent one of his officers to propose

---

[1] Hoffmann, Nov. 19, 1715.
[2] For the following cf. also official account circulated to foreign diplomatists and British representatives abroad; see, *e.g.* enclosure in Townshend's letter to Walpole at The Hague, Nov. 16/27, 1715.

a capitulation. General Wills refused to treat with the rebels who had killed many of His Majesty's subjects and must expect a similar fate. After long entreaties he at last agreed that if the rebels would lay down their arms and surrender at discretion, he would protect them from being cut to pieces by the soldiers, until further orders from the Government.[1] The Scots were enraged at Forster's pusillanimity, and the Highlanders almost rose in mutiny; had Forster appeared in the street, he would have been killed by them. But even the Scottish leaders lost heart; they saw no escape and Wills threatened, should they resist, to attack the town and give no quarter. The entire rebel army, English and Scots, gentry and tenants, surrendered unconditionally to the King's troops.

The question of the numbers of the opposing armies is puzzling. As General Wills approached Preston, the strength of the rebels was reported to him as 4000-5000; while his own army, according to Berwick, did not exceed 1000. This is an under-estimate and certainly does not cover the united forces of Wills and Carpenter. Wills alone had six regiments of horse and one of foot, and though it is not possible exactly to determine their strength, especially as five of the cavalry regiments were newly raised, the total strength must have exceeded 1000, while Carpenter's troops amounted to about 900. It is not certain that Carpenter marched with all his forces against Preston: according to the official report he joined Wills with three regiments of dragoons (those of Cobham, Churchill, and Molesworth). But Berwick's account is defective also in other respects, and the joint forces of Wills and Carpenter probably exceeded 2000 men.[2]

It is equally difficult to determine the strength of the rebel army; many of them must have been poorly armed or unarmed, and would not count in a serious battle. In consequence the number of prisoners proved much smaller than had been expected, and consisted of some 200 English and Scottish gentlemen and only about 1400 men. A certain number must have escaped, while in the case of others, and especially of natives of the neighbouring counties, their connexion with the rebels was not obvious and they could easily escape capture.

---

[1] See Wills's evidence, Howell, *State Trials*, xv. 854.

[2] Argyll reported on November 4/15, 1715: "When I arrived here . . . I found an army of about 1300 men. . . . I have been reinforced by three regiments of dragoons that did not make 500, and four regiments of foot under 1200. . . . These troops, my Lord, with the recruits that have been raised since my arrivall who are not yet cloathed amount alltogether to about the number of 3300 men" (S.P. 54, Bundle 10, No. 18).

Thus, while the rebels may have been superior in numbers, they certainly had no superiority in the military sense; otherwise the official report would undoubtedly have mentioned it in order to enhance the achievements of the Government troops. It was not a miracle which put an end to the rising in England—the Government forces were fully sufficient, and the mass of the people, even in the least well-affected districts of England, could not be drawn into a rising against the Hanoverian dynasty.

The success at Preston was complete; all resistance in England was at an end. In view of the numbers, it was not possible to prosecute all the prisoners. Many of the common people were set free, when they could no longer be dangerous; but many were transported to the Colonies. Less lenient was the treatment of the rebel nobility and of the officers in general. General Wills refused to act on orders received from London, to shoot out of hand all late officers of the Royal army or officers on half-pay; only a small number were executed at Preston. The greatest part were sent to London, and on December 20, some 150 gentlemen with 70 servants were marched through the streets; they were on horseback but "came in with their arms tied, and their horses (whose bridles were taken off) led each by a soldier". Fashionable society went to watch the sight, only those staying away who, like Lady Cowper, had relatives or friends among the prisoners. "The mob insulted them terribly, carrying a warming-pan before them [a hit at the Pretender], and saying a thousand barbarous things, which some of the prisoners returned with spirit." [1] Ten prisoners of the first rank were sent to the Tower, while the others were lodged in common jails, among them Old Borlum, and even Forster though he was a Member of Parliament. Reports were spread by the Ministers that an example would be made in their case.

Meantime the long-awaited battle was fought in Scotland. Lord Mar had wasted precious time, not being able to make up his mind to attack. He was one of those generals to whom chances never seem sufficiently favourable, and who wait till, in the end, they are forced to fight under much less favourable conditions. Mar hoped for a rising in England, waited for France to act, counted on the success of Ormonde's landing; he still wished to bring up reinforcements from the remotest parts of the Highlands in the north and west, but in the counties of Ross and Sutherland Lord Seaforth, who had declared

[1] *Diary of Lady Cowper*, p. 62.

for the Pretender, was opposed by Lord Sutherland, while in the West the vassals and adherents of Argyll had so far been able to prevent the Jacobites from joining the Rebellion. So long as Inveraray and Fort William were held by Royal troops, the rebels could hardly count on reinforcements from the Western Highlands. On one occasion Mar even attempted a negotiation with Argyll, who, however, said that he "neither could nor would speak with him", and caused the messenger to be imprisoned.[1]

The position of Argyll's army was not favourable either. Although the small body of 1300 men, whom he found on his arrival at Stirling, had been reinforced by three regiments of dragoons and four of foot, and by a small number of recruits, by the middle of November Argyll had only about 3300 men under his command. In London it was thought that he ought to crush the Scottish rebellion at one blow, and his regular forces were considered fully equal to four times the number of undisciplined troops. His enemies at Court did their best to discredit his generalship. Argyll replied that he was sent to Scotland "to make him look little in the eyes of the world".[2] His letters contained sharp strictures on Marlborough and the Ministers; the King himself felt offended;[3] Argyll's "animosity at last grew so high", wrote Lady Cowper, "that he made himself to be more in the wrong even than they had been".[4] He had to offer formal apologies, but at the same time put before the Ministers in detail the difficulties of his position.[5] He had nothing to reproach himself with and so far his conduct had at every step been approved by the general officers, who served with him:

... there are severall little spaces of plain ground, where we might have the use of our cavallry, yet those plains are divided by rough hilly grounds, and the River of Ern which covers Perth has but two bridges upon it, and three fords, which bridges they have entrench'd and may break in a few hours, the fords being at this time of the year only passable after two or three days fair weather, and the rebells have been these ten days working on a new entrenchment round the toun of Perth.[6]

[1] *Hist. MSS. Comm.* Rep. II, App. p. 26.
[2] S.P. 54, Bundle 10.
[3] Stanhope and Townshend to Argyll, Nov. 2/13, 1715, in reply to Argyll's letter of Oct. 18, O.S.
[4] *Diary*, p. 59.
[5] Argyll to Townshend, Nov. 4/15, 1715.
[6] Argyll to Townshend, camp at Stirling, Nov. 4, 1715, S.P. 54, Bundle 10, No. 18.

An attack against the position of the rebels seemed, therefore, impracticable to Argyll; nor did he think it feasible to draw nearer to Perth, as the enemy could by certain manœuvres force him to retreat. Moreover, "it is impossible to ly any time at this season of the year in this cold climate unhutted",[1] while the question of forage and provisions would present difficult problems on the other side of Dunblane (four miles from Stirling)—the soldiers would not be satisfied with the diet of the Highlanders, whose "naturall food is not bread", but meal and water; ". . . our chief hopes are, that either they will by advancing give us an opportunity of attacking them, or if they ly still that the common people will grow weary and retire home".[2]

On November 20, Mar, in his council of war, decided to take action. He was moved by two considerations. He had by now collected all the forces on which he could count; even Lord Seaforth had reached Perth with a few thousand men from the North, and General Gordon had managed, with a few detachments from the Western clans to pass by Inveraray and Fort William, whose Governor was mortified to see two bodies of rebels "with their five hundred men each" pass "under his nose", while he was quite unable to take any measures against them.[3] A few days later they joined the main army. Mar had by now abandoned the idea of a concentric attack against Argyll, and planned to attack him with all the forces under his command.

Mar had now upwards of 10,000 men, and thought himself greatly superior to the enemy. But he knew—and this was the second reason for his decision—that the balance would soon change. A Dutch army was shortly expected in Scotland, 6000 men having been promised by the States General in the Treaty of January 30, 1713, should they be required for the defence of the Protestant Succession. In October 1715, after some hesitation, the British Government decided to ask for the Dutch support. Horace Walpole was sent to The Hague, and was to claim 6000 men; their pay would come from the British Government, who wished to avoid placing themselves under excessive obligations to the Dutch.[4] The caution arose from regard to Charles VI, for hardly had Walpole's mission become known, when Hoffmann uneasily enquired about it with the Ministers. They hast-

---

[1] Argyll to Townshend, camp at Stirling, Nov. 4, 1715, S.P. 54, Bundle 10, No. 18.   [2] *Ibid.*
[3] *Hist. MSS. Comm.* Rep. III, App. p. 380.
[4] Bonet, Oct. 25/Nov. 5, 1715.

ened to assure him that the Dutch military succour would have no influence on the Barrier negotiations. In reality some interaction between the two questions could not be altogether avoided, and the German Ministers openly admitted it to Hoffmann.

Mar left Perth on November 21, N.S., crossed the Earn, and reached Auchterarder, where he held a grand review; here he was joined by the Western clans under General Gordon. He omitted that day to take possession of the strategically important Dunblane, as was originally intended, and it was not till November 23 that he advanced to the Roman camp at Ardoch, sending a few detachments under Gordon ahead to occupy the town. But soon intelligence reached him of the approach of the enemy who was said to have entered it. At first Mar, according to the rebel account of the battle,

judged it to be only some small party to disturb our march, ordered the guards to be posted, and the army to their quarters, with orders to assemble upon the parade any time of the night or day, upon the firing of three cannon. A little after the army was dismissed, the Earl of Mar had an account from Lieutenant-General Gordon, informing him that the Duke of Argyll was at Dunblane with his whole army; upon which, the General was ordered to hold till the Earl could come up to him, and ordered the three guns to be fired; when the army formed immediately, and marched up to Lieutenant-General Gordon, at Kinbuck [four miles from Dunblane], where the whole army lay under arms, with guards advanced from each squadron and battalion, till break of day.

The Royal troops received the news of the approach of the rebels with joy; "we that who are young soldiers", wrote Lord Rothes from Stirling on November 1/12, 1715, "think that tho' the rebells should venture to meet even the few regular troops we have they would not be able to stand it. . . ."[1] Another writer reported on November 11/22 when it was already known at Stirling that the rebels were approaching: ". . . our troops desire nothing more then a fair meetting with the rebells, but we are affraid they'll only act a cunning part, if E: Mar delay now doing something and return to Perth again, his men will desert very much".[2]

When on November 22 the Duke of Argyll heard about the approach of the enemy, he summoned a council of war, though there could hardly be any doubt what measures should be adopted. The Forth was beginning to freeze, and might soon offer no obstacle to

[1] Stirling, Nov. 1/12, 1715, S.P. 54, Bundle 10, No. 2.
[2] J. Cockburn, Stirling, Nov. 11/22, 1715, S.P. 54, Bundle 10, No. 41.

an enemy advance to the south. This had to be prevented, and a favourable battlefield had to be chosen which would allow the cavalry to deploy; for it was on his cavalry that Argyll relied to defeat the enemy, who outnumbered him in men nearly by three to one. Argyll now planned to fight a battle in the plain of Sheriffmuir, beyond Dunblane to the north-east. It was therefore resolved to advance towards it, but Argyll wished first to gather in all his available forces. He therefore ordered the small detachments, which were quartered in the neighbouring towns of Glasgow, Kilsyth, Falkirk, and Linlithgow—probably as protection against raids— to come up immediately to Stirling; but it was night before they had all assembled. The next morning the Duke started for Dunblane with an army of 3300 regulars and 150 volunteers. He found no enemy at Dunblane. But as it was his aim to reach the ground on the other side of the town, he drew up his troops in the exact order which he intended they should assume next day before the enemy, and then ordered them to lie down, each in his proper place upon the ground, with his arms ready beside him; and though the night was cold they spent it in the open. Thus the two armies camped that night within two miles of each other.

The Sheriffmuir is an uneven piece of ground but does not rise anywhere sufficiently to prevent the deploying of an army or a favourable use of cavalry. In the east it is bordered by the Ochil hills, in the west by the River Allan; near the hills the moor forms a peat marsh, as a rule almost impassable for infantry, and certainly for cavalry; but on the day of the battle it was frozen hard. No part of Sheriffmuir rises sufficiently high to offer a view of the entire plain.

Early in the morning of November 24 the two camps were astir.[1]

---

[1] Besides the usual sources, see for the battle of Sheriffmuir (1) *Hist. MSS. Comm. Rep. III. App.* p. 384 (and also p. 377); report of a volunteer who fought on the right wing of the Royal army. It appears that Montrose has made use of that report. (2) *Ibid.* p. 385. A report from the left wing of the Royal army— the only one extant for that part of the line. (3) *Ibid. Rep. VI. App.* p. 618; a short account.—Further in the Record Office: (4) Mar's letter to the Governor of Perth, Nov. 13/24, 1715; about the original of the document see *Hist. MSS. Comm. Rep. II. App.* p. 204. (5) *An Account of the engagement on the Sheriff-muir near Dumblaine the 13th Nov. 1715, betwixt the King's army commanded by the Earl of Mar and the Duke of Brunswick's commanded by Argyle,* printed at Perth by Robert Freebairn for the rebels; there is no copy of it in the British Museum, and only a manuscript copy in the Record Office; it is reproduced in James Hogg, *The Jacobite Relics of Scotland,* vol. ii. pp. 240-44. (6) *An Account of the Battle of Dunblain, in a letter from a gentleman at Stirling*

Lord Mar formed his troops in two lines; ten battalions of Highlanders, the flower of the rebel army, were in the centre of the first line; its right wing consisted of three regiments of horse, among them the Stirling squadron, which was composed entirely of gentlemen and bore the royal standard of James VIII; on the left were the Perthshire and Fifeshire squadrons. In the centre of the second line were again ten battalions of foot, commanded by their feudal chiefs, Lords Seaforth, Huntly, Kenmure, Tullibardine, Drummond, and others; on the right wing two squadrons under the Earl Marischal, and on the left the Angus squadron.

While the Army was forming [relates the rebel "Account"],[1] we discovered some small number of the enemy on the height to the westward of the Sheriffmuir . . . from which place they had a full view of our army. The Earl of Mar called a council of war, consisting of all the noblemen, gentlemen, general officers, and heads of the clans. . . .

Even at this council, at which Mar himself was for fighting, some

were heard to counsel a return to Perth, and a postponement of active warfare till next spring. But every negative voice was drowned in a general shout of "Fight, fight"; and, without waiting to make a regular resolution on the subject, the greater part galloped off to their different posts.[2]

Argyll's army was forming in the positions assigned to them the night before, with Dunblane on their left and the marshy eastern part of Sheriffmuir on their right, when intelligence was received that the rebels were drawing up along the River Allan, apparently with their front against the right flank of the Royal army. The Duke with his generals went up the hill to reconnoitre the enemy—this was the group seen by Mar. It was early morning and in the light of the

to his friend at Edinburgh (a pamphlet). (7) An Account of the engagement near Dunblain yesterday the 13th inst. betwixt the King's army under the command of H.Gr. the Duke of Argyll and the Rebels commanded by Mar (a pamphlet). (8) Argyll's reports to Townshend, especially that of Nov. 14/25, 1715, S.P. 54, Bundle 10. (9) Report from the Earl of Rothes, Stirling, Nov. 15/26, 1715, ibid.—In the Hanover Archives: (10) "Copy of a letter from Paris", Jan. 12, 1716. (11) A lengthy account in French starting with the words: "Vous avez vu, sans doute, mon cher Monsieur . . ."; judging by internal evidence it is by the Earl of Rothes.

[1] See previous footnote under No. 5.

[2] Chambers, p. 256. According to the rebel "Account"—"it was voted to fight the enemy nemine contradicente".

rising sun Argyll and his officers could easily distinguish, though at a distance of about two miles, the several bodies of the enemy army; and they had to admit that the rebels had drawn up their forces as well as any regular troops.

Lord Mar, having caught sight of the enemy on the height, decided to attack in that direction. Possibly he wished his Highlanders to bear down with all their weight against Argyll's right wing. Under normal conditions the moor would have offered sufficient protection against the attack, but this day it was frozen hard. Argyll realized the danger of the situation. He saw the dense masses advancing against his position, and as the right wing of the enemy was entirely concealed from his view by higher ground, he mistook them for the principal body of the clans, and thought that they intended to take his army in the flank. He consulted his general officers and, pointing out the movement of the enemy, asked them whether it would not be advisable to lead their own troops up the height where they could meet the rebels more directly in front.

They in general thought that it would be better to meet the insurgents on the high grounds, face to face; but most of them were of the opinion, that the troops could scarcely be brought forward, and formed anew, in time to receive them with perfect coolness. So completely, however, was he convinced of the propriety of advancing, that he determined to hazard this smaller danger.

Returning then at full gallop to the bivouack of his troops, he caused the drums to beat *the General*, which was a signal for them to start into fighting order.[1]

The Royal army was also formed in two lines. In the centre of the first were six battalions of infantry, all old troops, under General Wightman; on each wing three squadrons, on the right under the personal command of the Duke of Argyll, on the left under General Whitham. Behind the cavalry on the right was a body of volunteers under the Earl of Rothes. Argyll's second line consisted of only two battalions of foot with a squadron of dragoons on each wing. Lastly, another two squadrons were posted on the wings behind the cavalry of the first line.

It was almost twelve, an hour after the Duke's return to the camp, before his troops had begun to move. When they reached the top of the hill, the right wing alone, under Argyll's command, had time to re-form its lines. The centre and the left had lagged behind, and

[1] Chambers, *op. cit.* p. 255.

not come up to the positions assigned to them when the right was about to engage.

Meantime the rebels had reached the height in four columns. From an advance detachment Mar had received intelligence of the enemy approach, and therefore ordered his army to march very quickly. But while he advanced at the head of the right wing, "by the breaking of their lines in marching off, they fell into some confusion in the forming, and some of the second line jumbled into the first, on or near the left, and some of the horse formed near the centre".[1] It required some time to restore the previous formation.

In both armies the right wing, consisting of the best troops, and led by the Commander-in-Chief, had correctly carried out the advance and was ready for battle, while the left had fallen into confusion and required time to re-form. Another circumstance increased on either side the superiority of the right wing: the two armies had marched up the hill from opposite sides, north and south, without seeing each other, and their fronts did not tally, the right wings of either greatly out-flanking the enemy. Argyll had specially ordered the Greys to extend as far to the right as they could.

The rebels reached the height first, but let various detachments of Argyll's army march so close across their front that, as an eye-witness put it, partridges could have been shot at that distance. Argyll's cavalry meantime deployed for battle; otherwise neither army was as yet fully re-formed, when the rebels in the centre commenced action by firing a volley. Both wings followed the example and the second volley was even more effective than the first. Experienced officers allowed that they had never seen it surpassed by any regular troops. And when on the left wing the Highlanders attacked with their swords, the position became critical, although these were Argyll's best troops and he himself in command. Even Evans' squadron reeled a little; the horses, frightened by the firing, turned, causing confusion among the infantry. But Argyll quickly determined upon making a charge with his own cavalry and sent a squadron of dragoons circuitously across the frozen marsh, to strike in upon the flank of Mar's left wing, and at the same time Argyll's cavalry delivered a frontal attack against it. Not a shot was fired. The dragoons attacked both horse and foot with their swords. Evans' squadron valiantly returned to the battle, in which the famous Greys especially distinguished themselves. The rebels offered determined

---

[1] "Account of the engagement", Hogg, vol. ii. p. 242.

resistance. The cavaliers of the Perthshire and Angus squadrons fought bravely, and the fire of the rebel infantry, delivered at close quarters, worked havoc. But after an hour and a half of fighting the resistance of the rebels was broken. Their small country horses were unable to bear up against the weight of the English horses. The Royal cavalry broke into their ranks, the infantry followed; at first they retired disputing every inch of ground, but soon the retreat changed into a rout of the entire left wing. Many threw away their arms, and fled before their pursuers. Major Hay with his Grey Dragoons captured the rebel guns; a standard and many colours were taken. In some places the Highlanders held out with great bravery; forty of them gathered round a flag, refused to surrender though attacked by superior forces, and the flag was not taken till the last of them had been cut down. After three hours some 5000 rebels had been defeated by Argyll. The pursuit continued for three miles till beyond the River Allan. Many a man who had escaped the sword, perished in the river. Argyll, imagining to have won a complete victory, was intent on pursuing the enemy so long as the short November day would allow.

He acted like a dashing cavalry officer and not like a commander-in-chief—he failed to observe the development of the battle as a whole, and saw it only where he himself was engaged; when at last victorious in his part of the line, he would not desist so long as he saw an enemy in front. Warning voices were raised. Among the volunteers on the right wing, who followed the dragoons, it was asked what had happened to the left wing, about which nothing was known. It was suggested that the Duke should turn back with the infantry and part of his cavalry, for the remaining part would be sufficient to pursue the enemy, who was in complete flight. General Wightman, in command of the five battalions which followed Argyll, repeatedly reported to him that the left wing was in danger, which news was confirmed from other quarters. But Argyll still clung to the idea that he had defeated the entire rebel army. At last he had to listen to the others, and with the volunteers and a detachment of the Greys, he galloped back till he reached the hill from which he could survey the battlefield. Now he saw on the height, which had previously been occupied by the left wing of his army, a body of rebel troops forming for battle; nothing was to be seen of his own left wing.

Argyll immediately recalled his troops, horse and foot, from the pursuit of the enemy, and marched them back to the battlefield. He was at the head of five battalions and five squadrons; probably

N

his entire force amounted to something above 1500 men, while that of the rebels was estimated by him at 4000. Lord Rothes, the commander of the volunteers, thought that he should attack the rebels; their troops in that part consisted mainly of cavalry, which was inferior to their infantry. But Argyll's men were exhausted, the enemy was double their number, and held a more favourable position. No attack was delivered, and Argyll was able to give good reasons for this omission in his report to the Government. His chief concern was not to allow himself to be cut off from Dunblane, to which his left wing must have retired. He therefore slowly advanced against Dunblane, leaving the enemy on his left. He still hoped, having reunited with his left, to complete the victory the same day; but no news reached him, the rebels remained inactive, and Argyll finished by returning to the position which he had held in the morning. Night fell without a decision having been attained.

What had happened to the left wing of the Royal army? Here Mar had placed himself at the head of the clans, and when he found that the Royal troops were only forming their line, he decided to attack while they were at such disadvantage; he sent immediately to the chiefs of the various detachments ordering them to march up and attack. Then "pulling off his hat, he waved it with a huzza, and advanced to the front of the enemy's formed battalions". The Royal troops, not yet fully in position, were shaken by the furious attack of the massed clans, and even the effect of their murderous fire checked the advance but for a while. The rebels were incensed when they saw the chief of Clanranald fall. They threw themselves at the three regiments of Morrison, Orrery, and Clayton, which were unable to stand their ground. Colonel Ker and the other officers tried in vain to rally their men, but the horse falling back among the foot completed the confusion; "so that in seven or eight minutes", boasts the rebel *Account*, "we could neither perceive the form of a squadron or battalion of the enemy before us". In reality, the cavalry under General Whitham managed to cover the retreat, which was carried out in tolerably good order; even the cannon was saved. Only the men of the defeated regiments could not be stopped; in their flight many of them threw away their arms, and even their coats. Meantime they were told that the right wing under Argyll and the centre had been completely annihilated and that not one man had got away. When the defeated regiments reached Dunblane, Colonel Ker was for holding the bridge on the road to Stirling against the rebels. But Whitham, giving all over for lost, decided to regain the old position near Stirling. Thus the left wing were retiring, with no one in pursuit, when a gentleman sent by Argyll overtook them with the order to rejoin the Duke at Dunblane. The troops

gave three hurraes, which went thro' all our regiment, tho', at the same time, we scarce beliv'd it, abundance soldiers and officers having told us that the Duke was killed, and all the Grays except 6 that were taken. About half an hour after that, a gentleman came 2d express from the Duke, who gave the same account, and then all the horse and foot . . . returned.[1]

The same night at seven the Royal forces were reunited, but it was too late, and a further attack was impracticable.

The loss in dead and wounded was considerable on both sides, but it is hardly possible to give exact figures. Judging from the course of the battle, it seems likely that the rebel losses were double those of the Royal troops. Argyll seems to have underrated their losses when estimating them at 500 men; they are said to have amounted to 1200. The death-roll would have been even longer, had not Argyll ordered quarter to be given wherever it was asked, indeed even without its being asked. He felt it deeply when he saw his own countrymen massacred by the English during the pursuit. He himself parried three blows aimed by a dragoon at a Scottish gentleman who asked for mercy. The rebels were less humane and some of them cut down everybody, even those who wished to surrender. Lord Forfar, taken prisoner after having been wounded, was barbarously butchered and received eighteen wounds; he was sent back to Argyll's camp dying.

In the plain between Dunblane and the battlefield, Argyll made his troops spend the night once more in the open, hoping to complete the work the next day. But the same night the Duke learnt that the enemy had left the height, and by the next morning they had completely disappeared. During the night Mar had started his retreat towards Perth. Argyll now took possession of the battlefield, and the same day, retired to Stirling. The position at the front appeared to have reverted to what it had been for many weeks.

Both sides claimed a victory, and at the utmost admitted that it was incomplete. "Had our left and second line behaved as our right and the right of the first line did, our victory had been compleat", wrote Mar on November 24. Similarly Argyll asserted that had

[1] *Hist. MSS. Comm.* Rep. III. App. p. 385.

only the five squadrons and the three battalions of his left been
sufficiently near to join up with him, "the victory had been as
compleat as ever any was."[1] Undoubtedly Argyll had better ground
for speaking of a victory than Mar. The strategic success was with the
Royal forces. The rebels had failed to break through to the south;
no boasting reports could hide that fact and the Scots realized the
position. A contemporary song about Sheriffmuir starts as follows:

> There's some say that we wan, and some say that they wan,
> And some say that nane wan at a', man;
> But one thing I'm sure, that at Sherra'muir
> A battle there was, that I saw, man.
> And we ran, and they ran, and they ran, and we ran,
> But Florence ran fastest of a', man.[2]

And yet, indecisive as the battle of Sheriffmuir had been, it was a
heavy blow to the cause of the Pretender; for a half-success did not
hurt the purpose of the rising much less than a complete defeat would
have done, and after Sheriffmuir a real success was unthinkable.
"The Chevalier of St. George", wrote Stair, "becomes once more a
mere Pretender."[3] For now the Royal army could await the 6000
Dutch troops whose succour would enable them to defeat the Rebellion. "Had the Dutch troops been here," wrote Argyll on November 15/26, 1715, "there must have been an end of the affair, and I
most heartily wish for His Majesty's service they may arrive in time,
for indeed . . . we have not reason to expect that Providence will
work more miracles for our preservation."[4]

[1] S.P. 54, Bundle 10, No. 48.
[2] James Hogg, *The Jacobite Relics of Scotland* (1821), vol. ii. p. 1. According
to Hogg, "Florence" stands for the Marquis of Huntly's horse.
[3] Stowe MSS. 228, f. 184.
[4] S.P. 54, Bundle 10, No. 51.

CHAPTER VIII

FAILURE AND AFTERMATH

In January 1716, before reinforcements reached Argyll, James Edward landed in Scotland. A few months earlier his mere presence would have inspired his followers, now he came only to see with his own eyes that all was lost.

It had not been easy for him to find the means of effecting his crossing to Scotland. At the end of October 1715 he had left Lorraine for France, as his only chance of embarking seemed to be from a French port; for this the connivance at least of the Duke of Orleans was required. First he meant to go to St. Malo and see how Ormonde's attempt had succeeded; if the result was favourable, he meant to follow him to the West of England. When Stair learnt that James Edward had left Lorraine, he presented a memorial to the French Court[1] reminding them of Article IV of the Treaty of Utrecht which laid down that under no pretext was the Pretender to re-enter France. The Regent replied that, in principle, he was ready to make the Pretender return to Lorraine as soon as he learnt where he was, but could not be expected to raise a hue and cry for him as requested by Stair. Meantime James Edward was secretly given the hint that he could not sail from Normandy or Picardy, but that the rest of the coast was clear, and that he should try to get away before Stair got on his tracks; Marshal d'Huxelles agreed with Bolingbroke "how to banter Stair".[2]

At one time Stair thought he could name the day when the Pretender would arrive at Château-Thierry, and at his demand the Regent dispatched a reliable officer, Contades, to stop the Pretender and escort him back to Lorraine. When Contades reached the place

---

[1] Cf. Wiesener, i. 124. On November 5, the date of his Memorial, Stair wrote to Robethon that he did not believe James Edward to have left.

[2] Bolingbroke to the Chevalier, Nov. 8, 1715; Thornton, p. 410.

(proceeding, it is said, by a round-about way[1]) the Pretender was gone, from which it was again deduced in England that Orleans secretly favoured him.[2] At Nonancourt, a small place west of Paris, a few individuals were arrested on suspicion of plotting against the Prince on his journey; these were Stair's agents, and even at the Regent's Court it was openly alleged that the British Ambassador was scheming the murder of the Pretender. In reality neither Stair nor George I could be guilty of such knavery. "Of all the Princes in Europe, I serve the one least capable of giving such an order", wrote Stair to Robethon on November 28, 1715;[3] and one of these men, Colonel Douglas, wrote to Stanhope indignantly denying the accusation.[4] Stair thought that the sole purpose of these allegations was to justify the illegal measures taken against him—for how could the French otherwise have excused the arrest of his servants and the opening of his letters?[5]

A policy of extreme restraint was now practised by the British Government towards France so as not to supply a handle to the Regent for the break which seemed imminent. It was a sound idea to fight the ill-will of France by a quick defeat of the Scottish Rising; for this in itself would make the Regent hold a different language. Meantime Stair was not altogether to avoid the Court, but to appear seldom in it, and in general to remain aloof, even if the French attempted a *rapprochement*.[6] About the New Year Stair was refused the entry to the Louvre, but he made no formal complaint about it.[7] Further negotiations were clearly impossible; discussions concerning Mardyke were adjourned *sine die*, and the British Commissioner charged with them was recalled from France.[8]

Meantime the Pretender, in spite of all difficulties, had reached St. Malo. At first it was uncertain where he was to go, and, as that question depended on the changing circumstances in Great Britain, the views of his advisers varied accordingly. Immediately after the death of Louis XIV, Bolingbroke had thought that the Chevalier's

[1] *Mémoires de Berwick*, p. 251.
[2] Bonet to Hoffmann, Nov. 8/19, 1715.
[3] Stowe MSS. 228, f. 182.
[4] Dec. 14, 1715.
[5] Stair to Robethon, Nov. 28 and 30, 1715; Stowe MSS. 228, ff. 182 and 184.
[6] Stanhope to Stair, Nov. 26 and Dec. 15, 1715, O.S., F.O. 90/14.
[7] Same to same, n.d., probably Dec. 26/Jan. 6, 1716, *ibid.*
[8] Stanhope to Sir J. Abercrombie, Jan. 19/30, 1716, *ibid.*

landing "must be in Scotland".[1] "He must get ready to come to some
parte of the Island as soon as possible", even though the views to
French help were distant "as well as those of money from Spain and
troops from Sweden"; and whereas English Jacobites were intimidated, Scotland was ready to rise.

But while Bolingbroke had so far been under the influence of the
Scots, who ardently wished for James Edward's arrival, he came to
see the matter in a different light as soon as Ormonde prepared to
embark for England. He knew the situation too well not to see that
everything depended upon England; he now thought that if Ormonde
was "able to make a head", the Chevalier should "pass immediately
over to such place as the advices from those parts shall direct":

at worst, it is better to make a bold experiment so near to your retreat
as the west of England, than to abandon yourself to the Highlands of
Scotland . . . for these two propositions seem to me to be self-evident
—that England will not rise upon your marching into the north from
Scotland, if she will not rise upon your coming . . . into the west; and
. . . that the utmost efforts of Scotland, if England cannot or will not
rise, must end in a composition.[2]

However just, these considerations became irrelevant as soon
as the miserable failure of Ormonde's attempt was known; the
Chevalier could no longer think of landing in England, where he
would have been seized immediately, and had to risk an expedition
to Scotland, even if nothing more than a short-lived success could be
expected. Bolingbroke subsequently confessed that "no prospect of
success could engage him [James Edward] in this expedition: but it
was become necessary for his reputation".[3]

At Stair's advice ships were sent to cruise along the northern
coast of France to look out carefully for any suspicious vessel sailing
from a French port. When Ormonde, after his second expedition, had
been forced against the French coast, Stair reported to London that
the Duke would probably sail next from Morlaix, possibly taking the
Pretender with him. Immediately a few ships were dispatched to
cruise off Morlaix. The captain was ordered[4] "to look out for the
aforesaid ships and upon their coming out to follow them and

---

[1] "Memorandum sent to England by Lord Bolingbroke", Sept. 3, 1715;
Thornton, pp. 384-5.
[2] Bolingbroke to the Chevalier, Nov. 8, 1715; Mahon, i. App.
[3] *Letter to Sir William Windham*, p. 193.
[4] Admiralty Records, Adm. 2/48, p. 457 (Orders and Instructions).

intercept them, or to sink or destroy them in case they make resist-
ance . . . and to secure and bring to England such persons as he shall
find on board those ships". Also further east between Cherbourg and
Havre, and Dieppe and Calais, British ships kept constant watch.
How could it have been possible in these circumstances for the
Pretender safely to cross the Channel and reach the east coast of
Scotland? Once more he had to travel across France, and in disguise
he successfully evaded the spies of Lord Stair. He sailed from
Dunkirk.

The English and the French alike were glad to hear that the
Pretender had embarked. "The best news which I can report to you
from here", wrote Stair on November 28, "is that, unless the wind
changes, you will have the Pretender in a few days in Scotland." The
news was premature, but the attitude remained the same when
James Edward did actually embark. The French, according to
Bolingbroke, "were extremely eager to have him gone".

Some of those who knew little of British affairs imagined, that his
presence would produce miraculous effects. . . . As near neighbours as
we are, ninety-nine in an hundred among the French are as little acquainted with the inside of our island as with that of Japan. Others of
them were uneasy to see him skulking about in France, and to be told
of it every hour by the Earl of Stair. Others again imagined, that he
might do their business by going into Scotland, though he should not do
his own: that is, they flattered themselves that he might keep a war for
some time alive, which would employ the whole attention of our Government; and for the event of which they had very little concern.[1]

At the first attempt, in 1707, James Edward was conveyed by the
French fleet to his Scottish kingdom; now he had to elude his pursuers
by innumerable deceits. He reached Scotland in a single ship,
attended by half a dozen persons. This, however, was his best chance
to reach the coast unperceived. Even so the danger was considerable,
and after having crossed the North Sea he had once more to escape
the vigilance of British warships which were patrolling the Scottish
coast. About the height of Montrose he exchanged the first signals
with his friends on the coast; but the presence of a British man-of-
war caused his ship to stand off to sea and steer northward; it was in
the small harbour of Peterhead that on January 2, 1716, James
Edward set foot in Scotland.

[1] *Letter to Sir William Windham*, pp. 194-5.

He immediately sent one of his companions back to France in the same ship with the news of his arrival. He wrote to Bolingbroke:

I am at last, thank God, in my own ancient Kingdom. . . . Send the Queen the news . . . and give a line to the Regent. . . . I find things in a prosperous way; I hope all will go well, if friends on your side do their part as I shall have done mine.[1]

The next day he proceeded to join the army at Perth, preserving his disguise till he met Lord Mar, who had come to meet him and at the head of a small body did homage to his King. Everywhere he was received with enthusiasm. A Declaration was distributed, dated Commercy, October 25, 1715, in which James VIII, by the Grace of God King of Scotland, England, France, and Ireland, addressed his loving subjects. He beheld a foreign family, aliens to the country, ascend the Throne; in the midst of peace Great Britain feels all the load of a war. "Dutch forces are brought into these Kingdoms and by taking possession of the Dutchy of Bremen, a door is opened by the Usurper, to let in an inundation of foreigners from abroad, and to reduce these nations to the state of a province to one of the most inconsiderable provinces of the Empire." Now he, the rightful King, has come to preserve his subjects from those dangers and to relieve Scotland from "the hardships of the late unhappy Union, and to restore the Kingdom to its ancient free and independent state".[2]

In January 6/17, 1716, the Chevalier made a state entry into Dundee, with Mar on his right. People crowded the streets to see their King. He was civil and greeted everybody. But it was felt that he had not the Stuart gift of winning hearts by a friendly word or a smile. Adversity had made him serious. The Scottish women especially were disappointed;[3] they had imagined him lively and impetuous, and found him thin, pale, grave, and composed. No one felt attracted by him, and his cause did not gain much by his presence.

Comparisons were drawn between the Pretender and his father; but James II, in spite of his religious fanaticism, was a much better politician than his son. James Edward moved within a narrow compass of ideas. He would not forget for a moment the connexion between his hereditary rights and the interests of the Roman Church,

---

[1] James Edward to Bolingbroke, Peterhead, Dec. 22, 1715/Jan. 2, 1716; Mahon, i. App.

[2] The Declaration is reproduced in Tayler, *The Old Chevalier*, App. II, where it is misdated October 15, 1714.

[3] Mahon, i. App.

and started his short quasi-reign by favouring the Roman Catholics in a very marked degree; places and honours were bestowed on them. He refrained from attending Protestant Church service, and entertained a dislike of strong Protestants even when enlisted in his cause. Characteristic of his views is a letter which he wrote to the Pope a week after having landed in Scotland; he supplicates the Pope to help a devoted and obedient son, and "to save a suffering Church, whose weal is inseparably connected with mine, and which is almost irretrievably lost if I fail in this undertaking".

At the time of James Edward's landing the military position in Scotland was inauspicious. On January 8/19, 1716, he arrived at Scone, the spot where the ancient Kings of Scotland were enthroned and crowned. He too desired to be crowned there, and the date was fixed for January 23/February 3. There was colossal presumption in his simply ignoring the Union established in the reign of his sister. Meantime he fixed his residence at Scone, some two miles from Perth. He felt concerned and surprised when he learnt the size of his army—there were only 4000 men left with Mar. Another encounter with the Royal forces was bound to result in a complete defeat of the Jacobites. The troops themselves were dispirited—

if he was disappointed in us [wrote a "Rebel" in 1716], we were tenfold more so in him; we saw nothing in him that look'd like spirit; he never appeared with chearfulness and vigour to animate us: our men began to despise him; some ask'd if he could speak. . . . He car'd not to come abroad among us soldiers, or to see us handle our arms or do our exercise. . . . I am sure . . . had he sent us but 5000 men of good troops and never come among us, we had done other things than we have now done.[1]

No improvement in the situation was to be expected for the present. The declarations of the Pretender had little effect and his authority carried little weight. The order summoning all fencible men from sixteen to sixty to his banner was defeated by the clan organization. And yet James Edward realized that all was lost if he could not at least stay out the winter at Perth. But was this possible without reinforcements? France refused active support, nor did the Swedish help, on which he had reckoned, materialize. About the time of Sheriffmuir, Inverness had been captured by the Royal forces, whereupon Lords Seaforth and Huntly separated from the rebels at Perth, and returned home to defend their estates against the Earl of Sutherland, who was

[1] *True Account of the Proceedings at Perth,* written by a Rebel (1716), pp. 20-21.

appointed by the King to command in the north of Scotland. Asked by James Edward to return, they claimed not to be able to do so as yet; in reality they were about to make their submission to the Government. Others pleaded that the roads had been rendered impassable by heavy snow. In the first enthusiasm after the Pretender's landing, some Jacobite ladies had offered their jewels for a crown for James VIII. Soon no one talked any more about his coronation.[1]

Even with James Stuart at the head, the Scottish Rising could not hold out much longer after Argyll had been reinforced by 6000 men from Holland, including some Swiss troops. General Cadogan, Marlborough's favourite, who had lately been engaged in the Barrier negotiations, was ordered to embark the troops for England. The ships, however, were so bad that the men refused to proceed in them to Scotland. A few detachments, which had landed at Yarmouth, were immediately re-embarked in better ships; the rest had to travel on foot from Harwich to Scotland, which was a hardship, for the journey was reckoned at twenty-six days, and this was very nearly the worst time of the year.[2]

Cadogan was in command of the Dutch troops, though Argyll was Commander-in-Chief of all the forces. Old jealousies at Court and in the Army were continued in the field, with prejudice to the conduct of the war. There was constant friction between the two commanders, but fortunately the success of the campaign could no longer be jeopardized. The severe weather, not the rebel army, delayed the advance of the Royal troops; 2000 men were employed to clear the road from Stirling to Perth of snow. The ships with the heavy cannon for the army were long detained in the Thames by ice. None the less, Cadogan managed to persuade Argyll that the attack should not be delayed any longer. As a diplomat he weighed the dangers of the international situation; preparations to help the Scottish Rising were reported from France; it was said that if the Pretender could only hold out in Scotland till the spring, the Regent would openly succour him with arms and men, as presumably by that time Charles VI would be involved in a war with Turkey. And then, wrote Hoffmann, much disturbed, to the Emperor, France would be able "to play the master in Europe".

On February 9, 1716, Argyll and Cadogan set their army in motion.

[1] Cf. Bonet, Jan. 31/Feb. 11, 1716.
[2] Hoffmann's dispatches of Dec. 3 and 6, 1715.

The rebel forces, wearied with long waiting, rejoiced, and were loud and clamorous for battle. But their leaders thought that they were not in a position to meet the enemy in a general engagement, while a siege of Perth by the superior Royal forces might have resulted in another Preston. A retreat into the Highlands was therefore resolved upon. The men were bitter and indignant when they heard the decision. This was January 30 (O.S.), the day of Charles I's execution, *dies infaustus* in the history of the House of Stuart. Early next morning the rebels left Perth.

A few miles behind followed the Royal army, hampered by the discord between its two commanders. Argyll had previously expressed his intention to resign the supreme command but was now inclined to remain in order not to leave the credit of having extinguished the rising to a creature of Marlborough's. In letters to Marlborough, written in French so that the King should be able to read them, Cadogan complained of Argyll, saying that it was "almost impossible to live with him any longer". Now when it was merely a question of finishing off the rebellion, the Argyllshire men, who previously had not ventured to leave their country, were joining—they "go before the army a day's march, to take possession of the towns the enemy had abandoned, and to plunder and destroy the country, which enrages our soldiers, who are forbid, under pain of death, to take the value of a farthing, though out of rebels' houses. . . ." [1] The bickerings between the two generals continued, till at last Argyll was recalled, and the sole command transferred to Cadogan.

Meantime the sham reign of James Stuart had reached its term. The common soldiers in his army were told that he would proceed with them by way of Aberdeen into the Highlands. Should the enemy follow them into the hills, the horse being there useless, they were sure of victory. But the men became suspicious; instead of turning to the hills, they were marched along the coast; and when they reached Montrose and saw a few French ships at anchor near by, they feared that James Edward meant to sail and leave them to their fate—they declared excitedly that he, for whom they had fought, should not separate his fate from theirs. Their fears were well founded, for it had been decided in the council of the Pretender that he should re-embark. To put the soldiers out of doubt, his baggage was sent forward with the main body of the army, and his bodyguard was ordered to parade in front of his house as if he were about to

[1] Cadogan to Marlborough, Feb. 4, 1716; Coxe, *Marlborough*, iii. p. 612.

start. Meanwhile James Edward slipped out by a back door and proceeded to Lord Mar's house. They pushed from shore in a private boat and boarded the French ship; here they waited above an hour and a half for two of the other leaders; but as these did not come, they weighed anchor.[1] The Prince was assured by his advisers that his presence, far from being a help and support to the rebels, would rather be an occasion of hastening their ruin. He left behind him a commission appointing General Gordon commander-in-chief, and a letter to the troops explaining his action:

Your safety and wellfare was I may say with truth my only view. . . . I resolved not to lett your courage and zeal carry you so far as to serve for your own intire ruine at last without doing any good to mee or your-selves; and whereas I considered that there were no hopes att present of retriving our affairs the whole business was to securing your lives in such a manner as to be yet again in condition in appearing in a more favourable occasion. And as I look'd on my remaining amongst you not only as useless but as even distructive to you . . . I took the party to repass the seas.[2]

A sad scene, that desertion of men who had sacrificed their all in the cause of the Pretender. And yet it was true that his presence would have merely brought further disaster upon them. Now they had nothing more to care for than their own safety, and it was a small band which Cadogan pursued into the Highlands. Ruthless suppression was now the programme, and there was no longer any thought of treating with the rebels, as Argyll had intended after Sheriffmuir. The leaders tried to escape abroad, the men gradually dispersed, and there was no further serious engagement. A number of gentlemen took refuge in the Isles of Skye and Uist, but could not stay there long. By April 1716 the whole of Scotland once more recognized George I as its King.

The root of the trouble was in the clan system; five or six powerful chiefs had been able to raise an army of determined men who, at least in their hills, were a match for a regular army. Forts did not offer sufficient security, and the idea of abolishing the clan system was contemplated. Then alone would the Government enter into direct touch with the people in the Highlands, which now was even

[1] Mar to H. Straton, Feb. 10, 1716; Thornton, p. 422; and *Hist. MSS. Comm. Stuart Papers*, vol. i. pp. 508-9.

[2] MSS. of C. S. H. Drummond Moray, of Blair Drummond; *Hist. MSS. Comm.* Rep. X, App. I, pp. 157-8.

more difficult, since the government was carried on, not from Edinburgh, but from London. It is not clear why nothing was done in that direction after 1715; possibly the Government were afraid of antagonizing the chiefs of the clans. The Duke of Argyll, whose influence was still considerable, was certainly opposed to such a measure; and the Earl of Stair, so prominent in the history of those years, was likewise a keen Scotsman. In December 1715 he wished for a reassurance that the English did not contemplate a conquest, and that the hardships of the Union would be mitigated. The clan system survived till after the next Stuart attempt at a restoration.

As soon as the British Government had reason to believe that the Pretender would seek safety overseas, warships were sent to intercept him.[1] But his ship was a fast sailer, and although pursued by one of the men-of-war, easily made its escape.[2] On February 21, James Edward landed near Gravelines;[3] and Bolingbroke wrote to him when hearing of his arrival: "You are well, and the cause cannot dye, but will in God's good time revive again".[4]

While the Pretender was in Scotland, Bolingbroke had done his utmost to obtain effective help from the French Court. "The Regent", the Pretender wrote to him, ". . . can alone, but that with ease, sway the balance on our side, and make our game sure." [5] But all Bolingbroke's endeavours, his manœuvres and intrigues, were of no avail; with the Duke of Orleans regard for George I was now the dominant consideration. In an interview with Marshal d'Huxelles, Bolingbroke found that nothing was left but to "send them vessels, which with those already on the coast of Scotland might serve to bring off the Pretender, the Earl of Mar, and as many others as possible"; [6] when

---

[1] See Admiralty Records.   [2] Hoffmann, Feb. 25, 1716.

[3] The date of his landing appears from Mar's letter of Feb. 10/21, 1716, Thornton, p. 421. As for the place, it was supposed in England at that time to have been near Gravelines; thus it is stated in the King's speech of Feb. 17/28, and in all history books; cf. *Mémoires du règne de George I* (The Hague, ii. p. 206). The information is probably derived from a dispatch from Stair which has not been preserved. Similarly Bolingbroke's *Letter to William Windham* names Gravelines as the place of landing. I cannot therefore agree with Thornton that the Chevalier landed at Boulogne. If the letter published by him on p. 429 is at all from James Edward—which, judging by the contents, seems doubtful— it may have been written by him at Boulogne on his way from Calais to Abbeville and Paris.

[4] Bolingbroke to James Edward, March 3, 1716; Thornton, p. 430.

[5] Jan. 2, 1716; Mahon, i. App.

[6] *Letter to Sir William Windham*, p. 205.

shortly afterwards Bolingbroke informed d'Huxelles of the Pretender's return,

the first thing which the M. d'Huxelles said to me upon it was, that the Chevalier ought to proceed to Bar with all the diligence possible, and to take possession of his former asylum, before the Duke of Lorrain had time to desire him to look out for a residence some where else. . . .[1]

Bolingbroke shared the view; because of the impression which this would produce in Protestant England, nothing could be more disadvantageous to the Chevalier "than to be obliged to pass the Alps, or to reside in the Papal territory of Avignon".

Bolingbroke put these considerations to the Pretender on his arrival at St. Germain; but possibly his pious mother influenced him in favour of seeking a retreat in the Papal territories. Anyhow, according to Bolingbroke, he was in "no disposition to make such haste: he had the mind, on the contrary, to stay some time at St. Germain's . . . and to have a private meeting with the Regent". But the Regent "rose up in a passion" and "said that the things which were asked were puerilities, and swore that he would not see him".[2]

The Chevalier now declared that he would instantly set out for Lorraine, and asked Bolingbroke how soon he would be able to follow him. In reality the Pretender was deceiving his Minister:

Instead of taking post for Lorrain, he went to the little house in the Bois de Boulogne, where his female ministers resided; and there he continued lurking for several days, and pleasing himself with the air of mystery and business. . . . He saw the Spanish and Swedish Ministers in this place.[3]

A few days later, Ormonde suddenly came to see Bolingbroke and put into his hand a note to himself and a little scrip of paper directed to Bolingbroke, both in the Chevalier's handwriting. One of these papers, in a "kingly laconic style", declared that the Chevalier had no further occasion for Bolingbroke's services, the other was an order to him to give up the papers of his office. The late Minister of the Queen could only smile at these imitation orders from the sham King. Once more he was dismissed, as before by George I, with all signs of distrust; and this was the end of his schemes to regain through the Stuarts the power which was withheld from him by the Hanoverians.

What were the reasons of his fall? He was accused of treason against the Stuart cause. It was said that the Pretender was incensed

[1] *Ibid.* p. 210.   [2] *Ibid.* pp. 214-5.
[3] *Ibid.* pp. 212-3.

by some abusive expressions which Bolingbroke, in a state of intoxication, had uttered against him.[1] Much more serious was the charge of his having communicated the Jacobite schemes to Lord Stair; but Stair himself ridiculed this accusation.[2] Shortly after Bolingbroke's fall, several articles were drafted to prove his treason.[3] It was said that when informed from Scotland that they were "in the utmost distress for want of amunition and arms", though "the things demanded were in my Lord's power, not so much as one pound of powder was sent". A messenger dispatched by the Chevalier was "amused" by him "twelve days together", and was not introduced by him to any of the French Ministers. Arms and ammunition, which had been stopped at Havre, were put at his disposal, but were not shipped by him to Scotland; even merchants, who were prepared privately to undertake such transports, were discouraged by him. "The King's friends at the French Court had for some time past had no opinion of his Lordship's integrity and a very bad one of his discretion." The chief blame for the failure of the Scottish Rising was ascribed to him.[4]

Bolingbroke had little difficulty in refuting these charges.[5] He had done all he could in support of the rising, and with some success. If the Pretender had stayed in Scotland a few days longer, he would have received a considerable transport of arms, powder, and other stores. A year later Bolingbroke wrote his famous *Letter to Sir William Windham* with a view to justifying himself, first in the opinion of the Tories, and next of mankind. He could rightly assert that the Chevalier and Mar now tried to fasten on him the blame for their precipitate flight from Scotland. The Duke of Berwick, who was in the know of what happened at the Court of the Regent, testifies in his *Mémoires* that Bolingbroke moved Heaven and earth to procure help for his King. The jealousy of the other advisers of the Pretender, foremost of Mar and Ormonde, contributed to Bolingbroke's undeserved disgrace.

[1] Cf. Coxe, *Walpole*, i. p. 200.
[2] *Ibid.* ii. pp. 607-8. Further see Stair to Robethon, March 14, 1716: "Ils disent ouvertement que Bolingbroke les a trahis et qu'il m'a donné avis de tous leurs projets et entre autre du dernier, dont ils sont très fâchés. Ils ne veulent pas croire tout ce que je peux dire pour justifier Bolingbroke, ils prennent tout cela pour raillerie, je ne saurais que faire" (Stowe MSS. 228, f. 240).
[3] See *Hist. MSS. Comm.* Rep. X, App. I, pp. 181-2.
[4] See also *Hist. MSS. Comm.* Rep. IV, App. p. 526.
[5] See his letters in *Hist. MSS. Comm.* Rep. X, App. I, pp. 182-3.

But the main reasons for his dismissal flowed from another source. The charges emanated from that Court of St. Germain whose confidence Bolingbroke had never possessed. He was fully aware of his opponents having long been at work to remove him, and he knew who they were: the intimate circle of Queen Maria, "a whole tribe of Jesuits", and a few intriguing women who could not forgive him that he no longer paid any attention to them. His own outlook was diametrically opposed to theirs: for them the cause of the Stuart Pretender was identical with that of the Roman Church, while Bolingbroke was resolved from the first "to serve upon a Protestant and English bottom or not to serve att all".[1] He was against the House of Hanover; he was not an enemy of his nation. When faced by the proselytizing Catholicism of the Stuarts, Bolingbroke, though their supporter, proved himself a representative of the English nation. Whatever his ambitions, on that fundamental point he adhered to principles. He succumbed, he disappeared from the European scene, he changed into a mere political refugee. Yet at that very moment he was infinitely superior to the opponents who had brought about his disgrace. Much of his past is expiated by his fall.

James Edward light-heartedly discarded his best adviser—gratitude was never one of his virtues, and he speedily forgot services rendered to him. On the other hand, he was easily reconciled to those whom he needed. He had reviled Berwick; but afterwards had wished him in Scotland as from his leadership alone the Highlanders expected victory. He disparaged Ormonde after his unsuccessful expedition: now Ormonde stood once more high in his favour.

Bolingbroke's sudden dismissal was both ignoble and unwise. Mar, his successor, could not replace him. Even Queen Maria deplored his removal. "It would be insane", says Berwick, "not to recognize the serious blunder committed by King James when he dismissed the only Englishman fit to conduct his affairs. For whatever some may say who judge with more passion than understanding, the whole of England admits that Bolingbroke is one of the greatest statesmen that ever lived."

As the prospects of the Pretender sank, relations between Great Britain and France gradually improved, and so did Lord Stair's position at the French Court.[2] Still, the French continued to turn a blind

[1] Letter from Bolingbroke, April 8, 1715, *Hist. MSS. Comm.* Rep. X, App. I, p. 183; see also concluding part of his *Letter to Sir William Windham.*
[2] For the following see Stair's letters to Robethon, Stowe MSS. 228.

eye to what was done in France in favour of the Pretender. Arms, supplies, and even men were embarked without hindrance for the service of James Edward; though now the Regent, for his own part, refused to know anything about these matters. As early as January 7, 1716, Stair reported that he had called the Pretender a fool and all the Jacobites madmen. A fortnight later the Regent said that he would have nothing more to do with these affairs, and spoke to the British Ambassador with more freedom than he had done for a long time past; but he did not disguise from him the fact that the sympathies of the French nation were with the Pretender.[1] To please England he ordered the release of all the Protestants kept in the galleys, and thereby redeemed a promise given by Louis XIV to Queen Anne but of which it had hitherto proved impossible to obtain the performance; "that was the point in the world", Torcy had once said to Stair, "that the King was the most delicate upon".[2] The relations between the two Powers seemed to become more friendly than they had been since the war. "I assure you", wrote Stair to Robethon, "a great change has occurred here."

Thus a chance offered that Stair's persistent complaints would at last receive attention. He presented a Note dated January 31, 1716, in which he complained that, despite all promises, munitions and men were daily embarked in French ports for the service of the Pretender, and that Ormonde and James Edward themselves had been allowed freely to leave France. No written answer seems to have been given to him, and he thought that the situation in France was as yet doubtful; the Regent regretted his mistakes but a change was not easy and he had to do his utmost whenever the least chance of success appeared for the cause of the Pretender. Stair therefore advised to concentrate on crushing the rebellion.[3]

The British Court was dissatisfied with the Duke of Orleans. Stanhope instructed Stair to present a further Note—which was done on March 9—and recall once more the obligations under the Treaty of Utrecht. The Pretender was to be removed from France, and the Duke of Lorraine was not to be suffered to plead again the neighbourhood of France as his excuse if he chose once more to offer a refuge to the Pretender. The Regent, having read the Note, gave Stair all the assurances he desired.[4] The written reply, which this

---

[1] Stanhope to Stair, Jan. 23/Feb. 3, 1716.
[2] Stair to Stanhope, March 2, 1715, S.P. 78/170.
[3] Stowe MSS. 228, f. 230. [4] Hardwicke, *State Papers*, ii. p. 552.

time was explicitly demanded, contained similar assurances of a good disposition towards England; only no undue interference in Lorraine should be required from France. Still, the reply was such that the Court of St. James's could acquiesce in it. The only remarkable circumstance was that it was not, in accordance with diplomatic custom, given to Lord Stair in Paris, but was presented through d'Iberville in London. It was obviously intended to slight Stair, perhaps to obtain his recall. But Stanhope asked him not to mind it and declared that the Government were fully satisfied with him; and as the Regent, too, assured Stair of his personal favour,[1] his position remained unchanged.

The increased prestige of George I did not fail to make an impression on the Duke of Lorraine, who, deprived of French backing, no longer ventured to refuse the British demands. When, after dallying some time at St. Germain, the Pretender at last returned to Lorraine, the Duke himself called on him at Commercy, and explained to him the reasons why he could no longer harbour him in his country. George I thanked the Duke in courteous terms for having conceded his request.[2] Nothing was left to James Stuart but to turn to Avignon. "In the States of Your Holiness alone", he wrote to the Pope, "can I still find a peaceful and secure refuge." [3] He could not even await the Pope's explicit consent; his first letter to the Pope from Avignon, in which he asks for his blessing, is dated April 4. The Pope left him a free choice of residence within the Papal States. James Edward remained at Avignon.

But even here British inveteracy did not suffer his presence for long. Stair presented a Memorial to the French Court which concluded with the remark that Great Britain could not rest so long as the Pretender remained at Avignon or any other place on this side of the Alps. Negotiations on this point became connected with the question of the future international configuration of Europe. On March 25 Stair related in a private letter to Robethon that the French desired an alliance with England;[4] the two Great Powers were about to bury their old enmity and to form a friendship.

During the Scottish Rebellion the Government were careful to keep up the spirits of the people. When in November 1715 the Barrier

---

[1] Wiesener, pp. 181-4.

[2] George I to Duke Leopold, March 19/30, 1716, R.O.

[3] The letters from the Chevalier to the Pope are among the Gualterio Papers, Add. MSS. 20292.   [4] Stowe MSS. 228, f. 243.

Treaty between the Emperor and the States General was concluded through English mediation, the Government were pleased to have it known that the two Powers had combined in defence of the Protestant Succession.[1] News from the fighting zone was sent to the Court, and the public heard only as much as the Ministers thought expedient. The London public learnt of the Pretender's arrival in Scotland only eight days after the news had reached the Government, and after they had taken their measures.[2]

The King had reason to be satisfied with the attitude of the public. The disturbances of the previous summer were not repeated, and in November 1715 associations were formed all over England, pledged, in case of need, to take up arms for King George; the well-affected hastened to sign, and even many who at heart were for the Pretender felt obliged to profess adherence to the Government.[3] In London the population took every opportunity to make a show of its loyalty. When the news arrived "that the rebels had abandoned Perth and the King's forces taken possession of it", the public demonstrated at the Playhouse—"there was not a word that was loyal but what met with the greatest acclamations".[4]

The division between Church and Chapel had all along played its part in the popular commotions. George I was considered the natural protector of the Dissenters though, so far, he had done nothing for them. In many places, such as Oxford, the mob attacked their meeting-houses and tried to pull them down. For their own safety, the Dissenters became active champions of the House of Hanover; in some places they took to arms, and in Lancashire a minister "rallied together four hundred Dissenters, armed and equipped at his own expense, and took them to join the standard at Preston".[5] None the less nothing was done for the Dissenters after the Rebellion had been crushed—the Test Acts, the Occasional Conformity Act, and the Schism Act remained on the Statute Book—the last, it is true, only a few more years.

Even more important for the Government than the support of the Dissenters was the fact that during the Rebellion the Church of England ranged itself on their side. In November 1715[6] the Arch-

---

[1] Hoffmann, Nov. 26, 1715.   [2] Bonet, Jan. 10/21, 1716.
[3] Hoffmann, Nov. 26, 1715.   [4] *Diary of Lady Cowper*, p. 69.
[5] See Skeats and Miall, *History of the Free Churches of England, 1688–1891*, p. 224.
[6] *A Declaration of the Archbishop of Canterbury and the Bishops in and near London, testifying their abhorrence of the present Rebellion.*

bishop of Canterbury and thirteen Bishops, probably induced by
the Government, published a Declaration to testify their abhorrence
of the rebellion and to exhort "the clergy and people under their
care, to be zealous in the discharge of their duties to his Majesty
King George". The Bishop of Bristol, who refused to sign, was immediately removed from his see.

We are not surprised [reads the Declaration] that Papists should . . .
endeavour to set a person upon the throne, who will establish their
religion, and ruin ours . . . but that profess'd members of the Church of
England should joyn with them in this . . . is so vile and detestable a
thing, as may justly make them odious both to God and man. . . .

And is this a time to stand neuters when all lies at stake? Or is popery
become so innocent of late, that it is indifferent whether a Popish or a
Protestant Prince be on the throne? This we speak to those who have
owned the King's title, and have sworn to maintain it, and are ready to
do it again, as occasion offers . . . we will be active for him according to
our several stations . . . they who are call'd to be soldiers by fighting
couragiously for him; they who are magistrates, by using their authority
for his support; they who are ministers, by their prayers, by their
preaching, and by their admonishing those under their care, of their duty
to him. . . .

In Ireland the newly summoned Parliament seemed to compete in
zeal and loyalty with that of Great Britain. When a rumour arose
that the Pretender thought of coming to Ireland, a prize of £50,000
was promised to anyone who would seize him on his landing. The
King was invited by Parliament, as in England, to raise as many
troops as he thought necessary. Ireland had changed since the Battle
of the Boyne; the Protestants dominated Parliament and the country.
A proclamation of the opposition calling on all Irishmen to rise in
favour of the natural and legitimate sovereign against the atheistic
and tyrannical German usurper, received no response. James Edward
would have been no more welcome in Ireland than in England.

At the opening of Parliament on January 9/20, 1716, the King's
Speech claimed that Divine Providence had blessed the measures
taken against the rebels "with a series of suitable successes", though
"our enemies, animated by some secret hopes of assistance, are still
endeavouring to support this desperate undertaking", apparently
headed by the Pretender.[1] It was clear that French assistance was
meant, though France was not named, to avoid the imputation of
wishing for a new war. The Ministers had delayed the reopening of

[1] *Parl. Hist.* vii. 224.

Parliament, hoping to be able to announce the conclusion of a Triple Alliance with Austria and Holland; what was now said in the Speech about foreign relations was more modest but favourable:

The Treaty for . . . the Barrier . . . is now fully concluded between the Emperor and the States General, under my guaranty. The King of Spain has agreed to a Treaty, by which that valuable branch of our commerce will be delivered from the new impositions and hardships . . . and the Treaty for renewing all former alliances between the Crown of Great Britain and the States General is brought very near to its conclusion.

In reply the Court easily obtained the desired Addresses from the two Houses; the Commons readily promising "to grant such early and effectual supplies, as may enable Your Majesty to put an end to this unnatural rebellion. . . ."[1] And when threatening news arrived from France, about Scottish and Irish officers and other enemies of England awaiting an opportunity to embark for Scotland, the King, on January 21/February 1, again addressed Parliament:

. . . the accounts I have received . . . do put it beyond all doubt, that he [the Pretender] is heading the rebellion there [in Scotland] . . .; his adherents . . . confidently affirm, that assurances are given them of support from abroad.[2]

Again France was not named—as Townshend wrote to Horace Walpole on January 24, 1716, O.S.:

. . . though it may be easy to collect from his Speech, who is meant, yet it is worded so, as not to give any just handle for provocation, or to engage His Majesty in any thing directly against France.[3]

Similarly in the Addresses from the two Houses expressions offensive to the Regent were avoided, though in the debate some speakers embarrassed the Ministers by violent attacks against France, which the House received with loud applause. Stanhope wrote to Stair on January 23, 1716, O.S.:

. . . it was the business of the King's servants rather to moderate than to raise the passions of the House upon this occasion, for had they encouraged the temper which appear'd, I do verily believe a warr would have been voted before the rise of the House.[4]

The Commons renewed their previous assurances to grant such supplies

[1] *Parl. Hist.* vii. 245. [2] *Ibid.* vii. 276.
[3] S.P. 104/81. [4] F.O. 90/14.

as shall be sufficient not only to maintain such additional forces, and to defeat all attempts of your enemies, both at home and abroad, . . . but also to enable your Majesty . . . effectually to shew your resentment against any foreign Power, that shall presume . . . to abet or support the Pretender or his adherents.[1]

The Government now decided to raise a further 10,000 men in England and 6000 in Ireland, a measure which could hardly be interpreted otherwise than as directed against France—no such armaments were required any longer against the Scottish Rebellion.

The impression produced in France was considerable. The union between King and Parliament gradually caused peaceful tendencies to prevail, while the Regent himself had probably never been for war with England. On March 9, Lord Stair communicated to him further Parliamentary addresses calling on the King to show his "just resentment against any Prince or State" that shall give protection to the Pretender.[2] The British Government had, in fact, profited by the Scottish rising, their strength earned them the respect of Europe, and Prince Eugene seems to have been right in saying that nothing better could have happened for them.

Meantime proceedings had been started against the rebels in England. Many were executed, and their property was confiscated; hundreds of those taken at Preston were transported to the American Colonies. Their leader, Thomas Foster, as a Member of Parliament could have hoped to be sent to the Tower, but he was expelled the House, imprisoned in Newgate, and was to have appeared before an ordinary Court. A few days before his trial he managed, however, to escape with the connivance of the keeper, who was immediately taken up. The Ministers were greatly annoyed, and a price of £1000 was set on Foster's head, but to no effect. Similarly old Macintosh managed to escape with a few companions; flourishing a knife in one hand and the broken chains in the other, he is said to have driven off the warders, and to have fought his way to freedom.

It was deemed necessary to make the seven lords captured at Preston stand their trial. But by adopting the method of a Parliamentary impeachment, the Court hoped to shift from itself the odium, while the influence it had in both Houses would still leave the decision to it. Moreover, such procedure would relieve the King from having to grant or refuse a reprieve—after an impeachment this would have

---

[1] *Parl. Hist.* vii. 278-9.
[2] Address to the House of Lords, Feb. 20, 1715, O.S., *Parl. Hist.* vii. 289.

required an Act of Parliament. The very day on which Parliament met, January 9/20, 1716, Mr. Lechmere moved in the Commons the impeachment of Lord Derwentwater. He extolled the blessings of George I's reign—"that his Majesty has done more for the honour of the Church, and the true interest of his Kingdom, than any of his predecessors, in three times the number of years".[1] He contended that "in justice to the King, as well as to the people" the House ought to take the inquiry into the Rebellion "into their own hands, and not to entrust the prosecution of it with any body but themselves". His further argument can hardly have suited altogether the book of the Government, as it disclosed their policy—Lechmere quoted in favour of the proposed measure the fact "that no pardon under the Great Seal could discharge a judgment obtained upon the impeachment of the Commons". In support of his motion he flaunted at the House the Declaration of the Pretender in which "they were represented as the most illegal and infamous assembly of men that ever met together". Lechmere's motion was followed by six others; all the seven lords were to be brought to the bar of the House of Lords for High Treason.

A Committee of the House of Commons, of which Lechmere was chairman, was ordered to draw up Articles of Impeachment; and the next day the Earls of Derwentwater, Nithisdale, Carnwath, and Wintoun, Viscount Kenmure, and Lords Widdrington and Nairn, were brought to the bar, where they knelt, until the Lord Chancellor directed them to rise. After the Articles of Impeachment had been read to them, he asked them severally: "What they had to say thereunto?" Derwentwater replied by asking for a copy of the Articles "and such time to answer as the House should think fit; and that counsel might be assigned to assist him";[2] and so did the others. The request was granted, and on January 19/30 they were brought again singly before the House of Lords. Derwentwater was brought in first, and his answer was read.[3] He could not deny the charges which were based on fact, and his reply was much rather a plea of attenuating circumstances than a justification. He was "young and unexperienced", and had rashly engaged in the undertaking, but

after the sudden skirmishes at Preston . . . was solicitous to prevent any further destruction of the lives of his Majesty's subjects, and instrumental to inducing all in arms to submit to the King, provided they might be secured of their lives.

[1] *Parl. Hist.* vii. 231.   [2] *Ibid.* vii. 244.   [3] *Ibid.* vii. 266-7.

This they were encouraged to believe they would obtain from the King's mercy. He therefore trusted the two Houses "to use their mediation for mercy on his behalf". The paper was a humble subjection to the will of his judges. The Lord Chancellor asked him whether he pleaded guilty, to which he replied in the affirmative. Similarly the other lords admitted their guilt, and pleaded for the mercy of the King and intercession of Parliament. Lord Wintoun alone asked for a fresh respite, which was granted; and as it was found that no admission of guilt was to be expected from him, his case was separated from that of the other six accused.

The verdict over these six lords was to be pronounced in Westminster Hall on February 20, 1716. With much pomp the peers proceeded to the sitting, which was presided over by a Lord High Steward, appointed by the King for that occasion. This time it was Lord Chancellor Cowper—much to his vexation, as Lord Widdrington was a relative of his wife's. He wished Nottingham had been appointed, though, to judge from that lord's further behaviour, the matter would have been even more embarrassing for him. Still, Cowper had to submit to the King's order.

To each of the accused he had first to address the question—what he had to say for himself why judgment should not pass upon him according to law? Ultimately they all had to answer in the negative, but each spoke once more recapitulating the circumstances which seemed to entitle him to the mercy of the King and the intercession of the two Houses of Parliament. They spoke about their families; Lord Nairn, the father of twelve children, said: "I chuse rather to lay my whole stress upon the King's mercy, for which he is so renown'd, and which I was put in hopes of at the time of my surrender". Or again, Lord Kenmure argued that he had never been accessory to any previous design against the King, and begged Parliament to intercede for mercy that he may live and be the means to keep his "wife and four small children from starving".

When they had finished, Lord Cowper pronounced the verdict. He pointed out that "the whole body politick of this free Kingdom has in a manner rose up in its own defence, for the punishment of those crimes".

It is alledg'd by some of your Lordships that you engaged in this Rebellion without previous concert or deliberation, and without suitable preparations . . . that your men, horses, were not so well prepared, as they might, and would have been on longer warning; but your minds were.

Some argued that they had been driven into rebellion to escape imprisonment.

'Tis hard to believe that any should rebel merely to avoid being restrain'd from rebelling; or that a gentle confinement would not much better have suited a crazy state of health, than the fatigues and inconveniences of such long and hasty marches in the depth of winter. . . .

I must be so just to such of your Lordships, as profess the religion of the Church of Rome, that you had one temptation, and that a great one, to engage you in this treason, which the others had not. In that 'twas evident, success on your part must for ever have establish'd Popery in this Kingdom, and that probably you could never have again so fair an opportunity.

But then, good God! how must those Protestants be cover'd with confusion, who enter'd into the same measures, without so much as capitulating for their religion . . . and so much as requiring, much less obtaining a frail promise, that it should be preserv'd, or even tolerated.

In conclusion Lord Cowper, as Lord High Steward, had to pronounce over all the accused the "terrible sentence of the law", condemning them to death.[1]

Many members of fashionable society, and even the King and his son, had assisted at these proceedings. The Ministers had represented to the King that he should not exercise mercy in favour of these rebels who had conspired against his throne and life; what turned them most against the convicts was that they had refused to make any confession such as would have given an insight into the deeper causes of the rebellion. On February 28 the King confirmed the verdict against the six lords and the date of execution was fixed for March 6.

The fate of the condemned lords evoked pity. At first it was not believed that the matter would be pressed to the bitter end; and now the respite was eagerly employed to obtain a reprieve. No means were left untried by the wives, relatives, and friends of the six lords; but applications to the King and his Ministers, and to influential persons of either sex, alike seemed of no avail. On a later occasion Robert Walpole declared in the House of Commons that £60,000 had been offered to him if he could obtain the pardon of only one, Lord Derwentwater; and Bonet reports a similar offer of a present of £150,000 "to a foreign lady", presumably Mlle. Schulenburg. On

---

[1] *The whole Proceeding to Judgment upon the Articles of Impeachment of High Treason* (1716).

March 1 Lady Derwentwater threw herself at the King's feet as he was leaving the Chapel, in a last attempt to obtain a pardon for her husband. George I, who shrank from scenes, was much embarrassed and merely muttered, "I sincerely regret, Madam, to see you in this distressing position". At night another Cabinet Council was summoned, but all members, except Nottingham, declared against a reprieve, if merely because the convicts had refused to confess.

There were, in fact, valid considerations on either side. It seemed ungenerous to proceed to extreme measures against men who had surrendered because they expected mercy, and who might otherwise have fought their way through, or at least met an honourable death; and punishments and executions were already earning George I a reputation for cruelty. On the other hand, some thirty or forty men of smaller rank, captured at Preston, had been executed—should mercy, which was denied to the misguided poor, be extended to the instigators and leaders of the rebellion? or should not rather the chief rebels be punished as a deterrent for the future?

The impeachment in the Commons was started in order that the King should not be in a position to exercise mercy; and even if it was now argued that the clause of the Act of Settlement "that no pardon under the Great Seal of England be pleadable to an impeachment by the Commons in Parliament" aimed merely at preventing the Sovereign from shielding his Ministers, it clearly applied to other cases as well—here for once the limitation placed on the Royal prerogative answered the wishes of the Government.

But now an attempt was made through Parliament by the friends of the six lords to force a reprieve on the King. Parliament was bombarded with petitions, and should it declare for a reprieve the Crown could hardly refuse it. There was a strong inclination towards it in both Houses, for the idea of a public execution of the six noblemen was abhorrent to them. The unfortunate clause in the Act of Settlement had caused much confusion in the public mind, and in spite of that clause it was generally believed that the decision about the reprieve lay with the King. The intended debates in Parliament appeared as a mere attempt to press the King to grant it; and their moral effect seemed more important than the legal consequences of the proposed resolutions.

The Government would therefore have preferred not to let the matter come up in Parliament, and on February 21/March 4 they managed to prevent such a discussion. The next day, however, the wives of the condemned went with a great attendance to West-minster, to petition both Houses of Parliament. The Government again tried to cut short the discussion by moving to adjourn till March 1/12, by which time the executions would have been carried out; but they failed to prevent a debate on the petitions. In the House of Commons, where the impeachment had been recently carried, a majority now seemed inclined to mercy. The free surrender at Preston was quoted, and one Member asked ironically whether the King's mercy was meted out with gallows and the axe.[1] In the end, the adjournment to March 12 was carried, but by a majority of only seven votes, the smallest which the Government had ever obtained in that House.

In the Lords, they suffered defeat. A warm discussion developed over the question whether the petitions should be received and read; whether in the case of impeachment the King had the power to reprieve; and whether to address the King to grant such a reprieve? Townshend and other Court lords did their level best in opposing these motions, and might just have secured a majority had not Lord Nottingham come out in favour of the condemned, as he had, two days earlier, in the Cabinet. He said "he hoped the King would pardon the prisoners if they confessed; nay, he hoped that he would pardon them though they did not confess".[2] The motion for an adjournment was rejected, and an Address to the King was voted. All that the Government side obtained was that the Address to the King was not for a reprieve, but for a respite; and not in favour of all the six lords, but only of such as would prove worthy of the favour.

Thus the two Houses, recently prosecutors and judges, were now inclined to mercy, while the Crown, which had shrunk from prosecuting, insisted on the law taking its course. Parliament was satisfied with the verdict having been pronounced, but felt that to carry it out would be a harshness unworthy of the Crown; whereas the King was disappointed, having wished to destroy the rebels without himself appearing in the matter. Now a denial of mercy would load him with more odium than if the Crown had from the very outset acted as prosecutor. It was even rumoured that Lechmere had moved for an impeachment so as to enable Parliament afterwards to plead with greater weight with the King for mercy.

In view of the Lords' Address, it was not possible to proceed with

---

[1] Bonet.   [2] *Diary of Lady Cowper*, p. 82.

the execution on the appointed day. The King returned to them this
short answer: "I shall always do what I think most for the honour
of my Government and the safety of my Kingdoms". Still, on
March 6 only two of the six convicts were sent to the scaffold, while
the other four were granted an indeterminate respite. Derwentwater
and Kenmure were chosen as the most guilty, one among the English
and the other among the Scottish lords, to suffer the supreme penalty. Derwentwater, a mere youth, received the greatest amount of
sympathy from the public. He was the son of an illegitimate daughter
of Charles II, one of the richest peers, and a Roman Catholic highly
esteemed at Rome and in France. He had harmed his cause by fool-
ishly denying his connexion with the Pretender, which could be
clearly proved against him. Lord Kenmure had commanded the forces
by a commission from the Earl of Mar. Both maintained a steady
and composed demeanour to the very end. On the scaffold Derwentwater read a speech in which he declared his regret at having pleaded
guilty at his trial; for he had never had any other but King James III
for his rightful and lawful sovereign. "I only wish now, that the laying down my life might contribute to the service of my king and
country." Similarly Kenmure declared that "he prayed for the Pretender, and repented of his having pleaded guilty".[1]

The lives of the other four lords were saved by the debates in
Parliament. Lord Nithisdale was anyhow out of the Government's
reach. His wife, who had made every possible attempt to obtain the
King's pardon for him, the night before the execution went to the
Tower, as if to bid a last farewell to him. Then she remained in
his cell, while he escaped in her clothes. With the help of an officer
whom she had bribed, the flight was kept secret till Nithisdale had
reached safety. The Government, however angry, did not venture to
punish the woman whose courage was universally admired, and re-
leased her.[2] The other three lords were reprieved, while Wintoun
escaped from the Tower.

But the executions can hardly be called cruel—they were "a fatal
necessity". It is true that George I, impervious to sentiment, would
have liked best to see all the six lords executed, and was angry with
Lord Nottingham. Nottingham had never been in full agreement with
the other Ministers, but at first had considerable influence with
George I, being able to converse with him in French, though not

---

[1] *Parl. Hist.* vii. 284-6.
[2] Rapin-Tindale (1749), xiii. pp. 120-21; Hoffmann, March 6, 1716.

always with perfect ease. His opponents alleged that he harangued the King every day for an hour and a half,

concluding always with his hand upon his breast, and these words: "Sir, I have done my duty and discharged my conscience, after having laid the truth before your Majesty. If your Majesty will not follow my advice, I have nothing to do but to submit with resignation to your Majesty's better judgement."[1]

His colleagues tried to counter his influence, assisted therein by the German Ministers, who were more Whiggish than the Whigs themselves. Bernstorff declared as early as November 1714 that Nottingham's reign would soon be at an end. The other Ministers were confirmed in their dislike of him by his once more drawing closer to the Tories. The King and the Prince were much displeased with him, but he now took great pains "to insinuate the Tories into the Princess's favour"; and one day she told her lady-in-waiting that she did not see "that a Whig was more than a Tory for the King's prerogative".[2] After the debate in the Lords, Nottingham's presence could not be tolerated in the Cabinet any longer; "all the trouble we have had in favour of the condemn'd Lords", wrote Robert Walpole to his brother Horace, "arose from that corner".[3] The mild Lord Cowper was for giving Nottingham another trial, and dismissing him on the next occasion; but "Baron Bernstorff said it must positively be done now, for if they did not take this opportunity, they, may be, might not be able to do it when they would".[4] Nottingham, his sons, and his brother Lord Aylesford were all put out of their places.

The Whig Government now tried to consolidate their power by every means. Severe action was taken against non-jurors and Roman Catholics, and an Act was passed for "enforcing the laws now in being against Papists". Hoffmann tried in vain to stop it after it had passed the House of Commons, and finally comforted himself with the thought that the many amendments made by the Lords "had to a marked extent removed its excessive severity and hardships".[5]

Of infinitely greater importance was another Act passed in 1716: the famous Septennial Act, which was the most important constitutional change brought about by the Jacobite Rising. The term of Parliament was extended from three to seven years. Originally no limit was set to the duration of Parliament, except the dissolution on

[1] *Diary of Lady Cowper*, p. 30.   [2] *Ibid.* p. 65.
[3] Coxe, *Walpole*, ii. p. 51.   [4] *Diary of Lady Cowper*, p. 88.
[5] Hoffmann's dispatch of July 10, 1716.

the death of a sovereign.[1] "The King could keep a Parliament in existence as long as he pleased, and Charles II retained for seventeen years the Parliament called at his accession." [2] To prevent a repetition of this abuse, a Bill for Triennial Parliaments, which originated in the Lords, was passed by both Houses in 1693, but William III considered it an encroachment on his prerogative and withheld his assent. He gave it, however, when the Bill was passed by Parliament a second time in 1694. "Parliaments", said a speaker, "were like manna which the Lord had given to the Chosen People; it was delicious when fresh, but if kept too long it bred worms, and stank." Although at that time considerable importance was attached to frequent elections, the cardinal fact about the Triennial Act was that it set a term to the life of Parliament, which hitherto had been left to the sole determination of the King: this was an important step towards Parliamentary Government.

The Septennial Act was not based on theoretical preferences, but much rather answered a practical need. Under the Triennial Act of 1694, a general election would have occurred in 1718, and it was by no means certain that the results would have been favourable to the Government. George I was not popular. The Ministerial impeachments, the increase in the standing army, the severe methods adopted in the suppression of the Rising, were measures which, undertaken with the assent of Parliament, produced dissatisfaction against the dominant party. Although the greater part of the nation were convinced of the necessity of maintaining George I on the throne, the general election could, none the less, have raised a dangerous storm against the Whig Government, who, to say the least, would have been hard pressed to maintain their position. They therefore had recourse to the expedient of prolonging the term of the existing Parliament; and although both parties were chiefly concerned with the lifetime of that particular Parliament, the matter had to be argued on general grounds. In 1713 the Tories in office had thought of repealing the Triennial Act; [3] had they introduced such a Bill, they would undoubtedly have supported it by the same arguments which they passionately repudiated when employed by the Whigs in 1716.

---

[1] The Triennial Act of the reign of Charles I merely laid down that Parliament had to be summoned at least once in three years.

[2] Sir William Anson, *Law and Custom of the Constitution*, i. p. 68.

[3] Cf. Thornton, *The Brunswick Accession*, pp. 174-7.

It was essential that the Act should apply to the Parliament which passed it—but was it right for a Parliament to extend its own term without consulting the electors? Not according to our present conceptions, nor even according to those of 1715. If there was to be a change, it should only have applied to the next Parliament. This was felt by the opponents of the Bill in 1716: "If this House of Commons", said Lord Trevor, "continued themselves beyond the time for which they were chosen, they were no more the representatives of the people, but a House of their own making".[1]

On April 10/21, 1716, the Duke of Devonshire introduced the Septennial Bill in the Lords,

representing the inconveniences that attend the triennial elections of Members of Parliament; particularly, that they serve only to keep up party divisions, and to raise and foment feuds and animosities in private families; that besides, they occasion ruinous expences, and give a handle to the cabals and intrigues of foreign princes: That therefore it was becoming . . . to apply a proper remedy to an evil which might be attended with the most dangerous consequences, especially in the present temper of the nation, for though the rebellion was happily suppressed, yet the spirit of it remained unconquered. . . .[2]

The Bill was read a second time on April 14/25. The Tories fought it strenuously and argued that long Parliaments were contrary to the spirit of the British Constitution. The Earl of Nottingham, since his dismissal once more a Tory, declared that "frequent and new parliaments are required by the fundamental Constitution of the Kingdom".

Lord Trevor used the argument which Swift had employed with William III in favour of the Triennial Bill: "that long parliaments were always pernicious" to the King. A good deal was said about the Pensionary Parliament of Charles II, Lord Ferrers asserting that it

made King Charles II uneasy, by making him neglect the affections of his people; and concluded, he was afraid that the repealing the Triennial Act would have the same effect. . . .

As for the rebels, the Duke of Buckingham declared that

they and their friends were inconsiderable: that they, perhaps, might whisper discontent and treason in corners; but that . . . it was not . . . in their power to do harm. . . .

[1] *Parl. Hist.* vii. 298.   [2] *Ibid.* vii. 293-5.

Lord Nottingham replied to the argument concerning long Parliaments as an encouragement for foreign Princes to enter into alliances with Great Britain:

... foreign potentates may be deterred from entering into measures with us, when ... informed, by the preamble of this Bill, that the Popish faction is so dangerous, as that it may be destructive to the peace and security of the Government. ...

The Earl of Islay answered, from the Whig side:

That it is certain frequent elections occasion ruinous expences; and ... ruinous expences beget ... corruption; for when gentlemen have laid out their estates in elections, they must exert their industry to find out some means to make themselves amends: that besides . . . frequent elections are a great occasion of vice, debauchery, and decay of trade ... that ... they ... occasion great heats, and even implacable feuds and divisions between father and son, husband and wife, brother and sister; ... and ... render our government dependent on the caprice of the multitude, and very precarious.

The Duke of Argyll denied that the Rebellion was at an end, and observed "that the rebels had only shifted their headquarters from Perth to Paris or St. Germains".

After a debate which lasted five hours, the question that the Bill be committed being put, it was carried in the affirmative by 96 votes against 61; and on April 18/29 the Bill was carried by 69 votes against 36. 24 Lords entered a protest against it.

In the Commons, the Government was from the very outset assured of a majority. Mr. Lyddal, who opened the debate, declared that the Bill would "entirely break our parties and divisions and ... lay a firm and solid foundation for the future tranquillity and happiness of this Kingdom". Sir Richard Steele quoted the late Earl of Sunderland, who had said of the Triennial Act "that it had made a triennial King, a triennial Ministry, a triennial alliance", and thus described its working:

... the first year of a Triennial Parliament has been spent in vindictive decisions and animosities about the late elections; the second session has entered into business, but rather with a spirit of contradiction to what the prevailing set of men in former Parliaments had brought to pass ... the third session languished ... and the approach of an ensuing election terrified the Members into a servile management, according as their respective principals were disposed towards the question before them in the House. ...

P

The opponents of the Bill had no hope, but argued with great skill; in fact, in the absence of Robert Walpole, they seemed to have the best of the debate. Mr. Shippen, a Tory of high character, who was in the habit of giving his views without reserve, or even discretion, remarked that the Bill "has already got through the most difficult part of its passage"—he meant the House of Lords—but freedom of speech had to be practised "in this, perhaps, our last struggle for the liberties of those we represent". He went on to say that the dangers threatening Government both at home and abroad were urged as a reason for the Bill:

> If this argument be applied to the Ministry, I can only answer, that it is no concern of ours whether they have rendered themselves odious to the people, or not. They are more properly the object of our jealousy, than of our care. . . . But if it be applied to His Majesty, as it must be to make it any inducement to pass this Bill, I will venture to say, that none of those, who are called enemies to the Government, and abettors of the rebellion, could have offered an argument so injurious to His Majesty's honour. . . . But the assertion . . . is entirely groundless. For when these pretended disaffections were at the highest, it appeared how impotent they were, how far from being universal, by the easy and sudden suppression of the rebellion; and by consequence how absolutely His Majesty reigned in the hearts of his subjects.[1]

He talked about the reigns of Edward I and Richard II, discussing the age of the Plantagenets in terms of 18th-century Parliamentary life, and concluded his speech by declaring that "Long Parliaments . . . will naturally grow either formidable or contemptible".

Another speaker, Snell, quoted against the Bill a passage or two from Locke's *Treatise on Government*, that where a limit is set to the duration of the Legislature, the supreme power "at the determination of the time set . . . reverts to the society, and the people have a right to place it in new hands".

Similarly Bromley, who had been Secretary of State under Queen Anne, opposed the Bill. Another Tory, Archibald Hutcheson, recalled what an outcry had been raised against the last Parliament, on a mere suspicion that a repeal of the Triennial Act was intended. "What an inconsistency must it then appear, to see those very gentlemen, who were then the most zealous opposers of such an attempt, become now the most violent advocates for it?" [2]

But no oratory of the Tories could change the decision which

---

[1] *Parl. Hist.* vii. 314.   [2] *Ibid.* vii. 343.

was formed before the debate opened. A Bill so much favouring the party interest of the Whigs was certain of a strong majority. The debate lasted eleven hours, and was listened to by the Prince of Wales and many peers. There were nearly forty speakers. The Bill was referred to a Committee of the whole House, and in that Committee Stanhope skilfully foiled an attempt to throw it out. The third reading was passed in the Commons on May 7, by 264 against 121. In spite of later attempts to repeal the Septennial Act it continued in force till 1911.

Even among the Whigs there were many who were uncertain about the Septennial Act, but practical considerations silenced their doubts. It was comforting for those who hesitated that the great Lord Somers, a short time before his death in May 1716, had told Townshend that the Septennial Bill had his hearty approbation. And how could he feel otherwise? The system founded by the Glorious Revolution, and confirmed by the Protestant Succession, received further support through the Septennial Act. The Whigs were its chief beneficiaries and without it could hardly have established their régime for the next fifty years. In practice the Act resulted in an increase of the power of the House of Commons rather than of the Royal prerogative. Speaker Onslow "was frequently heard to declare, that the passing of the Septennial Bill formed the era of the emancipation of the British House of Commons from its former dependance on the Crown and the House of Lords".[1] Henceforth the House of Commons assumed more and more its modern position, its majority acquiring gradually a decisive influence on the character of the Cabinet.

The Government immediately felt the good effects of the Septennial Act. Their prestige had grown very considerably, and public confidence found expression in a sudden rise of the Government funds.[2] In Government circles enormous value was set on the Act, and even an improvement in public morals was expected.[3] Stanhope boasted in a letter to the British Ambassador in Spain: "His Majesty's affairs are, thanks be to God, at present in a more setled and prosperous condition than his most sanguine servants could ever have expected".[4]

Now George I no longer needed to deny himself the wish he had entertained for some time past, to revisit his home. He had not seen

---

[1] Coxe, *Walpole*, i. p. 75.   [2] Hoffmann, May 8, 1716.
[3] Bonet, April 27/May 8, 1716.
[4] Stanhope to Bubb, May 17/28, 1716, S.P. 104/136.

it since September 1714. Faced by English party struggles and by the dangers of the Rebellion, he may often have wished himself back in his quiet Electorate which had neither a Parliament nor Tories to embitter his life and reign. He had counted on going to Hanover in the summer of 1715: [1] but the Jacobite Rising forced him to remain in England. He now ordered his Ministers to consider what form should be given to the Regency in his absence. These, in a letter from Townshend to Bernstorff dated May 19, 1716, once more laid before the King their unanimous opinion concerning the prejudice which such a journey might cause to his interests; that the Rebellion was "rather smothered for a time than totally extinguished", and that the subduing and eradicating of that evil could best be achieved "by a constant, steady, and uniform application in every branch of the Administration towards working out the inmost causes of this distemper", but that "such a strict and vigilant application of powers distributed through so many different hands . . . can hardly be hoped for without the invigorating influence of His Majesty's presence and inspection. . . ." [2] George I was not greatly impressed by these objections, while the further remarks of the Ministers concerning the ill-effects of the King's absence on foreign policy were not even altogether correct. The alliance with the Emperor, to which great importance was attached, was concluded during the last weeks of the King's presence in London; while abroad George I's journey produced, if anything, a favourable idea of his power—clearly his throne had to be secure if he could venture to leave his Kingdom for a few months.

George was determined not to let himself be detained. Still, certain difficulties had to be overcome; in the first place there was the clause in the Act of Settlement which forbade the King to leave the country without the consent of Parliament. Now that for the first time the question had arisen, it was generally felt that no such humiliation could be inflicted on the King, and that, rather than have him apply to Parliament for permission, the clause should be repealed. This was done by an unanimous vote, without opposition from any quarter—the Tories, who had not lost hope of some day regaining office under the Hanoverians, were careful not to offend the King in this most personal matter.

A more serious difficulty arose from the jealousy which George I entertained of his son. If the King was to be out of the country for

¹ Bonet, April 5/16, 1716.   ² Coxe, *Walpole*, ii. pp. 51-4.

several months, provision had to be made for someone to replace him; and yet it went very much against his grain to appoint the Prince of Wales Regent with all the prerogative of sovereignty. The Ministers informed him that it would be contrary to precedent to join other persons with the Prince in the commission and thus to limit his authority; and although in consequence the King "reluctantly submitted to consign to the Prince the sole direction of affairs, yet, instead of the title of Regent, he appointed him *Guardian of the Realm and Lieutenant*, an office unknown in England since it was enjoyed by Edward, the Black Prince".[1]

Next a dispute arose concerning the form and rights of the Regency. The Prince absolutely refused to submit to any limitations. The Speech with which the King was to close the session of Parliament had been drafted and mentioned his impending journey to Germany and the lieutenancy of the Prince. The time for its delivery had come without the dispute between the two having been settled; its reading was therefore to be delayed. "Lord Sunderland would have that part relating to the Prince struck out of the Speech"; [2] the King talked of giving up his journey. The negotiations continued, Bernstorff acting for the King, and Cowper for the Prince. Half an hour before the meeting of Parliament the Prince gave way, and the Speech was read in its original form.

But the quarrel continued, aggravated by Court intrigues and personal feuds. The King wished to humiliate his son still further. George Augustus was intimate with the Duke of Argyll, whose generalship in Scotland was criticized at Court. The Ministers wished at all cost to separate him from the Prince Regent. The struggle between the factions of Marlborough and Argyll was fought out inside the Whig Government. Marlborough had recently suffered a stroke of palsy, and was not as yet fully recovered. His friend Cadogan was pitched upon to fill his place, and was trying to undermine Argyll at St. James's as he had done in Scotland. There were even rumours at Court that Argyll had sent a challenge to Cadogan. But to defeat Argyll's influence it was not sufficient to deprive him of the places he held from the King—he was still Commander-in-Chief in North Britain—the Prince had to be prevailed upon to dismiss him from the post of his Chamberlain; it was feared that otherwise the Duke

---

[1] Coxe, *Walpole*, i. p. 79.
[2] *Diary of Lady Cowper*, p. 108; see also letter from George I to his son, *ibid.* App. D.

of Argyll would have more power under the Regency than the Ministers. The King himself attached great weight to the matter, and
insisted on making his son part from Argyll. He threatened to send
over for his brother, Duke Ernest Augustus, "and make him Guardian
of the Realm and Duke of York".[1] The Prince had no choice but to
submit. Argyll and his brother Islay were both put out of their places;
George Augustus made his friend surrender his gold-key of Chamberlain.

The position of the Prince Regent was now sufficiently restricted
for the King to feel reassured that in his absence the Government
would be carried on according to his own wishes and those of his Whig
Ministers. The limitations on the Regent were raised to the level of
a principle by the King's declaration that they should serve as precedent on future occasions "when Princes of our House will be visit-
ing their German possessions". The King added, with more grace
than sincerity, that regard for his descendants and for possible future
dangers to the Crown did not permit him to allow his son such full
powers as his confidence in him would have justified.

The restrictions concerned, in the first place, foreign policy, in
which the Prince was to take no decision without the King [2]—George
Augustus himself had claimed no independence in this matter. What
galled him, however, was to be forbidden to fill any important em-
ployments, whether in the Cabinet or in the Privy Council, the Royal
Household, the Treasury, or at the Board of Admiralty. He was precluded from appointing any governor, or officer above a colonel, and
in the Guards, even a lieutenant. Should Parliament meet, he was
as far as possible to withhold the royal assent to bills until the return
of the King; though such assent was never refused under the House
of Hanover. But apparently the King was not as yet fully conscious
of this fact.

A few important places were filled by the King before his departure.
The Duke of Devonshire, who had recently introduced the Septennial
Bill in the Lords, succeeded Nottingham as Lord President of the
Council; and General Carpenter succeeded Argyll as Commander-in-
Chief in North Britain. Of the British Ministers Stanhope alone was

---

[1] *Diary of Lady Cowper*, p. 108; see also letter from George I to his son, *ibid.*
App. D.

[2] A copy of the document among the Coxe Papers (Add. MSS. 9133, ff. 32-4)
bears the heading: *Restrictions for the Prince of Wales as Guardian of the Realm,
St. James's, 5th July 1716.* The document itself is in French.

to accompany the King to Hanover. His place as Secretary of State was temporarily filled by Paul Methuen, who, the previous year, had returned from his embassy to Spain; that Townshend, the other Secretary of State, did not simply take over the work of Stanhope's office, seemed to point to a long absence of the King. Townshend and Methuen were to report regularly to Hanover, and to receive the King's decisions through Stanhope. Stephen Poyntz was to write to Stanhope on

such occurrences and observations as my Lord Townshend and Mr. Secretary Methuen think less proper to be inserted in their publick dispatches. I am never to write to you but by the hand of a messenger, and my Lord and Mr. Methuen, do most earnestly beg, that the letters you shall receive from me may not be communicated to any body, but to his Majesty only. . . .[1]

From the contents of these dispatches it can be inferred that they were kept from the Prince, and that, indeed, they were to provide the King with reliable information about his son's conduct. Thus provision was made for the six months which the King was to remain on the Continent; but the Ministers feared that the King would not return in time. "I hope", wrote Sunderland on July 24, 1716, ". . . that we shall see him early in the winter back again here, for without that there is no prospect, but of certain ruine and confusion."[2]

At last everything was settled and the King could start for Hanover. He was in mighty good humour. Lady Cowper writes: "When I wished him a good journey and a quick return, he looked as if the last part of my speech was needless, and that he did not think of it".[3] The next day all foreign Ministers were received in audience; only those of Denmark and Poland were to follow the King to Hanover.[4] In sign of reconciliation, George spent the last evening before his departure in the rooms of the Princess,[5] and met there his son whom he had hitherto carefully avoided. In the morning of July 18 the King left St. James's. Before the Palace he embraced the Prince of Wales, to show to all and sundry that they were parting friends. The Prince drove with the King to the Tower, where they took a boat for Gravesend. On board the yacht, the Prince, kneeling, kissed the King's hand with his eyes full of tears.

---

[1] July 28, 1716; Coxe, ii. p. 55.   [2] *Ibid.*
[3] *Diary*, p. 110.   [4] Hoffmann, July 17, 1716.
[5] Bonet, July 10/21, 1716.

So long as the King was on the high seas, he was assumed to be within his British Dominions. It was only when the news was received of the King having landed in Holland that the Prince formally assumed the Regency.

The journey of George I passed without incident and on July 26 he reached Hanover. Here he was back in his Electorate, among subjects of his own race with whose customs and language he was familiar; and here he was master, unrestricted in his prerogative. "The King", wrote Stair from Paris, "will enjoy his rest in Germany after all the excitements which our island has caused him." [1]

England now learnt in a different sense than under William III what it meant to have an alien King whose heart was in his old home. George I had left his Kingdom while it was still exposed to many a danger. This was the first of a long series of royal visits to the Continent which play such a peculiar part in the reigns of the first two Georges. Many months were spent by the King outside his Kingdom; he resided at Hanover, accompanied by only one or other of his British Ministers. Britain he seemed to leave completely to the British. But this was true of domestic affairs only; for foreign affairs presented a peculiar intermixture of British and Hanoverian interests, answering the personal inclinations of the two first Georges. They acted as Kings but thought like Electors.

[1] Stair to Robethon, July 27, 1716, Stowe MSS. 229, f. 3.

CHAPTER IX

THE BARRIER TREATY AND THE "OLD SYSTEM"

THERE is permanency in the creative conceptions of great statesmen; even if temporarily abandoned, they survive as long as the conditions continue for which they were devised. In a system based on the alliance of the two Maritime Powers with the House of Austria, William III found the means for protecting Europe against French domination; this system secured the victories of the War of the Spanish Succession, and till 1756 governed the policy of the Powers ranged against the House of Bourbon. It came to be known as the "Old System".

The Tory Administration of 1710–14 had given up William's policy and had drawn closer to France, thereby estranging Austria. But on the accession of the Hanoverians England immediately reverted to the Whig system, even in foreign affairs, and, suspicious of France, tried to establish a permanent connexion with Holland and Austria. But first a reconciliation had to be effected between these two Powers by means of a Barrier Treaty satisfactory to both.

The right of the States General to garrison a number of fortresses on the French border—Nieuport, Mons, Namur, Luxembourg, etc. —dated back to the days when, in view of Spain's weakness, a Dutch barrier was required against French invasion. But even this barrier failed of its purpose when, in February 1701, the French invaded the country in peace-time, surprising the Dutch garrisons; and only by recognizing Philip V of Spain were the States General able to preserve their troops from capture.

The same year the Great Alliance against France was formed, one article of the Hague Treaty stipulating that the Allies should use all their strength for the reconquest of the Spanish Netherlands, "a dam and seal *vulgo* barrier" [1] against France. While the traditional

---

[1] " . . . *ut sint obex et repagulum, vulgo Barrière.*"

terminology was retained, the States General seem to have aimed at more than the occupation of a few fortresses, which had proved insufficient for defence. They desired the possession of a considerable part of the Spanish Netherlands, which would have left to Austria little of the country assigned to her by Treaty except the burden of its administration. Here was material for future conflict.

In 1706, after Ramillies, the Allies, having gained possession of the best part of the Belgian provinces, had to settle their future. Their possession could not be permanently withheld from the Habsburgs, and the Archduke Charles was proclaimed as Charles III in the Netherlands, as he had been in Spain; but the Maritime Powers, who had conquered them, were as yet unwilling to hand them over to a Habsburg administration. All the endeavours of the Imperial Envoy were of no avail, and when the Emperor tried to attain his aim by appointing Marlborough Governor of the Netherlands, the Duke declined and the Dutch cried out at Habsburg treason. First, the Maritime Powers constituted themselves joint trustees for Austria; next, the Dutch assumed sole administration, but demanded England's guarantee for all they claimed to be covered by their "barrier rights" in these provinces. Difficulties arose, and the problem of the Dutch barrier remained unsolved for years. Nor was either side in a hurry—the Dutch were in possession of the country and of its resources, while Britain, through the unsolved problem of the barrier, coveted by the Dutch and claimed by the Habsburgs, was able to exercise pressure on her allies. The decision was still delayed when in 1709 the States General found themselves courted by both sides, Louis XIV offering them a favourable barrier as the price of peace, while England tried to forestall him and to preserve their alliance for war; Lord Townshend was instructed to conclude a Barrier Treaty. The Dutch managed to have a recognition of their claim inserted in their preliminary agreement with France. Five months later a Barrier Treaty was concluded between Great Britain and Holland; [1] the States General pledged themselves "to assist and maintain the Protestant Succession as ordained by Parliament", while England pledged herself to procure for the Dutch the towns and districts which "may be found necessary" as "a barrier and security" to the States. But the Dutch claims now surpassed all that had been conceded by previous or subsequent Treaties. Besides what

[1] Cf. also van Noorden, vol. i. p. 598 ff.; Gachard, *Histoire de la Belgique au commencement du XVIIIe siècle* (Brussels, 1880), p. 210 *seq.*

England had offered, the Dutch demanded and obtained the advantages which an agreement with France would have secured for them. A chain of forts along the French border, in the interior, on the coast, and in the north, was assigned to the States General (including Dendermonde—here Townshend exceeded his instructions). Besides they were promised all the places which might yet be conquered from the French; the Upper Quarter of Guelders was specifically mentioned, the right to garrison the citadel of Liège, and the fortresses of Huy and Bonn in the Electorate of Cologne (the permission of the Empire was not asked). This made the Dutch strategically masters of the Belgian Provinces. Further, a million livres a year, "out of the clearest revenues" of the country, was guaranteed to them for maintaining those garrisons. Lastly, while they retained the control of the Scheldt and the other waterways, as secured in the Treaty of Westphalia, all "commodities going in and coming out of the harbours of Flanders" were to be charged with Dutch duties—thus the commercial subjection of the Southern to the Northern Netherlands, too, was established. Even British trade would have been affected by this arrangement.

Without taking the Austrian view, altogether opposed to the Barrier, the terms of the Treaty can be called preposterous. Even in the spring of 1709, Prince Eugene said with regard to the British Barrier project that the Austrians should sooner abandon the Low Countries than take them on conditions "which would be equally expensive, shameful, and unacceptable to them". Such protests were, however, met by the Dutch with a shrug of the shoulders and a hint that they could reach an understanding with France. Even in England it was felt that too much had been conceded and, as Townshend had overstepped his instructions on several important points, the Government hesitated for some time whether to ratify the Treaty. But as Holland refused to relinquish anything, and France started bidding once more for a separate peace, the step had to be taken. The war-party had gained its point: the struggle was to be continued with vigour, and Holland, usually not to be trusted to exert herself in the field, was now most immediately interested, as part of her gains had still to be secured. Marlborough, though Ambassador at The Hague, did not sign either the Treaty or its Additional Articles, and declared to Baron von Heems that it had been concluded without his knowledge. He thought the Treaty necessary, but with an eye to British public opinion preferred others to shoulder the responsibility for it.

The extent of the Dutch Barrier depended on the political situation, but the Barrier problem as such had now become a concern of British policy; in future no Government, whether Whig or Tory, could evade the fundamental obligations of the Treaty of 1709; henceforth Holland could claim British support for her demands on Austria. The guarantee of the Protestant Succession was bound up in the Treaty with that of the Belgian Barrier.

The change of Cabinet in 1710 unfavourably affected the British attitude towards the Barrier problem, as the Tory Ministers looked upon the Treaty as one of the most vulnerable points in the record of their Whig predecessors. St. John placed it before the House of Commons, seeking in their resolutions support for his further measures; nor did he let himself be influenced by Bothmer, who was concerned for the Treaty because of its guarantee of the Protestant Succession. The House saw primarily that it was prejudicial to British trade, and declared Townshend "who negotiated and signed, and all others who advised the ratifying of this Treaty, enemies to Your Majesty and your Kingdom". In the negotiations which led to the Peace of Utrecht, the Barrier was a foremost point of contention. In view of the changed European situation, the Dutch were forced considerably to reduce their claims. Fortresses such as Lille, Condé, and Valenciennes could no longer be demanded from France; they had even to renounce Nieuport, from regard for British trade interests; and Dendermonde and other towns in the interior, to the advantage of the future Austrian administration. Even so they received a chain of important forts, such as Furnes, Ypres, Menin, Mons, Charleroi, Namur, Maubeuge, the Castle of Ghent, and the much-disputed Tournai. Moreover, the clause of 1709 was confirmed "that the States General shall have all the revenues of the towns, places, jurisdictions, and their dependencies which they shall have for their barrier" in territory conquered from France; only the cost of the Austrian civil administration was now excepted. The position of the Dutch with regard to trade remained strong; though the closure of the Scheldt did not reappear in the Treaty, the forts of La Perle, Damme, St. Donas, the Castle of Ghent, and the forts of St. Philippe and Knocke, gave them control of the most important trade routes. On the other hand, the States General were precluded from "laying on the said places any new impositions", *i.e.* they were not to raise tariffs on imports and exports; and the subjects of the Queen of Great Britain were in future to "enjoy in all the places of the Barrier . . . all the privileges, exemptions, libertys, and facilities . . . granted to the subjects of the

States General. . . ." Lastly, the Dutch once more pledged themselves to maintain the Protestant Succession in Great Britain. The Barrier Treaty of 1713, like that of 1709, rested on reciprocal guarantees.

The Dutch gains, however, still required the consent of the Emperor Charles VI; and by Article XI of the Treaty, the Queen of Great Britain undertook to "prevail upon his Imperial Majesty" to enter into a Barrier Treaty with the States General, and "to use her good offices until the said Treaty be concluded". This and the future guarantee of that Treaty were the main obligations undertaken by Great Britain. But it was not an easy task to obtain the consent of the Emperor. Why should he, who was not a party to the peace treaty, concede so strong a position in his Netherlands to the Dutch? Austria did not require Dutch assistance, while the Barrier, as demanded by the States General, was no longer the traditional ring of outposts round Holland, designed to keep potential enemies at a distance—a desire for conquest now entered into the plans of the Dutch; as Marlborough had said, they were about to carve out for themselves a small kingdom in the future Austrian Netherlands.

No settlement of the Barrier was to be expected so long as the Emperor had not made peace with France; but even after its con-clusion in 1714, the Dutch were reluctant to follow the procedure laid down in the Treaty of 1713. Their relations with Britain were so strained that they hoped to achieve more by direct negotiations with the Emperor than through British mediation. In London dissatisfac-tion was felt at the attempt to exclude England from the negotiations. On July 16, 1714, Bromley wrote to Strafford: [1]

It might have been expected the States would have desired the inter-vention of her Majesty's Ministers in negotiating and setling their Barrier, . . . since her Majesty is obliged by Treaty to procure them a Barrier, and to secure them afterwards the quiet enjoyment of it, which makes it proper she should be apprized of the measures taken in the setling it.

If they fondly flatter themselves that her Majesty will blindly guaranty any Acts they prepare without her participation, they will find them-selves very much mistaken. But whether her Minister is admitted into these Conferences or not, her Majesty will think herself concerned to take care of the trade of her subjects, and will see the same setled upon the foot of former agreements.

Such warnings did not fail to make an impression, and a week later Bromley wrote again to Strafford: [2]

[1] S.P. 104/81.   [2] *Ibid.*

. . . the Queen . . . is very much pleased to find, that notwithstanding all the artful contrivances of particular persons, the generality will retain a just sence of the obligations they have to her.

On the death of the Queen friendly relations were re-established between the Maritime Powers. The States General were ready to stand by their obligations with regard to the Protestant Succession, and George I started negotiations about the Barrier Treaty during his stay at The Hague, before he had ever set foot on English soil.[1] While the Queen was still alive, it was decided in Vienna to send a plenipotentiary, Count Königsegg, to negotiate with the States General, but Hoffmann was informed that Great Britain was not to be admitted to these negotiations; he was to assist Königsegg with advice in this difficult situation, as the Queen "presumably will not be willing to let herself be completely excluded from these negotiations, and moreover, on certain points her good services might prove useful". The Austrian attitude gradually changed on the undisturbed accession of George I and in view of the friendly assurances of the new British Government; it looked like a return to the years before 1710, and the Vienna Court, in its isolation, could not afford to refuse the British advances. There was no longer any question of rejecting British mediation; rather did the Emperor compete with the States General for the favour of the mediator. Hoffmann was instructed to declare that Charles VI placed his trust in England, and to explain to the British Court how greatly it was in the general interest that the Emperor should soon enter into possession of his Netherlands. He talked to Marlborough and Townshend, and pointed out to the author of the Barrier Treaty of 1709 how the times had changed: while there was hope of conquering the entire Spanish Empire, the Emperor could afford to be more liberal with regard to Flanders; but now, he remarked pointedly, Lord Townshend himself would hardly wish to enforce to the terms of his own Barrier Treaty. Townshend replied that the mediation would proceed with perfect impartiality.[2] Great Britain became the arbiter between the contending parties.

The Dutch imagined they could now demand whatever they pleased—they thought themselves the strongest support of the throne of George I, and were out to obtain a profitable Barrier Treaty as

---

[1] Instructions to Hoffmann, Aug. 6, 1714, Vienna Arch.
[2] Hoffmann's dispatch, Oct. 19, 1714, Vienna Arch.

their reward. They had previously withdrawn a draft presented by them to Baron von Heems, when it was declared unacceptable by the Austrians; but now they advanced new demands which by far exceeded those of the draft: the occupation of Dendermonde, toleration of the Protestant religion, the cession of the entire Upper Quarter of Guelders, an extension of their frontier in Flanders, and the assumption of heavy financial obligations by the Emperor. In Vienna such conditions were considered disgraceful and utterly unacceptable.[1] Königsegg was to declare to the British Plenipotentiary that this would not lead to an enduring friendship between the two Powers and that, under the pretext of a Barrier against France, the Republic was about to raise one against the Emperor and the Empire in the Emperor's own territory. "We are expected", wrote Charles VI, "to nourish, support, and maintain this distrust of ourselves from our own purse." Even more emphatic was the letter of the Vienna Court to Heems:

Indeed, what confidence can we entertain towards a Republic which in war deserts us in despite of sacred alliances, and in peace time under professions of friendship and the pretext of security still further tries to deprive us of what the enemy has left us? who, when our help is required have nothing for us but coaxing words and promises; but at the first appearance of a favourable turn, when they think themselves secured by another alliance, immediately fly at us and do not hesitate to treat us in an offensive and contemptuous manner.

Such was the state of the negotiations at Antwerp when William Cadogan appeared as mediator. Like Stanhope he had distinguished himself in the War of the Spanish Succession, and was both soldier and statesman; he had served under Marlborough at Höchstedt and Malplaquet, and had established personal relations with Prince Eugene, which was a recommendation for the Antwerp negotiations. King George, when passing through Holland in September 1714, had appointed General Cadogan plenipotentiary to mediate for the Barrier Treaty;[2] he was likewise accredited to the States General, for the King considered that "he might conveniently do the business of both places", The Hague as well as Antwerp; it seemed unsafe to leave Strafford, a reputed Jacobite, at the Hague Embassy. Strafford was now informed that his services were no longer required and that he

[1] Instructions to Königsegg, Oct. 31, 1714, Vienna Arch.
[2] Hoffmann's dispatch of Sept. 28, 1714, Vienna Arch.

should prepare to leave; [1] and when six weeks later he was still at The Hague, he was told by Townshend "that his Majesty is very much surprized, that you have so long delay'd to deliver your letters of revocation, and to take your leave of the States". [2]

The security of the Netherlands being of first-rate importance to Great Britain, Cadogan was instructed [3] "to encourage and support all such proposals as shall tend to the increasing the numbers of troops to be kept in the Southern Netherlands". A speedy conclusion of the Treaty was specially desired so that the Imperial troops stationed in Bavaria and the Electorate of Cologne (which were to evacuate these territories, peace having been concluded with France) could immediately be moved to the Netherlands. It was expected that in the next war with France, which did not seem distant, Belgium would once more suffer invasion, and a defence was to be supplied for it, stronger than the Dutch Barrier and of a European character. Further, Cadogan was to watch over British commercial interests, and he was given the draft of a commercial treaty to be concluded, if possible, simultaneously with the Barrier Treaty.

Still, a reconciliation between Britain's old allies, Austria and Holland, and a renewal of her understanding with them, was the foremost diplomatic task of the new British Government. But the more distant this aim, the more extravagant were the plans connected with it—the overthrow of the Treaty of Utrecht, a renewal of the war against France, an integral revival of the entire Whig programme. The States General and the population of the Protestant Netherlands had sincerely welcomed King George; but the attitude of the Austrians was still far from favourable. They distrusted the new rulers of Great Britain and expected little from them. In the Barrier negotiations the accession of the House of Hanover had so far merely raised the terms of the States General. Doubting the stability of the new dynasty, the Austrians, though they did not think of supporting the Pretender, hesitated to enter into closer relations with the Protestant Government of Great Britain. The Emperor agreed as yet with those who thought that whoever was considered and recognized as King in England should be considered

---

[1] Townshend to Strafford, Nov. 9/20, 1714, S.P. 104/81; cf. Hoffmann's Report of Oct. 5, 1714, Vienna Arch.

[2] Townshend to Strafford, Dec. 14/25, 1714, S.P. 104/81.

[3] Oct. 11/22, 1714, F.O. 90/32.

and recognized as such by the Austrians—*i.e.* he would remain a neutral spectator.

The Secretary of State, General Stanhope, to win over the Emperor, decided to go to Vienna to communicate his schemes to him. Great Britain was about to resume diplomatic relations with the Imperial Court, and Sir Richard Temple, who had been created Lord Cobham at the Coronation, was to go as Ambassador to Vienna. Stanhope went with him. Naturally his journey made a great stir throughout Europe and he himself seemed intent on heightening the impression. Hearing Stanhope talk, it was hard to believe that the hastening of the Barrier negotiations or preparations for a defensive alliance were his purpose. This was the time when the French works at Mardyke were making much noise in England; and six days before leaving for Vienna, Stanhope threatened the French Ambassador, d'Iberville, that, if the building of the canal was not stopped, England would form an alliance which would raise 100,000 men to fill in that canal.[1] These words were immediately reported to Paris, where they naturally produced considerable excitement; and even more at The Hague, where the French Ambassador, Chateauneuf, assiduously spread them about. He declared that England had fired the first shot. This caused great consternation with the Dutch peace party; they did not doubt that the English wanted war, but the Dutch would not be involved in it, at least not on such a pretext. This view was clearly conveyed to the Great Pensionary and other statesmen who were reputed to wish for war.[2] Even in England a new war was believed imminent, and quotations on the Stock Exchange dropped.[3] The Ministers hastened to assert England's pacific intentions;[4] it was alleged that d'Iberville had misunderstood Stanhope; a new, more innocuous but hardly plausible, version of Stanhope's remarks was circulated;[5] but the fact remained that he was going to Vienna and the general anxiety was not allayed.

This, in fact, was not unfounded. Although Stanhope could not set himself a clear aim, it was his general intention to carry the Austrian statesmen with him as far as he could, and act according to circum-

[1] D'Iberville to Chateauneuf, Oct. 16, 1714, quoted in a letter from Duvenvoirde to Robethon, The Hague, Oct. 23, 1714; Stowe MSS. 227, ff. 488-91.
[2] Strafford to George I, Oct. 23, 1714.
[3] Hoffmann's dispatch of Oct. 30, 1714, Vienna Arch.
[4] *E.g.* Townshend to Strafford, Oct. 22/Nov. 2, 1714, S.P. 104/81.
[5] Hoffmann's dispatch, Oct. 30, 1714; dispatch from Meinertzhagen (Prussian Minister at The Hague), Nov. 6, 1714, Prussian State Archives.

stances. He sought clearly to ascertain the views and plans of the Imperial Court, to find out what concessions could be wrung from the Emperor concerning the Barrier, and to hasten its settlement. Circumstantial rumours had been recently circulated in England of the Austrians wishing to give up the Netherlands altogether by exchanging them against Bavaria. England was absolutely opposed to such an exchange, and Stanhope wished to discover how much truth there was in these rumours. Further, he desired to ascertain the attitude of Vienna towards a renewal of the previous alliance, and whether this would lead to war with France. Not all these plans and intentions were openly avowed, and only part of them can be traced in the written instructions which Stanhope and Cobham took with them to Vienna.[1] Still, most of the conjectures formed concerning Stanhope's journey contained a measure, or at least a grain, of truth. Probably the sensation it created was intended by Stanhope, who wanted to show that the new British Government was pursuing a new policy and, if provoked, would not shrink from war.

A few days before leaving, Stanhope had a conversation with Hoffmann, to whom he mysteriously declared that his commission would not be displeasing to the Emperor. He spoke about the talk which his journey had undoubtedly produced, and the allegations that a new war was intended: neither England nor the Emperor could engage in it at present, but it was necessary to reach an understanding in good time.[2] On October 21, O.S., the day after the coronation of George I, Stanhope left London. He broke his journey at The Hague, and in conversations with the Dutch statesmen tried to remove the impression which his words to d'Iberville had produced. To convince them of England's desire for peace, he showed them his altogether unexceptionable instructions,[3] and declared that the most important, indeed the only, aim of his mission was to prevail on the Emperor to conclude a Barrier Treaty satisfactory to the States General, as a basis for an alliance of the two Powers with Great Britain. The Dutch admitted that a defensive alliance of the three States would be the best guarantee of peace; but for their part they refused to take any steps to meet the Austrians, and all their efforts were centred on the Barrier, their most tangible gain from the last war. They could see no further. "Unless we act for them", wrote

[1] Dated Oct. 18, 1714, F.O. 90/3.
[2] Hoffmann's dispatch of Oct. 26, 1714, Vienna Arch.
[3] Duvenvoirde to Robethon, Nov. 6, 1714, Stowe MSS. 227, ff. 493-4.

Stanhope, "nothing will happen. There is no one among them who dares to assume responsibility." [1]

Stanhope was cordially received by the Emperor. The friendly relations between them had continued since the time when the General was one of the most effective champions of Charles III in Spain. Charles himself had recently expressed the wish to welcome Stanhope in Vienna,[2] and Stanhope based his hopes for the success of his mission on the personal good-will of the Emperor. But in political matters an understanding was not easy, and Stanhope soon perceived what a deep distrust he had to overcome. The Emperor listened coldly to what he had to say about the desire of George I to enter into close relations with the Imperial Court, and about the necessity to conclude the Barrier negotiations. Nor did the first conference with Prince Eugene yield favourable results.[3] Stanhope communicated to him his more secret plans and obviously went further than directed by his instructions,[4] and than he subsequently admitted in his reports to London. He urged on the Prince the necessity of renewing the previous Triple Alliance between Austria and the Maritime Powers. The King of England offered the Emperor a defensive alliance to which the States General were to accede. This was at first to be concluded for the preservation of the *status possidendi*, but in future was to be changed into an offensive alliance. Naturally these intentions were to be kept secret. It was in a way the utmost which the British Minister had to say and to offer to the Emperor; it contained an entire programme of far-reaching schemes and of military plans. Everything else proposed by Stanhope appeared subsidiary to the one great aim. Stanhope therefore pressed for a speedy conclusion of the Barrier Treaty, to open the way to a reconciliation between Austria and Holland. Entering into details, he urged that the States General, who had given in on other points, would not insist on the occupation of Dendermonde—a point violently disputed at Antwerp. Stanhope asked that the maximum of concessions which the Emperor was prepared to make to the Dutch should be communicated to him. Lastly, he demanded that a guarantee of the Treaty of Utrecht should be inserted in the Barrier Treaty. But he soon learned from Prince

---

[1] Stanhope to Townshend, Nov. 6, 1714; Mahon, i, App.
[2] Hoffmann's dispatch of Oct. 30, 1714, Vienna Arch.
[3] Stanhope to Townshend, Vienna, Nov. 13/24, 1714; Mahon, i, App.
[4] Report on the Conference of Nov. 27, 1714, dated Nov. 29, Vienna Arch.
Further cf. Weber, *Die Quadrupel-Allianz vom Jahre* 1718, p. 3.

Eugene how much the Vienna Court disliked this demand, which amounted to a recognition of Philip V—how could the Emperor be expected to renounce the rights for which he had fought with such determination, and had continued to fight, even when deserted by his allies?

The Secret Conference met to consider Stanhope's proposals and decided upon the reply that the Emperor was favourably inclined to a defensive alliance; "for though his Imperial Majesty had lately received very bad treatment from England, he had preserved his respect for the nation, and knew how to distinguish between the previous and the present Government and Cabinet". But before an alliance could be concluded, the Emperor had to obtain possession of his Netherlands. The Barrier Treaty had to come first. Stanhope was determined to ascertain, before leaving Vienna, the extent of concessions which the Emperor was prepared to make, and, on his way through The Hague, the same with regard to the Dutch. On the other hand, in the report of the Conference it is said that an attempt must be made "skilfully to elicit from Stanhope the true intentions of the British Court and the States General with regard to the ultimatum".

The Vienna Court fluctuated between two extreme views: the one was not to wait for the conclusion of the Barrier Treaty but march Austrian troops into the Netherlands; and this might have been done had not Cadogan at Antwerp sharply declared to Count Königsegg that England would consider it an open breach. The other view, favoured by Prince Eugene, was that the possession of the Netherlands was of no value after the best fortresses had been ceded to the Dutch; the Prince, in his last talk with Stanhope, openly declared in favour of exchanging Belgium for Bavaria. Henceforth it was Stanhope's endeavour to stop Austria from either measure, a premature occupation or an abandonment of the Netherlands.

On November 28, Stanhope and Cobham were invited to dinner with Prince Eugene, who adopted a more conciliatory tone, and showed himself inclined to an alliance with England but not to the Barrier Treaty. Stanhope replied that if a treaty was to be concluded between the three Powers guaranteeing the acquisitions made at Utrecht and Baden, the best and most discreet manner of doing it would be by inserting one or several articles to that effect in the proposed Barrier Treaty. He further wished to add an article whereby the House of Austria would agree never to alienate the Southern Netherlands. The Prince's manner did not altogether please his

British guests, to whom his ceremonious dignity appeared as offensive pride. They preferred Count Sinzendorff, but Stanhope fared best of all with Charles VI, who professed himself England's greatest friend at the Vienna Court.[1] Stanhope thought he could rely on him not to agree to an exchange of the Netherlands against Bavaria.[2]

When after a fortnight in Vienna Stanhope found the Barrier problem no nearer a solution than on the first day of the Antwerp Conference, he applied for an audience with the Emperor and declared that he had completed his mission, and could only repeat the wish of his King for a close connexion with the Emperor. Charles replied that he too thought the alliance necessary and for that purpose intended to send an envoy to England, who had his full confidence. But almost a year was to elapse before the Imperial Ambassador, Count Volkra, appeared in London; and the alliance between the two Powers was not signed till June 1716.

Stanhope's departure from Vienna was postponed for another few weeks. Not to let him leave empty-handed, a draft of the Barrier Treaty was prepared which was to embody the utmost concessions of the Emperor. Other political problems were also discussed between Stanhope and the Austrian Ministers, foremost the conflict in Northern Europe—Charles XII had just returned from Turkey. The Austrians showed little interest in these matters, but the Emperor promised Stanhope to decide about them only in an understanding with George I. Shortly before Christmas Stanhope received the promised draft of the Barrier Treaty, which he meant to communicate personally to the Dutch; Prince Eugene and Sinzendorff had added marginal remarks to every single article. In the last audience with the Emperor, Stanhope was assured once more that the Emperor meant to preserve a permanent union with the King of England. He was dismissed in the most gracious manner, and given a picture of Charles VI set with diamonds.[3]

Stanhope's stay at The Hague was short. After Count Königsegg had raised hopes in England and Holland that the "dernière résolution" of his Court would be satisfactory, the one brought by Stanhope from Vienna came as a disappointment to the States

---

[1] Stanhope's letters to Townshend of Nov. 17/28, Dec. 15, O.S., 1714, S.P. 80/32.

[2] Stanhope to Townshend, Dec. 8, 1714; Mahon, i, App.

[3] Stanhope to Townshend, Vienna, Dec. 5, 8, 12, 19, 22, O.S., 1714, S.P. 80/32.

General, and was declared by them unacceptable.[1] Should no agreement be arrived at, some Dutch statesmen were for asking King George to guarantee the Barrier; and should he refuse, they would know to whom to turn[2]—a hint at France. On January 12/23, 1715, Stanhope returned to London, having achieved little either in bringing about an understanding between Holland and Austria or in re-establishing the old alliances. D'Iberville's contention was not altogether wrong when he asserted that Stanhope had tried to gain the Emperor for a new war, and that his attempt had failed.[3]

The negotiations at Antwerp had been hampered rather than promoted by Stanhope's journey. At first news was awaited from Vienna; and next a draft was brought by Stanhope which, if it was really the last word of the Emperor's, seemed to preclude an understanding. The Austrians, in their turn, seeing Britain's endeavours to bring about an agreement, tried to amend the Barrier Treaty to their own advantage. Hoffmann declared that the Emperor had said his last word, while Stanhope asserted the contrary to his face.[4] No less troublesome were the States General, which insisted on Dendermonde and the Castle of Ghent, and had to be reminded that the days of the Barrier Treaty of 1709 were over.[5]

The British mediators now demanded certain concessions from the Vienna Court as a basis for further negotiations with Holland, and, to hasten matters, the discussion was transferred from Antwerp to Vienna, where, after Stanhope's departure, Cobham had tried in vain to wring concessions from the Austrians.[6] Cadogan was to proceed to Vienna, not because of Cobham's insufficiency, but, as Cobham was assured, because Cadogan had particular knowledge of the subject. In this respect he was undoubtedly preferable as a negotiator to Stanhope, who attended to the broad outlines of policy, but treated details with a certain impatient superficiality. Moreover, Cadogan's friendly relations with Prince Eugene were likely to prove useful. He was specially instructed to ascertain how much truth there was in the rumour which ascribed the delay not to the Emperor's dissatisfaction with the offer but to secret negotiations with France and Bavaria, alleged to cover half Europe: wide territories in Italy, Bavaria, and

[1] Cobham to Townshend, Feb. 2, 1715, S.P. 80/32.
[2] Hoffmann's dispatch of Jan 18, 1715, Vienna Arch.
[3] Hoffmann's dispatch of Jan. 15, 1715, *ibid.*   [4] *Ibid.*
[5] Townshend to H. Walpole, Jan. 18, 1715, S.P. 104/81.
[6] Cobham's reports of Jan. and Feb. 1715, S.P. 80/32.

also some Swabian and Franconian districts were to be assigned to
Austria, while the Belgian provinces were to be partitioned between
France and the Elector of Bavaria. The Pretender was to be married
to an Austrian Archduchess and to be played off against England.
Lastly, Charles XII of Sweden was to be saved by the Franco-Austrian
alliance from his numerous enemies. This scheme would raise the
power of France to an unprecedented height; the Princes of the
Empire and the States General would have to submit to French
leadership. George I might hold out for some time—the general
election had gone in his favour—but ultimately even he would sink
before such superior force.

Whatever truth there was in these rumours, their influence on
British policy was considerable;[1] they were believed, however much
contradicted by Hoffmann. Why then, he was asked, does the
Emperor delay the signing of the Barrier Treaty? Was it really impossible for him to renounce the small remainder of Upper Guelders
which, in view of the cessions made to Prussia at Utrecht, was
of no value? Hoffmann dolefully reported[2] that he was now in
almost as bad odour in London as in the last four years of the
Queen's reign.

Should Cadogan's mission fail to elucidate the intentions of the
Vienna Court, the idea was discussed of sending no less a person
than the Duke of Marlborough to try whether he could succeed in
making the Emperor accept the Barrier Treaty. Subsequently the
intention was denied—it was viewed by some as another proof of
Britain's warlike intentions[3]—but Hoffmann had heard it from a
Minister and had immediately reported it to Vienna.[4]

Cadogan succeeded better than he and his Government had expected.[5] He arrived in Vienna on February 22 and was given a friendly
reception. He had several conferences with Prince Eugene and Count
Sinzendorff, dwelt on the urgency of the matter, and declared that
the Dutch would accept the draft communicated through Stanhope,
provided the Emperor conceded to them a frontier rectification in
Flanders, payment of the Dutch garrisons, and possession of the

---

[1] About the mission of Count du Luc to the Vienna Court see his instructions
dated Jan. 3, 1715, in *Recueil des instructions données aux ambassadeurs et
ministres de France. Autriche*, pp. 154-83.
[2] March 2, 1715, Vienna Arch.
[3] Bonet's dispatch of March 4/15, 1715, Prussian State Archives.
[4] Hoffmann's dispatch of March 8, 1715, Vienna Arch.
[5] Cadogan to Townshend, March 2, 10, 20, 1715.

districts of Venlo and Stevensweert. Cadogan exerted himself to persuade the Vienna Court, and spoke of the unfavourable interpretation placed by some on Austria's marked reserve. On March 8 a note was presented to him,[1] practically accepting his demands; only to the financial clause certain objections were raised. But even these were soon removed, and on March 20 Cadogan was able to report to his Government that he had succeeded in settling the three points according to the King's wishes. The next day the Emperor wrote to Count Königsegg [2] that he had gone so far in his concessions as to feel uneasy in his conscience and fear the judgment of posterity. The concessions were made presumably to disprove the suspicions of a secret understanding with France, the existence of which was emphatically denied by the Imperial Ministers. They assured Cadogan that the Vienna Court was determined to enter into a lasting alliance with the Maritime Powers,[3] but that England must now do her part and take a firm line with the States General should they raise any further difficulties. Cadogan proceeded to the Netherlands and continued the laborious task of mediation at Antwerp, The Hague, and Brussels, while Horace Walpole, who in the meantime had acted as *chargé d'affaires* in Holland, returned to England.

The British Court was highly pleased with Cadogan's unexpected success at Vienna, and urged the States General to accept the Austrian offer; they, however, refused to renounce Dendermonde and Huy, which placed the British statesmen in an embarrassing position, as they had hitherto given out in Vienna that they were sure of the Dutch agreeing provided only the Emperor conceded those three points. They seemed now in honour bound to the Emperor, and, as the King informed Hoffmann, they would not hear of the Dutch objections; and when Hoffmann enquired whether the King would not in the end make some further concessions to them, George replied emphatically: *"en rien, en rien, il faut qu'ils s'en contentent"* [4]— Hoffmann and the King, both Germans, as diplomats conversed in French. But the Dutch demands, especially with regard to Huy, received after all British support, and the Emperor was urged to concede this as a "further *douceur*" to the States General, burdened as they were with debt; the Treaty should not be endangered over such small

[1] Enclosed in instructions to Hoffmann of March 19, 1715, Vienna Arch.
[2] Instruction of March 9, 1715, Vienna Arch.
[3] Cadogan to Townshend, March 20, 1715.
[4] Hoffmann's report of April 23, 1715, Vienna Arch.

points. When in June 1715 instructions were drafted for General Carpenter, the new British Ambassador to Vienna, the Barrier was mentioned as a matter which would presumably be settled before Carpenter's arrival at the Imperial Court.

Yet many months were to pass before an agreement was reached. First the Emperor complained of England's not having kept her word, and of Cadogan's having made concessions to Holland which exceeded the Emperor's "final resolution"; a Dutch Minister, declared Hoffmann,[1] could hardly oppose the Emperor's interest more strongly than Cadogan. Königsegg was sent on a special mission to London, and as Cadogan was there too, London was for a time the centre of the negotiations. It was urged by the English that Cadogan had acted on orders from the King and that it was impossible to go back on it without disavowing the King.[2] The Emperor requested the British Court, should the States General refuse his "ultimatum", to give up the mediation, recall the British troops from the Netherlands and admit the entry of the Austrians. Bernstorff answered evasively that there was hope of a speedy settlement.

On August 16, the Secret Conference met in Vienna and took a new decision, which was described as final, and which they professed to hope would satisfy the States General. On August 20, a courier left for Antwerp. Königsegg produced the new "ultimatum" declaring that it had to be accepted within six weeks. The Dutch Ambassadors in London now complained "in very strong terms" and the British *chargé d'affaires* in Vienna, Luke Schaub, had to demand that the Imperial Court should "at least make no scruple to lengthen the time".[3] This provoked the indignation of the Austrians, who considered that they had anyhow shown too much patience and gone too far in their concessions. The Emperor felt inclined to drop the negotiations and march an army into the Netherlands, but the majority of his Ministers opposed this. The Emperor therefore adhered to his "ultimatum" but added an "explanation" of a conciliatory character. None the less no understanding was reached. The question of religion in the parts of Flanders and Guelders to be ceded to the States General was now the point at issue. In the conversations

---

[1] Report of June 28, 1715, *ibid.*

[2] Instructions to Hoffmann, June 26, 1715; Hoffmann's Report of July 19, 1715, Vienna Arch.

[3] Tilson to Schaub, Sept. 23/Oct. 4, 1715; Townshend to Schaub, Sept. 30/Oct. 11, 1715, S.P. 104/42.

with Schaub and the Imperial Ministers hard words were used about the Republic, its obstinacy and conceit. Prince Eugene declared that the Dutch had played the masters in Imperial territory too long and that they delayed negotiations only in order to continue their dominion, and Sinzendorff thought that too much leniency had been shown to them—he knew their nature: they had to be kept in awe.[1]

In some measure the British attitude in these negotiations was bound up with the international situation. If in the spring of 1715 British mediation was more favourable to the wishes of the Emperor than to those of the States General, this was because the King-Elector needed the concurrence of the Emperor in his Northern policy. But the position changed with the outbreak of the Jacobite Rebellion, of which no one could as yet foresee the extent; the States General were guarantors of the Protestant Succession and were now asked by England for 6000 men, which help they readily promised. But naturally the Dutch now raised their demands with regard to the Barrier. Hoffmann was urged to move the Emperor to new concessions; King George put it to him as his personal request; Bernstorff and Bothmer stressed the fact that the dispatch of the Dutch troops depended on the settlement of the Barrier. Even Lord Nottingham tried his best to impress Hoffmann: the Emperor apparently hated the Dutch because of the treatment experienced from them during the peace negotiations, but the blame for it fell on the Tory Ministers, who were about to be punished. Surely the Emperor was interested in preventing the return of a Government amenable to French influence, and from whom, in case of need, he could expect no support. He should therefore now, for England's sake, make concessions to the Dutch. The argument was cogent but based on a wrong premise: the resentment of the Emperor did not go back to the late Peace Treaty but was caused by the attitude of the States General in the Barrier negotiations, and, as Hoffmann asserted, would not outlast them.[2] Meantime progress had been made at Antwerp. On November 7, Cadogan reported that everything was settled, and on the 15th the Barrier Treaty was signed. Negotiations had lasted eighteen months, and the Antwerp Conference had met forty-eight times, but, as it often happens, the decisions had been reached elsewhere—in London, Vienna, and at The Hague.

[1] Schaub to Townshend, Oct. 19, 23, 1715, S.P. 80/32.
[2] Hoffmann's dispatch of Oct. 9, 1715, Vienna Arch.

The new Barrier Treaty differed widely from that of 1709, when the Dutch were courted by several Powers, and Great Britain had to accept their demands. Even in 1713 the position of the States General remained favourable. This time, however, Holland had to face not Great Britain with a merely indirect interest in the matter, but Austria, the future owner of the Southern Netherlands. Britain acted the more or less impartial mediator and, except for her commercial interests, wished for nothing but to see the Treaty concluded, as a necessary basis for her further European schemes.

The Treaties of 1709 and 1713 seemed forgotten, and in the preamble to the Barrier Treaty of 1715 only the Hague Alliance of 1701 was mentioned, while Article XI of the Treaty of 1713[1] was passed over in silence. A curtain was drawn on the antecedents of the Barrier Treaty, and the contents of the Hague Treaty were deliberately mis-stated. It was said in the preamble to the Barrier Treaty that in 1701 the Allied Powers had intended to provide for the security of the Southern Netherlands "so that they should serve as Barrier to Great Britain and the United Provinces". In reality, the Barrier was then named as a protection for the United Provinces only, while the real part played by Great Britain in the affair of the Barrier was left unmentioned. This new interest was invented in order to explain her mediation and participation in the Treaty. The Emperor now at last obtained possession of the Belgian Provinces assigned to him by the Treaties of Peace; it was explicitly stipulated in Article II that the Emperor should never alienate the Belgian Netherlands, or any part of them, from the hereditary possessions of the House of Austria (this was to prevent an exchange against Bavaria). The Dutch, for a long time masters in the Catholic Netherlands, had to evacuate them, but were to be partly responsible for their security: the Emperor was to supply three-fifths of the troops to be employed in the defence of the Southern Netherlands, and the Dutch two-fifths. The Emperor admitted their right to garrison a chain of fortresses along the French frontier, but not all those promised in 1713; Mons and Charleroi were not among them, still less those conceded in the Barrier Treaty of 1709. The States were to keep garrisons at Furnes, Knocke, Ypres, Warneton, Menin, Tournai, and Namur, and the Emperor promised to pay 500,000 thalers a year for that purpose. Further provisions were made for effective defence by the States General in case of an enemy attack. In peace time they were free to import neces-

---

[1] See above, p. 229.

saries for their troops free of duty, a privilege liable to open the door to illicit trade. The States General had insisted on obtaining Dendermonde, which Austria neither would, nor could, cede as Dendermonde was "the key to all Brabant";[1] in the end it was agreed that Dendermonde was to be jointly garrisoned by equal numbers of Austrians and Dutch under a Governor appointed by the Emperor, who was, however, to take an oath also to the States General.

In the Barrier fortresses the Dutch were given powers implicit in a military occupation, while Austria retained control of civil and religious matters. Certain parts of Flanders and Upper Guelders between the sea and the Scheldt were, however, ceded outright to the States General and could no longer be counted as part of the Barrier in the accepted sense. Cadogan had succeeded in overcoming the bitter opposition of the Austrians, the alleged ground for the cession being the need of an effective organization of the flooding system for the military defence of Holland. In reality another aim achieved by this cession was the complete control of the Scheldt which the Dutch tacitly assumed for the future. Cadogan had told the Emperor that it was a question of a few villages only, and Königsegg was instructed to ascertain whether nothing more important was implied; but in matters of commerce the Dutch were undoubtedly superior to the Austrians.

Another important success of Cadogan's was to have obtained from Austria the cession of the parts of the Upper Quarter of Guelders, situated on the Meuse. Their loss meant less to the Emperor than their gain to the States General: it gave them the strategic control of the lower Meuse—Namur was a Barrier fortress, Maastricht had long been in their possession, and though Huy was retained by the Austrians its fort and the citadel of Liège were to be razed; lower down the Dutch obtained Stevensweert and Venlo, and Fort St. Michel on the other side of the river. Upper Guelderland was now partitioned between Austria, the States General, and Prussia —this constituted Prussia's interest in the Antwerp negotiations. Bonet watched over her interests in London, but King Frederick William I demanded also the admission of a Prussian Plenipotentiary to the Antwerp negotiations. England and the Emperor agreed, and so did the States General after some resistance. The Prussian representative managed to obtain that in Article

[1] Swift, "Some Remarks on the Barrier Treaty," *Works*, v. p. 124.

XVIII, dealing with the cession of Upper Guelderland, the rights of Prussia, as established in 1713, were expressly recognized and confirmed.[1]

Article XXVI of the Barrier Treaty stipulated that until the arrangement of a new commercial treaty the duties on the exports and imports of the Maritime Powers should continue to be paid on the present footing. The King of Great Britain guaranteed the entire Treaty.

The signing of the Barrier Treaty did not put an end to the wrangle between the Emperor and the Dutch. Article XXIX stipulated that the Treaty should be ratified within six weeks; but the term expired without the ratification by the States General having reached Antwerp; for the British ratification had not come yet and the Dutch meant to await its arrival. A new difficulty had arisen over the duty to be paid on heavy English cloth, and the English, tenacious about trade, meant to delay the ratification of the Barrier Treaty till their interests were secured. General Cadogan had left the Netherlands for Scotland to fight the Jacobites; but he was again consulted by his Government and from the camp at Stirling sent his observations to London.[2]

The new delay was not without danger, as France was trying to counter the growing connexion between the Maritime Powers and the Habsburgs. The proposal was made to the States General to drop the Barrier Treaty, to withhold the Belgian Provinces from the Emperor, and make them into a neutral State. Their High Mightinesses, however, replied that they would first have to communicate this proposal to King George and the Emperor, which was tantamount to a refusal. The attitude of France after the Treaty of Ryswick was recalled by Townshend "when the terrible apprehensions of a new war made us and the Dutch run into the measures of a Partition Treaty, which was believed might be a wonderful preservation against war, but in effect proved the source, and the chief occasion of it".[3] Even stronger displeasure was naturally felt at the French proposal in Vienna. The Emperor professed to know that the French merely meant to coax the Dutch in order to detach them from the Triple Alliance, and England was asked to "stiffen up" the Republic in its

---

[1] Cf. Bonet's dispatches for 1715 and enclosures; further, cf. Gachard, p. 245 seq.

[2] Cadogan to Townshend, Stirling, Dec. 31, 1715.

[3] Townshend to Walpole, Dec. 27, O.S. 1715, S.P. 104/81.

resistance to the French.[1] And still the ratifications of the Barrier Treaty had not been exchanged. The patience of the Austrians now broke. On January 16, 1716, Count Königsegg wrote a letter to the Dutch deputies "in so vehement a style" as made Townshend think "it proceeded from Monsieur Heems' impetuous temper and not from his own, which has a more gentle and complaisant turn".[2] He threatened, "in a very peremptory manner", that the Austrians would "take possession of the Low Countries the 19th, in case they were not ready by that time to exchange the ratifications with him".[3] But two days earlier, on January 14, a courier had left London for Brussels with the King's ratification.[4] It did not seem worth while endangering the Barrier Treaty and opening the door to French intrigue in Holland, for the sake of the British woollen trade. Ratifications were exchanged before the term set by Königsegg had expired.

The Barrier Treaty was a humiliation which the Emperor had to undergo because of the international situation. The British contention, that Dutch garrisons were indispensable for the defence of the Netherlands, was incorrect. The Barrier and the frontier rectifications in Flanders and Upper Guelderland were the Dutch share in the booty of the Spanish War of Succession.

Austria had reluctantly taken over the Belgian Provinces, and the idea continually recurred of exchanging them against Bavaria—at that distance, the Netherlands were a burden rather than an asset to the Habsburgs. They were a province with its fortresses in the occupation of a foreign Power, which had moreover to be paid for garrisoning them. The best trade route was under the control of that Power; and in 1731 the closure of the Scheldt was explicitly renewed.

When in the War of the Austrian Succession the French attacked the Netherlands, the Dutch garrisons surrendered the fortresses practically without resistance. Subsequently these fortresses were completely neglected; while the Barrier itself became superfluous after France had, in 1756, become Austria's ally. The Vienna Court had long wished to free themselves of the Barrier Treaty, and Joseph II, soon after he had become sole ruler of Austria, unilaterally

[1] Instructions to Volkra, Jan 11, 1716, Vienna Arch.
[2] Townshend to Walpole, Jan. 17/28, 1716, S.P. 104/81.
[3] Walpole to Townshend, Jan. 21, 1716, enclosing Königsegg's letter, S.P. 84/253.
[4] Reports from Hoffmann and Volkra, Vienna Arch.

denounced it. The Barrier had not *become* obsolete—it was obsolete when the Treaty of 1715 was concluded.

The Barrier Treaty formed the basis for a new system of alliances planned by George I; and firm support abroad was valuable at a time of internal upheaval in Great Britain, especially in view of the semi-hostile attitude of France in the first months of the Rebellion.

In Austria a renewal of the "Old System" was desired perhaps even more than in England. Stanhope's remarks in 1714 about an Anglo-Austrian alliance had made a deep impression in Vienna; the idea was never altogether abandoned by the Austrians. A complete draft of an alliance between the Emperor and the Maritime Powers was made and given to Stanhope for submission to his Court. But nothing was heard about it for some time. A few months later, in April and May 1715, when the Barrier negotiations had reached an impasse, it was suggested in Vienna that an Anglo-Austrian alliance might be concluded before the Barrier was settled. Count Sinzendorff put this to Lord Cobham, mentioning at the same time a pacification in the North, but the Ambassador could see that, having secured an alliance with Great Britain, the Austrians would stiffen in the negotiations with Holland, and there would be no end to them. He therefore courteously but firmly refused the offer—stating that the King was merely waiting for the conclusion of the Antwerp negotiations before he approached the question of the alliance. The reply was fully approved of in London—"it will be time enough to think of a new alliance when that Treaty is concluded".[1]

There was a special reason why the Emperor now wished for a British alliance. He had not abandoned the hope of acquiring Sicily, which at Utrecht had been assigned to Savoy; without it the possession even of Naples seemed insecure. There was much political discontent in the island; but what encouraged the Emperor most to attempt its conquest was the help promised by the Pope, who had quarrelled with the King of Savoy. The time seemed ripe for action; and yet it could not be attempted without a fleet, *i.e.* without the support of Great Britain. In April 1715 Hoffmann was therefore instructed to approach the British Government with a request for the support of the Mediterranean fleet.[2] He spoke to Bernstorff and

---

[1] Cobham to Townshend, May 1, 1715, S.P. 80/32; Townshend to Cobham, May 10, 1715, S.P. 104/81.

[2] Instructions to Hoffmann, April 17, 1715, Vienna Arch.

Bothmer, and to Stanhope who did not in principle reject the idea
but thought the time inexpedient as England had only four warships
in the Mediterranean.[1]

A few weeks later the Austrians remembered the draft Treaty
which the previous year had been entrusted to Stanhope and which
in its second secret article stipulated that Great Britain and Holland
should, so far from opposing the Emperor if he tried to regain the lost
parts of the Spanish Empire, do their best to support him in his
undertaking. This applied more particularly to Sicily. Possibly it was
this ticklish article which at the time had made Stanhope entirely
suppress the draft Treaty. But when, in May 1715, in connexion with
the Northern conflict, the old idea of an alliance between the Maritime
Powers and the Emperor was brought up by England, the opportunity
was taken by the Austrians to enquire after that draft Treaty of
December 1714, Hoffmann telling Bernstorff and Bothmer that the
Emperor had long ago expressed in it his ideas concerning an alliance.
The two Hanoverians were greatly taken aback—they had never
heard of such a draft. At their request Hoffmann supplied them with
a copy, and, at the first opportunity, challenged Stanhope why he
had failed to submit it to his Government. He received the mysterious
answer that he should preferably not mention the matter at present
"for the time had not yet come to speak about it".

Although this was professedly the draft for a defensive alliance,
the secret article in itself shows that an offensive alliance was
planned. Stanhope himself had held out the prospect, and the
Austrians merely followed his lead. But soon the British Government
denied all warlike intentions; though these were not really abandoned
and Stanhope remained their foremost exponent at the Court of
George I. And in spite of all this reticence, the subject would be
occasionally mentioned. In 1715 Pope Innocent XII offered the
Emperor to mediate between him and Philip V of Spain. Hoffmann
communicated this offer to the British Court, because Charles VI
would not do anything in that matter without the approval of his
future ally, George I.[2] But the British Ministers advised delay.
Bernstorff said to Hoffmann "that the King of France might die and
a great revolution ensue"; and Stanhope was even more explicit—
Hoffmann reported on June 25, 1715: "He said that the King of
France was wasting away, and that within six months the situation

---

[1] Hoffmann's dispatch of May 10, 1715, Vienna Arch.
[2] Instructions to Hoffmann, May 29, 1715, *ibid.*

here may have changed so much that this nation will be for war rather than for peace".[1] The sense is clear: the leading British statesmen desired a renewal of war against France, but preferred to await the death of Louis XIV and the chaos which could be expected. England would then presumably be in a mood to renew the war, but that time had better be awaited. Meantime, the conclusion of peace with Charles VI and Philip V had to be avoided, as that conflict would offer a convenient starting-point for a general war. For this reason a discussion of the unambiguous Austrian draft Treaty was inexpedient for the present, as it would have forced the British Government to declare for or against war. Neither British public opinion nor the European situation was ripe for openly avowing the resumption of the full Whig programme in international affairs.

In the last months of the Queen there had been negotiations for a grand alliance with France and her satellites against Austria; after the accession of George I, British statesmen merely waited for the death of Louis XIV once more to unite half Europe against the House of Bourbon. But the scheme was never to materialize. The news of the death of Louis XIV on September 1, 1715, was an occasion for open joy and mutual congratulations at the British Court—but this was inspired by a feeling of relief, not an adventurous desire for a new war. The British Government was faced with a Jacobite rebellion and dreaded most of all French interference on behalf of the Pretender. Louis' successor was a child, and the right to the Regency was contested; hence there was little danger from that side. Yet for England this was not a time for warlike undertakings either.

Great Britain was as yet isolated among the European Powers; for her own defence it was necessary to conclude at last the alliance with Holland and Austria. Even before the signing of the Barrier Treaty on November 15, 1715, an Imperial Ambassador had

---

[1] Hoffmann's dispatch of June 25, 1715. The importance which Hoffmann attached to these pronouncements is shown by his using a cypher which he otherwise employed sparingly.—Stanhope spoke in a similar sense also on other occasions. Hoffmann, under date of January 2, reports him as having said that time would prove England to pay as little regard to the Bourbon Courts as to Savoy, and that then she would help the Emperor in every way (this was after Charles VI had asked for help against Sicily). Again, on July 16 he reported Stanhope to have said that a change might occur sooner than was expected and a state might arise in which the King would leave no indignity unavenged.

been sent to England—there had been none since the failure of Prince Eugene's mission to England in 1712. The Resident, Johann Philipp Hoffmann, though not a statesman, had done his work sensibly and well. From long experience he was equally well acquainted with the various currents and persons at the British Court as with the wishes of the Emperor.

Very different from Hoffmann was the new Imperial Ambassador, Count Volkra. Inexperienced as a diplomat, he was haughty and arrogant in his intercourse with the British Ministers, who repeatedly complained about his making difficulties where there were none, and insisting on demands which the Emperor himself had relinquished. Writing to Vienna Townshend remarked "that this allyance might have been brought to bear before now had we had such a man with us as Count Königsegg; with whom we might with pleasure and ease transact more business in a month than with our present Envoy in a year".[1] Prince Eugene admitted that Volkra had been a wrong choice. He was said to have entertained a secret correspondence with the Spaniards at the Vienna Court and through them with the Emperor, and by such means to have received instructions behind the back of the State Conference. From the day of Volkra's appointment the German Ministers of Charles VI worked therefore for his recall, and the difference between the two Austrian Envoys in London, traceable in some of their concurrent reports, reflected differences within the Austrian Government. On the one hand, they were about to enter into an understanding with the Powers which had concluded the Treaty of Utrecht, but on the other, they refused to relinquish their old claims to the entire Spanish Empire. Although Volkra was regarded in London as the most obstinate exponent of the Imperial claims, in his inexperience he would occasionally go too far in adopting the English view. This would earn him bitter reproaches from the Emperor—he should not "so easily fall in" with everything which was put to him in London. On one occasion it was even proposed to remind him in a rescript from the Emperor that it was for him to do the Emperor's business, and not that of the British Government; but in the end these words were deleted as excessively severe. He was directed in his instructions to work for a return to the old friendship between the two Courts and for a close alliance; but he was cautioned not in any way to recognize the Treaty of Utrecht, concluded "to the detriment" of the Empire and the House of Austria. Volkra was to

[1] Townshend to Schaub, Feb. 17, March 20, 1716, S.P. 104/42.

declare that the Emperor stood by the Treaty of Baden, but neither could, nor would, take cognizance of that of Utrecht as a *res inter alios acta*.

When Volkra arrived in London, the Scottish rebellion was at its height. In the first audience with George I, Count Volkra in the Emperor's name congratulated him on his accession.[1] Next, the conversation turned to the Barrier Treaty, which had just been concluded, but did not contain the mutual guarantee of their possessions which at times had been planned. The King thought that it had better be done in a separate Treaty. But this, too, presented difficulties; a Triple Alliance was intended, but the States General were not as yet prepared for it. At first the British Ministers replied evasively that proposals from the Emperor were awaited; next, that the Dutch would have to be brought more effectively into it.[2] The signing of the Barrier Treaty was followed by new discussions. Cadogan had left Holland, and Horace Walpole returned to The Hague to settle contentious or obscure points. The attempt to conclude the Triple Alliance before the meeting of Parliament failed[3] and the renewal of the old alliance with the States General was contemplated.

The relations between the Emperor and the Republic had still further deteriorated because of the continued Dutch occupation of the fortress of Bonn, in the Electorate of Cologne, a right conceded to them in the Treaty of Utrecht; but as it was not mentioned in the Treaty of Baden, the only one recognized by the Emperor and the Empire, the Archbishop-Elector refused to suffer the continued presence of the Dutch troops in his capital. In November 1715 Cologne troops entered the town, and on December 11 the Dutch had to withdraw. The same day the Elector, Joseph Clement, entered it, enthusiastically acclaimed by the population. The *coup* caused much excitement; the States General protested, presented a note in London, and declared everywhere that the Elector could not have acted without the connivance of the Emperor. This was emphatically denied in Vienna, the Emperor professing himself as much surprised as anyone else. But there were some who openly applauded the Elector. Count Stahremberg, intensely hostile to the Dutch, said that they had obviously to be dragged into everything. Further annoyance was caused to the Dutch by the news that the Emperor, in contravention

---

[1] Volkra's dispatch, Nov. 15/26, 1715, Vienna Arch.

[2] Volkra's dispatches, Nov. 29/Dec. 10, and Dec. 6/17, 1715, *ibid*.

[3] See above, pp. 205-206.

of the Barrier Treaty, intended to cede the Duchy of Limburg to the Elector-Palatine.

In these circumstances Austria and Holland were not likely to participate in a Triple Alliance. But England did not want to risk the Dutch being gained over by France, and therefore decided to conclude an alliance with them as basis for a Triple Alliance; and the British Ministers tried to convince even the Austrians that this step was necessary. There was no difficulty in renewing the old alliance between the Maritime Powers, and in January 1716 a Treaty was agreed upon between the British Ministers and the Dutch Ambassador. It was sent to The Hague, was soon returned with the necessary full-powers, and was signed on February 6/17, 1716. This was the first of a series of alliances concluded by George I with the Great Powers—the first step towards the system of the Quadruple Alliance of 1718, which was for some time to dominate the European situation.

The Treaty of February 6, 1716, confirmed all the agreements concluded between the two Powers, from the Peace of Breda in 1669 to the Barrier Treaty of 1715, with the proviso that previous stipulations stood in so far as not superseded by later ones. The Treaty of March 3, 1678, was named as the basis for common defence in case of attack against one of the contracting Powers; and a secret article stipulated that the case should be considered to have arisen not merely when an actual attack was suffered but even if another Power armed, or threatened to arm, against one of the contracting Powers. Open or secret hostilities from the Duke of Orleans were daily expected in England, and the article was obviously designed to make the Dutch arm as soon as the Regent declared for the Pretender.

Austria, meantime, sulked because of Britain's independent action. Similarly, the conclusion of the Anglo-Spanish Commercial Treaty in December 1715 caused much annoyance in Vienna, though the British Government truly asserted that it contained "nothing but what relates to our trade".[1] Charles VI feared that he could not in future count on British help against his enemy, Philip of Anjou; and to him the underlying plans for a common offensive were the main point of the proposed alliance. The British *chargé d'affaires*, Luke Schaub, had to listen to angry speeches. Prince Eugene declared that after the experiences of the Barrier Treaty and after an understanding had

---

[1] Townshend to Schaub, Dec. 20/31, 1715, S.P. 104/32. Schaub to Townshend, Jan. 29/Feb. 9, 1716, S.P. 80/33.

been established between Great Britain and Anjou, there could be no talk about a debt of gratitude owing to King George from the Emperor. Now the Emperor was expected to accede to the alliance between the Maritime Powers. But British diplomacy was not specially particular about questions of form, and did not care in what way this was done. Article IV of the Treaty foreshadowed the adherence of other States which would either ask to be admitted or be invited to accede to it; nor would there have been any objection to concluding a new Triple Alliance on similar lines. But the mere proposal of acceding to the Treaty caused offence at the Imperial Court, and an awkward report from Volkra enhanced the annoyance. This, said Prince Eugene, was the way to treat a princeling, not the Emperor.[1] In reply Townshend explained in a long dispatch to Schaub that Great Britain had concluded the Dutch Alliance in an understanding with Volkra; "the King thought he had been doing a service to the Emperor and paving the way to the Guaranty he aimed at when he entered into his Treaty with Holland; and his Majesty had not the least intention of prescribing the method how the Imperial Court should come into it". England had nothing against a new agreement. But the Vienna Court should "hereafter distrust those who may think it matter of sagacity, to give the worst turn to the honest, well-meaning proceedings here".[2]

After this the Emperor could hardly be expected simply to accede to the Treaty of February 6. He wrote to Volkra that he had much rather expected to be invited as *pars contractans principalis* in the proposed defensive Triple Alliance. During the next months this was discussed in London and Vienna. The negotiations in Vienna were conducted by Luke Schaub, a clever and experienced diplomat who knew how to penetrate the clumsy forms of Austria's foreign policy and fathom their true intentions—a man who even in times of excitement could find the ground on which the conflicting wishes of the two Powers could be made to agree. In London the British Ministers had much difficulty with Volkra, who conducted business in a fussy and arrogant manner, and with little judgment. His conduct was condemned almost as severely in the Imperial rescripts as in Townshend's letters to Schaub, and the negotiations were still further complicated by the changing views as to whether or not Holland should be included in the Treaty.

[1] Same to same, Feb. 8, 1716, S.P. 80/33.
[2] Townshend to Schaub, 17 Feb. 1716, O.S., S.P. 104/42.

At first an agreement *à trois* was alone contemplated, and a draft presented by Volkra was amended by the British Ministers to render it acceptable to the Dutch. Townshend thought that "if the Emperor would write an obliging letter [to the States General] upon the finishing of the Barrier Treaty with such expressions of friendship and union, as such an occasion may suggest . . . I believe our friends at The Hague might be spirited up to such a degree as to overcome all the opposition of the partisans of France. But if the Imperial Ministers continue cold and disobliging, I cannot hope for any complyance in that Republick".[1] In Vienna, however, it was thought that the Emperor could not write such a letter;[2] though Marquis Prié, who was about to proceed as Governor to the Austrian Netherlands, was to be instructed to pay some compliments to the Dutch. Soon afterwards Horace Walpole reported from The Hague complaints[3] by the Pensionary about the harsh and haughty language of the Austrians. Special offence was given by Königsegg declaring at the exchange of ratifications of the Barrier Treaty that the Emperor could not "treat them any longer as *celsi et potentes*" as it was "beneath his Imperial Majesty to give this Republick a higher title than what they can obtain from France";[4] and while the behaviour of the Austrian diplomats thus seemed calculated to offend the Dutch, the French Minister, Chateauneuf, tried his best to gain them for a French alliance and thereby overturn the Triple Alliance before it was ever concluded.

The unfavourable news from Holland produced in England the decision now to conclude an alliance with the Emperor alone, as had previously been done with the States General, and afterwards to invite the Dutch to accede to it. Instructions to Volkra, including three different drafts for the Triple Alliance, could only have been in his hands a few days when the British refused to discuss them any further. On February 24, 1716, O.S., Lord Townshend, in the presence of the two German Ministers, explained to Volkra the most recent developments of British policy. He suggested that the Emperor should conclude an alliance with George I alone, and "by an article particularly invite the States General into it. But as in all Treatys his Majesty makes, he expects that the succession to the

[1] Townshend to Schaub, Jan. 31, 1716, O.S., S.P. 104/42.
[2] Schaub to Townshend, March 5, 1716, S.P. 80/33.
[3] Walpole to Townshend, Feb. 18, 1716, S.P. 84/253.
[4] Same to same, Feb. 28; Townshend to Schaub, Feb. 14, O.S., 1716.

Crown as established here should be guarantyed. . . ."[1] The Emperor was not to be asked explicitly to guarantee the *Protestant* Succession, but the succession as established by the laws of England. Moreover, there was to be a general reciprocal guarantee of possessions. Here Bernstorff and Bothmer intervened and declared that the guarantee would have to extend to the German possessions of the King, "since the King would be engaged to support the Emperor in whatever he possesses in Italy". Even more, the Emperor was asked to extend his guarantee to Bremen and Verden, recently conquered from Sweden. If the Emperor found some difficulty in "giving his guaranty for the new acquisitions upon the account of the constitutions of the Empire, . . . some expedient may be found out by which his Imperial Majesty may give the King some assurance of his being favourable to him in this particular."[2] The Hanoverian statesmen undoubtedly had the matter much at heart, and it was for the sake of Hanover that King George wished for a speedy conclusion of the alliance with the Emperor. This was well known to the Austrians but did not surprise them, as the distinction between King and Elector was not made on the Continent.

Volkra naturally raised difficulties; these matters, he thought, should be dealt with in a separate Treaty in which the Emperor would receive a *quid pro quo*—presumably in Italy. The same day Townshend wrote to Schaub[3] in the sense in which he had spoken to Volkra. Schaub was reporting a more friendly attitude at the Vienna Court and a growing dissatisfaction with Count Volkra, who was disowned by everybody except the Spaniards. Prince Eugene declared that if the alliance was to be concluded in London, Volkra should sign but not negotiate it, so as to avoid any "contributions of his".[4]

The offer of an alliance with Great Britain alone was welcomed in Vienna, as reports were received of hostile intentions on the part of Philip V against Italy, in which case the help of the British fleet was necessary, indeed, indispensable to the Emperor; especially as war with Turkey too seemed inevitable. The Secret Conference met on April 4 and joint instructions were drawn up for Volkra and Hoffmann authorizing them immediately to sign the Treaty of Alliance. All previous drafts from either side were scrapped, and a new text was sent to them, the acceptance of which they were to procure in

[1] Townshend to Schaub, Feb. 24, 1716, O.S., S.P. 104/42.
[2] *Ibid.*   [3] *Ibid.*   [4] Schaub to Townshend, March 18, 1716.

London.[1] The distrust of Volkra was expressed in that he and Hoffmann were categorically forbidden to change a single word in the document.

The draft stipulated that in case of a hostile attack the two Powers were to succour each other; but not only territories and rights, even "the honour and dignity" of the contracting rulers were to be protected. These words *honor* and *dignitas* were open to various interpretations. To the Emperor they may have covered his claims to Spain, "the ideal Spain", as it was frequently termed in those days, an interpretation which could hardly have proved acceptable to England. The draft Treaty stipulated that in case of an attack against England the Emperor was to supply 12,000 men; in the opposite case, Great Britain was to send 10,000 men and 20 warships of the second and third classes—a heavier commitment. The States General were to be invited to adhere to the Treaty. The possessions of the two rulers which were to be covered by it were not mentioned either in general or in specific terms, neither the Austrian possessions in Italy nor the German possessions of George I and his newly acquired Duchies of Bremen and Verden. While the Emperor wished to secure British help in case of an attack against Italy, he tried, by silence, to evade such commitments in Germany. Nor was the Hanoverian Succession mentioned in the draft. Still, despite the omission of the two points in which George I was primarily interested, the draft became the basis of the Treaty.

The Austrian Ministers were not altogether honest in their discussion of those two points with Schaub. After having sent instructions to Volkra with a speed quite unusual at Vienna, they amused Schaub for some time with vague talk, professing that they could not as yet say anything about the question of the Succession and the Bremen Duchies. They were awaiting the issue of Volkra's negotiations, or rather of the categorical instructions sent to him and Hoffmann. In case of failure concessions could still be made to Schaub; and they did not guess that he saw through their game.[2]

Meantime the British Government had again changed their intentions and once more favoured a Triple Alliance. Horace Walpole continued to report from The Hague about Chateauneuf's endeavours to gain the friendship of the States General; even England was

---

[1] Enclosure in the dispatch to Volkra and Hoffmann of April 4, 1716, Vienna Arch.

[2] Schaub to Townshend, April 18, 1716, S.P. 80/33

courted by the French, and her statesmen themselves began to take kindly to the idea of a French alliance. But they thought that the three old allies should start by drawing closer together. On March 30, O.S., Walpole received full powers to sign the Treaty of the Triple Alliance; afterwards a *rapprochement* with France would be welcome. A new system of British policy was being prepared.

But now the Dutch, sensing the possibility of a French alliance, were once more making difficulties. Volkra, therefore, pressed the British Ministers to conclude immediately with the Emperor. Stanhope and Bernstorff favoured this solution, Townshend and Bothmer opposed it. On May 5 Horace Walpole reported from The Hague that the States of Holland had decided—the city of Amsterdam had given the casting vote—to insist that negotiations for two defensive Triple Alliances should be conducted simultaneously, the one with George I and the Emperor, and the other with Great Britain and France. Soon afterwards it was clear that the States General would cling to that programme. Chateauneuf felt sure of success and declared that he would shortly be in a position to submit a plan of alliance, to which even the British could not object. When this news reached London, the Ministers hastened to conclude with Volkra. The King intended to go to Hanover that summer, but his Ministers would not let him leave before the Austrian Alliance was concluded. They also desired a connexion with France, but Great Britain was to enter it, while holding a strong position in Europe and not standing in need of France to attain it. The Austrian Alliance was to be sprung as a surprise on the world.

When on Saturday, May 19/30, Townshend met Volkra and Hoffmann [1] at Court, he explained to them the circumstances and urged that the alliance should be concluded before the mail left on Tuesday. On Monday he came to Volkra and repeated his declaration. The two Austrians gave the correct answer, that they were fully prepared immediately to sign the draft Treaty sent by the Emperor and communicated by them to the British Court, and added that they were not free to make even the smallest change in it. If that was so, replied Townshend, it would be sheer waste of time to talk about the matter, for the words *honor* and *dignitas* could not be suffered to stand in the Treaty, and there had to be parity between the obligations undertaken by the contracting Powers; he argued that the un-

---

[1] The following account is based on the dispatch of Volkra and Hoffmann about the conclusion of the Alliance, May 25/June 5, 1716, Vienna Arch.

equal distribution of burdens in the last war continued to provoke diatribes against the previous Cabinet whenever the size of the national debt was mentioned in Parliament. The Austrians seemed to think there was nothing in the sending out of warships for those who possessed them; but in fact the fitting out and manning of 20 warships, as demanded by the Emperor, was equal to sending an army of 16,000 men; and besides, England was to supply 10,000 men, while the total offered by the Emperor was only 12,000. It was no good discussing such demands. Townshend rose in ill-humour and was about to leave.

But this was merely the bluff common in classical diplomacy. Volkra and Hoffmann had been ordered by the last Imperial rescript to conclude the Alliance as soon as possible but "without betraying too anxious a desire for it". Consequently they adopted a firm attitude, which did not, however, deceive Townshend—he knew that Volkra was as desirous to conclude as he was himself. On Townshend rising to go, Volkra begged him to arrange still a conference with the other Ministers. Townshend saw that he had won, and replied that he could see no purpose in it; but that he did not wish to oppose further discussion and would at 6 P.M. come with the other Ministers to Count Bothmer's house.

After he had left, Hoffmann reproached Volkra and said that he would much rather drop the matter for the present than, contrary to their positive instructions, admit of any changes in the draft; and that the Treaty was not of such importance to the Emperor that they could not await further orders from Vienna. He thought that the British Ministers exaggerated the danger of France gaining over Holland and suspected some hidden British designs. But as it often happens with novices in diplomacy, Volkra was bent on concluding this important Treaty. He answered Hoffmann that it would be unpardonable in him not to try to counteract French and Anjou intrigues and to let the Treaty founder because of some details, when there was agreement on fundamentals; he would much rather assume sole responsibility for that independent decision, and indeed sacrifice himself, rather than render such bad service to the Emperor.

The same day Volkra and Hoffmann attended the conference at Bothmer's house. Besides the two Secretaries, Townshend and Stanhope, there were present the Duke of Marlborough and the indispensable Count Bernstorff. Two hours were spent in an excited argument about the words *honor et dignitas*. Townshend declared emphatically that these words as well as the word *jura* must be deleted, for there was no limit to the alleged rights and claims of the Emperor, and neither England nor Holland could guarantee them without involving themselves in an endless war; but it was their wish to avoid anything pointing to warlike intentions. Still, Volkra and Hoffmann persisted, and at 8 P.M. the conference was adjourned; it was resumed an hour later. After much talk, Stanhope at last took the pen and recast Article II into a form which was ultimately agreed to by all those present. The words *honor, dignitas,* and *jura* were allowed to stand, but their import was reduced—the Article started by emphasizing the defensive character of the future Alliance. Agreement was further reached concerning the mutual obligations in case of war, the main difficulties being circumvented rather than solved. Each side was pledged to supply 12,000 men but, if required by the character of the war, England was to replace by warships the whole, or part, of its contingent, and the maintenance of such succour should answer the expense of the troops thus replaced. The Treaty did not define the ratio between the two services.

Otherwise the Vienna draft remained unchanged, except that an Article IX was added, inviting the adhesion of the States General. The Austrians further accepted an Additional Article relieving Great Britain of any obligation to succour the Emperor in a war against Turkey. However obvious, the point had to be made to save the British Levant trade from being endangered by the imminent war with Turkey. Neither the Protestant Succession nor the Bremen Duchies were mentioned, the British Ministers being satisfied with what was attainable at the time. Even Count Volkra would not have dared to saddle the Emperor with such guarantees; and were he to apply for new instructions a delay of several weeks would have ensued. Satisfied with the results, Townshend wrote to Horace Walpole that the King had directed him and Stanhope "to try how far we could carry the negotiation with Count Volkra" and that now, after several conferences, they had at last "the good fortune to bring him to reason . . .".[1]

The conference broke up late at night. The next morning they met once more at Bothmer's house, to discuss the way in which the Treaty was to be signed. Volkra proposed that he and Hoffmann should sign without presenting their full powers, in the hope that the Emperor would approve. The British Ministers could hardly expect

[1] May 22, 1716, O.S., S.P. 104/81.

anything more from the Austrians, who had gone counter to the positive terms of their instructions. The signature even of this, rather irregular, Treaty had to be delayed for a few days as the Lord Chancellor, who had to append the Great Seal to the full powers of the British Ministers, was out of town. None the less the conclusion of the Treaty was reported to Holland by the mail on Tuesday, May 22, O.S., as had been intended; but the formal signing took place at Westminster on May 25, O.S. That in the hurry the date was named in the Treaty according to the Old Style was one of the points for which Volkra and Hoffmann were blamed by the Emperor.

In reality great satisfaction was felt at the Vienna Court on hearing that the Treaty was signed. Count Sinzendorff communicated the news to Schaub with joy, though several articles had been considerably modified and the help promised by England was reduced. Sinzendorff placed the right value on the alliance when he said that it laid a firm foundation for further agreements which the contracting Powers may in time find it necessary to conclude for their security.[1]

Volkra, however, received a rather ungracious communication [2] from the Emperor, who found much to object to in the Treaty and thought that the intended advantages could hardly accrue from it. Although no guarantee of the Protestant Succession and of the Bremen Duchies was mentioned, the Emperor feared that his guarantee of the King's possessions in their present state (*eo quo sunt statu*) would some day be interpreted as covering these new acquisitions. The apprehension was groundless—George I had concluded the Treaty as King of England, and not as Elector of Hanover, which is proved by the British Ministers alone having received full powers to sign the instrument; the Hanoverian Ministers, whatever their share had been in the negotiations, did not sign the Treaty.[3] On the other hand, the Emperor professed himself disappointed by the British guarantee covering his possessions in their present state only. The Vienna Court still hoped to recover Spain, and these hopes, according to the Emperor, had been nourished by Stanhope and Cadogan. Now nothing was left to him of Spain but a title, and to defend that, no considerable forces were required. Further, Charles VI was dissatisfied with the succour in war promised by Great

[1] Schaub to Townshend, June 17, 1716, F.O. 80/33.
[2] Instructions of June 30, 1716, Vienna Arch.
[3] Cf. dispatch from Volkra and Hoffmann, July 17/28, 1716.

Britain; his somewhat superficial reading of the Treaty was that England was to supply either "men for ships or ships for men".

But in spite of all these doubts, which were expressed to Volkra more strongly than they were felt, the Emperor was careful not to reject the Treaty and so involve himself in embarrassing complications. On the contrary, his ratification was dispatched to London without much hesitation. At the exchange of the ratifications Volkra and Hoffmann were merely to express the hope that England would now refrain from concluding an alliance with France, or otherwise safeguard in it Austria's interests; more especially the Emperor's position in the Southern Netherlands was not to be drawn into the negotiations. The declarations ordered by the Emperor were made at the exchange of the ratifications, and Volkra repeated them even to the Prince of Wales[1] (the King having left for Hanover) and received the assurance that the British Court would never do anything disadvantageous to the Emperor; the Prince even added that the French alliance would, if possible, be altogether avoided. In reality preparations for it were in full swing.

The conclusion of the Anglo-Austrian Alliance made so unfavourable an impression in Holland that the British Ministers nearly came to regret their precipitate action. But the displeasure of the States General was soon dispelled when they saw that England continued no less inclined to the French alliance which they desired. They therefore paid little attention to the invitation to accede to the Treaty of May 25, especially as England no longer made "the negociation with France depend in point of time upon the States accepting the Treaty with the Emperor".[2] In fact, they never acceded at all to the Anglo-Austrian Alliance.

Similarly in France the conclusion of the Treaty of May 25 produced pained surprise. England had just entered into negotiations with the French for an alliance and now had concluded one with Charles VI, who was as hostile to the House of Bourbon in France as in Spain. D'Iberville openly expressed his surprise, but Stanhope replied that England could not be expected to separate from her old ally, the Emperor, and to refrain from concluding with him at least a defensive alliance. Similarly, Lord Stair was told he "may very freely aver . . . that it is an alliance purely defensive".[3]

[1] Dispatch from Volkra and Hoffmann, July 17/28, 1716.
[2] Townshend to Walpole, June 5/16, 1716, S.P. 104/81.
[3] Stanhope to Stair, May 27/June 7, 1716, F.O. 90/14.

The French were soon reassured, and the negotiations took their course.

Great Britain had now regained an independent position among the European Powers. The armed rebellion at home had been defeated, a loyal Parliament supported the King. The throne of George I was secure, and after so many storms he could leave England to revisit his home. England had made it up with her old allies, Holland and Austria, while the continued bickerings between them made Britain their mediator. Moreover, a *rapprochement* had been effected with France; and in that quarter England was free to accept or refuse an alliance. If George I demanded that the harbour of Mardyke be destroyed and the Pretender sent across the Alps, the Duke of Orleans had to agree. There was continuous interaction between the domestic and foreign policy. The defeat of the Stuart Rebellion and the Septennial Act raised George I's position abroad, while foreign alliances strengthened his position at home. Similarly favourable was the effect on the German interests of George I: the Bremen Duchies could not be retaken from the King of England. In less than two years the Hanoverian dynasty, to which many serious politicians had given a short life, had asserted itself, and the basis was laid for an international system controlled by Great Britain.

CHAPTER X

SPAIN AND THE COMMERCIAL TREATIES

SELDOM has the peculiar influence of historical tradition counted for more than in the early days of the Hanoverian dynasty in Great Britain. The uncertain attitude of foreign Powers and the lack of security at home left the new Government with few fixed directives; but the less they were able to develop a clear programme of their own, the more they adhered to the traditional Whig principles and tried to resume the foreign policy pursued during their last tenure of office, which, based on an alliance with Austria and Holland, had aimed at destroying the preponderance of France for all future time. The new Secretaries of State, James Stanhope and Lord Townshend, reverted to this system, aiming in the first place at reconstituting the old alliance, and next, at renewing the war. But it gradually became clear that the British nation would not tolerate a new war, and after the Rebellion had been suppressed and the old alliances reconstituted, an unexpected opportunity offered of good relations with France, her new ruler, the Duke of Orleans, seeking British support for his personal position. Two years after the accession of George I, the traditional Whig policy towards France was given up, and to great advantage.

A similar evolution occurred with regard to the Spanish Bourbons. Originally the Whigs had insisted on Spain being placed under Habsburg rule; they would have fought to the bitter end rather than concede to the Duke of Anjou an inch of territory in the Peninsula. But the Tory Administration had concluded peace, and recognized Philip V, and the Government of George I had to make terms with this King as he could no longer be removed. It was hardly to be hoped that relations would be restored on as profitable a basis for England as had existed under Carlos II. With the accession of Philip V a considerable and beneficial change had been wrought in

Spain, where foreign influence was required to put fresh life into the decaying State. A self-reliant Government was set up by men trained in the school of Richelieu and Louis XIV, intent upon restoring unity to the Kingdom and on subjecting the provinces to the Crown; they were not prepared to concede wide privileges either to the ancient Fueros of Catalonia, or to foreign Powers in their commerce with the Spanish dominions. The new Spain had managed to establish friendly relations with Queen Anne and her Tory Administration; but naturally the Spaniards did not expect much good from the Whig party, which had insisted on driving out the Bourbons from Spain, and at first the relations between the two countries were very distant. Under Queen Anne negotiations had been started, from which Spain had expected considerable advantages, but they were broken off by order of the Regency Council, and King George drew closer to Charles VI of Austria, the mortal enemy of Philip V. Peace between these two had not yet been made, each of them hoping some day to acquire all the territories which had belonged to Carlos II; their hostility was to be for years one of the pivots of European policy. Spain had therefore little to expect from an England friendly to Austria, and a Stuart restoration in Great Britain was hoped for at Madrid.

Since 1705, when Peterborough had captured Barcelona for the Habsburgs, the Catalans had faithfully adhered to Carlos III, even after he had left the country and his chances in Spain had practically vanished. Moreover, the Spaniards at his Court took care that the Catalans were not forgotten; and in 1714 the anniversary of the capture of Barcelona was celebrated in Vienna almost like that of its own relief from the Turks. Still, the Emperor was not in a position to do much for them, and could merely advise them to await the death of the Queen. In fact, representations in Paris on behalf of the Catalans were one of the first measures taken by the Regents —an armistice should be concluded and an attempt be made by an amicable arrangement to save a people which otherwise was determined to perish fighting.[1] Louis XIV replied that his attempts with his grandson to preserve the ancient privileges of the Catalans had been of no avail; but besides, he reserved to himself the right to furnish auxiliary troops for the capture of Barcelona. The French reply was presented in London by d'Iberville, who communicated it

---

[1] Mémoire by Prior, presented in the name of the Regents; Paris, Aug. 26, 1714; S.P. 78/159.

also to Hoffmann; and in doing so he underlined the fact that Louis had never bound himself not to assist in the "reduction" of the Catalans. In the end, the Austrians had nothing better to say than that "the destroying of these poor people" was surely not the way to gain the friendship of England.[1]

Prior continued to urge the French Government, which remained, however, impervious; finally, Louis XIV warned England that excessive pressure in favour of Catalonia might result in his grandson withdrawing his renunciation of the French throne.[2] While these diplomatic *pourparlers* were proceeding, the news arrived of the fall of Barcelona. The Catalans had resumed the struggle, and in a way declared war on the Duke of Anjou—the only title which they accorded to Philip V—and on the King of France. The Duke of Berwick conducted the siege, and his Memoirs bear witness to their brave resistance. Repeated attacks were repulsed, and successful sorties were undertaken. All Europe watched them with sympathy, but from nowhere did they receive any effective help. They turned to London, and also to the British Admiral commanding the Mediterranean fleet;[3] and in September, Hoffmann was still endeavouring in vain to obtain orders for Admiral Wishart to succour the city. On September 12 Berwick undertook a general assault against it; the ground was contested inch by inch; one bastion was taken and retaken eleven times. In the end the city had to surrender unconditionally. The Catalans had suffered 6000 casualties and the attacking forces 10,000. The victorious troops were restrained from excesses, and the town was treated leniently, but there was an end to its privileges and liberties.

The only effect of the attempted mediation had thus been to force the pace of the siege, though British sympathy may have had a mitigating influence on the fate of the conquered city, Louis XIV exhorting his grandson to mercy towards the besieged;[4] for during the siege Philip V and his Ministers had repeatedly declared that no quarter would be given to the rebels. Still, relations between Britain and Spain remained highly strained; Stanhope's journey to Vienna

---

[1] Hoffmann's dispatch of Dec. 7, 1714, Vienna Archives.
[2] See Courcy, *La Coalition de 1701 contre la France*, vol. ii. p. 437.
[3] For the letter from the city of Barcelona to Admiral Wishart see *ibid.* p. 612.
[4] Cf. Baudrillart, vol. i. pp. 651-3, and the letters from Louis XIV to Philip V, published by him.

caused serious anxiety at Madrid, and when he returned to London without visible success, Philip declared that the British Minister had tried to induce the Emperor to enter into an alliance for making a new war, but had failed.[1]

British interests suffered more than those of Spain by the unfriendly relations between the two States, as commerce with Spain and her colonies was one of the principal branches of British trade. Under Carlos II, practically the whole of the Spanish trade was in the hands of Dutch and English merchants, who carried on Spain's foreign trade, exported their own manufactures to Spain, and, under cover of Spanish firms, even those of other European countries to the Spanish colonies, and enjoyed numerous privileges and many illicit advantages, while the weak government of the Spanish Habsburgs was helpless against the preponderant commercial Powers. In fact, British and Dutch merchants reaped the harvest of Spain's colonial riches, while the Spanish Crown had the trouble of administering them; the bullion which, every year, the flota brought home from the colonies, found its way into the coffers of foreign merchants.

Though much had changed since those days, the securing of trade interests remained the foremost concern of English statesmen in their relations with Spain. This had been one of their main objectives in the War of the Spanish Succession; and hardly had the Austrian Archduke set foot in Spain as King Carlos III, than negotiations were opened for an Anglo-Spanish Treaty of Commerce, according preferential treatment to British merchants. One thing only Carlos refused: direct trade between England and the Spanish West Indies; on all other points he gave way, and by the Treaty of July 10, 1707, all the advantages were secured to the English merchants which they had enjoyed under Carlos II, while other nations, especially the Dutch, were practically debarred from competing with them in the Spanish trade.

But in the end it was with Philip of Anjou that Great Britain had to negotiate, and not with the Habsburgs. By the Treaty of Navigation and Commerce of November 28, 1713, previous Treaties, and especially that of 1667, were renewed, and commerce was generally to be re-established on the pre-war basis. None the less, considerable divergencies were admitted, and new regulations for duties to be levied on British imports were laid down in three Explanatory

[1] Burch, British *chargé d'affaires* at Madrid, to Stanhope, in a cipher letter of Feb. 11, 1715; S.P. 94/83.

Articles. These, especially after the death of Queen Anne, were given in practice a twist thoroughly disadvantageous to British merchants. Their position became intolerable, and soon after the accession of George I it was decided to send an envoy to the Spanish Court to seek redress.

The first Envoy was Paul Methuen, son of the diplomat whose name is affixed to the famous commercial treaty with Portugal. His Instructions [1] clearly show the aim of his mission (and incidentally indulge in a number of hits against the previous Administration):

> Whereas the preservation of the commerce between the Kingdoms of Great Britain and Spain was one of the chief motives which induced our two Royal Predecessors to enter into the late long, expensive war and one of the principal benefits expected by our people from the conclusion of a peace after such a glorious and uninterrupted course of successes . . . And whereas by a late Treaty of Navigation and Commerce . . . concluded at Utrecht, November 28, 1713, and particularly by the three . . . Explanatory Articles the ancient usage and custom of stating and paying the duties upon merchandises imported into Spain together with the gratias and abatements constantly made . . . to the British merchants is entirely subverted and destroyed, and a new exorbitant method for paying the duties is erected, that must necessarily, if put in execution, render the commerce between the two nations . . . impracticable [contrary to various Royal Ordinances, and especially to the Treaty of 1667 confirmed at Utrecht], you are to use your utmost application and endeavor . . . to obtain . . . a full confirmation of all the privileges and concessions . . . to the British merchants . . . and . . . that the three Explanatory Articles . . . be annulled as having been inserted and obtained in a very extraordinary manner. . . .

Next, the various branches of British trade to Spain are discussed, and while, generally speaking, Methuen is to work for the restoration of conditions as they existed in the reign of Carlos II, on certain points further concessions are desired.

He is further instructed to use his best offices with the King of Spain on behalf of the Isle of Majorca,

> and to mediate, if possible, an accommodation on such terms as may preserve to these poor people their laws, rights, and privileges; you may observe to that Court how agreeable this will be to us. . . .

He was particularly to endeavour "to bring the Treaty of Peace

---

[1] "Instructions" dated Jan. 15, 1714/5, S.P. 104/135, pp. 72-102; and "Additional Instructions", Feb. 1, 1714/5, *ibid.* pp. 102-7.

between the Crowns of Spain and Portugal to a conclusion", this being a matter in which the King's honour was engaged. Lastly:

You shall diligently observe the motions and conduct of the Court where you reside, and use your best skill to penetrate into their secret views and designs, and particularly you are to apply your self with the utmost care and diligence to understand the views and dispositions of that Court with relation to France and the situation of the settlement of Succession there in case of the Dauphin's death or of the Regency in case of a minority by the death of the French King.

Methuen, on his arrival in Spain, encountered nothing but difficulties. The Spanish Court was entirely under the influence of France—even the Court ceremonial distinguished between the Ambassadors of France and those of other States. Methuen therefore thought that it would be best for him merely to make use of his credential letters without taking the character of Ambassador until the ceremonial was adjusted to his satisfaction, and he was confirmed in that intention by the Spanish First Minister, the Cardinal de Giudice.[1]

Meantime he daily received complaints from the British merchants,[2] which he found, however, difficult to reconcile "to the trade they drive"—they "continue to overstock all the markets with goods they cannot sell". Still, the oppressions they suffered from the Spanish officials were growing worse every day, new and arbitrary duties were levied, their goods were confiscated,their ships were seized or were forced into the Spanish service without any compensation to the owners, and their warehouses were broken open and their goods taken away, "without any previous agreement or satisfaction for them afterwards".[3] These proceedings he ascribed very largely to French influence—"they will always have power enough here to destroy our trade in Spain and lay it on the obstinacy of this Court, so that I see no remedy but war, and you are the best judges at home whether that be practicable or no".[4]

This seems to confirm that a new war was seriously contemplated by British statesmen in the first year of the reign of George I, as the British Ministers abroad must have known the intentions of their

---

[1] Methuen to Stanhope, Portsmouth, Feb. 14, 1715; Cadiz, Feb. 26; Madrid, April 8, 1715; S.P. 94/83.

[2] Methuen to Stanhope, May 20, 1715, S.P. 94/83.

[3] Methuen to British Consuls in Spain, enclosed in a letter to Stanhope, June 3, 1715, *ibid.*

[4] Methuen to Stanhope, May 20, 1715, *ibid.*

own Government. Lord Stair's reports from Paris, in the spring of 1715, were apt to encourage England to a new war with France, and it is possible that Methuen pursued a similar aim in his reports from Spain. Presumably there was an understanding between them and Stanhope, and their reports may have been intended to serve as his justification if he decided to go to war.

But a revolution was preparing at the Court of Madrid. The Queen, Elizabeth Farnese of Parma, was young and ambitious, and exercised absolute dominion over her husband, Philip V. She herself was influenced by Giulio Alberoni, the Envoy of Parma, and it was he who was solely responsible for the overthrow of the hitherto so powerful Princess Orsini; he had insistently urged her dismissal on the Queen as the only means whereby she could save herself from perdition. At the first meeting with the proud Princess, the Queen flew into a passion and ordered her to be immediately exiled from the Kingdom.[1] This, the first action of the young Queen in Spain, astonished Europe, and Alberoni was soon the most influential man at Court, since Elizabeth had declared that she would see to it that he remained in Madrid, even if he ceased to be Envoy of the Duke of Parma. At first he naturally kept in the background, but he soon came out into the open and as First Minister of Spain conducted a bold policy at home and abroad, till it broke down against the united opposition of Europe.

As yet he did not interfere in foreign policy, which retained its French outlook, especially with regard to Great Britain. The King of Spain could not think of conducting a war, and his provocative attitude can only be explained by the belief in the imminent fall of George I. Spain was a centre of Jacobite intrigues, and Frenchmen and Jacobites vied in assuring the Spaniards that the Stuart King would restore to them Port Mahon and Gibraltar. The Spaniards remained in constant touch with the Jacobites in Great Britain, and were kept informed of their activities and chances. The King of England was criticized at Madrid for having discarded the Tories, and there was approval and praise for the flight of Bolingbroke, from

[1] The scene is similarly described by St. Simon and other contemporaries, including Prior, in a report from Paris, Jan. 11, 1715, S.P. 78/159; still it will probably never be fully cleared up in its details. The origin of the conflict is, however, known from the letters of Alberoni, published by E. Armstrong in the *Eng. Hist. Review*, 1890. See also Armstrong's *Elizabeth Farnese*, 1892, pp. 25 *seq.*

whom much was expected. Spain shared the delusion of the Jacobites that a Stuart Restoration was imminent.

In Spain Methuen met with constant disappointments, and the relations between the two States remained the very worst. The point of entering into serious negotiations was never reached, and the Envoy soon felt that he was not equal to the situation. He fell ill, and on May 20 he wrote to Stanhope about his "entire loss of . . . health . . . occasioned either by the air of this place . . . or by the multiplicity of business, or perhaps too much application to it. . . ." "I therefore hope His Majesty will be graciously pleased to recall me." And in a private letter he wrote the same day: "I am now reduced to so miserable a condition that every body thinks I shall not live to receive your answer to this. . . . I must own . . . I have contributed to it my self by . . . passing whole days and nights in writing." His recall was granted, and he himself recommended George Bubb for his successor, advising that the instructions [1] which had been given to him should be renewed. Methuen had not been able to work any change in the situation, and the task fell to his successor.

Only two points included in Methuen's instructions did not need to be repeated. The first concerned peace in the Peninsula. Great Britain had long endeavoured to effect a reconciliation between her ally, Portugal, and Philip V, but so far without success. When, however, Methuen, who was enjoined to work for such a peace, landed at Cadiz, it had already been signed at Utrecht, on February 6, under the influence of Louis XIV, who thus had taken a further step towards the general pacification of Europe.

Methuen had further been instructed to work for an agreement between Philip V and the island of Majorca. Barcelona had fallen, but the islands of Majorca and Iviza, which had been ceded to Spain in the Treaty of Utrecht, held out, hoping for Austrian, and possibly for British, help. The Emperor sympathized with them, is said to have supported them with money, and after the fall of Barcelona had tried to gain British naval help for Majorca. Unfounded rumours were current of Admiral Wishart having declared to Marshal Berwick that any attempt against the islands would be treated as a hostile act against Great Britain. With the help of the British fleet, Charles VI planned to send from Naples to Majorca 1000 men with artillery and munitions. The Treaty of Utrecht, of March 14, 1713, included the Islands in Catalonia, but the Imperial Court would not

[1] Dated May 31, 1715, O.S., S.P. 94/83.

admit it; and as Majorca refused to surrender to the Duke of Anjou, in instructions sent to Hoffmann, it was declared worthy of support.[1] He was told that if the British Government pointed to the agreement to evacuate Catalonia, he should reply that the Emperor had agreed to such an evacuation but had not precluded himself "from re-conquering them in the future or sending them help after they had been evacuated".[2]

The British Government refused to let themselves be drawn into such reasonings, and avoided suspicions of warlike intentions, which would have done much harm to Great Britain, even more than actual war. They declared that they would preserve strict neutrality and that they were as much bound by the Treaty of Evacuation as Charles VI himself.[3] The Emperor ordered 1000 men from Naples to Majorca, while Hoffmann had to make a last attempt to obtain English succour for the islands; and should this prove impossible, he was at least to secure a capitulation assuring free egress for the German troops and a full amnesty for the Spaniards under arms, and confirming the ancient privileges and liberties of the islands. This, according to the Emperor, could best be promoted by Great Britain also landing some troops in Majorca.[4]

Stanhope declared any military action in favour of Majorca im-possible, but entered into the idea of a capitulation; and added that similar instructions had been given to Methuen. The next day the Cabinet met and resolved to instruct Lord Stair to offer British mediation to France, representing it as a suggestion of their own accepted by the Emperor. He was to negotiate with the French Ministers, and Great Britain and France were to be the contracting parties.[5]

Louis XIV politely accepted the declaration that George I, by his offer to mediate, meant to give further proof of his peaceful intentions (which, in reality, were disbelieved in France), and said he would inform his grandson of it. In doing so, Louis XIV enquired what concessions he was prepared to make to the Islands. Philip replied that he could not favour the inhabitants of Majorca beyond

---

[1] Instructions to Hoffmann, May 4, 1714, Vienna Archives.

[2] Instructions to Hoffmann, Nov. 14, 1714, *ibid.*

[3] Townshend to Hoffmann, Nov. 26, Dec. 7, 1714, enclosed in Hoffmann's report of Dec. 11, 1714. See further Hoffmann's report of Jan. 18, 1715.

[4] Instructions to Hoffmann, Feb. 16, 1715.

[5] Hoffmann's report of Mar. 15, 1715, Vienna Arch.; instructions to Lord Stair of Mar. 4 and 21, 1715, F.O. 90/14.

his other subjects—they might retain their municipal rights, but he had to assert his supremacy in government and war, finance and justice, and could admit of no infringement of the Royal prerogative in such matters. In fact, Philip did not mean to accept a mediation, being determined to deal with Majorca as he had done with Barcelona; while his grandfather himself, though the negotiations had started in Paris, significantly wrote to Madrid that the King of Spain should examine his military forces and act accordingly.[1]

Relations even between England and France were strained, and the argument about the Mardyke Canal was conducted with so much heat that Lord Stair's departure from Paris was repeatedly discussed.[2] None the less, after the King of Spain had formally declared his readiness to accept the mediation, negotiations were opened in Paris. Lord Stair was given full powers and instructions by the Emperor.[3] In these the "King of Spain" naturally was not mentioned, as that title was claimed by the Emperor, and the person of Philip V was merely alluded to under "the King of France *and his allies*". But though for Charles VI he was the Duke of Anjou, Great Britain had recognized Philip V—what forms was a British diplomat to adopt when acting on behalf of, and under instructions from, the Emperor? The position was eased by Stair receiving special powers from George I, which recognized the King of Spain, without offending the Emperor.[4]

The Emperor's instructions to Stair assumed that Philip V could obtain possession of the islands in no other way than their voluntary surrender. He was to confirm the islands in their rights and liberties, grant a full amnesty, continue all and sundry in their offices and dignities, and allow free egress to the Austrian troops and even to the armed Spaniards. Even more: Lord Stair was to demand concessions for Barcelona and Catalonia as part of the price to be paid for the islands—the Emperor seemed to forget that Barcelona had surrendered unconditionally. In London the demands concerning Catalonia were immediately declared impracticable,[5] and Stair was

[1] Courcy, vol. ii. p. 448.

[2] Hoffmann's report of Mar. 29 and April 30, 1715, Vienna Arch.; Stanhope to Stair, April 30, 1715, O.S., F.O. 90/14.

[3] Dated April 6; enclosed with instructions to Hoffmann dated April 6, 1715, Vienna Arch.

[4] St. James's, April 30, 1715, O.S., F.O. 90/14. Further cf. Hoffmann's reports of May 7 and 14, 1715, Vienna Arch.

[5] Hoffmann's report of May 10, 1715.

instructed to adapt the Imperial demands to the facts of the situation. He had previously declared in Paris that Majorca might have to be content with part of her privileges, and he was now instructed by his Government to try and save as much of them as possible, but was not to press impracticable demands. A special article of the Treaty was to secure for the inhabitants of the island of Minorca, since 1708 in English possession, free access and trade with Majorca and Iviza as enjoyed under Carlos II.

Meantime Philip V had decided to forestall the work of diplomacy. In May 1715 a strong Spanish fleet, much superior to the few British ships in the Mediterranean, was sent against Majorca, carrying Spanish and French troops which outnumbered by far the Austrian garrison in the islands. "The Archduke and the King of England", wrote Philip to Louis XIV, "are much mistaken if they think that I cannot procure myself satisfaction." The landing in Majorca was effected without encountering any resistance, and the troops marched against the capital, Palma; everyone there favoured surrender except the Governor Marchese Rubi, who, in the end, was forced to it by the inhabitants. Practically all the troops in the island were taken prisoner.[1]

A highly painful impression was produced in Vienna and London by the Spanish expedition, and yet no one could deny that Philip had acted within his rights; but the fact that he had accepted mediation rendered it contrary to international custom. The Imperial Court refused to believe that Spain had undertaken the expedition for the sake of Majorca and Iviza alone, and suspected that the aim was to regain all the late Spanish dominions. Hoffmann was instructed to secure the protection of the British fleet for the Imperial possessions in Italy;[2] while the British Government kept "a watchfull eye for the security of Minorca".[3]

But in reality Spanish intentions on this occasion went no further, and the size of the armaments was merely determined by the fear of British or Austrian support for the islands; though, in fact, the futile diplomatic mediation was all that Britain was prepared to undertake. The Great Powers of Europe hesitated, while the King of Spain had both the will and the strength to act. Great Britain did not as yet hold that position which a few years later enabled her to dictate to the

---

[1] Cf. Courcy, *La Coalition de 1701*, vol. ii. p. 452; and *Theatrum Europaeum*.
[2] Instructions to Hoffmann, July 31, 1715, Vienna Arch.
[3] Stanhope to Stair, July 3, 1715, O.S., F.O. 90/14.

Continent. The easy successes of 1714 and 1715, and the weakness shown by Europe on these occasions, probably contributed to the idea that the lost dominions of Carlos II could be recovered by a bold policy on the part of Spain.

The increased self-reliance of Philip V and his Court still further impaired relations between Spain and England. The British merchants had to suffer for it, and George Bubb declared their position untenable, and advised them to renounce all trade with Spain.[1] The Jacobite rising imposed caution on the British Government; according to Bubb, French intervention would have produced a rupture with Spain, and in that case, despite all treaties, the property of British merchants would have been immediately seized.[2]

On the death of Louis XIV, on September 1, 1715, the treaties which guaranteed the separation of the Crowns of France and Spain were put to a test: Philip V was determined not to observe them, and desired, if not the Crown, at least the Regency of France. In May 1715 he had sent Prince Cellamare to Paris to form for him a party in the capital and the provinces; and Cellamare was to enter a solemn protest if the last will of Louis XIV proved unfavourable to Philip. The Envoy made little progress, and when the King's death was approaching, people at Madrid expected Philip to appoint his wife Regent and draw closer towards the French frontier, so as to be near when the moment came. But it seems that Louis, though dying, managed to make his grandson desist from such action.

Should Philip go to Paris, the British Ambassador proposed to offer to go with him,[3] though he did not think that the offer would be accepted, nor did he expect the Spanish people to oppose the King's journey; but in that case he intended to present a Note with a solemn appeal to Europe invoking the renunciation originally made by Philip V. Had Philip established himself in France, George I could hardly have opposed him, in view of the rebellion at home, and it is very doubtful whether the Emperor alone would have dared to undertake a war both against France and Spain. Europe might have finished by admitting a union of those two States for the prevention of which it had carried on a war for ten years.

But this time the obstacle to Philip's ambitions lay in France.[4] The

---

[1] Bubb to Stanhope, Aug. 26, 1715, S.P. 94/84.
[2] Same to same, Sept. 23, 1715, *ibid.*
[3] Same to same, Sept. 6, 1715, *ibid.*
[4] Cf. Armstrong, *Elizabeth Farnese*, pp. 58-9.

Duke of Orleans became Regent on behalf of Louis XV, with powers wider than the late King had intended. The whole of France sided with him, and Philip V, to assert his claims, would have had to plunge the country into civil war. "I left the Ministers in the utmost concern . . . at the measures they heard were already taken in favour of the Duke of Orleans", wrote Methuen to Stanhope from Lisbon on September 27, 1715.[1] Philip V had to renounce his views on France: "I am persuaded", wrote Bubb to Stanhope on September 16, "that the King will not leave Madrid." [2] The idea of an attempt at a more favourable moment was still entertained at the Court of Philip V for a long time to come, and the rivalry between the two Bourbon princes was the cause of the profound estrangement which set in between France and Spain. The adherents of Philip V were henceforth called in France "the Spanish Party", and Orleans considered them his most dangerous enemies. When two years later Spain was at war with the Emperor, Alberoni said that if his King was unsuccessful and had to leave Spain, there remained to him France, where he and his four sons would find compensation for what they had lost in Spain. Such pronouncements naturally contributed to embitter the relations between the Regent and his Spanish cousin. When Philip of Anjou went to Spain as King, he had said "*Il n'y a plus de Pyrenées*"; more than any other event, the death of Louis XIV re-established the Pyrenees, and the separation of the two Crowns was better secured by the rivalry between Orleans and Anjou than by any treaties. But Philip V, having lost the support of France, had to seek good relations with other States, in the first place with the Maritime Powers. An attempt was now made by Spain to effect a *rapprochement* with the Government of George I. It was at this time that Alberoni rose to supreme power at the Spanish Court, and it proves his sound political judgment that he should have championed this new policy.

The negotiations were started in the greatest secrecy, which was preserved as long as possible; British trade to Spain naturally formed their main subject. On September 30, 1715, at 10 P.M. Bubb sat down to write a report on the subject to his Government: [3]

. . . the Ambassador of Holland has been with me and is just gone away. . . . He tells me that he receiv'd a message this afternoon, to

---

[1] Methuen to Stanhope, Lisbon, Sept. 27, 1715, S.P. 94/84.

[2] Bubb to Stanhope, Sept. 16, 1715, P.S., S.P. 94/84.

[3] Bubb to Stanhope, S.P. 94/84. For the following transaction cf. also Armstrong, *Elizabeth Farnese*, p. 71 *seq.*

come to Court; that there was a person that waited to speak with him there, by order of the King. He went immediately, and found a gentleman of great consequence, who he says show'd him a power from the King which authoriz'd him to talk to him as from His Majesty. They talk'd a pretty while about the Dutch affairs to which very full satisfaction was promis'd; and afterwards the gentleman told him, that he desir'd him to come to me, this evening, and tell me, as from the King, that he was resolv'd to live in a perfect good correspondence with the King my master, and to give His Majesty all imaginable proofs of it. He was ready to consent to the annulling the Explanatory Articles, and do all things that were reasonable to continue a good intelligence between His Britannick Majesty and himself; and the gentleman desir'd that I would give His Majesty an account of it to-night.

To this Bubb added a cipher postscript:

P.S.—*La personne ordonné de dire ceci à l'Ambass. d'Hollande était Alberoni, envoyé de Parme, qui gouverne absolument la Reine; le Cardinal ne sait rien du tout de cette affaire.*

Cardinal Del Giudice and Monteleone, the Spanish Minister in London, were as yet kept in the dark about these negotiations, carried on at Madrid by the Dutch Ambassador between Bubb and Alberoni, who in Bubb's dispatches to Stanhope is usually referred to merely as "this gentleman". On October 11, 1715, Bubb sent home the "Heads" of the commercial treaty which Alberoni proposed to obtain for Great Britain, and they were so favourable to British interests that London had nothing to add to them.[1] These "Heads" became in fact the basis of the Treaty. Still, gradually the secret leaked out, and Del Giudice, who felt his position threatened by Alberoni, tried his best to stop, or at least impede, the negotiations; "whatever we settled with the King in the morning", wrote Bubb, "the Cardinal and his party undid at night".[2] Moreover, exaggerated news about the Jacobite rising and about the serious danger which threatened the throne of George I were assiduously spread in Spain and rendered the Government untractable. Still, Alberoni's influence had grown so strong that he was able to overcome all the difficulties. The proposals were soon drawn up, and a Latin translation of Bubb's own proposals was given to him—"which is what they say they will stand by, if they do, you will see the worst piece of Latin, which

[1] Stanhope to Bubb, Oct. 19, 1715, O.S.
[2] Bubb to Stanhope, Dec. 15, 1715, S.P. 94/84.

ever appear'd, since the monks time". He similarly imputed to the
Spaniards the blame for "the ill-French, that the whole is full of".[1]
On December 14, 1715, the Treaty was signed, and it was received
with much joy in England. The end was as theatrical as the beginning—on the Spanish side it was difficult to find a proper person
willing to sign it, while Alberoni could not do it as, so far, his position at the Spanish Court was merely that of Envoy of Parma.
Finally full powers were made out for the Marquis of Bedmar, a
man of distinction and character, but at that time removed from
politics,

and as soon as it was ready, in the evening, we mett at that gentleman's
house (who keeps his bed and I fancy never heard anything of the
matter, till dinner time), and there, after the reading the Instruments,
they were signed. . . .

The Treaty placed Anglo-Spanish commerce more or less on the
footing on which it had been before the last war in the time of Carlos II.
Article I declared that British subjects trading with Spain "shall not
be oblig'd to pay greater, or any other impositions" on imports and
exports than those that they paid in King Carlos II's time. Article III
conceded to them the right previously enjoyed of raking salt on the
island of Tortuga[2]—this was a point "certainly of no consideration
to them: but I am sure I have had as many disputes about it, as if I
had ask'd a Province of Spain".[3] By Article IV British merchants
were to pay no greater and no other impositions than those paid by
Spanish subjects; in the course of the negotiations Spain demanded
"that the Spanish subjects should be used in the same manner in
Britain", but Bubb replied that other nations enjoyed that privilege
in Spain, while "no one nation enjoy'd it" in Britain. Article V
assured the most-favoured-nation treatment to either side, a thing
which was, however, of much less importance to Spain, with her
undeveloped commerce, than to Great Britain. It was specially
mentioned that other nations should pay the same duties on imports
or exports by land as the British by sea—"which, I believe", wrote
Bubb on December 9, "they [the French] never did, by near a quarter
part". And on December 15 he added, referring to this clause, that

---

[1] Bubb to Stanhope, Dec. 9 and Dec. 15, 1715, S.P. 94/84.
[2] The Treaty and Correspondence give the name as "Tortudos", but clearly
what is meant is the island of "Tortuga" in the Caribbean Sea.
[3] Bubb to Stanhope, Dec. 15, 1715, S.P. 94/84.

"it must be a stroke to the French trade here and particularly their wool trade". With regard to Article VI, which stipulated that all innovations in the commerce were to be carefully removed, everything depended on whether it was honestly observed on the part of Spain.

The King was mighty desirous that I should specify what they were . . . but I always declin'd it, because I knew it would be difficult to make him understand it . . . after several messages between us, I said, that I would make it all very plain to His Majesty, if he would be pleased to shutt himself up with me, two or three hours every afternoon, for six months. . . .

The seventh and last Article annulled the three Explanatory Articles of 1713.

Thus the Treaty contained all that England could wish for, and seemed to offer what the Treaty of Utrecht had failed to secure, conditions as favourable as had obtained in the Habsburg days. No wonder if during the negotiations Bubb received much encouragement and praise from his Government. On October 11, 1715, he had reported that Alberoni's "chief design" in intervening in these matters was "the getting of money"; and that he would obtain for Great Britain a favourable Treaty of Commerce if he was given 4000 pistoles on the signing of the Treaty, and 10,000 on its ratification. Stanhope replied on the 19th that he had prevailed with the King to consent to Bubb's promise of 10,000 pistoles, "4 to be given to him at the signing of the treaty, and 6 at the ratification"; to which he added a postscript—"rather than miscarry I would not advise you to break off for 4000 pistoles more". The British Government was highly satisfied when the Treaty was signed; it was immediately ratified, and on February 17 the ratifications were exchanged at Madrid, and the money probably paid out which was to have gone to Alberoni. "Though we gave them a silver box for a dirty piece of paper," wrote Bubb to Stanhope on February 19, 1716, "I hope we shall have no reason to repent our bargain." [1] The Ministers at home naturally ascribed the success to their own merit and steadiness,[2] while the Speech at the opening of Parliament on January 9, 1716, boasted with a certain measure of exaggeration that British commerce with Spain

---

[1] Bubb to Stanhope, Feb. 19, 1716, S.P. 94/85.
[2] Report from Hoffmann, Jan. 3, 1716, Vienna Arch.

will stand settled, for the future, on a foot more advantageous and certain than it ever did in the most flourishing time of any of my predecessors.[1]

In the rest of Europe the Treaty produced amazement and jealousy. It had been believed by some that the throne of George I was unsafe, and the Jacobite Rising, not yet quelled, seemed to bear out that assumption. And now a leading European Power had conceded to England a Treaty of Commerce on such advantageous terms. The understanding between the two Powers seemed to contain certain dangers and to clash with other political combinations which were looked upon as natural. On February 6, 1716, Stanhope wrote to Bubb:

I had the other day a letter from the Earl of Stair, wherein he writes to me that in a conference which he had with the Regent, His Royal Highness told him speaking of Spain, "so then you are friends with Spain, however I can tell you that Spain has done things for the Pretender which I would not do, and I could give you proofs of it". My Lord Stair answer'd him, "Sir, I don't say the contrary, but now we are nevertheless very well assur'd that the Court of Spain is very far from doing any thing in favour of the Pretender". This I thought fit to communicate to the Marquis de Monteleone, not out of any distrust our Court entertains of that of Spain, but on the contrary to shew the real confidence the King has in the assurances his Catholick Majesty has given him of his friendship, on which His Majesty intirely relyes.[2]

Thus the Spaniards were informed of what was said about them, and that they had now to merit the confidence of England.

Most painful was the impression which the Spanish Treaty of Commerce created in Austria. In view of the good relations with England, the Vienna Court felt slighted when they heard of it only after the event; but as the Emperor was not in diplomatic relations with Spain, he could not have heard of it earlier. He hardly knew what to think of the policy of Great Britain; he had thought that he was about to conclude an alliance with her who had just mediated the Barrier Treaty; and now George I had drawn closer to his worst enemy. It was believed in Vienna that this was merely a beginning; and the news from Hoffmann, who this time was misinformed, sounded ominous.[3] He reported that in future expeditions the Spanish fleet would be accompanied by British ships; and that England would not allow her alliance with the Emperor to be given an anti-Spanish turn. Vienna would not therefore trust the English assurances that the Treaty was merely of a commercial nature, and that there was no ground for suspicions.[1] Count Sinzendorff insisted that the English were now friends of the Duke of Anjou, and similarly Prince Eugene spoke bitterly to Schaub about the Commercial Treaty.[2] Only after repeated assurances from Great Britain,[3] and when the Austrians saw that there was no sequel to the Treaty, were their fears gradually allayed.

In fact, the British Government never thought of making the Commercial Treaty with Philip V as starting-point for a new political system; for of what use would the Spanish Alliance have been to them at a time when Spain was hostile to the Empire and estranged from France? Bubb, intoxicated by his success, was probably the only British diplomat who advocated political co-operation with Spain. In a remarkable letter to Stanhope he developed the following argument: if the Emperor tried to make himself master of Italy, as was expected, Spain was resolved to oppose him with arms; nor was it in the British interest to let Italy fall "into the hands of a Prince extreamly powerfull already". It was now in King George's power to render Spain dependent on him, and to be looked upon as her protector. Philip V's Queen, Elizabeth Farnese, should be won over by the inheritance of the Grand Duchy of Tuscany being secured to her descendants—here Bubb put forward a suggestion which was to be realized later on. In exchange, Spain should be made to guarantee the Hanoverian succession in Great Britain; thus a strict alliance could be made with Spain which would favour British commerce more than ever, a valuable guarantee could be gained for the Protestant Succession, and France and Spain could be entirely disunited "and most effectively so". His Majesty would thereby

do more good for his people with relation to Spain in one year, than our late mis-managements have done us hurt here in four.[4]

And in a separate letter to Stanhope he tried to flatter the late British Commander in Spain:

[1] Townshend to Schaub, Dec. 20, 1715, O.S., S.P. 104/42.
[2] Schaub to Townshend, Jan. 29, Feb. 1 and 5, 1716, S.P. 80/33.
[3] Townshend to Schaub, Feb. 14, 1716, O.S., S.P. 104/42; Volkra's report of Feb. 21, Mar. 3, 1716, Vienna Arch.
[4] Bubb to Stanhope, Feb. 19, 1716, S.P. 94/85.

I think that it is just that you, who have twice drove the King of
Spain out of his capital, when he would not be our friend, should have
the glory of establishing him there, more firmly than ever, now he
will.

Stanhope was not inclined to play the part. England was about to
renew the old alliance with Holland and Austria, and there was no
room for Spain in that system. Bubb's plan would probably have
meant war in Italy between Charles VI and Philip V, which might
easily have led to a new European war. This England wished to avoid,
and in Italy she meant to preserve the neutrality stipulated in 1713.
Thus there could be no thought of a Spanish alliance. On the contrary,
an alliance with the Emperor was concluded, and it was Bubb's task
to explain its purely defensive character to the Spanish Court, which
was seriously perturbed by it. Stanhope wrote to Bubb on May 17,
1716:

'Tis not many months since we had scarce an ally abroad and a dangerous Rebellion at home, in which circumstances the Emperor frankly and
handsomely offer'd to assist us. But no difficultys . . . could ever divert
the King from his fixed resolution of keeping himself free, and absolutely
master of the resolutions he shall think proper to take when any disturbance shall happen amongst his neighbours. . . . And since His
Majesty's affairs are, thanks be to God, at present in a more setled and
prosperous condition than his most sanguine servants could ever have
expected, I believe they [the Spanish Court] can hardly think, that, in
such circumstances the King would be so ill advised, as to contract any
engagement which could possibly lead him to quarrel with a nation whose
friendship and commerce hath ever been esteem'd the most beneficial to
England.[1]

The pursuit of trade interests was thus for the present the main, in
fact almost the sole, object of British diplomacy in Spain. The so-
called Asiento Treaty required thorough revision. The right to import
negro slaves from Africa to the Spanish Colonies, which had formerly
been vested in the Dutch and Genoese, and lately in the French
Guinea Company, was assigned by the Treaty of 1713 to the English
South Sea Company. During a period of thirty years, 4800 negroes
were to be imported every year to Spanish America, and sold at a
fixed price. Other branches of British trade with the Spanish Colonies
were also dealt with in the Asiento Treaty, which, however, was
unclear on these points and unsatisfactory to the British merchants.

[1] Stanhope to Bubb, May 17, 1716, S.P. 104/136.

T

No sooner had the new Treaty of Commerce been concluded than the British Government decided to take advantage of the favourable attitude of Spain and, on December 29, 1716, O.S., Stanhope, when sending the ratification of the Treaty to Bubb, added that to complete the friendship between the two monarchs and their subjects, a just settlement of the Asiento problem was required. The next day he added in a private letter that for this he was authorized to pay Alberoni the same sum as he had for the Treaty of Commerce. The negotiations now took a similar course, and on May 26, 1716, Bubb signed with the Marquis Bedmar the new Asiento agreement. All that the British South Sea Company desired was granted, and Bubb received the highest praise for having brought this affair to a successful conclusion. High hopes were now entertained for the future of British trade with Spain.

These hopes were, however, soon disappointed; trade with Spain did not recover and British merchants continued to complain about the damage suffered. It seems that deceit had been practised on Great Britain in that matter, and that the Treaty was concluded without Philip V, or rather Alberoni, seriously intending to carry out its provisions. In 1715 no one realized the overgrown ambitions and monstrous plans of this man, and British statesmen, almost to the very end, mistook his real intentions. He was not after money—it was subsequently proved with fair certainty that the sums paid for him did not reach him, and that Bubb had been cheated by an intermediary. And yet the loss of a few thousand pounds was the least disappointment—it was much more serious that all the ill-practices and extortions which had been specifically condemned in the Treaty, continued to be practised on British subjects, and diplomatic representations in that matter were of no avail. Most probably Alberoni's purpose in concluding the Treaty was to make the English believe that he was their friend and that it was in their interest to favour his rise and to strengthen his position, till the time when even the hostility of England would no longer prevent the carrying through of his far-reaching plans. He knew that he could not conquer Italy against the British fleet, and he therefore put into the Commercial Treaty anything England could wish for; and, being a comparative new-comer and stranger in Spain, he hardly realized which of these articles were capable of realization. But then, in the pursuit of his great aim, he did not care about details; and he failed to see that ultimately his action was bound to result in even greater

estrangement from Great Britain. But for the moment he had won
her sympathy, and even Stanhope continued until 1718 in the belief
that he was a friend of this country, and wished him to be made a
Cardinal and First Minister, for it was expected that he would carry
out the Commercial Treaty concluded by him.

CHAPTER XI

IN 1745, at the time of the Peace of Dresden, Frederick the Great asked the pointed question whether the King of England was to be looked upon as one person or as two; for George II, considering things purely from the angle of his Hanoverian Electorate, tried secretly to thwart the policy of his British Ministers, who had the British interests in view. Relations between England and Hanover were then the subject of public discussion. The Opposition declared in noisy debates in the House of Commons, and in widely circulated pamphlets, that since the Hanoverian accession the foreign interests of Great Britain and her glory had been sacrificed to the Electorate—an assertion to which writers in the service of the Court could give no convincing reply. A dynastic union had been established between two countries whose interests and needs differed on almost every point. Great Britain was a World Power, with colonies and trade in both hemispheres, while Hanover was a secondary German State without access to the sea, and with a policy which hardly made itself felt beyond the limits of the Lower Saxon Circle. They had nothing in common except the person of their ruler. He was, however, absolute in Hanover, and even in Great Britain, in spite of the limitations on the Royal Prerogative, the influence which the monarch was able to exercise was by no means negligible, and was greatest in the sphere least accessible to public control, *i.e.* in foreign politics, which were, besides, much more intelligible to George I than British domestic affairs. Lastly, there alone points of contact were to be found between England and Hanover, which called for his personal intervention.

An attempt had been made in the Act of Settlement to guard against a Hanoverian King trying to subordinate English policy to the interests of the Electorate.[1] But while he was precluded from

[1] See above, pp. 3-4.

openly waging war for the sake of Hanover, it would have been difficult to prove if he surreptitiously employed the resources of his Kingdom in the service of the Electorate. The strict observance of the Act
depended, therefore, on the honesty of the King, and on this point
the first two Georges were not over-scrupulous.

The Northern policy of George I is an early example of such
evasion. In August 1714 Charles XII of Sweden was still in Turkey,
where, after the vicissitudes of a remarkable career, he had spent five
years in voluntary exile, while his enemies busied themselves conquering the scattered dominions of the Swedish Crown. When all his
outlandish plans had failed, he returned home. The journey was
extraordinary, like everything undertaken by Charles XII: he crossed
Central Europe on horseback, covering more than nine hundred miles
in a fortnight. On November 22, 1714, he appeared in his fortress of
Stralsund. His legs were so badly swollen that his boots had to be cut
open. The old wound in his left foot had reopened, but his strong
constitution conquered the after-effects of this terrible ride.[1]

Charles immediately resumed the direction of military and diplomatic affairs. The best part of his German dominions was lost; and
he was at war with Russia, Denmark, and Poland. The young King
of Prussia, Frederick William I, had entered into treaties of alliance
with the enemies of Sweden, and, by seizing Stettin, had taken a
step which was practically bound to lead to war. And now George,
Elector of Hanover and King of Great Britain, joined the Northern
Allies.

For a long time past the Guelph dynasty had had an eye on the
Swedish Duchies of Bremen and Verden. In 1712 they had been conquered by Denmark, but were now claimed by Hanover. The Danish
King was at first reluctant to cede them, but agreed when on the return of Charles XII the attitude of George I became a matter of
serious concern to the Northern Allies.[2] Charles XII, who could hardly
hope to regain the Duchies, might offer them to George I as the price
of an alliance, and Denmark preferred to forestall him. Thus all the
Northern Princes were to profit at Sweden's expense. Moreover, the
territorial interests of the German Princes agreed with the German
national desire to expel the Swedes from Germany.

In November 1714, George I, as Elector, concluded a Treaty with

---

[1] Report of the English Envoy, Jefferyes, from Stralsund, Dec. 4, 1714, O.S.,
Stowe MSS. 227, ff. 528-9.
[2] Cf. Havemann, iii. p. 491.

Prussia which secured for him Bremen and Verden.[1] In May 1715, Hanover, by an alliance with Denmark, definitely joined the enemies of Sweden, though war was not formally declared till October. Hanover was to receive the Duchies from Denmark against financial compensation, and in return guaranteed the possession of the Duchy of Schleswig to the Danes. In the ensuing war the Elector of Hanover employed the resources of his British Kingdom, which was not at war with Sweden. England had watched the struggle in Northern Europe, but while engaged in the War of the Spanish Succession, had tried to localize it, lest it should reduce the exertions of her allies against Louis XIV. Only during the concluding years of Queen Anne had England shown an interest in the wars of Charles XII.

In the spring of 1714 the French proposed to Frederick William I an alliance with Charles XII:[2] in Prussia's own interest Sweden should be protected against Russia's preponderance. In return, Charles XII was to cede Stettin and its hinterland to Prussia. France was Sweden's old ally, but hopes of help from other Powers were also held out, even from England, which under the Oxford-Bolingbroke Administration had become connected with France, and was at that time negotiating for an alliance with her, Spain, and Sicily. The problem of the British Succession formed the background to the new Anglo-Swedish friendship: Sweden's help might be valuable in an attempt to exclude the Elector of Hanover from the throne. In accord with the policy of Louis XIV, the British Government started negotiations with Prussia. The British Minister in Berlin[3] was instructed to declare that the Queen

cannot sit still and see with indifference the total ruin and overthrow of that Kingdom [Sweden] and tho' she cannot afford his Swedish Majesty the immediate assistance she is inclined to do . . . yet she will not be wanting to use those means which in the present juncture may be most serviceable. . . .

If in reply to a Danish attack on Schonen Prussia threatened Denmark in Holstein, and if this provoked the Tsar to hostilities against her, England would come to Prussia's assistance.[4]

But Frederick William I, having been offered Stettin both by Sweden and Russia, could choose from whom to accept it. Tsar Peter

---

[1] Droysen, iv. 2, pp. 101-2.   [2] *Ibid.* pp. 87 ff.
[3] Bromley to Breton, May 4, 1714, O.S., S.P. 104/53.
[4] Cf. Droysen, iv. 2, p. 93.

offered him, moreover, a treaty of mutual guarantee: Frederick William I accepted. "I may fare ill," he declared, "I don't mind; the Swedes must clear out of Germany." Two months later, the death of Queen Anne caused a complete reversal in England's Northern Policy. George I was as Elector on the brink of war with Sweden, and could not as King engage in opposite measures. Even the most insular of English politicians had to pay some regard to Hanover—to do much more they were forbidden by the Act of Settlement. George I and the Continental rulers thought differently: for Prussia and Denmark the importance of Hanover's adherence lay in the expectation of English support against Sweden, which could be given most effectively by sending a British fleet into the Baltic.

The programme of the Northern Allies for 1715 was to conquer Stralsund and Rügen, which would have left the King of Sweden with Wismar as his only base in Germany. But it was doubtful whether even the joint fleets of Russia and Denmark could establish a superiority over that of Sweden in the Baltic; Tsar Peter spoke with contempt of the Danish fleet.[1] The mere presence of the British fleet would be of great value. Frederick William I wished for it, moreover, as a counter-weight to the preponderance of his Russian ally, and so did George I, because Hanover was at war and a Swedish success might cost Bremen and Verden. A few months after his arrival in England, the decision was taken to send a British fleet into the Baltic the following year. The idea originated with Bernstorff and not with the British Ministers, and the Prussian Resident[2] expected that the presence of the British fleet would facilitate the attack against Stralsund and Rügen, and harass the Swedes.

The true purpose of that naval expedition was on no account to be talked about in England, though the annexation by Hanover rather than by Denmark[3] of the Duchies, on the left bank of the Lower Elbe, would have been favourable to England's trade with Hamburg. Still, this did not justify the expense of sending a fleet into the Baltic, which had to be explained on grounds of British policy; it was therefore alleged that British trade in the Baltic was in need of protection. It had suffered severely during the Northern War, numerous merchant ships having been captured by Swedish privateers. The legality of these captures was disputed, for the fact that the ships

---

[1] Cf. Droysen, iv. 2, III, Note 2.
[2] Bonet, Dec. 17/28, 1714, Prussian State Archives.
[3] Cf. Erdmannsdörffer, *Deutsche Geschichte*, ii. pp. 338-9.

were bound for Russian ports was no sufficient justification, as, barring war contraband, direct trade between neutrals and belligerents was admitted. The Swedes were on firmer ground when they claimed that all those ports were blockaded, though this was not the effective blockade, postulated by some jurists, but a mere "paper-blockade".

In 1711 Jefferyes, the British Minister to Sweden, was instructed to demand freedom of trade with the Baltic ports for the British merchants, but his representations were met by a flat refusal, both verbally and in writing; [1] and while the Swedish blockade caused constant friction, the British Government complained, but took no serious measures, and in 1714 was even prepared to help Sweden in her distress. Nor was the naval expedition of 1715 really undertaken on behalf of the injured merchants: according to Bonet "the first step was to make the merchants claim protection for their trade", which, when asked, they were naturally very willing to do.

The expedition into the Baltic was decided upon in January 1715, before Parliament had met, indeed before it had been elected. The Dutch were invited to do the same in the interest of their own trade. Bernstorff, however, addressed to Bonet the naïve and self-complacent question whether the King was not doing a great deal when, besides supporting the operations by land against Stralsund, he sent a fleet to help in the conquest of Stralsund and Rügen, and moreover offered a considerable sum of money to Denmark for the conduct of the war.[2] It looked as if the Elector of Hanover had acquired the right freely to dispose of the resources of Great Britain to the advantage of his German principality.

A few months passed before the fleet was ready to sail. It was intended to appear off Stralsund in May in order to facilitate, perhaps even assist in, the operations of the allies. Although it was for Englishmen alone to settle this matter, the Hanoverian Ministers took the lead in it. Bonet discussed the Baltic squadron with Bernstorff alone, and elicited from him repeated assurances that Great Britain pursued the double aim of protecting her trade and promoting the operations against Rügen and Stralsund. When Bonet pointed to the rather small share of Hanover in the military operations in Pomerania, he invariably received the reply that the naval expedition more than

[1] Sweden, retrospect of the English-Swedish relations, 1711–1719, S.P. 95/19-25.

[2] This probably refers to the purchase money for Bremen and Verden.

balanced the account.[1] A special Envoy, Baron Eltz, was sent from
Hanover to Berlin, and was instructed, together with the Hanoverian
Minister Heusch, to declare that the fleet was intended to assist in
the operations against Sweden.[2] King Frederick William was not
satisfied with the verbal assurances, and demanded a written agreement defining the extent to which he could count on the support of
the fleet. But naturally the real intentions could not be officially
stated: this was a British fleet and Great Britain was not at war with
Sweden. Heusch was, however, instructed to make at Berlin the
following classical declaration in the name of George I:[3] " We promise
his Prussian Majesty upon our Royal word and faith, that the said
squadron shall in every way second the operations against Sweden,
and we hope that his Royal Majesty will trust our word, seeing that the
result would prove that there shall be no shortcoming in redeeming it.
We cannot, however, enter on this point into a written engagement
with his Prussian Majesty because the action of this said squadron
concerns us as King, and were we to put anything about it in writing
we could not therein employ our German Ministers, but would have
to let it pass through the hands of our Ministers of British nationality."

Contemporaries may possibly have been deceived about the purpose of the naval expedition, for the utmost caution was observed.
In international law the case of 1715 is quoted to show how Great
Britain as a neutral Power employed her fleet to convoy merchant-
ships in the Baltic and to protect them against Swedish privateers.[4]
In reality the case presents an even more interesting aspect: a neutral
State effectively supported a belligerent, without abandoning its
neutrality and without incurring a declaration of war from the State
against which it acted.

The British Ministers, placed between the personal wishes of the
King and their own responsibility towards the nation, were in an
embarrassing position. It was by no means easy to find a way to
render the fleet serviceable in the war against Sweden without Great
Britain appearing to do more than protect her trade and take reprisals for damage suffered. Frederick William I, who had little

---

[1] Bonet's reports, Feb. 11/22, March 8/19, March 29/April 9, 1715; cf. also
Droysen, iv. 2, p. 126.

[2] Instructions to Eltz and Heusch, March 21/April 1, 1715, Han. Arch.

[3] P.S. to instructions to Heusch, April 5/16, 1715, Han. Arch.

[4] Cf. Heffter, *Das Europäische Völkerrecht*, 7th ed., by Geffken (1882), p. 374.

understanding for this fine distinction, demanded in a personal letter to George I, dated May 1, 1715, that the dispatch of the fleet should be hastened and that the Admiral should be instructed to act in exact accordance with the wishes of the King of Prussia! Bernstorff conferred with the British Ministers and reminded Bonet that it was the Elector of Brunswick, and not the King of England, who was at war.[1] None the less, in practising reprisals the British ships would attack every Swedish vessel they encountered whether man-of-war or merchant-ship. Further, by lying off the island of Rügen the British squadron would in fact render the same service as if Great Britain had declared war. The Hanoverian Residents in Berlin and Copenhagen were instructed to speak in the same sense.[2] "Seeing that we have not declared war in our character of King, it is hoped that we shall not be expected to order Admiral Norris to undertake superfluous and unnecessary hostile demonstrations against Sweden, as such procedure would embarrass us here, and be of no help over there."

Sir John Norris was placed in command of the fleet. But when his instructions were to be drafted differences of opinion arose between the German and the British Ministers over the instructions to him, the British Ministers having to think of Parliament.[3] The instructions for Norris, dated May 6 and 12, O.S., were of an unexceptionable appearance. He was directed to convoy the British merchant-ships safe into the particular ports and harbours for which they were bound, and to give them all the protection they required. The ships were to unload and reload without loss of time. Meanwhile the warships were to lie at anchor off Reval or any other suitable port. When the ships destined for St. Petersburg were ready, the fleet was to start for home, calling at the various ports for the merchant-ships, and to convoy them back to England. In his additional instructions he was directed immediately on his arrival in the Baltic to dispatch an express to the King of Sweden at Stralsund demanding "in the most pressing manner satisfaction without any further delay for the ships and effects of our subjects taken and confiscated, and also insist

[1] Bonet, May 6/17, 1715.

[2] Instructions to Heusch and the Hanoverian Resident at Copenhagen, London, May 10/21, 1715, Han. Arch.

[3] Bonet, May 13/24, 1715: "*Les instructions de cet amiral ont souffert plus d'une difficulté de la part des ministres anglais, qui auront un jour à en répondre au Parlement*".

that the freedom of trade to the Baltick may be restored and preserved for the future" (*i.e.* the revocation of the Edict issued by
Charles XII on February 19, 1715, was demanded). He was further
to inform the King that in the meantime he was ordered to stop
and detain all Swedish ships, that he was able to meet with, until
such time as the British demands for reparation and security were
granted.

No accusations against the Ministers could ever have been raised
in Parliament because of these instructions. Still, the hopes which
Denmark and Prussia founded on the intervention of the British fleet
would have been very incompletely realized if Norris had strictly
adhered to his instructions. King Frederick William, to whom it seemed
obvious that an Admiral had to act according to his instructions,
ordered Bonet to ask that they should be shown to him. The British
Court hesitated for a while, and finally refused the request. Bernstorff,
however, gave verbally the desired information, and was in a position
to reassure the Prussian Minister whom the contents of the written
instruction could hardly satisfy; he said that he had summoned the
Admiral and explained to him what he should do to promote the
King's interests; in his presence Norris had to take notes of the main
points to which His Majesty attached the greatest weight.[1] Thus,
short, "extra-secret", additional instructions were given, more important for the movements of the fleet than those which bore the
signature and the great seal of George I; and Parliament knew nothing about them. The naval expedition was in fact contrary to the
spirit of the Act of Succession—England was drawn into war for
the defence of dominions which did not "belong to the Crown of
England".

George I was not punctilious as to his duties towards his British
subjects; whereas the British Ministers, out of regard for his wishes,
partly supported him and partly gave in to him; in the end they
were glad if only a form could be found which would enable them
to accept responsibility towards Parliament. None the less, their
actions seem highly questionable. At the very time when Bolingbroke
was impeached for having given the Commander-in-Chief secret instructions contrary to his overt orders, King George in secret directed
the Admiral in the Baltic to assist in the operations against Sweden,
exceeding thereby his strict instructions. In their own interest, the
Ministers had to see to it that the part which the British fleet was

[1] Bonet, May 17/28, 1715.

to play should remain a secret.[1] Under the heading of reprisals Norris was instructed to attack any Swedish ships he met. "Clearly," said Bernstorff to Bonet, "if the co-operation of the British fleet is desired, you must not say to the Admiral: 'Please help us in this or that operation', but simply: 'We know of the presence here of Swedish ships. Please come and attack them.'"[2]

On May 29 Sir John Norris sailed for the Baltic,[3] his departure having been delayed by a few weeks as the ten merchant-ships, which were to start under a convoy of twenty men-of-war, were not all ready. On the high seas Norris joined with the Dutch squadron, which acted as convoy to a number of merchant-ships. The States General had, however, given no instructions to their Admiral with regard to action to be taken against the Swedes; and with them the protection of trade was in fact the only purpose of the expedition. Norris, however, did his best to obtain Dutch support for the major aim of his mission.

Off Helsingör the two Admirals held a council of war. It was agreed that the fleets should take the first opportunity of wind and weather and sail to Kjöge Bay, south of Copenhagen; and then, from such intelligence as could be obtained, take further resolutions.[4] At the same time Norris sent a ship to Stralsund to inform the Swedish King through the British Envoy that the British fleet had arrived in the Baltic, and that it would seize all Swedish ships which it met, until Charles XII had made proper compensation for the damage done to British trade and revoked the Edict of February 19. Naturally no one expected any results from this threat. Charles XII, so far from meeting the British demands, ordered his own fleet to attack British ships wherever possible.[5] Norris's message to Stralsund was a mere matter of form. Four days later it was resolved by the Admirals in another council of war to convoy the merchant fleets to their respect-

[1] Bonet, Feb. 11/22, 1715: "*Je fus confirmé que cet armement est très-reél mais il (Bernstorff) souhaite qu'on le ménage avec tout le secret possible*".

[2] Bonet, May 17/28, 1715.

[3] For the following account see correspondence between Townshend and Norris, S.P. 42/70, and Adm. 2/48. Extracts from Norris's reports are published in the Townshend MSS. *Hist. MSS. Comm.* Rep. XI, App. Part IV. p. 89 *et seq.*

[4] "At a Council of War held aboard his Majesty's ship the *Cumberland* at Elsenure the 31st May 1715", Adm. 1/2; S.P. 42/70.

[5] Norris to Townshend, June 2, 1715: "I hear from all hands in these parts that the King of Sweden has directed his naval force to attack us". Further see Townshend to Norris, June 14/25, 1715.

ive harbours, and accordingly the two fleets crossed the Baltic. On June 12 they threw anchor in Danzig Bay, having brought the merchant-ships bound for Danzig and Königsberg to their destinations. A week later they reached Reval. Four British warships convoyed the merchantmen destined for St. Petersburg across the Bay of Finland. After the fleet had reassembled, it sailed together with the Dutch in a southerly direction, called at Riga, and on July 10 arrived again off Danzig to receive news and instructions from the shore. On the 20th, after another council of war, they returned to Reval, and sent once more four warships into the Bay of Finland. They were now about to collect the merchant-ships from the various ports where they had discharged their cargoes and taken new freights aboard, in order to convoy them home.

Meantime Norris had not lost sight of his other task; but he could not start by fighting the Swedes. "The protecting the trade and convoying the merchantships safe into their several ports", wrote Townshend to him on June 14/25, 1715, "is to be your first and chief point of view." But after that, "you should apply your self with all the diligence and earnestness you are able to execute that point of your instructions which relates to reprisals".[1] When the British fleet entered the Baltic, the campaign on land had anyhow not yet started. Prussia had declared war on May 1, but through the fault of the Danes, the allied armies effected a junction before Stralsund only on July 13. The King of Sweden himself took charge of the defence of the fortress; the besieging forces were 50,000 strong, the Prussians under command of their King.

An opportunity now offered to Admiral Norris to support operations against Stralsund and Rügen while the merchant-ships placed under his care remained in the Baltic ports. The Danes and Prussians counted on such help, and Frederick William wrote from the camp before Stralsund to George I that it would be useful if the British fleet approached nearer to the coast with a view to closing in Stralsund more completely from the sea. In two letters the King urged Norris to join the Danish fleet, which was too weak for the Swedes.[2] Norris was willing to do his utmost, and was sure of the approval of the King. But he had to think of Parliament and sought his justification by co-operating with the Dutch. So long as he acted in conjunction with the Dutch Admiral, no one could assert that the British

---

[1] Diplomatic Instructions, Sweden. Camden Series, vol. 32, pp. 78-9.
[2] Norris to Townshend, July 8, 1715, S.P. 42/70.

fleet was employed in the service of Hanover.[1] But it was not the intention of the States General to intervene in the war. On June 24 Norris wrote in high delight that he had persuaded the Dutch Admiral to cruise with him in the Baltic in such a manner as would, if time permitted, besides securing trade, render possible the pursuit of the other aims of His Majesty. The two Dutch Ministers in London informed the King that the States General were determined to let their fleet in the Baltic act in perfect concert with the British.[2] The news was sent to Norris: "I have accordingly used my utmost sollicitation with the Dutch Rear-Admiral, to get him to promise, if occasion should offer to attack the Swedes, to join with me in the action; but he says . . . that until he receive such orders from the States . . . he can't join with me in any such action offensively".[3] And when the Dutch Admiral received the news from Danzig that the States General intended "to keep an exact neutrality", all prospect of co-operation was gone.[4]

This was the time when the support of the British fleet was specially required.[5] The Danish Admiral Rabe did not dare to oppose his sixteen ships of the line to the twenty-two of the Swedish fleet, which had sailed from Karlskrona, and he withdrew to Moen. Meantime, between the dyke of Peenemunde and the islet of Ruden, a smaller Danish squadron was placed by the approach of the Swedish fleet in a highly precarious position. Norris, however, lay with his squadron off Danzig and did not effect the junction with the Danes for which Rabe had hoped, nor was he, having only fourteen warships, sufficiently strong without the Dutch to attack the Swedish fleet, even had he wished to do so. He remained inactive awaiting further instructions from his Government. Denmark and Prussia were much disappointed, and the King of Prussia, in a letter written from the camp before Stralsund, and dated July 27, 1715, asked his father-in-law, George I, that he should not allow the British fleet to leave the Baltic while the success of the Prussian operations was endangered by the Swedish fleet. He naïvely added that surely those must not prove to have been right who maintained that the British naval expedition had been undertaken exclusively for the protection of British trade.[6]

[1] Bonet, Aug. 2/13, 1715.
[2] Townshend to Norris, July 5/16, 1715.
[3] Norris to Townshend, July 8, 1715, S.P. 42/70.
[4] Same to same, July 13, 1715. *Hist. MSS. Comm.* Rep. XI, App. IV, p. 92.
[5] Cf. Droysen, iv. 2, pp. 132 *seq.*   [6] Han. Arch.

Before a reply could be received from England, the situation in the Baltic had changed once more. On receipt of fresh instructions from London, Norris tried again to persuade the Dutch Admiral together with him to attack the Swedes, but the Dutch Admiral had just received the explicit order from the States General in no way to assume the offensive, and not even to practise reprisals.[1] Norris therefore gave up the idea and both fleets left Danzig for Reval to convoy the merchantmen, which had meantime discharged and taken on cargoes; they reached Reval on June 23.

Next day there arrived at Reval the Russian fleet, consisting of nineteen warships, with Tsar Peter himself on board the flagship. The relations between Great Britain and Russia, which had been unfriendly during the concluding years of the Queen's reign,[2] had improved on the accession of George I. In 1710, as Elector, he had been an ally of Russia; now they were ranged on the same side, and in October 1715 a new alliance was concluded between Russia and Hanover. Whatever jealousy was felt in England of the rising Russian power and of Russian trade competition in the Baltic, the interest of Hanover prevailed with George I, and even as King of Great Britain he cultivated the friendship with Russia. When Norris met the Russian fleet, he asked permission to wait on the Tsar. Peter invited him on board his ship, and returned the visit of the British Admiral. He was received by the salvoes due to a monarch. Norris admired the Tsar's keen interest in naval matters, and the progress which the Russians had made in naval construction. He saw three Russian ships of sixty guns as good as any in the British fleet.

Meantime they had been rejoined by the merchant-ships from Petersburg, and next all the other ports were visited from which merchant-ships were to be convoyed home. Without taking part in the fighting round Rügen and Stralsund, the fleets of the Maritime Powers traversed the Baltic. They left Danzig on August 25, and lay off Bornholm from August 27 till September 1. Norris reported that the winds were unfavourable, but possibly his stay aimed at helping the allies by the mere proximity of his fleet; for George I, in a letter to Frederick William, dated August 2,[3] expected that Norris had by that time "settled near Bornholm, which will cover the operations

---

[1] Two letters from Norris to Townshend off Reval, July 30, 1715.
[2] Cf. Martens, *Recueil des traités et conventions conclus par la Russie avec les puissances étrangères. IX, Traités avec l'Angleterre*, p. 23 *seq.*
[3] Han. Arch.

against Rügen and Stralsund". Probably this point was mentioned in secret instructions given to the Admiral by Bernstorff. On September 1, Norris resumed his course and next day he was once more in the Bay of Kjöge. Here he met the Danish fleet and received from its admiral a letter with important instructions from Townshend.[1]

The complaints of Frederick William I about insufficient support from the British fleet made an impression in London. Could George I and his German Ministers have acted as they wished, they would gladly have left the British fleet in the Baltic till the last inch of German territory had been recovered from the Swedes. This was demanded by Denmark, and was the condition for the cession of Bremen and Verden.[2] But to the British Ministers the convoy for the Baltic trade, and at the utmost the taking of reprisals, were the purpose of the naval expedition, and they failed to see how any further employment of the fleet in the Baltic could be justified in Parliament. Anyhow the Tories would say, wrote Hoffmann, that hardly had the King mounted the throne, when already "British naval power is used, at British expense, for the profit and advantage of his Electoral possessions".

To facilitate matters for Bernstorff and Bothmer, Bonet complained only verbally that so far the British fleet had done nothing to assist in the conduct of the war, whereas his master, the King of Prussia, had relied on their support. He drew a comparison with the line taken by William III in 1700, when the fleets of the Maritime Powers, without being at war, had made their weight felt in the Baltic, and had forced Denmark to conclude the Peace of Travendal. How much more justified would George I now be in attacking Swedish ships without declaration of war, when he had grounds to demand satisfaction for infringements of international law, committed by Sweden in seizing British ships.[3]

Bonet's intervention was welcome to the German Ministers, who now energetically demanded that Norris should not return without having attacked the Swedes. The British Ministers, conscious of their responsibility, answered with a determined refusal. In this conflict between British and Hanoverian interests, George I himself gave the decision.[4] He summoned both sides, and declared to his British and German Ministers that the capture of so many merchantmen could

[1] *Hist. MSS. Comm.* Rep. XI, App. IV, p. 93.
[2] Hoffmann, July 19, 1715.   [3] Bonet, Aug. 2/13, 1715.
[4] Hoffmann, Aug. 20, 1715.

not be left unavenged. If not the entire fleet, part of it at least should join the Danes in the fight against the Swedes. The British Ministers submitted to the verdict of the King. The Hanoverian interest had prevailed.

Fresh instructions were sent to Sir John Norris. His previous conduct and even his having refrained from attacking the Swedes without Dutch support, received the King's approval. Now it was "of the last consequence to the nation" that the fleet of merchantmen from the Baltic "should be conducted home in safety (since if they should miscarry such a scarcity of navall stores must ensue as would disable His Majesty from fitting out a fleet next spring upon any event)". This, therefore, was the acknowledged intention.

But as you cannot but be sensible that one part only of the necessary and important services which you was instructed to perform will by this means be executed, the King of Sweden not having as yet returned any answer to the representations that you sent by His Majesty's order . . . for obtaining reparation for the losses sustained by his subjects and the revocation of the unjustifiable edict published by the Swedes . . . and His Majesty having considered that by returning home with your whole squadron . . . the Swedes would by that means become masters of those seas and the commerce of the British subjects be exposed to the same violence and interruption which it has suffered these last two years.

To prevent this happening, Norris was, if possible, to leave eight ships in the Baltic "under the command of some discreet officer", to join the Danish fleet.

These instructions reached Norris in Kjöge Bay on September 2, and he immediately selected eight of his best ships, and under the command of Captain Edward Hopson, sent them to join the Danish fleet; [1] Captain Strickland was sent with Hopson. Also the other six captains would, wrote Norris, do their duty towards the person and Government of the King, as they had all received their commissions since his accession from the new Board of Admiralty. Norris drew up instructions for Captain Hopson, dated September 3, 1715,[2] ordering him to join the Danish fleet with a view to obtaining compensation from Sweden and making them cancel the edict; naturally no other aims were mentioned in the written instructions, as these might easily some day be called for by Parliament. Much more was said in Norris's letter to Townshend: the eight ships were to remain in the Baltic till October 21, "before which time, in all probability, the affair

---

[1] Norris to Townshend, Sept. 3 and 5, 1715.   [2] S.P. 42/70.

of Rügen will be over, and after that I don't see that the squadron can be of more service to Denmark for this year".[1]

Although these eight British warships did not engage in battle with the Swedish fleet, they effectively contributed to the success of the campaign. Their junction with the Danes seems to have given the allies a decisive superiority over the Swedish fleet which could no longer interfere with the operations against Rügen and Stralsund. After a battle between the Danish and Swedish fleets off Jasmund[2] on August 8, the Swedes had retired to Karlskrona without having suffered real defeat. Had it not been for the accession of the eight British warships, the Danes would probably have had once more to meet the Swedes who had to prevent, as long as possible, a landing in Rügen. Now, however, the united Danish and British fleets cruised between Zeeland and Rügen.[3] About the middle of October it was rumoured that the Swedes had put to sea; the Danish and British ships immediately sailed for Rügen, but when nothing was heard of the Swedish fleet, they returned to Kjöge Bay. The bad state of the Danish ships made it impossible to remain off Rügen,[4] but even so the aim was achieved, for the Swedish fleet had to stay at Karlskrona, and on November 15 the island was captured. Nor could Stralsund, defended by Charles XII, hold out indefinitely; it surrendered on December 22, 1715. The campaign had achieved its purpose, and the Ministers in London could claim that this would not have been possible without the assistance of the eight British warships.[5] And yet no overt infringement of the Constitution had been committed: there was nothing in the instructions of the naval commanders about fighting for Rügen and Stralsund; it had been the tasks of Norris to convoy merchant-ships, and of Hopson, to make reprisals.

In October 1715, the Swedish Minister in London, Count Gyllenborg, presented a Note complaining of the help given by Great Britain to the enemies of Sweden; he openly told the English that they had violated the Act of Settlement. He received a severe rebuff, was told that the King had to protect British trade and exact compensation, and was ironically thanked for the lesson on the meaning of Parliamentary Statutes.

[1] S.P. 42/70.   [2] See Droysen, iv. 2, pp. 134 *et seq.*
[3] See Hopson's reports, S.P. 42/70.
[4] "*Conclusion prise dans le conseil de guerre tenu à bord de l'Éléphant,* 12ième de Nov. 1715", S.P. 42/70.
[5] Bonet, Feb. 14/25, 1716.

As a result of the British naval expedition Hanover, after long negotiations, received in October 1715 the reward promised by Denmark. She had delayed handing over the Duchies, even after the conclusion of the Treaty in May, but changed her attitude when the British fleet under Norris appeared in the Baltic, and still more when Hopson was left there with his squadron. But to obtain the legal title to the Duchies an investiture by the Emperor was required, and it was only in 1733 that George II received this from Charles VI.

The acquisition of Bremen and Verden was of immense advantage to the Electorate. What had been pursued in vain in 1648, was now achieved: access to the sea was secured and with it valuable territory. The new subjects had reason to be satisfied with the change.[1] Since 1648 they had been treated by the Swedish Government as territory which could hardly be permanently held and had therefore to be exploited while the occupation lasted. The two Duchies had to raise enormous contributions for the wars of the Swedish Kings. During the Northern War of 1700–1712, 76 tons of gold, equal to 7,600,000 thalers had been extorted from them. In 1712 the Swedish garrison of Stade had surrendered to the Danes after a brave defence. But the promised "mild and gracious" government of the new ruler, King Frederick IV of Denmark, started by demanding, under the well-sounding name of "don gratuit", 4000 thalers from Stade, and 20,000 from the other towns. In the three years 1712–15 the Danes extorted no less than $1\frac{1}{2}$ million thalers from the country. The union with Hanover was therefore welcomed; it was a natural junction with the neighbouring German territories. The new Government endeavoured to restore their well-being and the country recovered during the ensuing period of some twenty-five years of peace.

In England distrust rather than joy was felt at the increase of the Continental possessions of George I. There were many who could not rid themselves of the idea that the King aspired to absolute dominion in England, such as he exercised in Hanover,—would he not perhaps attempt it some day by bringing Hanoverian troops across to England? This would undoubtedly be facilitated by Hanover now having access to the sea. It might have been natural during the Scottish Rebellion, instead of raising new regiments in England and inviting Dutch help, to bring across troops from Hanover; and

---

[1] Cf. Havemann 3, 495. Tobelmann and Wittpenning, "Gesch. der Stadt Stade", *Archiv des Vereins für Gesch. und Altertümer der Herzogtümer Bremen und Verden und des Landes Hadeln* (1869).

this was in fact suggested by Lord Stair.[1] In reality the Government could not have done so without arousing suspicion. When Hoffmann suggested the idea to Stanhope, he received the reply that England was still "able to hold her own ground".[2]

Bremen and Verden were acquired, but the war was not over, and Sweden was by no means prepared to make the extensive cessions demanded from her. Three more times during the life of Charles XII British fleets entered the Baltic with a view to co-operating against the Swedes.

In the autumn of 1715 the King of Denmark had approached the British Court with the request that the eight ships should remain in the Baltic for the winter with his own fleet. Prussia supported the request, which was, however, more than England could grant. George I and his German Ministers were not disinclined, but the British feared Parliament, and the reply was given that the eight ships should remain in the Baltic till Rügen was taken, but that it was impossible to leave them there for the winter. England would, however, send another fleet the next year to join the Danes.[3]

Captain Hopson returned to England with his eight ships after Rügen had been conquered and before Stralsund had fallen; but a new naval expedition for the next year was already planned. The wish was expressed by the Prussians that this time the British fleet should openly attack the Swedes. The British Court replied that this was only possible if Prussia in turn assumed obligations towards Great Britain. A treaty was now discussed whereby Prussia was to guarantee the British Succession and promise help against all overt and secret abetters of the Pretender.[4] At Bernstorff's desire Bonet presented the British Court with a Note outlining such a treaty. It made a considerable impression, and the previous doubts of the British statesmen seemed suddenly forgotten. Townshend expressed his joy to the Prussian Minister at having been given the means to reconcile the wishes of His Majesty with the interests of his country. Lord Orford, First Lord of the Admiralty, who in 1715 had for a long time refused to sign the instructions to Admiral Norris, and had indeed threatened to resign before he let himself be persuaded to do so, now spoke in favour of sending a stronger fleet to the Baltic than the

[1] Stair to Robethon, Feb. 10, 1716, Stowe MSS. 228, f. 230.

[2] Hoffmann, Feb. 4, 1716.

[3] Bonet, Oct. 14/25, Dec. 2/13, 1715; instruction to Heusch, London, Oct. 4/15, 1715, Han. Arch.   [4] Cf. Droysen, iv. 2, 147.

previous year. The German Ministers of George I rejoiced most; they could now hope to drag England into the war against Sweden. In March Bernstorff said to Bonet that he could not as yet specify the strength of the fleet, but that he would do his best to make it sail as soon as possible; and the instructions of the Admiral should this time be unexceptionable.

The joy turned into disappointment when Frederick William I refused to agree to any Treaty of Guarantee; and when at last he was prepared to consider it, this had no longer any influence on the course of events. The fleet was fitted out, the instructions drawn up, and on May 25, 1716, Norris left England with twenty-one warships, including seventeen ships of the line. He himself had asked for a stronger force.[1] The British Navy had grown since the accession of George I. In May 1715 the House of Commons had voted considerable supplies for the construction of new warships, and when numerous ships were required to patrol the British and French coasts during the Rebellion, there was no need to recall the fleet from the Baltic. It would therefore not have been difficult to send out a stronger squadron in 1716, when England had no longer anything to fear at home.

As in the previous year, the instructions for Admiral Norris had produced a conflict between the English and German Ministers. Bonet once more asked in vain to be shown the instructions, but he, like the Ministers of all the other interested States, was merely told their purport: to convoy British merchant-ships, to repeat the demands made of Charles XII, and, if necessary, to take action against the Swedes. Moreover, after the experiences of the Rebellion, the demand was added that the King of Sweden should renounce giving any support to the Pretender. Lastly, Great Britain demanded that Charles XII should declare his readiness to conclude peace. Should he for that purpose send an Envoy to the Congress of Brunswick, which had sat for some time but with little prospect of success, Great Britain would assume the part of mediator.

No one could have expected the British demands to be accepted. Charles XII returned unopened the letter which Norris had written him in accordance with his instructions, and further forbade the Senate at Stockholm to reply to a note presented by the British Minister, Jackson. Besides protecting the British trade, Norris had therefore to consider taking forcible measures against Sweden. The situation was radically different from that of the previous year.

---

[1] *Hist. MSS. Comm.* Rep. XI. App. IV. pp. 96 *et seq.*

Even Wismar, the last outpost which in 1715 the Swedes had retained in Germany, was captured before the British fleet had entered the Sound. This year, Charles XII directed his thoughts to the conquest of Norway, which was under Danish rule. The attempt miscarried, and Sweden had to prepare to face an attack against Schonen in which a strong Russian contingent was to take part. But the powerful intervention of Russia gave a new turn to the Northern War —the Tsar's allies were disturbed by his ambitious plans, and feared that he might acquire a preponderance in the Baltic greater than that of Sweden had ever been. Bonet compared Tsar Peter to Philip of Macedon, and added that it would be well if only he had no Alexander for successor. It was the jealousy among the allies which saved Sweden from destruction; the descent on Schonen was laid aside before it was ever started.

In these circumstances no great task awaited the British fleet, and this year its activities were subordinated still more to the interests of Hanover. Townshend thought Norris had better keep to the neighbourhood of Bornholm and not far from Karlskrona, from where he could closely watch the movements of the Swedish fleet; while the Dutch who again had a squadron in the Baltic, should convoy the merchantships. The London merchants naturally complained to the Government that Norris was not giving them adequate protection.[1] Norris was not to interfere with the landing in Schonen, but his mere presence would in fact have served as a check on the Swedish fleet had they attempted such interference. In December 1716 Norris returned to England leaving, like the previous year, a small squadron of six ships in the Baltic with instructions to assist the Danes if necessary.

Thus for two years England had co-operated in the war without nominally being at war—this appeared only as a distant affair, of no concern to Great Britain, in instructions which in 1715 and 1716 were given to Ministers accredited to the Prussian Court.[2] The allies, on the other hand, took it for granted that they would have the help of the British fleet in the Baltic; in fact, they complained of having received insufficient support from it. In a dispatch to Bonet the King of Prussia wrote that he would do his share "if only the Hanoverian Court would get to work and follow our example better than hitherto,

[1] Bonet, Aug. 17/28, 1716.
[2] To the Earl of Forfar on July 3, 1715; to Lord Polwarth on May 14/25, 1716; and to Charles Whitworth on July 6/17, 1716.

for the squadrons sent into the Baltic in two consecutive years made great show and much noise, but in reality have not inflicted the least harm on the King of Sweden". George I naturally did not wish to have his Baltic expeditions considered in this light. Moreover, there was bad humour between the Courts of Hanover, where George was at the time, and of Berlin, because of the *rapprochement* recently effected between Frederick William and Tsar Peter. When now the King of Prussia, in a letter to his father-in-law, spoke with excessive confidence about a British expedition to the Baltic in the coming year, George I pointedly called his attention to the fact that he was not at war with the King of Sweden and therefore could not be "expected" to send a fleet.

Hitherto I have done so without any obligation incumbent on me, merely to set a good example to my Northern allies, and with a view to promoting peace in the North; similarly it will depend on my good pleasure whether I shall send ships, and if so, how many, into the Baltic, and I hope it will not be taken amiss if, before I decide, I first consider what my allies, and especially your Majesty, to whom the Lord has given great force and means, intend to contribute to the operations against Sweden.[1]

This was nothing more than a declaration of principles; for the dispatch of a fleet into the Baltic was intended for the coming year. The valuable Baltic trade seemed in need of protection against the growing boldness of the Swedish privateers. The merchants themselves repeatedly petitioned for it; and the action of the Government seemed still further justified by the fact that the States General, which were not concerned with Bremen and Verden, sent there a fleet every year. In reality the Dutch did so merely because they did not wish to leave the advantages of the trade to the English alone. In fact, England was generally expected to enter the war against Sweden in 1717;[2] and this gained very much in probability on the discovery, early in the year, of an extensive plan by Swedish diplomats directed at the overthrow of George I and the restoration of the Pretender.

Since the beginning of the Scottish Rising, the Swedes had main-

[1] Frederick William I to George I, Berlin, Dec. 5, 1716; George I to Frederick William I, Hanover, Nov. 29/Dec. 10, 1716, Prussian Archives.

[2] "It is for this reason that the return of the King to England is desired and the King himself declares that he will do his best and will endeavour to draw Great Britain into the war against Sweden, and that with a view to this he will hasten his return to England" (Instructions to Bonet, Nov. 29, 1716, Prussian Archives).

tained contact with the Jacobites. This was their reply to the policy of George I—if the Elector of Hanover used the British fleet against Sweden, they naturally tried to deprive him of this, his foremost, weapon. In 1715, the sending of a strong Swedish contingent from Gothenburg to Scotland was intended, but Charles XII, hard pressed at Stralsund, had not the necessary forces; nor could he carry out the plan during the following year.[1] But the idea of thus striking at the King-Elector was not forgotten in Sweden, and whatever danger arose for England from that side, resulted from the Hanoverian policy of George I.

Count Gyllenborg was the Swedish Minister in London. His relations with the English Court were unfriendly, as they were bound to be at a time when the two nations were in fact, though not in form, at war. Gyllenborg was naturally a friend to anyone who tried to distress the British Government. He was universally suspected of having instigated a pamphlet published in the autumn of 1716, which severely criticized the Northern policy of George I, the use of the British fleet in the Baltic, and, most of all, the leaving there of the eight ships in 1715. It was soon discovered that he himself was its author, and that he had ordered it to be printed at The Hague in three languages.[2]

It was the practice of the eighteenth century to open and examine in the Post Office the correspondence of foreign Ministers when important news was expected. As this was universally known, diplomats tried to cover their secrets by the use of cyphers; but this too, worked only so long as the cypher remained undiscovered. Thus, late in 1716, Gyllenborg's correspondence was opened and, in a measure, deciphered in the London Post Office. Most objectionable things were found: that Gyllenborg had been in touch with the Jacobites was known to the Government; but now it was discovered that the Swedish Minister had been negotiating with some of them plans for a new rising, which was to be supported by a Swedish invasion. King George, and with him Stanhope, were still at Hanover, and Townshend sent them this important news. More followed, clearly proving

---

[1] Cf. Berwick's *Mémoires* and Bolingbroke's *Letter to Sir William Windham*.

[2] Its title was *An English merchants remarks upon a scandalous Jacobite paper* published in the *Post-Boy*, under the name of "A Memorial presented to the Chancery of Sweden by the resident of Great Britain". Compare letters in *Parl. Hist.* vii. 398; and Bonet's dispatches, Sept. 14/25 and 18/29, 1716, Prussian Archives.

the existence of extensive plans.[1] The Prince of Wales summoned a Cabinet Council and

the Lords were all unanimously of opinion . . . that all possible precautions should be taken both at Hanover and in England to put it out of the power of Sweden to execute the design framed by Count Gyllenborg and the Jacobites.

They advised to close

with the proposal lately made by the Tsar . . . for making a descent from Finland next spring, which, especially if seconded by a descent on Schonen at the same time, will in the opinion of the Lords give the King of Sweden his hands full of business, and put him out of a condition to spare any forces towards supporting the cause of the Pretender.

The King, on his side, should engage immediately to send a strong fleet into the Baltic—England was by now so deeply involved in the Northern War that even the conscientious Townshend considered direct participation in it unavoidable.

At home precautions had to be taken, and troops and money kept in readiness. The best defence lay in the complete discovery of the conspiracy; after that further measures would have the full approval and support of Parliament. Information derived from letters which were opened in the Post Office could not well be quoted, and it was therefore necessary to obtain evidence which could be published. The Government decided on a coup, which amounted to a serious transgression of international law. Gyllenborg's house was surrounded in the night, and two officers demanded and obtained admission to the Minister, who was still up writing despatches. One of them immediately declared that he had orders to put a guard on the person and secure the papers of Gyllenborg, who expostulated with great warmth about the Law of Nations being violated in his person, but had to submit to force. His house was searched and his papers seized, however carefully they had been locked away or hidden; and he was kept a prisoner in his house, cut off from intercourse with the outside world.

The case being of a very extraordinary nature, made a great noise in the world, and the most famous writers on international law, Grotius and Wicquefort, were quoted by the friends of the Government to justify their action; it was argued that an ambassador who acts counter to the duties of his position, forfeits his privileges. Thus

---

[1] Coxe, *Walpole*, ii. pp. 113 and 120 *seq.*

Grotius writes: "If the ambassador use armed force, he may undoubtedly be killed, not in the way of punishment, but in the way of natural defence".[1] Still, in Gyllenborg's case "natural defence" did not require such drastic measures as were adopted; it would have sufficed to expel him. The measures taken against him were almost as irregular as the activities in which he had engaged; for he could not be divested of his diplomatic privilege.[2] Sweden, however, committed an even worse violation of international law, when they, in turn, arrested the British Minister at Stockholm, for reprisals are inadmissible in such a matter.

The news of Gyllenborg's arrest produced a sensation among the public and consternation in the diplomatic body in London, as affecting them all. Most of them decided to stay away from Court till a sufficient explanation was given of the incident; [3] even Hoffmann and Volkra did so, though the reasons had been communicated to them by Bernstorff. Stanhope now wrote a circular letter to the foreign Ministers justifying the proceeding, and most of them acquiesced in it. Bonet, however, returned a non-committal answer; while the Spanish Ambassador asserted that "arresting the person of a Publick Minister and seizing all his papers" were facts which "seem very sensibly to wound the Law of Nations".[4]

Shortly after Gyllenborg's arrest his chief fellow-conspirator was seized at the demand of England. It was Baron Görtz, a confidant of Charles XII, one of the worst intriguers of his time, shrewd and inscrutable, best known in history by his doubtful financial operations in Sweden and by his tragic end. He was now actively engaged in working against George I in Western Europe. When Gyllenborg's plot was discovered, the British Government asked the States General for the arrest of Görtz and of a few associates. Görtz was about to embark for England; now chase was given to him. Finally he was run to ground at Arnheim, while a part of his papers had already been seized during the pursuit. His arrest, though it was not made by the Dutch in their own interest, was less objectionable than that of Gyllenborg, as Görtz was not an accredited representative with the States General, and therefore could not claim diplomatic privilege.[5]

[1] *De jure belli ac pacis*, ii. p. 18; iv. p. 7.
[2] See also Holtzendorff, *Handbuch des Völkerrechts*, iii. pp. 650-51.
[3] Hoffmann, Feb. 12, 1717.
[4] See Boyer, *Political State*, xiii (1717), pp. 147-54.
[5] Holtzendorff, *op. cit.*

For several weeks nothing more was heard in England about Gyllenborg's intrigues. The Tories once more started the story that it was all an invention of the Court to prevent a reduction of the Army. The Government, however, quietly took measures to meet a Swedish invasion, should it be attempted even after the plot had been discovered. A strong expedition to the Baltic was prepared, and troops were moved from the interior of England to the most exposed points on the coast. Actually there was no imminent danger; a merchantship claimed to have met 30 Swedish ships off Yarmouth, but later on it was found that in a panic harmless Dutch merchantships had been mistaken for a Swedish fleet, about to enter the Thames.[1]

Still, the extent of the danger was disclosed when, on the reassembly of Parliament on February 20/March 3, 1717, Stanhope laid before the House of Commons letters which had passed between Count Gyllenborg, Baron Görtz, and some associates, among them a brother of Gyllenborg's, who too, had been arrested in Holland. The letters were printed,[2] and foreign diplomats received them in two copies, one for their own use and the other for their Governments. The range and boldness of the plan produced general amazement. It was found that Gyllenborg had for some time past been in touch with the Jacobites with a view to overthrowing George I; "ten thousand men transported hither from Sweden", he wrote "would do the business." And in another letter: "The male-contents require but a body of regular troops to which they may join themselves. That body . . . will cause a general revolt."[3] The Jacobites who were providing the money would do so "as soon as I shall shew them a line from the King, with assurances under his own hand, that he will assist them". Görtz in reply declared that Sweden was determined to help: "We have in Sweden troops more than enough for that purpose;"[4] what suspended their entering into action was the lack of transports, of means of maintaining the troops when landed, and of horses for the cavalry. But at last on January 8, 1717, Görtz reported from Paris that all was clear and that 12,000 Swedes would be employed in the expedition—8000 foot and 4000 horse. "Now or never," he wrote, "as well for our friends as our enemies." Having fixed this affair, Gyllenborg was to meet Görtz in Holland. The Swedes hoped for Russia's assistance. The Pretender was informed of these preparations, entertained

---

[1] Hoffmann, Feb. 26 and March 2, 1717.
[2] Most of them are reprinted in *Parl. Hist.* vii. 397-421.
[3] *Parl. Hist.* vii. 399.   [4] *Ibid.* 409.

the best hopes of success, and was prepared to contribute to the expedition any means he could raise. It was argued that the support of Protestant Sweden would improve the chances of the Catholic Stuart. James Edward, for whom a further stay at Avignon was rendered impossible, would have liked to go straight to Stockholm, but was restrained from doing so by the objection that this would have amounted to an open and formal declaration of war.

The two Houses of Parliament in their Addresses expressed their indignation at the conspiracy. What added to it was the pretence that the enterprise was in defence of English liberties against the prerogative of the Crown; as Sir John Brownlow said in the Commons—"we had no need of the King of Sweden to maintain the English liberties and support the Church of England." [1] And in a pamphlet it was pointed out that Swedish soldiers who were slaves in their own country were not fit tools to support freedom elsewhere.

The danger to which England had been exposed arose solely from the fact that her King had tried to extend his German possessions at the expense of Sweden. Each of the Baltic expeditions of the preceding two years, in reality undertaken for that purpose, had cost Great Britain more than £200,000, and now the country had to face an open war with Sweden, or, at the least, further expensive armaments. She had to pay a heavy price for Bremen and Verden. Görtz wrote to Gyllenborg on December 11, 1716:

Pray, Sir, which way can the King of Sweden better secure himself the recovery and possession of his said Duchy, than by reducing King George to be nothing more than an Elector of the Empire? [2]

But as the result of a conflict within the British Government England did not enter the war in 1717, nor was the fleet sent into the Baltic so strong as the King would have wished.

This time Admiral Norris was not placed in command of the expedition, though he certainly was the fittest man for it. Lord Orford had picked for it Sir George Byng,[3] an Admiral of great merit, but hardly suited to the part which, in the last two years, England had played in the Baltic as an auxiliary of Hanover. The King naively accepted the nomination. Byng's instructions sounded warlike:—he was to attack the Swedes wherever he met them. But the execution

[1] *Parl. Hist.* vii. 422.
[2] *Ibid.* vii. 410.
[3] Bonet, March 29/April 9, 1717; Hoffmann, April 6, 1717.

was weak. On April 13, the British fleet put to sea: the capture of a Swedish ship in July marked the first encounter between the British and Swedish naval forces. In November Byng returned with the fleet, having left in the Baltic six ships to reinforce the Danish fleet.

In 1718 Sir John Norris again commanded the Baltic expedition. Still, the practical results fell short of those in previous years. Another squadron was sent to the Mediterranean, a region far more important for Britain's European position than the Baltic, and therefore only a dozen ships were available for the other expedition. Moreover, secret negotiations for a separate peace had been started between George I and Charles XII. In March 1718 the Swedish General Dücker came to London, and the Hanoverian Secretary Schrader, returned with him to Sweden. The secret could not, however, be concealed from the allies. Russia also, which now appeared far more dangerous than Sweden, was engaged in negotiations with Charles XII. In August 1718 Norris was instructed to prevent a junction between the Russian and Swedish fleets; and in November he returned to England without having delivered any decisive blow. Nor had peace been concluded. The death of Charles XII, at the siege of the Norwegian fortress of Friedrichshall, radically transformed the situation. There was a chance of concluding a favourable peace with the new Swedish Government. The British nation was thoroughly sick of this quasi-war which, though never declared, had imposed on it heavy burdens in the service of Hanover.

It is remarkable that no formed attack was delivered against the Government and its Hanoverian policy—the affair had been too skilfully managed. Who could prove that the protection of trade and the justified desire to take reprisals against the Swedish privateers had not been the sole motives of the Baltic expeditions? Occasionally the Tories contemplated attacking the Government on these grounds. Late in 1716 a document was published by the Danes seriously compromising the British Ministers—it showed that they had tried to obtain the co-operation of Russian troops for the intended descent on Schonen. The Government now expected to be attacked by the Tories; but nothing happened.[1] Incidental malicious remarks show

[1] Bonet, Oct. 23/Nov. 3, 1716; Hoffmann, Nov. 6, 1716: "The Danish declaration shows that the English Court had worked for an invasion of Schonen, and thus shown itself as a declared enemy of Sweden, for no other reason than with a view to maintaining its hold on the Duchies of Bremen and Verden". See further Whitworth to Townshend, Berlin, Oct. 9/20, 1716: "The passage

that the Opposition realized where was the most vulnerable point of the Government: on December 15, 1717, the Jacobite Shippen made the remark (inappropriate on that occasion) that certain propositions in the Speech seemed "rather calculated for the meridian of Germany, than of Great Britain".[1] He added: "It is the one misfortune of His Majesty's reign, that he is unacquainted with our language and Constitution, still he must not think that he can rule us like his Germans." [2] The speech gave offence and several Members declared "that those words were a scandalous invective against the King's Person and Government".[3] Shippen, having refused to retract or excuse what he had said, it was ordered that he be committed prisoner to the Tower. This happened at a time when even one branch of the Whigs had joined the Opposition.

where 'tis mentioned, how earnestly the British minister and Sir John Norris press'd to have the descent made in Schonen, might very well have been omitted in such a sort of manifest; since the Crown has yet no declared war with Sweden;" (S.P. 90/7).

[1] *Parl. Hist.* vii. 508.

[2] This sentence, which does not appear in the *Parliamentary History*, is here quoted from a dispatch of Pendtenriedter, London, Dec. 17, 1717, Vienna Arch.

[3] *Parl. Hist.* vii. 511.

CHAPTER XII

THE QUADRUPLE ALLIANCE

IF proof is required of the extent of the Royal power under the first two Hanoverian Kings, it can be found in the Northern policy of George I, which he was able to shape to suit his own views, against the wishes of the nation and of the Ministers, imposing heavy burdens on Great Britain, and dragging the country into a war for interests alien to it. Similarly, about the middle of 1716, a sudden and surprising change was wrought by him in the relations between Great Britain and France: to the average Englishman France was the enemy, or at least a Power which required careful watching; but this traditional view was brushed aside, and although the dislike of the public for the new policy was, if anything, even stronger on the other side of the Channel, the heads of the two States effected a *rapprochement*, which was soon to mature into an alliance. Still, this was not a return to the Treaty of Dover—this time England was to be the leading partner in the alliance.

Although the Regent had given no overt support to the Scottish Rebellion, French sympathies had been with the Pretender, and the British Government, expecting a French attack, had armed on a scale for which there was no other explanation, especially after the Jacobites had been defeated; but no provocation was given to France. Lord Stair alone, her most inveterate enemy, was, early in 1716, thinking once more of war. The Imperial Ambassador in Paris, Pendtenriedter, reports a conversation with him on February 6, 1716, in which Stair in a rather roundabout manner put forward a scheme for partitioning French territory.[1] He told Pendtenriedter a fantastic story of how the plans of the Sardinian Court had been conveyed to him, and how he had arranged the details with the Sardinian Minister.

[1] See G. Syveton, "Un projet de démembrement de la France en 1716", *Revue d'histoire diplomatique*, vol. vi.

Victor Amadeus was to cede to the Emperor Sicily and all the other territories acquired in the late war, and to receive in return Provence and the Dauphiné—thus Marseilles and Toulon, with their Levant trade, were to go to Savoy. In the North and East, France was to lose important towns and districts to Holland and the Emperor.

Pendtenriedter did not relish the scheme and refused to report it officially to Vienna; pressed by Stair he admitted, however, that the time could not be more favourable for war against France. But Charles VI would not hear of it; Austria was about to engage in war with Turkey, where chances seemed more promising than in the West; if France was weak, so much the better—this left Austria a free hand in the East. Lord Stair's scheme fizzled out completely, and it is not certain whether it was ever so much as seriously considered by the British Government,[1] which would not engage in war, least of all while the Emperor, taken up by the Turkish campaign, would be of little value as an ally. What George I wished most, was to leave for Hanover. Circumstances were favourable to the scheme of a Franco-British alliance.

Since March 1716, France had tried to enter into negotiations for a Triple Alliance with the Maritime Powers, the Regent seeking foreign support against Philip V and the Spanish party in France. This he hoped to find easiest with the States General, where the ill-humour against Austria over the Barrier negotiations still persisted; Buys was at the head of the party which favoured a French alliance, and it was through Holland that England was first approached. While Stair reported from Paris that France wished for a British alliance, the Dutch diplomats worked in the same sense. But when the plan was submitted to Horace Walpole, the British Minister at The Hague, he pointed to the course which relations between the two countries had taken since the death of Louis XIV to prove the impossibility of such an alliance. George I, who had approached the Regent with confidence, had been deceived, and was now bound to distrust him.[2] Was it perhaps the purpose of the French offer to thwart the alliance with the Emperor? Walpole urged the need of concluding the understanding with the Emperor before discussing an alliance with France.

---

[1] Syveton assumes the British Government to have favoured the scheme and to have, to say the least, suffered Stair to proceed with it. But the matter is not even mentioned in the extant British official records.

[2] H. Walpole to Townshend, Mar. 31, 1716, S.P. 84/253.

The British Government fully approved of the answer given by Walpole;[1] and a similar reply was given to the Dutch Minister, Duvenvoirde, in London. France was suspected of trying to hoodwink England and Holland, which must not let themselves be dissuaded from the alliance with the Emperor. Closer relations with the Regent can be established afterwards, once he has given real proofs of his friendly disposition. The conditions on which Stair was to negotiate, should the occasion arise, were summarized in a dispatch from Stanhope, dated April 16, 1716:[2]

. . . I am by his Majesty's orders to tell you, that you are to insist, that previous to any negociation his Majesty have full satisfaction in the three points you have already mentioned, viz. the article of Dunkirke, the sending the Pretender into Italy, and refusing to allow his Majesty's traiterous and rebellious subjects to stay in France.

Still, the Dutch gathered from these replies that England was not in principle disinclined to a French alliance, and they now hoped to negotiate simultaneously a treaty between the Maritime Powers and the Emperor on the one hand, and France on the other. On May 5, 1716, Walpole reported this resolution of the States General. But a difference arose between England and Holland over the question whether the treaties were to be discussed simultaneously or successively. The English threatened, should Holland prove obdurate, to conclude a separate alliance with the Emperor, which they did on May 25, 1716.[3]

The alliance with France was now considered, irrespective of Holland's adherence to the Treaty of May 25, and in spite of the Emperor's intense dislike of such an alliance. It was sheer pretence when Count Volkra was told "that by protracting these negotiations it was hoped to make them fail, and thereby to prove to the Emperor the true affection which was felt for him by His Majesty the King, and by the British Ministers". The Prince of Wales, after the King's departure, similarly tried to make the Imperial Envoy believe that Great Britain sought to avoid an alliance with France.[4] But Hoffmann was not taken in, and remarked to one of the Ministers that he now understood their hurry in concluding the Treaty with the Emperor—they

---

[1] Townshend to H. Walpole, Mar. 27, O.S., S.P. 104/81.
[2] Stanhope to Stair, Mar. 28, 1716, F.O. 90/14.
[3] Volkra to Hoffmann, July 17/28, 1716, Vienna Arch.
[4] *Ibid.*

wished to enter into negotiations with France, but pay him the compliment of precedency.[1]

Attempts were made to reach a speedy agreement with France. Originally it was intended to discuss it in Paris through Stair,[2] but the French Court signified their unwillingness to negotiate it with him; nor did London, where the matter had been discussed between Stanhope and d'Iberville, seem the most suitable place. As the initiative had come from the States General and their mediation seemed desirable, the negotiations were transferred to Holland. On June 16, Townshend sent Horace Walpole the draft of a defensive alliance with the remark that he would receive full powers to sign it as soon as France had made reparation "for what has lately past there relating to the Pretender by obliging him to retire beyond the Alps . . .";[3] for George I insisted that to sign without this would be derogatory to his honour.

The demand was humiliating, but not dangerous for the Regent— it meant that he had to start by repairing a wrong he had committed, and acknowledge that he, much more than George I, required such an alliance to strengthen his position. But the Regent thought otherwise. Lord Peterborough, who was in Paris in May 1716, expatiated on the importance of the French alliance for England, and although he had no official status, his talk convinced the Regent that it would be unnecessary to remove the Pretender before the alliance was signed.[4] He said to Stair that such action would be dishonourable, that he would not do it, and that this was his last word; and he even added a proud remark about a possible war which he had no reason to fear.[5] In these circumstances negotiations in Holland did not advance. The French Minister, Chateauneuf, refused Walpole's demand because the Regent would find it difficult to account for the removal of the Stuart Prince if afterwards the treaty was not concluded. Walpole, on the other hand, would not listen to the French offer that the expulsion should be ordered between the signing and the ratification of the treaty.[6]

The methods of eighteenth-century diplomacy were elaborate and clumsy. Intercourse by letter was slow, it was difficult to preserve secrecy, diplomats were bound by their instructions, and were fond

---

[1] Hoffmann, June 19, 1716, Vienna Arch.
[2] Stanhope to Stair, May 31, 1716, O.S., F.O. 90/14.
[3] Townshend to H. Walpole, June 5, 1716, O.S., S.P. 104/81.
[4] Stair to Robethon, May 26, 1716, Stowe MSS., 228, f. 284.
[5] Cf. Wiesener, i. pp. 226-7.   [6] *Ibid.* p. 235.

of manoeuvring for positions; insincerity was inherent in the forms of their intercourse, and clearness was not easily attained. A man like Stanhope, who himself shaped his policy, would often lose patience and set out to negotiate personally with foreign statesmen. But this time, when negotiations in Holland reached an impasse, it was the Regent who had recourse to new methods.

The Abbé Dubois now entered the scene. Of humble extraction, but a man of culture and understanding, he had been tutor to the Duke of Orleans, and became his life-long friend; it was natural that he should play a part under the Regency. The accepted view about the two is that they were clever and vicious, and that their policy was determined by their personal interests. It is difficult to defend Dubois' moral character—the judgment of his rival, the Duc de St. Simon, is confirmed by other contemporaries; *e.g.* Elizabeth Charlotte, the mother of the Duke of Orleans, called Dubois the greatest scoundrel and cheat in Paris.[1] But his policy was dictated by the position of his master, and no British pension was required, as was alleged by St. Simon,[2] to make him advocate the British alliance.[3]

Dubois was entrusted by the Regent with the confidential task of resuming negotiations with England. He had old connexions with Stanhope, and had written to him a few times in the spring of 1716.[4] At first he received cold replies, while subsequent letters were left unanswered; none the less, this was considered an opening for renewing relations. Stanhope accompanied George I to Hanover and Dubois tried to intercept him at The Hague. To Dubois secrecy was the soul of diplomacy, and he adopted an elaborate disguise.[5] He professed to have come to The Hague as a bibliophil and art collector, and even in the French Legation only Chateauneuf was informed of the purpose of his journey. He took immense trouble to discover when the King and his Secretary of State were expected—which must have been common knowledge. And when at last Stanhope, guessing immediately the purpose of his visit, agreed to receive him, Dubois still thought that he had to continue his game of make-believe.

[1] In a letter to the Electress Sophia, dated Nov. 19, 1713, Ranke, *Collected Works*, vi. p. 306.

[2] Edition of 1844, vol. xxxi. p. 146.

[3] Cf. Wiesener, vol. i. p. 260.

[4] See de Sevelinges, *Mémoires secrets et correspondance inédite du Cardinal Dubois* (Paris, 1815).

[5] Besides Sevelinges (vol. i. p. 186 ff.) see Aubertin, *L'esprit public au* XVIIIe *siècle*, p. 68 ff.

In their several interviews at The Hague, they talked about art and science, about problems of European policy and the internal affairs of various States. Dubois began by professing great joy over the purchase of Poussin's "Seven Sacraments" from a Dutch dealer, who had bought it in Paris. Next, the conversation touched upon public finance, Stanhope arguing the value of public credit; he declared that some day the British national debt would be much greater, without causing more embarrassment to the Government. Dubois replied that none the less the French King was richer, for he could consider himself the owner of all the land in his Kingdom.[1] "Abbé," jested Stanhope, "you seem to have learned your public law in Turkey!"

Stanhope was intellectually superior to Dubois, who thought that by his clever conversation he had brought the British Minister to open himself on the problem of an Anglo-French alliance. Stanhope acted cautiously,[2] and consulted Bernstorff on the line to adopt with Dubois. He paid proper regard to Holland and, at the wish of Heinsius, saw Dubois a second, and even a third time. In these talks Stanhope explained that the King's original confidence in the Regent had been deceived by the French attitude during the Scottish Rebellion. Dubois tried to excuse it by the regard which had to be paid to French public opinion. But when he spoke of the cause of the deadlock in the negotiations, Stanhope made the surprising remark that personally he considered the removal of the Pretender a matter of complete indifference—"I do not care whether he is at Avignon, or Rome, or Bologna. If France ever tries a coup against England I would wish, in order to assure its failure, that the Pretender should lead the expedition." Still, this was merely the personal opinion of the Minister, for George I was determined not to sign any agreement so long as the Pretender remained on this side of the Alps. To Stanhope the main difficulty lay in that France wished to base the agreement on the Peace of Utrecht, which England had to refuse from regard for the Emperor.

Such informal talks could hardly result in a formal treaty; still, they brought the leading statesmen into personal touch, and facilitated further negotiations. Dubois promised, on his return to Paris, to send Stanhope an explanation of a somewhat obscure point concerning the Port of Mardyke, and if that satisfied Stanhope, Dubois would return

---

[1] Cf. R. Koser, "Die Epochen der absoluten Monarchie in der neueren Geschichte", *Hist. Zeitsch.*, 61, p. 270.

[2] Cf. Wiesener, vol. i. p. 472 ff.

with full powers to The Hague, or come to Hanover if Stanhope wished it. Meantime the Ambassadors in Holland received instructions to keep the negotiations alive, without pressing them to a point.[1]

George I now proceeded to Hanover, where he stayed nearly half a year.[2] The Court acquired a splendour, not known in Electoral days. Numerous English company had come to Hanover, forming there a close circle, in which Stanhope was the foremost person. Bothmer was left behind in England by the King "to keep all things in order, and to give an account of everything that was doing";[3] while Bernstorff went to Hanover, now the centre of Anglo-Hanoverian politics. The female favourites accompanied George I, and Mme. Kielmannsegge, very angry that her rival, Mlle. Schulenburg, recently created Duchess of Munster, ranked so much above her, was determined to apply to Parliament for naturalization, with a view to acquiring a British title. Even sharper was the conflict between Mlle. Schulenburg and the beautiful Countess Platen, a previous favourite of George I, who had not followed him to England.[4] Their rivalry split the Court into a Schulenburg and a Platen faction. Every night there were receptions at Herrenhausen and during the long winter evenings, by order of the King, comedies were given at Hanover by a French troupe. The King greatly enjoyed the stay in his own home, dined in public, was invariably good-humoured and gracious, and seemed happy to have shaken the dust of England from his feet. Lord Peterborough, who was received by him at Hanover, thought that the King and his family had completely forgotten the misfortune which had befallen them on August 1, 1714.

Relieved from party strife, George I turned to the problem of England's international position. Here British and Hanoverian interests converged, and the King was pleased to be able to work on the policy of the two countries without continually encountering opposition; for of the British Ministers, Stanhope alone had accompanied him, and he was too much a man of the world sharply to stress the British point of view, instead of meeting the King's wishes wherever possible.

Thus George I was able to take a leading part in the negotiations

[1] ". . . till we see what is the issue of which is in hand with the Abbé Du Bois." Townshend to H. Walpole, July 17, 1716.

[2] Cf. J. Clavering's "Letters from Hanover", App. E. to the *Diary of Lady Cowper* and *Lady Mary Wortley Montagu*, vol. i. p. 135 *et seq.*

[3] *Diary of Lady Cowper*, p. 121.

[4] Lady Mary Wortley Montagu, *Account*, pp. 8-9.

for an Anglo-French alliance, which Stanhope's talks with Dubois at
The Hague had turned into something like a personal transaction
between the two heads of the States—the matter had passed out of
the hands of the regular diplomats into those of the confidants of the
Princes. On Dubois' return to Paris, the Duke of Orleans decided to
let him continue the negotiations, and, in August 1716, shortly after
the arrival of George I and Stanhope, Dubois came to Hanover at
Stanhope's invitation. This time he had full powers from the Regent
to sign a treaty, but until then the negotiations, and even his presence
at Hanover, were to remain a strict secret. In reality the diplomatic
world soon came to know that the Abbé Dubois, charged with important instructions, was at the German Court of George I.[1]

The negotiations started immediately. Mardyke formed the chief
obstacle. After the Hague conversations Stanhope had written to
London that he hoped the French would give in on that point.[2] But
the two Secretaries of State, Townshend and Methuen, did not believe
that the Regent would consent to demolish Mardyke in the manner
specified by England.[3] Indeed, the proposals brought by Dubois suggested a way which in Stanhope's view would have enabled the French
in a very few days, to restore it to its previous state.[4] Stanhope refused
to negotiate on this basis, and all Dubois could offer was that a French
representative, equipped with the technical information, should discuss the matter in London. Stanhope replied in the King's name that
if they sent anybody to England they should be heard; but at the
same time gave him no manner of hopes that anything in the British
demands would be receded from. Under this proviso and as a concession to France, he was prepared to discuss the other points of the
future agreement. From regard for the Emperor, he refused Dubois'
demand of a guarantee of the Treaty of Utrecht. Vienna declared
that, barring such a guarantee, they would not, despite their apprehensions concerning a Franco-British alliance, take it ill if the two
countries mutually guaranteed their respective Successions. Consequently, Stanhope prepared an article whereby Great Britain,
France, and Holland were "to guaranty all and every the articles of
the Treaty of Utrecht, so far forth as they concern the interests of

---

[1] Stanhope to Townshend, Aug. 11/18, 1716. Wiesener, vol. i. p. 477,
Bothmer to Robethon, Sept. 4/15, 1716. Stowe MSS. 229, ff. 96-7.

[2] Wiesener, vol. i. p. 474.

[3] S. Poyntz to Stanhope, July 31, 1716, Coxe, *Walpole*, ii. p. 73.

[4] Stanhope to Methuen, Han. Aug. 24, 1716, *ibid*. ii. p. 68.

each of the three Powers, and the successions to the Crowns of Great Britain and France".[1] It cost him three days' wrangling to make Dubois accept it. With regard to the removal of the Pretender, France offered three expedients of which George I promised to accept one, when the article of Mardyke should have been settled to his satisfaction.

Thus the main provisions of the Treaty and its form were fixed. The mutual territorial guarantees were framed in such a way as to extend the French guarantee to George I's new acquisitions in Germany. This was not said; but to make it impossible for France to withdraw from it subsequently, Stanhope had the preliminary results fixed in a document which was signed by the negotiators. The completion of their work now depended on an agreement being reached in London about Mardyke.[2]

Small hopes with regard to that point were entertained in London, and the Ministers thought that it was over Mardyke that the Regent's insincerity would be proved. In fact, it was thought it might be best to break off the negotiations over that point, for this would relieve the King from difficulties with regard to other matters. The negotiations in London were started between d'Iberville and the two Secretaries of State, and at first took an unfavourable turn. Stanhope, hearing of it at Hanover, asked Dubois whether he himself would not go to Paris or London. The Abbé replied that he would go even further, if this were of any use; but before a decision was taken the surprising news came from London of d'Iberville having handed in a paper

by which he consents to ruine the fascinages and to reduce the sluice to the breadth of 16 feet, which in the opinion of the most skilful of our sea officers as well as engineers, will more effectually exclude ships of war and privateers, than what was first proposed in the paper annexed to his Majesty's project.

Poyntz added the triumphant remark that France had thus undertaken "a solemn engagement of destroying that work which . . . the late French King intended, should stand to ages to come as a perpetual check to our island, and a lasting monument of his superior policy and glory".[3] The King naturally accepted the offer, and merely wished the Ministers would hasten the conclusion of the treaty.

---

[1] *Ibid.* p. 70.

[2] Stanhope to Methuen, Aug. 24, 1716, *ibid.* ii. pp. 67-72.

[3] Poyntz to Stanhope, Hampton Court, Sept. 11/22, 1716, *ibid.* ii. pp. 82-3.

Abbé Dubois, who had hitherto been received by him in secret only, was now introduced at Court.

A fresh motive had arisen for George I to seek the French alliance. Hitherto the English, while not disinclined to the French proposals, looked upon them with a certain unconcern, or even professed a wish that the negotiations should fail. The position in the Baltic now produced a change. There was intense jealousy between Denmark and Russia, whose power seemed a menace to Northern Europe. In September 1716, it was found that a descent on Schonen could not be undertaken any more that year, and the Tsar declared that he would quarter his army of 40,000 men in Denmark, Holstein, and Mecklenburg. This aroused apprehensions even in Hanover.

. . . the King of Denmark [wrote Stanhope to Townshend] . . . prays that Sir John Norris may stay with him. . . . Mr. Bernstorff thinks it necessary to crush the Czar immediately, to secure his ships, and even to seize his person to be kept till his troops shall have evacuated Denmark and Germany. . . . The King now wishes, and so doth your humble servant, very heartily that we had secured France . . . I was, you know, very averse at first to this treaty, but I think truly as things now stand we ought not to lose a minute in finishing it.[1]

And a fortnight later Stanhope wrote expressing his satisfaction at the "business of Mardyke" being happily concluded:

Nothing could happen more seasonably for the King's interest; for the affairs of the North have given his Majesty of late no small uneasiness; and it was very much to be apprehended, that France taking advantage from thence, might have laid hold on such an occasion not only to break off the negociation, but to have fomented and abetted new disturbances in Brittain, to prevent which his Majesty thinks no time should be lost in fixing the Regent, and tying his hands, by this treaty.[2]

Thus the situation in the North acquired peculiar weight in the negotiations for an Anglo-French Alliance, and Hanoverian interests came to affect a problem of British foreign policy; though, as the outstanding issues had already been settled, the alliance with France cannot be said to have been made for the sake of Hanover.

When the news reached Hanover that the business of Mardyke was happily settled, an agreement was concluded by Stanhope and Dubois that the Treaty of Alliance should be signed as soon as the Abbé arrived at The Hague; and if the States General refused to join,

---

[1] Stanhope to Townshend, Sept. 25, 1716, N.S., Coxe, ii. pp. 84-5.
[2] Stanhope to Methuen, Hanover, Oct. 8, 1716, N.S., *ibid.* p. 100.

it should be concluded without them. The King now agreed that the Pretender should not be removed from Avignon until after the treaty was signed. Stanhope wrote to London that proper powers should be immediately sent to the British Envoys in Holland, Cadogan and Horace Walpole, if those which they had were not sufficient for signing without Holland. George I was loath to lose a minute in concluding the treaty.

On October 11 Dubois left Hanover, full of the King's goodness and the courtesy of his Minister. On the 16th he arrived at The Hague expecting the treaty to be signed immediately—but three more months were to elapse. Horace Walpole declared to Dubois that so far he had not received full powers from London which would enable him to sign; and even when they were received, the conclusion of the treaty was still distant. Walpole was unwilling to act without the States General, after having pledged his word that the treaty should not be signed except by the three States jointly—he had thus kept the Dutch from embroiling the negotiation at Hanover. The Pensionary now asked him "what he should say, when some people in the States would charge him and his friends with having been the dupes in this whole affair".[1] In numerous letters to London and Hanover, Walpole begged that he should not be forced to break his word and declare himself a villain under his own hand. "I had rather starve, nay dye, than doe a thing that gives such a terrible wound to my honour and conscience." [2] Officially he asked leave to return to England for reasons of health.

This request could hardly be admitted. Orders from London and Hanover demanded that Walpole and Cadogan should sign with Dubois on receipt of the necessary powers. And yet Walpole was sure at least of the silent approval of his brother-in-law, Townshend.

. . . his Lordship owns [wrote Poyntz], if it were his own case, he should be under pretty much the same difficulties as you, but he thinks you cannot well decline the King's positive commands. . . . But . . . if you think it absolutely necessary to decline signing, you may find excuses without removing from the Hague, which would make too much éclat.[3]

Townshend did not lose hope that by the time the necessary powers had been received, the States General would "by the pressing

[1] Coxe, ii. p. 105.
[2] Walpole to Stanhope, Hague, Oct. 17, 1716, Coxe, ii. p. 107.
[3] Oct. 9/20, 1716, *ibid.* pp. 112-13.

instances of the King" be brought to sign the treaty at the same time; as those instances owed "their rise to the exigency of the Northern affairs, and not to any design of slighting the States. . . ."

It went anyhow against the grain of Townshend and Walpole that these matters, which concerned Hanover alone, should influence British policy. Townshend was as much averse to the new plans for active British intervention in the Northern War, as he had been to the Baltic expeditions in 1715 and 1716. He advised the King to make peace with Sweden, even at a price; warned against breaking with Russia; and would not hear of Admiral Norris's fleet continuing in the Baltic during the winter, still less of the extreme measures which Bernstorff had proposed against the Tsar. This, he thought, was Denmark's affair, and not England's. In an outspoken letter on October 21, Horace Walpole wrote to Poyntz that a messenger had arrived with orders from Hanover to sign with the Abbé;

and the only reason that I find for it is, least the Czar should become master of the nobility of Mecklenbourgh. I can't for my life see the connection between our immediate signing and that affair, or why the whole system of affairs in Europe, especially in relation to the interest of England, must be entirely subverted on account of Mecklenbourgh. God knows what will be the consequence of such politicks. . . .

Thus certain differences now arose over the Baltic problem between Stanhope and Bernstorff[1] on the one side, and Townshend and Horace Walpole on the other.

When powers to sign reached The Hague, it was Dubois who asked for a delay. The news had been received that the Pretender had fallen ill at Avignon and that an immediate operation was required. Suspecting a pretext, the Regent immediately dispatched a famous Paris surgeon to Avignon, while Dubois wrote to Hanover that George I was free to do so likewise and ascertain the truth concerning the alleged illness.[2] This, of course, was not done, but Paris learned that an operation was really required, and that the Chevalier was not in a condition to travel. None the less English suspicions were not entirely allayed, and Lord Stair told the Regent on October 27, that he heard "that operation was to be a pretext for the Pretender staying all the winter at Avignon".[3] Meantime, news was arriving about

[1] Horace Walpole to Stephen Poyntz, Oct. 21, 1716, Coxe, ii. p. 112.
[2] Wiesener, vol. i. App. p. 502 ff.
[3] Stair to Methuen, Oct. 28, 1716, S.P. 78/160.

extensive Jacobite plans; "as to Sweden", wrote Stair, "I have been assured that the King has a Treaty with the Pretender . . ." It was further asserted by the Jacobites that the article of the Treaty relating to the Pretender would not be carried out, and that the Pope would "thunder from the Vatican if the Regent should use violence against His Holyness's territorys".[1] The Regent contradicted these rumours and declared to Stair that the Pretender would leave in six weeks. In fact, the illness seems to have been genuine and the best informed Jacobites in Paris at one time looked upon him as "being in very great danger".[2] But he recovered, and was now willing to remove beyond the Alps; for the Regent had the means to enforce his compliance: while the Pretender professed that he would not leave "but by force", the pension which the widow of James II received from the French Court was stopped, and payment was not resumed till James Edward had complied.

Horace Walpole made use of the delay quietly to remove from Holland. The Government suffered him to do so, this being the only way in which he could escape from his embarrassment without compromising himself or the Ministers. Cadogan, who had come at a later date and was not bound by any promises, remained at The Hague, ready, if necessary, to sign the treaty with Dubois. But this was not the end of the difficulties. Stanhope had written to Dubois to wait another eight or ten days, and see whether the States General would not join in signing it. In reality there was no prospect of their doing so, especially since Marquis Prié, the Governor of the Austrian Netherlands, had come to The Hague and canvassed everybody to stop the Dutch from entering an alliance with France.[3] But an unexpected obstacle arose even with regard to the Franco-British alliance. When Dubois declared himself ready to sign and Cadogan presented his powers, the Abbé, having carefully examined them, declared them insufficient: they were drawn up in general terms, without making express mention of the treaty with France. Cadogan suspected that Dubois was playing for time, and asked him to draft a form of powers acceptable to him. Dubois did so, and solemnly declared that on Cadogan receiving such powers, he would sign immediately.[4]

George I and Stanhope, who had impatiently expected at Hanover

[1] Same to same, Nov. 7, 1716, S.P. 78/160.
[2] Same to same, Dec. 7, 1716, S.P. 78/160.
[3] Cf. Sevelinges, i. p. 223.
[4] Cf. Wiesener, i. p. 389.

the conclusion of the treaty, were much upset at the new delay. They admitted that Dubois had acted correctly—but why had the London Cabinet and Townshend committed that fatal mistake of form? Stanhope, and also Sunderland who was at Hanover, confirmed the King in his judgment. The post of Lord Lieutenant of Ireland, which was offered to Sunderland at the accession of the King in 1714, had not satisfied his ambition; he remained in England, but ranked in the Cabinet below Townshend and Stanhope. In 1715, on the death of Lord Wharton, he would have liked to exchange his post for that of Lord Privy Seal, which similarly carried with it a seat in the Cabinet. He was jealous of Townshend, who was looked upon as First Minister, and welcomed any opportunity to undermine his position.

George I had reluctantly allowed Sunderland to come to Hanover.[1] Here, however, he entered into closer touch with the King, and reached a complete understanding with Stanhope. Now he tried to profit by the annoyance caused at Hanover by the delay. Townshend was known to oppose the concluding of the treaty without Holland, and was now suspected of using these petty contrivances to upset it. Stanhope himself thought that his policy was countered from London, and offered his resignation. This, of course, was refused by the King, who unreservedly took sides with Stanhope and Sunderland. The three worked themselves up into violent indignation against Townshend: the King himself expressed his dissatisfaction in a letter to Townshend which has not been preserved, Stanhope and Sunderland expostulated with him and demanded an explanation.[2] After all that had happened, it was difficult to believe that the general form of Cadogan's full powers had been chosen unintentionally. Now France could easily "take a pretence, from these delays, to avoid signing at last; and, . . . say it is not their fault".[3]

In connexion with the Gyllenborg conspiracy, Townshend had written on October 16/27[4] that it was impossible "even to set this Northern business in such a light, as may induce the Parliament not to look on it with indifference", and that

if the Northern affairs were brought into Parliament by His Majesty's order upon the foot they now stand, His Majesty would be so far from

[1] Stanhope to Poyntz (not the other way round, as erroneously stated by Coxe), Sept. 8, 1716, Coxe, ii. p. 79.

[2] *Ibid.* pp. 126-7.

[3] Sunderland to Townshend, Nov. 11, 1716, *ibid.* p. 128.

[4] Townshend to Stanhope, Oct. 16/27, 1716, *ibid.* pp. 118-19.

obtaining any assistance on that head, that there would be great danger from such a step of ruining his credit and influence in both Houses.

It was further obvious from the letter that he himself was opposed to such a policy, and his argument was approximately this: that England may, and indeed must, send again a fleet to the Baltic in 1717, but that to wage war, both against the Tsar and Sweden over Baltic affairs, was not a scheme which Parliament could be made to engage in.

In reply to this letter Sunderland wrote on November 11, N.S., that

the King is very much surprised at the strange notion that seems at present to prevail, as if the Parliament was not to concern themselves in any thing that happens in these parts of the world, which he looks upon not only as exposing him to all kinds of affronts, but even to ruin: and indeed this notion is nothing but the old Tory one, that England can subsist by itself, whatever becomes of the rest of Europe, which has been so justly exploded ever since the Revolution.[1]

In reality Townshend voiced the general English dislike for excessive regard being paid to Hanoverian interests. Nor was the reproach that he wished to scuttle the treaty with France justified—it was not his nature to engage in such "a pitiful artifice and evasion"; but it seems to have been his aim to throw off all responsibility for the treaty—Stanhope, its author, was to bear it. He therefore refrained from ever mentioning in his letters the agreement concluded between Stanhope and Dubois, and gave to the powers for Cadogan the general form which referred to no specific treaty, and thus did not implicate the London Cabinet. In answer to the letters from Hanover of November 11, N.S., Townshend wrote on November 11/22:

. . . my heart is so full with the thoughts of having received this usage from you, to whom I have always been so faithful a friend, that you will excuse my not saying any more at this time. I pray God forgive you; I do.

P.S. Lord Sunderland will, I am persuaded, excuse my not answering his letter.[2]

The same day, in a letter to the King, he explained the circumstances in which he had acted, and refuted the accusation of having deliberately delayed the conclusion of the Treaty. He was able to

---

[1] Coxe, ii. p. 128.   [2] *Ibid.*

quote previous occasions on which "full powers in the same general form" had been given, without being questioned by the other side. "Mr. Methuen himself, concluded the Treaty with Portugal, in virtue of such a full power, and several others have done the like." [1]

Anyhow the conclusion of the Treaty could not be delayed much longer by questions of form. Townshend had "a second full power" sent to Cadogan, drawn up "in the form prescribed by the Abbé", and he himself had countersigned the warrant to the Lord Chancellor for appending the Great Seal. But Dubois, whose suspicions were roused, objected that these powers were not signed by the Prince, nor countersigned by Townshend, and was not satisfied till he received a written declaration from Townshend that such was the usual practice, and that the Treaties of Utrecht, Ryswick, and Nymwegen had been signed upon the credit of similar powers. The road was now clear at last, and it seemed for a moment that the States General would join in signing the treaty. But they did not, and on November 28, 1716, Great Britain and France concluded the alliance on the lines laid down in the Preliminaries signed at Hanover by Dubois and Stanhope. Stanhope suggested that the treaty should be kept secret for a month, in the hope that in the meantime the States General would be ready to sign in conjunction with Great Britain. But their cumbrous constitutional procedure and various intrigues, largely of Austrian origin, caused delay—were they to accede first to the alliance of May 25, or to that of November 28? And however natural it would have seemed to start with Austria, this was not done. The Austrians themselves, seeing that the Triple Alliance of the Western Powers could not be prevented, set little store by Holland's accession to the Anglo-Austrian Alliance. Prince Eugene told the British Ambassador "that he thought they had treatys enough already with the Dutch".[2] The States General acceded to the Franco-British Alliance on January 5, 1717;[3] the province of Zeeland alone did not sign till January 12.

The Treaty offered considerable advantages to Great Britain, France guaranteed the Hanoverian Succession, and the Pretender had to remove to Italy at a time when, owing to Swedish activities, his chances appeared better than at any time since the collapse of the Rebellion. If Article IV, which embodied the agreement with d'Iber-

[1] Coxe, ii. p. 131.

[2] Stanyan to Townshend, Jan. 9, 1717, S.P. 80/34.

[3] Cadogan to Methuen and Stanhope, Jan. 5, 1717, S.P. 84/255.

ville about Mardyke, was honestly carried out, England would be rid of a serious danger. Lastly, the Alliance assured George I of the benevolence of France in European, and especially in Northern, affairs. If anything, the Treaty was of even greater value to the French Regent, who found in it the much-needed support for his personal position—the interest of France was subordinated to that of its governor. For the Treaty hardly enhanced the prestige of France, Britain being the leading partner in the Triple Alliance. But the Duke of Orleans was overjoyed at its conclusion, and he and his mother are said to have kissed the parchment in high delight.

Meantime a serious crisis was brewing in England,[1] such as a year earlier might have endangered the domestic peace, or even the Hanoverian dynasty. The jealousy between George I and the Prince of Wales, which had increased during the King's absence from England, played a part in it. The Prince and Princess of Wales, sociable by nature, made for themselves a Court such as the King had not. From the beginning of August till the end of September they resided at Hampton Court, both for business and pleasure. Lord Townshend was there in constant attendance on the Prince Regent; Methuen called twice a week, and other Ministers still less frequently. The Prince seemed to aim at appearing different from his father. He and his wife dined in public, gave frequent receptions, entertained people without distinction of party, and showed the same courtesy to all. The Prince seemed unconcerned about the judgment of the world and of his father. The Duke of Argyll, in disgrace with the King, had his ear and confidence, while the Ministers who had caused Argyll's fall were treated with marked coldness. Most remarkable was the countenance which he showed to the Tories, though himself no less a Whig than the King; but he wished to appear unprejudiced. Still, his behaviour was amazingly unwise; he caused uneasiness among the Whigs and became suspect to his own father.

In view of the sharp political divisions, such an approach to the Opposition by the heir-apparent was bound to raise hopes that he might be used against the King's policy. In various counties addresses to the Prince were promoted—"the general tenour of them will be to compliment the Prince upon his Regency and upon his shewing himself disposed to be a common father to all his people, in

[1] The main authorities for the following account are: Coxe, *Walpole*, vol. ii.; the *Diary of Lady Cowper*; the dispatches of Hoffmann (Vienna Archives); Bonet (Prussian Archives); and Bothmer's letters to Robethon, Stowe MSS.

spight of the artifices and insinuation of such as delight in war or bloodshed".[1] But when the first Address was presented to the Prince, though it contained nothing "very liable to objection", the Prince was prevailed upon to reply that "he was obliged to the gentlemen for their zeal and attention, but desired [to] lett them know, that it was more agreeable to him to have all things of this nature addressed to the King". Robert Walpole added in his letter: "It cost some pains to bring His Highnesse to this temper, and will be a great disappointment to the managers of this affair".[2]

What rendered the position worse was that divisions had arisen among the Whigs themselves, which could easily prove fatal to their rule. Since the accession of George I, there had been constant rivalries between their leaders—there always were some like Lord Halifax, who thought that their merits had not been duly rewarded. Since the King's departure a faction was formed among the Whigs which worked deliberately at overthrowing the Administration; at their head were Lord Sunderland, impatient at being reduced to take a second place, and General Cadogan, created a peer after his Scottish campaign and appointed Ambassador to the States General. The Duke of Marlborough was behind these intrigues, though, paralytic and weak, he could no longer take an active part. This, however, was done by his Duchess, who was as good at Court intrigues as she had been in the days when she dominated the Court of Queen Anne. She now lavished on her friends her husband's money—he himself had never been so easy with it. It was planned, on the return of the King, to displace Lord Townshend and his brother-in-law, Robert Walpole, and perhaps also Stanhope, Cowper, and some minor Ministers. The Ministers clearly understood the danger and feared to lose the support which they had in the King, for his favour was decisive; and he could make his choice on personal grounds, for no political principles were involved in the matter.

The Germans at George I's Court had their share in the intrigues. Though they themselves were debarred from office by law, their power was considerable, and they naturally favoured those through whom they hoped to maintain and enlarge their influence and pursue their personal interests. Robert Walpole distrusted Bernstorff, who had gone with the King to Hanover, while Townshend said about

[1] Stephen Poyntz to Stanhope, Hampton Court, Aug. 21/Sept. 1, 1716, Coxe, ii. p. 75.

[2] Walpole to Stanhope, Aug. 30/Sept. 10, 1716, *ibid.* pp. 77-8.

Bothmer that "he has every day some infamous project or other on foot to get money"; and Bothmer had remained in England with the Prince of Wales and Townshend. By his reports to the King and his letters to Robethon he could aid or injure the British Ministers; and it was to him that Townshend subsequently ascribed the responsibility for his being removed from the Secretaryship by the King. Robethon, a clever, crafty man, faithful to the King, was hated by the English, to whom he was no friend, at least not further than suited his own interests. Walpole wrote: "Robethon's impertinence is so notorious, that we must depend upon it he does all the mischief he possibly can . . ." [1] Lastly, the newly created Duchess of Munster was very angry at not being an English duchess, and she imputed the whole to Lord Townshend, and expressed a particular resentment against him. [2]

Thus personal relations at Court rendered the position of the Ministers insecure. Their attitude in the Northern question and to the French alliance had roused the King against Townshend, and after the correspondence which had passed between Townshend and Stanhope, harmony could hardly be re-established between them. The offensive conducted by Sunderland and his faction against the Ministers was in full swing, and Stanhope's accession was bound to render it fatal to Townshend. A new Administration was prepared at Hanover, with Stanhope and Sunderland at their head. George I could not forgive Townshend for having obstructed Hanoverian interests.

For the present, however, Townshend's explanation was admitted to be sufficient—Stanhope said as much to Horace Walpole, who was on a visit to Hanover, and asked him to effect a reconciliation. Subsequent events, however, throw doubt on Stanhope's sincerity, or else Sunderland and the King soon succeeded in bringing him round once more. The King was annoyed at the Prince for countenancing Argyll and other people who had incurred his displeasure, at his hunt for popularity, and his wish to open the next session of Parliament with the full powers of a Regency. With Robert Walpole misunderstandings arose over financial problems. Bothmer's reports must have confirmed George I in the belief that the ultimate responsibility for it all lay with Lord Townshend; and Stanhope and Sunderland seemed much more amenable to the King's wishes with regard to Hanover and England. George I decided to change his First Minister.

[1] Robert Walpole to Stanhope, July 30/Aug. 10, 1716, Coxe, ii. p. 59.
[2] *Ibid.*

This was "a tryal between the English and German councils".[1] The Hanoverian interest won against that of England, and the peculiar system which was to continue under the first two Georges was established. On December 15, 1716, Townshend was dismissed from his office of Secretary of State. The King, who was about to return to England, wished to settle the matter beforehand, as had been done with regard to Bolingbroke. Townshend was graciously appointed Lord-Lieutenant of Ireland, and was, according to Stanhope, to retain his seat in the Cabinet.[2] In England, the transaction produced general consternation. But the King persisted. "They may possibly unking their master, or . . . make him abdicate England," wrote Stanhope to Methuen on January 13, 1717; "but they will certainly not force him to make my Lord Townshend Secretary."[3] But Townshend, "for domestic reasons" and in spite of the advice of his friends, declined the Irish office. In a letter to a friend he said that his "accepting the Lieutenancy of Ireland, under the circumstances above-mention'd, would have appear'd to the world like a confession of some degree of guilt".[4]

The final solution of the ministerial crisis was deferred till the return of the King. His long absence was highly unpopular and, according to Hoffmann, it was said in explanation "that this country did not suit him". George had to return for the opening of Parliament unless he was prepared to give fuller powers to his son; for this reason Parliament did not reassemble till after Christmas. At the end of January 1717, the King landed in England, solemnly greeted by his principal servants and by the Prince with the same honours as on his departure. Lord Townshend, graciously received by the King, complained of Sunderland not having acted honourably towards him. But as it was essential to settle the crisis before the opening of Parliament, everything was done to restore unanimity in the Cabinet. Townshend allowed himself to be persuaded to accept the Lord-Lieutenancy of Ireland, while Methuen remained in office in spite of Stanhope's return.

But real confidence could not be restored and a divided Cabinet could not carry on for long. Stanhope and Sunderland were ranged against Townshend and Walpole; the decision, however, had to be

[1] Thomas Brereton to Charles Stanhope, London, Dec. 1716, Coxe, ii. p. 150.
[2] Stanhope to Robert Walpole, Hanover, Dec. 15, 1716, *ibid.* p. 140.
[3] *Ibid.* p. 156.
[4] Townshend to Mr. Slingelandt, *ibid.* p. 161.

postponed in order not to weaken the Government in Parliament, and especially in order to retain Walpole's support in the Commons. But when on April 9, 1717, on the discovery of the Gyllenborg conspiracy, Walpole gave only a cold and formal support to the Government demand for measures against Sweden, and a number of Whigs voted with the Tories, reducing the Government majority to only four votes, the King took action; the same day Townshend was dismissed from his Lord-Lieutenancy. The next morning Walpole waited upon the King, to resign his office of Chancellor of the Exchequer. The King was greatly embarrassed; Walpole was wellnigh irreplaceable as financier and debater, and would prove dangerous in Opposition. The King, speaking in Latin, begged him not to leave his service, saying repeatedly *"rogo te, rogo te"*, and returned the seal which Walpole "had laid upon the table in the closet, into his hat . . . ten times". But Walpole persevered, and told the King "that, were he ever so well inclined, it was impossible to serve him faithfully with those Ministers, to whom he had lately given his favor and credit".[1] They parted, both greatly disturbed and agitated.

Walpole's example was followed by other Ministers. The Administration broke up, and a new one had to be formed. Stanhope and Sunderland, together with Cadogan, for a short time had the lead. Stanhope became First Lord of the Treasury, Sunderland and Addison Secretaries of State; Lord Berkeley replaced Orford at the Admiralty, Cowper remained Lord Chancellor. There were changes also in other posts. The Government was considerably weakened. One branch of the Whigs joined the Opposition, and Townshend and Walpole did not find it against their principles to embarrass the new Administration; they became the leaders of the disaffected Whigs. Yet such was the strength of the Whigs that not even this division among them could shake the Government.

England's position abroad was not affected by these internal difficulties and disputes. Her foreign policy followed its course, and, to the general surprise, soon placed George I and his kingdom at the head of Europe. England assumed a central position among the Great Powers, was allied to each of them, and called upon by circumstances to solve the extant problems. George I was to succeed where Louis XIV had failed, and to complete the work of pacification undertaken in 1713 and 1714.

[1] Horace Walpole to Rev. H. Etough, Wolterton, Oct. 12, 1751, Coxe, ii. p. 169.

Deeply engrained ideas had to be revised—most difficult of all was it for Charles VI to renounce Spain. The Austrians had watched with suspicion the negotiations carried on at Hanover, London, and The Hague, and Hoffmann repeatedly asked the embarrassing question how England could at the same time be an ally of Austria and of France when the interests of these two Powers were diametrically opposed ; and when told that George I only guaranteed the succession in France, *i.e.* the exclusion of Philip V from the French throne, he objected that this implied a tacit guarantee of the Duke of Anjou's right to Spain. The Imperial Minister, Count Sinzendorff, explained to the British *chargé d'affaires*, Luke Schaub, the system which, he thought, England should adopt: no alliance with France was to be concluded, except jointly with the Emperor, and on terms agreed between them. To this Sinzendorff added the cryptic remark that, should the European situation prove unfavourable, Austria would not be able to conclude the Turkish war soon, *i.e.* that her support would not be available for her allies in the meantime.

These pointed remarks received a sharp reply from London. Townshend wrote to Schaub on October 5, 1716, O.S.:

. . . after all the immense effusion of blood and treasure which this Kingdom has made in supporting the Emperor's interests in particular, and making acquisitions for him, it seems very hard that we cannot secure our selves from the dangers on the side of France, with respect to the Pretender and Mardyke without creating such strange alarms at Vienna; whereas we might with more reason expect from our good friends there that they should be pleased that our procuring these advantages to Great Britain, and particularly that point of demolishing the sluyces at Mardyke; which alone is sufficient to justify our allyance with any one that wishes us well; since unless we could have taken that thorn out of our sides in the manner we have, we should have been so curbed and awed, that instead of being able to assist our friends on occasion, we should have been insecure at home, and continually exposed to dangerous attempts on our own coasts.[1]

The Austrians, who had no reason for anxiety, now changed their tone, and merely criticized the way in which the alliance had been concluded; next, they argued that England ought to have at least communicated its text to Vienna beforehand; and finished by being convinced that George I must have had urgent reasons for hastening the conclusion of the treaty. In November, Prince Eugene, back from

[1] S.P. 104/42.

his victorious campaign against the Turks, was very willing to learn from Schaub how necessary the treaty had been, and accepted this view because of the situation in the Baltic. The last doubts must have been dispelled by Hoffmann's dispatch from London, of November 18, about the Northern complications having been, as was put to him by a British Minister, "the true key to these hasty negotiations".

To reconcile Charles VI with the Bourbon King of Spain was now the foremost task of British diplomacy; still, an understanding had first to be effected between the Emperor and the King of Sicily. The Vienna Court was determined not to renounce Sicily, which by the Treaty of Utrecht had been assigned to Victor Amadeus, who, however, since George I's accession could no longer count on being protected by the British fleet in its possession;[1] and without that he could not hold the island. But if he was to lose it, he meant at least to obtain compensation for it. An Envoy of his appeared at Hanover, and Stanhope with pleasure reported to Townshend: "we may boldly offer Sicily to the Emperor".[2] The discussions at Hanover became the pivot for negotiations concerning practically the whole of Europe.[3]

In November 1716 a new British Ambassador, Abraham Stanyan, arrived in Vienna; Lord Cobham had been recalled in April 1715, and Luke Schaub had since acted as *chargé d'affaires*. In accordance with the agreement reached at Hanover, Stanyan was instructed to speak to the Austrian Ministers about a reconciliation with Victor Amadeus. Sicily was not mentioned, and his approach met with an unfavourable reception. Prince Eugene remarked ironically that "he did not wonder that any person who had taken possession of another man's estate should afterwards desire to be friendly with him again without restitution";[4] but he declared in the name of the Emperor that he was not averse to negotiation, provided two points were settled first, Sicily and the Spanish Succession. In no case would the Emperor

[1] See above, p. 65.

[2] Coxe, ii. p. 124.

[3] For the history of the Quadruple Alliance, see Weber, Wiesener, vol. ii., and Baudrillart, vol. ii. A contemporary documentary digest by Bothmer has been published by R. Doebner in *Forschungen zur deutschen Geschichte*, vol. 26. The copy in the Hanover Archives is not in Bothmer's hand, but apparently in that of a copyist occurring in many documents signed by Bothmer; and there is no occasion to doubt Bothmer's authorship.

[4] Stanyan to Townshend, Dec. 19, 1716, S.P. 80/34.

allow the House of Savoy to be next to Anjou in the Succession of Spain. Talking about it, the Prince added

that it appeared by the King's accession to the Crown of Great Britain, as well as by the probability of the Duke of Orleans's coming to that of France, that it would be very imprudent to quit any just pretention to a Kingdom tho' the prospect were at a great distance.[1]

Meantime the great problems of European policy were discussed at Hanover. St. Saphorin, a Swiss by birth employed in the Hanoverian diplomatic service, had been to Vienna and had considered with the Ministers the possibilities of an understanding with Spain. As a result a special Envoy, the Imperial Councillor von Pendtenriedter, was sent to Hanover to establish contact with Stanhope.[2] Lord Stair described him as a man of engaging personality who knew how to transact important business with prudence and skill.[3]

Pendtenriedter arrived at Hanover on December 16, 1716, and his first talk with Stanhope naturally dealt with the recent Anglo-French alliance. He was instructed to speak of it "with a touch of pained surprise, but in measured terms expressing hurt friendship rather than reproach".[4] The discussion took a sharper turn only when Pendtenriedter set forth the old objection that the Treaty secured to the Duke of Anjou the throne and for ever excluded the Emperor from Spain. Stanhope blamed the Emperor's scheme with regard to Spain, the possession of which no one now allowed him or could procure for him. He, as British Minister, might have to pay for it with his head if he started a war against Spain, whereas he could undertake to obtain within forty-eight hours the consent of Parliament to a war against France. He finished by appealing to the Emperor that he should learn at last to pursue real, and not chimerical, advantages. This was the view now universally held in England. The Imperial Envoy could not possibly admit the argument—why, then, had millions been spent on the conquest of Spain, and why had the Tory Ministers been impeached? What change had occurred in these two years, since the time when Stanhope himself had, in Vienna, told the Emperor the opposite of what he was now saying? Spain had long been in the possession of the House of Austria; and possible apprehensions concerning an excessive increase in the power of the

[1] Stanyan to Townshend, Jan. 9, 1717, S.P. 80/34.
[2] Cf. Weber, *Quadrupel-Allianz*, pp. 28-9.
[3] Stair to Robethon, Dec. 18, 1716, Stowe MSS. 229, f. 333.
[4] His instructions are dated Nov. 25, 1716, Vienna Arch.

Emperor could easily be met by dividing his dominions. The discussion was warm, for both men knew its fundamental importance. The Emperor's renunciation of Spain was a necessary premise to the system which Stanhope was about to put before Pendtenriedter.

Charles VI was to renounce for ever all territories in the possession of Philip V. Stanhope already spoke of Philip as the King of Spain, which was resented by the Imperial Envoy; Sunderland, with more regard, referred to him as the Duke of Anjou, the description used in Vienna. The Emperor was to make peace with Philip, effect a reconciliation with Victor Amadeus, and guarantee the French Succession to the Regent, as had been done by England; lastly, something was to be done for the Queen of Spain, who completely dominated her husband. In return France and Spain were to guarantee the Emperor's dominions, Spain renouncing all her claims to them; and he was to receive Sicily. As the House of the Medici in Tuscany and the male line of the Princes of Parma and Piacenza were about to become extinct, and the character of Imperial fiefs of these States was disputed, these problems, too, were to be settled in favour of the Emperor and the Empire. The Emperor himself was to determine the future of Tuscany; while Parma and Piacenza might be given to one of the sons of Elizabeth Farnese—three sons by Philip V's first wife preceded them in Spain. The Princess from the House of Farnese, now one of the most powerful persons in Europe, was to regain for her children the rank of her ancestors. Thus all contradictions and uncertainties left over from the War of the Spanish Succession were to be settled. Nor were Stanhope's plans Utopian; suggestions had come to him from others, but it was he who distinguished what was feasible from the impossible—and he knew that the position of England was now such that she could play the leading part in all European problems.

Pendtenriedter raised many serious objections, and declared at first that he could not even suggest to the Emperor a renunciation of his claims to Spain. Finally, the entire plan was embodied in a memorandum drawn up by St. Saphorin and transmitted by Pendtenriedter to the Vienna Court.[1]

The Imperial Court was faced with a serious decision. The Secret Conference, which was immediately summoned, declared for continuing the negotiations,[2] as they offered the Emperor advantages

[1] Pendtenriedter's dispatches, Dec. 24, 1716, Vienna Arch.
[2] Reports of the Conference, Jan. 5 and 16, 1716, *ibid.*

such as could seldom be obtained without a long war. It would have been much more profitable if the initiative had come from the Emperor; but this could not be changed any more, now that England was in alliance with France and assured of Dutch support. He was not to renounce Spain—the Conference advised him merely to recognize Philip V as her King. But even this was too much for Charles VI. The new instructions for Pendtenriedter[1] probably expressed the Emperor's own mind—he would not hear of a renunciation or a recognition, but was prepared to declare that he would leave Philip V and his lawful descendants in undisturbed possession of Spain. On other points the Emperor was willing to meet Stanhope—he would even admit the candidature of a Spanish Prince to Parma and Piacenza. Pendtenriedter was, however, to try to recover Montferrat and the parts of the Duchy of Milan which had been ceded to Victor Amadeus; while the Emperor would in return cede to him Sardinia, which, after the loss of Sicily, would restore to him the royal title. This was the first time that the Royal Crown of Sardinia was mentioned in the negotiations; and Charles VI added in his own hand a postscript to the instructions, that Pendtenriedter should discuss this matter direct with the Savoy Minister present at Hanover.

By the time the new instructions reached Hanover, George I and his Ministers had left—he had hastened his departure because of the Cabinet crisis in England, and the intrigues of the Prince of Wales. Stanhope had asked Pendtenriedter not to follow the King, so as to avoid the appearance of the Emperor desiring the negotiations to be continued. He thought it better to be able to say to France afterwards that it would be difficult to obtain the Emperor's consent to the scheme. Pendtenriedter could therefore merely acquaint St. Saphorin with his new instructions, and communicate the Emperor's answer to Stanhope in writing. He returned with St. Saphorin to Vienna.[2] Some time now elapsed before the negotiations were resumed, but a basis had been found for the future.

The Vienna Court had expected the English to settle with them the details of the Treaty before approaching France. But such was not Stanhope's intention; on his way back to England, he met the Abbé Dubois at The Hague, and explained to him his scheme. It was now with France rather than with the Emperor that the Treaty had to be negotiated. The Regent wished it to be concluded in an under-

[1] Reports of the Conference, Jan. 5 and 16, 1716, Vienna Arch.
[2] Pendtenriedter's reports from Hanover, Jan. 9-23, 1716, Vienna Arch.

standing with Spain; and the friendly relations which England entertained with Madrid since the rise of Alberoni made Stanhope expect that he would be able to gain Spain for his scheme. The better part of 1717 elapsed before the negotiations were properly started. The French idea to draw Prussia into the alliance was displeasing to Vienna and apt to produce new difficulties. But in the summer of 1717 an event occurred which clearly proved the need for the Treaty: Philip V renewed the war against the Emperor.

The coming of Alberoni had worked a marked change in the Spanish Government. He was convinced that Spain could play a great part in the world, if enabled to employ her resources. He found her administration in a miserable condition—"this Government is completely destroyed by a canker, and if a cure is possible, it must be by iron and fire".[1] Alberoni's reforming activities extended to all branches of administration. In future the treasure of the Indies was not to enrich foreign nations; a national industry, the lack of which had impoverished the country, was promoted; and the system of taxation and finance was remodelled. These activities might have vastly improved the condition of the people had they been limited to peaceful pursuits. But under the ambitious direction of Queen Elizabeth and Alberoni, Spain reverted to the long-renounced Habsburg policy of conquests. Italian territories were to be regained. Alberoni "night after night . . . forced the King and Queen to consider his reforms. He convinced them that Spain should be a naval Power and not a military Power."[2] Foreign ships were purchased and work was pressed on in the Spanish shipyards. By the summer of 1717, Spain had a fleet of respectable size in the Mediterranean.

It is remarkable how Alberoni had managed so far to disguise his intentions. The Pope was made to believe that an expedition against the Infidels was intended: Alberoni hoped to be made a Cardinal— this was to raise his position in Spain and abroad; he was made one in July 1717. The position in Southern Europe was closely watched by all nations; but on August 9, after the fleet had long left Barcelona, George Bubb still thought that it was bound for Italy. He did not expect much to happen this year; but he expected that in the following spring Italy would become the scene of a war as great and bloody as the last.

[1] *Lettres intimes de J. M. Alberoni adressées au Comte J. Rocca*, ed. by E. Bourgeois (1892), p. 540.
[2] Cf. Armstrong, *Elizabeth Farnese*, p. 102.

The moment was not unfavourable for an attack against the Emperor's dominions. Austria, at war with Turkey, could hardly spare considerable forces for the defence of her Italian possessions. Moreover, Alberoni could point to the Emperor's having recently shown a hostile attitude towards Spain; the Grand Inquisitor Molines, when passing through Milan, had been arrested and kept prisoner.

The Spanish fleet, comprising twelve warships and a hundred transports, sailed against Sardinia. As yet Alberoni thought it risky to attack the Italian mainland, for Charles VI might have quickly concluded peace with Turkey and brought up his troops from Hungary. But Sardinia could not hold out against the Spaniards. The people were still attached to their old masters and assisted in the conquest of the island; which it took, none the less, several months to effect. Bubb reported under date of October 11:

I saw the Cardinal and he seemed to be in a very good humour, so that the little success of the enterprise against Sardinia has made no impression to his prejudice, or else he knows very well how to dissemble it.[1]

In Vienna the news about the Spanish armaments and the attack against Sardinia produced consternation. Only the Spanish courtiers rejoiced, as the war, on which they had pinned their hopes, now seemed unavoidable.[2] On second thoughts, the Austrian Ministers did not believe that there was ground for serious apprehension. Should the Spaniards land in Italy, they would be expelled before the winter, while in Sardinia the climate would prove fatal to their troops. As for the French Regent, Vienna was satisfied that he had no concern in the matter; nor did Stanyan fail to point out that this was primarily owing to the Anglo-French alliance, and Sinzendorff readily admitted that the Vienna Court had gone back on its previous condemnation of that alliance.

By the Treaty of May 25, 1716, O.S., England was undoubtedly under an engagement to help the Emperor against Spain, especially if a friendly mediation proved unsuccessful. Volkra and Hoffmann were instructed to remind the British Court, by word of mouth and in writing, of the *casus foederis* having arisen. Their Memorial was to show "neither contempt for the danger, nor indecent fear".[3] The two Imperial Envoys strictly carried out their orders;[4] even before, they

[1] S.P. 94/86.
[2] Stanyan to Sunderland, Aug. 28, 1717, S.P. 80/35.
[3] Instructions to Volkra and Hoffmann, Aug. 11, 1717, Vienna Arch.
[4] Their Memorial bears the date of Aug. 17/28, *ibid.*

had acted in that sense. At their instance[1] a courier was sent to Madrid on August 10, with instructions to Bubb to enter a protest with Alberoni. As the British Ministers still always considered him a zealous friend of England, Bubb was to make his representations in a friendly form and, should there be need of a memorandum for the King, he was to couch it in the most respectful terms. When Sunderland and Addison read out the dispatch to Hoffmann, he could not withhold from them that in his view "a wrong emphasis attached" to the words *amicable* and *respectful*.

Alberoni wished to preserve the good reputation which he enjoyed in England. He assured Bubb that "he had no part in this enterprise but the execution" and that "the King was absolutely bent upon it, and all he could say had not weight enough to dissuade him from it".[2] Alberoni played his part skilfully, and it is hardly astonishing that contemporaries believed him till facts proved the contrary; it is more surprising that attempts should have been made in recent times to absolve Alberoni of the responsibility for Spain's reckless policy.

The reply to Bubb's Memorandum[3] described at length how for years the Emperor, in defiance of all treaties, had insulted the King of Spain and provoked him, starting with the wrongful defence of Majorca and finishing with the recent arrest of the Grand Inquisitor. It concluded with the disingenuous promise that King Philip, to prove that he did not wish to profit by the "Archduke's" being engaged in war with the Turks, would limit himself to the occupation of Sardinia, and refrain from sending further forces to Italy.

However unsatisfactory was the reply, a break between Spain and England was still distant. The Secretaries of State had declared to the Austrian diplomats that this was not possible until Holland had acceded to the alliance with the Emperor; otherwise the Dutch would alone enjoy the advantages of trade with Spain and the West Indies, a situation for which the Ministers could not accept responsibility towards their country.[4] None the less, quietly and gradually, a sufficient number of warships was to be sent to the Mediterranean, which would enable England to take decisive action. But the hope of a

[1] Addison to Bubb, July 30, 1717, O.S., S.P. 104/136; Hoffmann, Aug. 13, 1717, Vienna Arch.

[2] Bubb to Addison, Aug. 30, 1717, S.P. 94/87.

[3] It is dated Aug. 26, 1717; the answer to it in the form of a letter from the Marquis de Grimaldo to Bubb, is dated Sept. 7, 1717, *ibid.*

[4] Volkra to Hoffmann, Aug. 30/Sept. 10, 1717, Vienna Arch.

peaceful settlement was not abandoned. Colonel William Stanhope, a cousin of the Minister, was to be sent to Spain as Bubb's successor. In his private instructions he was directed, should he find any inclination to a peaceful settlement, to hold out to the Spaniards the advantages discussed between Stanhope and Pendtenriedter at Hanover: the candidature of a Spanish Prince to Parma and Piacenza, an agreed settlement of Tuscany, and the declaration of both as fiefs of the Empire. Should it prove possible to reach a compromise on that basis through Alberoni, Colonel Stanhope received secret instructions to offer him, in the name of the King, a present of 40,000 pistoles. So much did the British Ministers misjudge the character of Alberoni.

Late in 1717, under the impression of the Spanish expedition, negotiations were resumed on Stanhope's great scheme. The Emperor stood in need of the other Great Powers, while these were favourably inclined to the Habsburg Empire after Prince Eugene had, by his recent victory of Belgrade, re-established the reputation of the Austrian Army. It was now incumbent on the Ministers of George I to mediate between Austria and France. The Regent was represented by Dubois, and the Emperor by Pendtenriedter.

Pendtenriedter left Vienna on October 7, and arrived at Cologne on the 20th; he intended to proceed to England by Ostend, when he received a letter from Baron Heems from The Hague, asking him to go by way of Holland, so that the States General should not think that he meant to keep the impending negotiations secret from them. Relations between Austria and Holland were not as yet satisfactory: there were disputes concerning the implementing of the Barrier Treaty, and consequently the States General had not, so far, acceded to the Anglo-Austrian Alliance—which was desired perhaps even more by the English than by the Emperor. When the Spanish expedition against Sardinia became known in London, Cadogan was sent to The Hague as Envoy Extraordinary; it was his task, as he informed Pendtenriedter,[1] to remove the difficulties and make the Dutch, should war break out with Spain, take part in it, if merely by sending a few ships to the Mediterranean.

Pendtenriedter made friendly professions to the Dutch, and continued his journey. He arrived in London on November 1. As Dubois, who had been in England a month, was staying at Hampton Court, rooms were prepared there also for Pendtenriedter, who, however,

[1] Pendtenriedter's report, The Hague, Oct. 26, 1717, Vienna Arch.; Cadogan's instructions, Aug. 21, 1717 (O.S.), F.O. 90/32.

remained in London.[1] His instructions reproduced in the main those
sent to him to Hanover under date of January 16, 1717; in broad
outline, the Imperial Court had accepted Stanhope's scheme. Three
draft treaties were inclosed with the instructions, the first two for
concluding with or without Spain, and the third to meet the new
situation created by the conquest of Sardinia. The prospect of acquiring Sicily had gained the Emperor's assent to Stanhope's plan; but as
"the acquisition of Sicily is the main advantage resulting to Us from
the Treaty", Charles VI refused to undertake any obligations until
he was satisfied on that point. The support of the other contracting Powers was to be promised should the island have to be conquered
from the Duke of Savoy; Pendtenriedter was "emphatically to declare
in the negotiations that this was the central point, and was to insist
on it as a *conditio sine qua non*". He was further to use his "earnest
endeavours" to recover for the Emperor the district of Montferrat,
ceded to Savoy in 1703; though this was not an absolute condition.

In return, Charles VI would guarantee the British Succession
though without naming its Protestant character—this the Roman
Emperor could not do; the old formula was to be used, promising to
recognize as successors to George I those designated and acknowledged by the laws and Parliament of Great Britain. With regard to
Philip V, the Emperor would make no other declaration but that he
would give no disturbance to him or his legitimate descendants in
their possession of Spain. If possible, the hereditary claim of the
House of Austria was to be recognized, in case the Anjou branch
became extinct or left Spain. Lastly, the Emperor, in his own hand,
added to the instructions the remark that now, after Spain had
broken the peace, she should not be admitted to the Treaty unless
she made reparation: besides restoring Sardinia she was to cede to
him Majorca, or at least Porto Longone, *i.e.* the part of Elba which
by the Treaty of Utrecht had been left in Spanish possession.[2]

The first conversations with the British and Hanoverian Ministers
and with Dubois proved to Pendtenriedter how very far he still
was from his goal—almost insuperable difficulties arose in every
direction. When he recalled the obligations assumed by Great Britain
a year ago in the alliance with the Emperor, he was told that there
was no intention to shirk them, but that England could not engage in
war with Spain without the States General, which would otherwise

---

[1] Hoffmann, Nov. 2, 1717.
[2] Instructions to Pendtenriedter, Sept. 27, 1717, Vienna Arch.

capture the entire Spanish trade; and the remark, current in those days, was added by the British Ministers, that they could not dare to give such advice without risking their heads. "What then", Pendtenriedter would reply, "was the sense of concluding the Treaty?"[1] Stanhope replied that even hitherto England had not been inactive, and pointed to the negotiations of Bubb and Colonel Stanhope at Madrid. Surely it made no difference to Austria whether her aim was attained by arms or by negotiation.

But there was little chance of a peaceful solution. Alberoni met Colonel Stanhope in a haughty manner. He would not hear of the proposed conditions which were communicated to him. This would soon change the whole of Italy into an Austrian province; Britain and France should much rather use the opportunity offered by King Philip to establish a better balance of power in Italy. Alberoni flattered himself with the hope of being able to make war on Charles VI, against the wishes of England, but in an alliance with France and Holland.[2] The English were taken aback, and thought him mad; worst of all, there were suspicions that he was encouraged by the British Opposition with a view to embarrassing the Administration.[3]

But even an understanding with France was as yet distant. Dubois declared to Pendtenriedter that the Regent could not conclude a Treaty with the Emperor without a guarantee of the throne for Philip V, *i.e.* without the Emperor renouncing Spain. Nor could the Duke of Orleans promise Sicily to the Emperor, for this would be against the Treaty of Utrecht, on which his own position was founded. The attitude of the Regent was dictated by the dangers of his position. The so-called Spanish party did their best to stop him from concluding the treaty; Dubois maintained that there were not two Frenchmen in twenty who would not prefer war to it.[4] It was said that in France 40,000 soldiers were living on the fat of the land doing no service—would it not be better to send them to Italy where they could live at other people's expense? This view was voiced even in the Council of the Regent.

Even some of the suggestions made by British Ministers were considered unacceptable by Pendtenriedter. They too demanded that

[1] Pendtenriedter's reports in Vienna Arch.

[2] Cf. Weber, p. 48.

[3] Pendtenriedter to the Marquis de Rialp, London, Nov. 2, 1717, Vienna Arch.

[4] Pendtenriedter to Königsegg, Nov. 18, 1717, Vienna Arch.

the Emperor should renounce Spain. The British, declared Sunderland, would not concede an increase of territory to the Emperor, powerful as he was anyhow—this was after the victory of Belgrade—unless they were assured that he did not aim at the conquest of Spain. When on November 23, Stanhope and Sunderland came to Pendtenriedter and submitted to him a new draft treaty,[1] whereby the Emperor was to recognize Philip V, guarantee the Protestant Succession, and compensate Victor Amadeus with Sardinia, Pendtenriedter enquired of the Emperor whether any useful purpose was served by his further stay in London.

A week later, Abbé Dubois left England. He went to Paris to find out, in a personal talk with the Regent, whether he at all desired to conclude the Treaty. Recently he seemed to have come entirely under the influence of the Spanish party, which wished to drive him into a war with the Emperor, or at least to prevent his concluding the treaty. There was talk of a French invasion of the Austrian Netherlands, unsupplied as they were with troops. But Dubois' influence sufficed to bring back the Regent to his previous policy.[2] He declared his readiness to conclude the treaty if only the Emperor showed the necessary regard for Spain; he should renounce his claims, and concede Parma and Piacenza, and also Tuscany, to a son of Philip V. The Abbé returned to London on December 31, 1717, with full powers for signing the treaty.

But Pendtenriedter was still without reply to his report of November 23—he had to wait for it till February 1, 1718. On receipt of his report the Conference was summoned in Vienna, and in view of the uncertain European situation, they declared for continuing the negotiations.[3] Pendtenriedter was instructed to work for an offensive alliance with England, or at least to obtain the dispatch of the British fleet to the Mediterranean. In return, should Dubois demand it, Pendtenriedter was empowered formally to declare the Emperor's renunciation of Spain in favour of Philip V and his lawful descendants; but nothing more, as this would suffice to secure the Regent's succession to the French Crown. The Emperor was not as yet prepared absolutely and unreservedly to renounce his claims to Spain.[4]

By the time Pendtenriedter was ready to resume negotiations with

[1] Enclosed in Pendtenriedter's report of Nov. 23, 1717, *ibid.*
[2] See Wiesener, ii. pp. 118-120.
[3] Cf. Weber, pp. 55-6.
[4] Instructions to Pendtenriedter, Jan. 17, 1718, Vienna Arch.

the British Ministers, they refused. After Dubois had left Paris, the Spanish party once more gained in influence; altogether the attitude of France was changeable and vacillating; the warlike intentions of Spain, the attitude of Alberoni, a serious illness which had recently endangered the life of Philip V, the victories of the Imperial armies over the Turks—everything had its influence on the Regent. Therefore Stanhope, who even as First Lord of the Treasury retained control of foreign policy, decided to settle with the Regent, without awaiting the Austrian reply, and only afterwards with the Emperor; for the Emperor was at least steady in his policy—one concession after another had to be wrung from him. After Stanyan's arrival in Vienna, Luke Schaub returned to London; and in him Stanhope found the skilful negotiator he required. A third draft was prepared, in the form of an alliance between Great Britain, France, Holland, and the Emperor—a Quadruple Alliance. Schaub was to take it to Paris, and, if he reached an agreement with the Regent, to proceed with it to Vienna. To this plan Stanhope now desired to adhere. A day before Schaub's departure the new instructions reached Pendtenriedter; but the British Ministers would not see him, and Pendtenriedter could only report to the Germans in the presence of Schaub. Stanhope and Sunderland did not receive him till after Schaub had left London.[1]

The Duke of Orleans was very willing to accept the treaty now submitted to him. In six conferences Schaub and Lord Stair went with him through all its details. No change was made in any vital point. The Regent, seeing the near conclusion, felt sufficiently strong not to be intimidated by the opposition of his advisers, most of all of Marshal d'Huxelles, whose attacks against the whole scheme and against its single points, were sharply answered by Schaub and Stair; the Regent subsequently expressed his satisfaction to them. He saw in the treaty an effective support for his personal position, and therefore promoted its conclusion. When Schaub suggested that after the work was completed those who had been hostile to it would have to be removed from the Government, and added that this was a hint which King George felt it his duty to send him—"This", declared the Regent, "is the advice not of a friend but of a father. You may assure the King that I shall act accordingly when the treaty is concluded." In fact, the Regent, having adhered to the policy of George I, could no longer have dispensed with England's support.

<hr>

[1] Pendtenriedter, Feb. 8, 1718, Vienna Arch.

Schaub arrived in Paris on February 8, and on the 18th continued his journey to Vienna. He found the Imperial Court in ill-humour. Not altogether without reason: they felt slighted by the British Cabinet having set a third draft treaty in circulation without awaiting the Emperor's reply to the second.[1] Jointly with St. Saphorin, the new British Ambassador in Vienna, Schaub started negotiations, and presented to the Austrian Ministers the latest draft, approved by the Regent, with a note[2] in which all the advantages of the treaty were explained once more. "You have forgotten nothing in it", remarked Prince Eugene with a smile; and they hardly knew whether this was meant as praise or as a reproach. They had little hope of success, and in view of the cumbersome procedure of the Vienna Court, had anyhow to be prepared to wait a month for a reply.[3] In the meantime they canvassed individual Ministers. Two things were most difficult for the Vienna Court to accept: the absolute renunciation of Spain, and the demand of Tuscany for a son of Philip V, especially as the Regent had deleted a clause inserted by Stanhope, whereby Pisa was separated from Tuscany (a few other points objected to by the Austrians were given up by the Regent on application from Schaub).[4] Even the Emperor having to give Philip the title of Spain, whereas Philip still used to refer to him as the "Archduke", could form no serious obstacle. Schaub and St. Saphorin did all they could to gain the consent of Charles VI to the Treaty, St. Saphorin going even so far as to threaten that, in case of refusal, the Emperor was not to expect any British help against Spain—although this was promised to him by Treaty.[5]

Another negotiation, carried on at the same time, to some extent endangered the success of the British diplomats. Charles VI had informed Victor Amadeus *via* London,[6] that he was not disinclined to a direct understanding, and was prepared to receive his Envoy. Victor Amadeus naturally agreed, and it was rumoured that his Minister was negotiating with Prince Eugene, and that he had brought with him a considerable sum of money—this, St. Saphorin believed, one

---

[1] See Schaub's "*Relation de ce qui s'est passé dans les conférences que Mylord Stair et moi avons eues avec le Régent de France*", dated Vienna, Mar. 14, 1718, S.P. 80/36.
[2] Schaub to Stanhope, Mar. 19, 1718, S.P. 80/36.
[3] St. Saphorin and Schaub to Stair, Mar. 16, 1718, S.P. 80/36.
[4] Stair to St. Saphorin and Schaub, Paris, April 1, 1718.
[5] St. Saphorin to Stanhope and Sunderland, Mar. 23, 1718.
[6] Instructions to Pendtenriedter, Jan. 17, 1718, Vienna Arch.

of the Austrian Ministers had the kindness to accept. There was talk of a marriage between the Prince of Piedmont and an Archduchess. Had Charles VI thus obtained Sicily, he could not have been gained for the Quadruple Alliance. Schaub and St. Saphorin made every effort to fathom these dangerous negotiations,[1] and openly declared to the Ministers that in view of the Stuart descent of the House of Savoy, King George would look upon this match just as if the Archduchess married the Pretender himself.[2]

But on April 4, the two British diplomats were most pleasantly surprised by Count Sinzendorff declaring to them that, though some of the clauses of the proposed treaty were hard, the Emperor had decided to accept it; he agreed even to the articles concerning Spain and Tuscany. He would, however, have to ask for a few minor amendments in the draft, on which points he hoped King George and the Regent would meet him. Pendtenriedter was to communicate this decision to the British Court, and ask for the immediate dispatch of the fleet to the Mediterranean, as had been promised. This Schaub now urged on Stanhope, saying that he would attain immortal fame by having built up the Quadruple Alliance.[3]

The resolution of the Emperor was welcomed both in Paris and London. Hoffmann reports the reception accorded to him and Pendtenriedter at Court—"which shows how seriously they were afraid of a new great war should your Imperial Majesty have rejected the proposed Treaty. Your Majesty's moderation and desire to preserve the peace of Europe are highly praised and valued more than the greatest victories which your Majesty could have won over your enemies." The British Ministers declared that the fleet should sail to the Mediterranean. Dubois wrote to St. Saphorin full of the most complimentary expressions.[4]

Still, the negotiations concerning the changes desired by the Emperor presented many difficulties; the details had to be gone through in long conferences, the Austrian Ministers tenaciously defending the interests of the Emperor. Repeatedly the British diplomats

[1] Extract from a letter of the French *chargé d'affaires* du Bourg to Huxelles; Vienna, Mar. 26, 1718, S.P. 80/36.

[2] St. Saphorin to Robethon, Mar. 26, 1718, *ibid.*

[3] St. Saphorin to Sunderland and Stanhope, April 5, 1718, *ibid.* Instructions to Pendtenriedter, April 6, 1718, Vienna Arch.; Schaub to Stanhope, April 5, 1718, S.P. 80/36.

[4] Stair to Stanhope, April 14, 1718; Hoffmann, April 19, 1718; Pendtenriedter, April 22, 1718; Dubois to St. Saphorin, London, April 12, 1718.

had to remind them of the Emperor's promise not to ask for vital changes, and to protest against Austria taking away with one hand what she had given with the other. They refused the Austrian demand that the article which placed the House of Savoy next in succession to Philip V and his descendants should be deleted; nor did they allow the German possessions of George I, or even Bremen and Verden, to be excluded from the Treaty guarantees. The preamble, however, which declared the right of the Great Powers, on their own authority, to settle points in dispute between other States, was deleted at the Emperor's desire; nor did the Emperor promise, as suggested in the draft, to *procure* the assent of the Empire to a Spanish Infante succeeding to Parma, Piacenza, and Tuscany (this, the Austrians declared, would exceed his powers) but merely that he would *earnestly endeavour* to obtain such assent. The news reached Vienna[1] of the Regent having offered the King of Spain, should he accept the treaty, to allow Spanish garrisons to be stationed in the strong places of the three States, before the Infante had succeeded to them. This the Austrians would not admit, and the denial by Schaub and St. Saphorin of the idea having been entertained, did not satisfy them; it had to be explicitly disallowed by a secret article—Charles VI had written to London that under no condition would he desist from that demand.[2] Possibly the Imperial Court still hoped that the treaty would fail, in which case the House of Bourbon was not to have gained a footing in Italy.

Although the Emperor had in principle accepted the treaty on April 4, it was not till May 22 that the British Ministers were in a position to report his final terms to London.[3] They now tried to represent his amendments (however much previously contested by them) as so unimportant that England was bound to support them with the Regent; especially as the position of Austria had considerably improved since April 4. The Emperor, if he wished, could make peace with the Turks within a month, and transfer, still this year, a considerable army to Italy. Also the Northern crisis was less acute. Lastly, it was open to the Emperor to make his bargain with Victor Amadeus—the promise of a marriage with an Archduchess and of

[1] Probably through the Savoy Minister. Stair in his letter to Stanhope, June 12, 1718, S.P. 78/161, declares that the Emperor had undoubtedly heard about that suggestion.

[2] Instructions to Pendtenriedter, Apr. 30, 1718, Vienna Arch.

[3] Two reports from St. Saphorin to Stanhope, May 22, 1718, with enclosures.

the succession to Tuscany for the Prince of Piedmont, would secure him Sicily. Replying to Dubois' flattering letter of April 12, St. Saphorin wrote that a refusal by the Regent of the proposed amendments might once more unsettle everything. "If because of such questions of form I had to begin anew, I would find myself in the position of that Pharaoh who suffered his sons to be massacred, and his daughters to be violated, and only cried when his favourite slave was to be executed. He said that his misfortunes had exhausted his strength, so that he could not bear any further mishap."

London followed with impatience the long-drawn negotiations— "In Vienna", said the King to Pendtenriedter, "they require more time for a single decision than in London to fit out a whole fleet"; to which Pendtenriedter pertly replied that in London more was asked in one hour than could be conceded in Vienna in a year.[1] When at last the draft was returned to London with the dispatch of May 22, and examined by the Ministers, the "Remarks on the Alterations made in the Treaty by the Imperial Court" which they drew up for the Regent were, on the whole, favourable to Austria; they obviously agreed with St. Saphorin and Schaub that the amendments did not infringe on the fundamentals of the treaty. In France, too, the delay caused anxiety.[2] Schaub now returned to Paris, where he arrived on June 11, and the next day, together with Stair, had a conference of three hours with the Duke of Orleans. The Duke readily accepted many of the Austrian amendments, with regard to some he let himself be persuaded by Schaub and Stair, but some he absolutely refused. With regard to the garrisons, he was bound by a promise of his Ambassador at Madrid and had therefore to take up a position diametrically opposed to that of the Emperor. Finally, he suggested that neutral, instead of Spanish, troops should be stationed in those Italian towns, an idea which had been considered in England, but was not to be put to the Vienna Court as coming from the Regent. The Duke spoke of Swiss soldiers, while Stair was for using British troops.

But soon a change supervened in the attitude of the Regent. At the second conference with Stair and Schaub, Marshal d'Huxelles, the worst opponent of the treaty, was present, and the Duke of Orleans treated them with visible coldness. "Counter-Observations"

[1] Pendtenriedter's dispatch of June 13, 1718, Vienna Arch.
[2] Stair to Craggs, May 25, 1718, S.P. 78/161; Craggs to Stair, May 22/June 2, 1718.

to the English "Remarks" had been drawn up in Paris, and while Stair and Schaub expected that these would now be discussed with them, the document was sent direct to London. The Regent having thus transferred the negotiations from Paris to London, Schaub's presence had become superfluous, and Stair decided to send him home to explain the position.[1] The Regent granted a further interview to the two diplomats. Stair declared that a miracle was required if the treaty was still to be concluded, but that no blame for it attached to King George or the Emperor. "Nor to me either," retorted the Regent. "But to your Ministers", replied Stair, "whom you have countenanced."

It was understood in London that the Regent was once more under the influence of the Spanish party, and that there was little hope for the treaty. Dubois felt the ground shake under his feet. Stanhope now decided to proceed to Paris,[2] in order to reconvert the Regent and to help him in eliminating the opposition from the Government. Dubois begged him to go, and so did Pendtenriedter, who saw how much Stanhope expected from his presence in Paris. Stanhope thought of proceeding next to Madrid, as the attitude of Spain was threatening. If anything could be done there, Stanhope alone could do it.

Schaub accompanied him to Paris.[3] The news of Stanhope's impending visit made a favourable impression on the Regent. When Stair complained of lack of confidence, the Regent spoke of him in flattering terms. He received Stanhope with the honours due to his rank; and was further influenced by the fact that a British fleet had sailed to the Mediterranean and that the mediation of the Maritime Powers between Austria and Turkey seemed to promise a speedy result. Without difficulty Stanhope managed to persuade him to drop the new demands of the "Counter-Observations". The further negotiations the Regent wished to conduct with Stanhope alone, i.e. to the exclusion of Stair. At first Stanhope refused, but on July 1 he

[1] Stair to Stanhope, June 18, 20, 1718. Schaub's "Relation" of July 15, 1718, S.P. 78/161.

[2] In appearance it was Dubois who seemed to urge Stanhope's visit to Paris, but in reality it seems to have been his own idea, and he merely wished to be asked to do so.

[3] The following is based on material in the Record Office and especially on Stanhope's letters to Stair and Craggs, June 30, July 1, 6, 12, 16, 18, and 19, 1718; Schaub's "Relation" to St. Saphorin, July 15, 1718; Stanhope's letter to Craggs, July 1, 1718.

agreed to a secret meeting with the Regent in his Cabinet. A convention proposed by England, and resembling that which Stanhope and Dubois had signed at Hanover in October 1716, formed the subject of their conversation. This time England and France were to agree to sign the Treaty of the Quadruple Alliance as soon as the Emperor's adherence to it was received. Stanhope had inserted in his instructions full powers to conclude such a convention. The Austrian Ambassador, Count Königsegg, considered it necessary to make certain that the Regent would authorize Dubois to sign the Treaty as it stood and without any further change, as soon as full powers were received by Pendtenriedter. The Regent was ready to agree, except that he would not undertake to give armed support to the Emperor before he had acceded to it; Stanhope agreed with this demand. After further correspondence with the London Cabinet, the convention was drafted. The Regent instructed Huxelles, as the Minister in charge of foreign affairs, to sign. But when on the morning of July 6, Stanhope and Stair went to him, Huxelles drily declared that he could not sign the convention. They went straight to the Palais Royal, to the Regent, who was as much taken aback as they had been. Huxelles' action corresponded to the views of his party; especially the generals of Louis XIV did all they could to defeat the Quadruple Alliance. Villeroy had openly told Stair his opinion, and the famous Villars had tried, when Stanhope and Stair dined with him, to ridicule the whole negotiation.

The Regent was indignant at Huxelles' refusal, scolded him in opprobrious words, and declared that someone else would be found to sign. Stanhope wrote to London that Dubois should be told he would have to take the place of Huxelles at the Foreign Office. The Marquis de Cheverny, instructed by the Regent to sign, replied that he could do so as his servant, but not as Minister. For a moment the Regent thought of Dubois; but Stanhope and Stair did not think that Dubois would dare to do in London what others refused to the face of the Regent. The Duke therefore sent to Huxelles telling him either to give up his place or to sign. The Minister said he would comply. But when on July 14, the Treaty was to be signed in the presence of the Regent, Huxelles raised new difficulties, and the matter had once more to be adjourned to the next day, when he again refused.

It seemed that the Quadruple Alliance would founder; for Huxelles' action, apart from his jealousy of Dubois, was due to the influence of the Spanish party and of public opinion. This was why the Duke of

Orleans found it so difficult to ignore him—against Huxelles' objections he felt unable to approve of the secret articles. Stanhope and Stair now suggested a way to shift the responsibility on to others: let him submit the Treaty of the Quadruple Alliance, including the secret articles, to the Regency Council for their decision. The Regent was at first startled by the idea, but having, in his mind, run through the list of the Regency Council, found that he could count on a majority in it. To pin him down, the British told him that Count Königsegg would immediately send a courier to Vienna to announce his decision. The Council was to meet in two days, on July 17.

The Regent opened it; next, Huxelles spoke in favour of the Treaty. Stanhope and Stair had seen a draft of Huxelles' speech and confessed that they themselves could not have made it more favourable. There was an almost unanimous vote in favour of the Quadruple Alliance; even Villars submitted to the opinion of the Regent, and Villeroy merely asked for delay. The Duke of Maine alone, the old opponent of the Duke of Orleans, declared that the Treaty would be fatal both to the State and the Regent. The next morning, July 18, the convention was concluded, Huxelles and Cheverny signing for France, and Stair and Stanhope for Great Britain. The convention declared in four articles that the two Powers could communicate the appended draft of the Quadruple Alliance to the Emperor as an ultimatum; that they would sign it as soon as the necessary full powers were received by the Imperial Ambassador; that in the meantime they would try to gain the accession of Spain, Sicily, and other Powers; and that this convention was to be ratified within fifteen days. Moreover, Stair and Stanhope accepted a declaration signed by the French representatives "that the most Christian King would not hold himself bound beyond the space of three months by this convention if the Emperor did not sign the Treaty within that time".[1]

The Treaty itself was to be signed in London; Pendtenriedter thought that he could assume the responsibility for doing so without awaiting new full powers from the Emperor.[2] On August 2, 1718, he and Hoffmann signed the Treaty; Dubois signed on behalf of Louis XV; while ten British Ministers were authorized to sign on behalf of George I. As the Treaty was to restore peace in Europe, it settled the form in which the Emperor was to conclude it with the Kings of

---

[1] S.P. 108/84; J. M. Graham, *Annals and Correspondence of the First and Second Earls of Stair*, vol. ii. p. 72.

[2] Pendtenriedter and Hoffmann, Aug. 2, 1718.

Spain and Sicily. Charles VI's renunciation of Spain secured the position of Philip V, but also the lasting separation of the two Bourbon Kingdoms. The position of the Habsburgs in Italy was strengthened by the acquisition of Sicily, but impaired by the re-establishment of the Bourbons in the Peninsula. Victor Amadeus was to be compensated by Sardinia, and thus remain a King. Secret articles prescribed the way in which the Treaty was to be executed.

The States General appeared in the Treaty as a contracting party, though in reality they were still far from acceding to it. The British Ministers were satisfied with the mere name of the States General being inserted—politically they had ceased to count and their effective support was not required, but commercially they were important and it was inadmissible that, should British commerce with Spain be stopped by war, the Dutch should reap the advantage. "Their nominal accession", said a British Minister to Pendtenriedter, "is necessary to allay the jealousy of the nation with regard to such lop-sided commerce." [1] Cadogan, who in April 1718 went as Ambassador to Holland, was to try to obtain the concurrence of the States General in the British expeditions to the Baltic and the Mediterranean, "altho' but one ship of war belonging to the States General should go alone with our fleet into the Mediterranean".[2]

It now depended on Spain whether the changes agreed upon in the Quadruple Alliance were to be peacefully effected, or whether the peace policy of the Allied Powers would have to be enforced by war. Alberoni was half-statesman and half-adventurer; with an acute sense of reality, he knew how to turn to advantage the resources of Spain and the European situation. And yet his fundamental conceptions were visionary. Under his leadership Spain tried once more to recover her greatness; but his powerful personality could not recall the past, and the inherent mistake in his policy was the more fatal, as the desire for conquest had taken the place of the higher motives which had previously actuated and in a way sanctified the Spanish bid for power.

The news which reached Spain in November 1717 of England intending, the following year, to dispatch a fleet to the Mediterranean, caused anxiety; while the contention that this was merely to obtain satisfaction for the arrest of Lord Peterborough in the Papal territories received no credence. Even greater was the excitement when

---

[1] Dispatch of April 27, 1718, Vienna Arch.

[2] Instructions to Cadogan, April 18, 1718, F.O. 90/32.

the next year a British fleet was actually fitted out and dispatched
to the Mediterranean; the fear which it evoked might have made
Spain accessible to the plans of the Great Powers.

In March 1718, on the arrival of the new French Ambassador at
Madrid, the Treaty of the Quadruple Alliance was formally communicated to the Spanish Court. Alberoni

upon receiving the proposals . . . expressed the utmost indignation at
Sicily's being given to the Emperor, alledging that by this means the
Emperor would become absolute master of all Italy. . . . Nor did he
receive the giving of Sardinia to the Duke of Savoy with more temper,
urging that the King of Spain could never consent to so great a dishonour. . . .

He would not have believed that Lord Stanhope would approve of
such proposals even if St. Paul had come down from Heaven to tell
him that.[1] The answer which he dictated to the French Ambassador
Nancré was of the most offensive character.[2] He hinted at a secret
connexion between the Regent and the King of England which
caused him to be guided by England and act so much against the
interest of France. The King of Spain, from respect for his grandfather and love of peace, had concluded the Treaty at Utrecht where
a few Englishmen laid down the law, but he would not do so a
second time, as God had given him sufficient independence and
strength not to accept the yoke of his enemies to the shame and
indignation of his subjects. Alberoni's rodomontades to the British
Ambassador were becoming more and more menacing. He hinted at
the possibility of Spain supporting the Pretender.[3] When Colonel
Stanhope refused Alberoni's demand for Sardinia, he replied that in
that case His Catholic Majesty would attack the Emperor with all his
might, even if all Europe threatened him with war; and if they tried
to act upon it, the King would withdraw to his own country and
defend it. Alberoni tried to impress the Ambassador with the enormous
military and naval resources of Spain. He declared that as soon as
the British fleet was sighted, the effects of the British merchants in
Spain would be seized. Either England or Spain must perish, he
repeated in wild excitement.[4]

Pendtenriedter tried to secure the dispatch of the British fleet, at

---

[1] Colonel Stanhope to Lord Stånhope, April 27, 1718. Graham, vol. ii. p. 353.
[2] Inclosure in the above, S.P. 94/88.
[3] Graham, ii. p. 353-4.
[4] See dispatches from Colonel Stanhope, Mar. till June, 1718, S.P. 94/88.

least early in 1718. He turned to the British as well as to the German Ministers and appealed to the King not to miss that opportunity "to show himself to the world". But the attitude of the Ministers was becoming increasingly uncertain—they feared a break with Spain—the mere rumour of it caused the shares of the East India Company to drop by several points. Urged by Pendtenriedter, the Government decided to bring the matter into the House of Commons. In a message to the House the King expressed the hope that "in case he should be obliged, at this critical juncture, to exceed the number of men granted this year for the Sea-Service, the House will at their next meeting provide for such exceeding." [1] An assenting Address having been moved, Robert Walpole opposed it and said that "such an Address had all the air of a declaration of war against Spain". Alluding to the Northern policy of the King, he said that war in the South was now necessary to obtain security in the North.[2] As, however, Walpole was isolated in his opposition, the Address was carried by a considerable majority.

The Government now proceeded to fit out the fleet, which was to consist of twenty of the largest warships under the command of Sir George Byng. Fresh delay was caused by the uncertain attitude of the Emperor towards the Quadruple Alliance. But when in April the news was received of his having accepted it in principle, the utmost dispatch was promised. The fleet did not, however, sail till June 12.

The Spaniards too had fitted out a fleet this year, as the year before; and again its destination was known to very few people. It caused universal surprise when on July 1, 1718, troops were landed in Sicily, and soon the greater part of the island was conquered. Strategically it may have been correct to start the invasion of Italy with Sicily; politically it was certainly a mistake, as Savoy, still the owner of the island, was thereby infallibly thrown into the arms of the Quadruple Alliance.

When Byng sailed, the destination of the Spanish fleet was not known in England. A similar argument concerning the instructions of the British Admiral developed between the British Ministers and the Austrian Ambassador as was usual with the Prussian and Danish Ministers whenever an expedition was sent to the Baltic. Pendten-riedter pressed that the British naval support should be made as effective as possible. The King himself having urged Pendtenriedter's

---

[1] *Parl. Hist.* vii. 555-6.
[2] Hoffmann, Mar. 29, 1718, Vienna Arch.

request on the Ministers, he could well be satisfied with the instructions to Byng. In fact, they were so favourable that he, on being given a copy, asked the King whether the original instructions did not perhaps contain other orders in secret articles, which George emphatically denied. The Admiral was instructed to inform the King through the British Ambassador at Madrid of his arrival off the Spanish coast. From Port Mahon, in the Island of Minorca, he was to inform the Viceroy of Naples and the Governor of Milan of his having come to defend the neutrality of Italy. He was to use all efforts in his power to bring about a cessation of hostilities, but should his friendly endeavours prove ineffectual, and hostilities have actually commenced, he should by openly opposing the Spaniards, defend the Emperor's territories from any further attempts.[1]

On one point did Pendtenriedter find the instructions deficient— there was no order to attack the Spanish fleet whatever the circumstances might be. And it so happened that nothing was said in them about the very case which had arisen—a Spanish attack against Sicily. Stanhope, who was in Paris, was of opinion that the provision for Byng's conduct "in case the Spaniards should . . . have landed any troops in Italy", ought to govern him "in the present case of their having landed in Sicily". On the advice of the Regent he sent, however, this letter to London, where it received full approval and caused additional instructions to be sent immediately to Byng. Pendtenriedter's doubt whether the British fleet would take decisive action against the Spaniards was soon appeased. He had tried to appeal to the English feeling with regard to naval power by reminding them how Charles II had been blamed for having suffered the French navy to grow, instead of destroying it at an early stage. Now that an occasion offered, it was decided completely to destroy the rising naval power of Spain. This intention could not be openly declared in the formal language of the instructions, but the Austrian Ambassador was assured by the Ministers "that Byng would do his duty, or otherwise would have to pay for it with his head, as besides his instructions he had been given verbal orders; and that he was to go straight to work and not be afraid of doing too much". King George himself expressed to Pendtenriedter the hope that Byng would destroy the Spanish fleet.

[1] The instructions to Sir George Byng, May 26/June 6, 1718, are inclosed in Pendtenriedter's reports in the Vienna Arch.; see also Graham, *Annals*, ii. p. 77.

The same was said in so many words in the additional instructions. The Secretary of State, Craggs, referred Byng to the orders which he would receive from Stanhope, from France or Spain. "Should you be directed to attack the Spanish fleet, you should waste no time on single ships, but try, with the first blow, to destroy their entire fleet." Similarly, on August 6, Craggs wrote to Byng to wait till the entire Spanish fleet was together and to destroy it at one blow.[1]

It might seem incongruous that at this juncture Stanhope should have decided to proceed to Spain. But he was sincerely anxious for her to join the Quadruple Alliance, and if there was to be war, the British Government would have a better case to place before Parliament if it had first used its utmost endeavours to bring about a peaceful settlement. The Regent, too, advised him to go, and on July 21 Stanhope left Paris, accompanied by Schaub. It was not without concern that George I and the Emperor learned of this journey, fearing lest Stanhope should be seized and detained by Alberoni. It was wished in London that the passport which was demanded for him by Colonel Stanhope should be refused; and indeed Alberoni was indignant at the request.

The King of Spain could not suffer such an indignity, as to admit of a chief Minister of England to come hither, when the two nations were in a state of warr, that he took it for granted, that your Lordship had sent orders to the fleet at least to suspend entring upon action whilst you were treating for an accommodation.[2]

Finally, Alberoni could not refuse, and Stanhope went to Spain.

Real success was hardly to be expected. Towards Stanhope Alberoni did not display his usual violence, and very nearly succeeded in convincing Stanhope that he was merely carrying out the orders from the King and Queen, and himself would renounce all conquests in Italy. But whoever it was who determined Spanish policy, so much was certain that there was little chance of Spain joining the Quadruple Alliance. The Treaty and its secret articles were communicated to the Court. Stanhope and the French Ambassador Nancré enquired, seeing that a term of three months was offered in the Treaty for Spain, whether they wished for an armistice for that period. When this was refused, Stanhope's mission was clearly at an end. He was graciously dismissed by the King and Queen; Alberoni shed tears on parting

[1] For extracts from Craggs's letters to Byng, of July 2/13 and 14/25, 1718, see below, Appendix No. 4, pp. 380-81.

[2] W. Stanhope to Craggs and to Lord Stanhope, Aug. 1, 1718, S.P. 94/86.

with him and promised to let slip no occasion that might offer of adjusting matters. On September 2, Stanhope returned to France, taking the route of Bayonne.[1]

Meantime the decisive battle had taken place between the Spanish and British fleets. Sir George Byng, acting on his orders, had informed the Spanish Government of his arrival off the coast of Spain and offered his services with a view to accommodating the differences with the Emperor. He was answered drily that Chevalier Byng might execute the orders of the King, his master.[2] The Admiral therefore continued his voyage. On arriving at Naples he learnt that a large part of Sicily had been conquered by the Spaniards, and that Victor Amadeus was prepared to join the Quadruple Alliance. To leave nothing untried, Byng sent an officer to the Spanish commander in Sicily, Marquis de Lede, offering a cessation of arms for two months, but received a refusal. He therefore decided to attack the Spanish fleet.[3]

The next morning, August 10,[4] when approaching Messina, he saw two of the Spanish scouts, and "having intelligence from shore that the Spanish fleet lay open", he stood after these scouts. By noon, he had a fair view of the entire Spanish fleet drawn up in a line of battle, "in which they lay untill we came near them, and then they bore away, but in line of battle". Admiral Byng decided to chase them, and ordered the four best sailers in the fleet ahead, to make what sail they could so as to come up with the Spaniards, while the rest followed. The pursuit was continued throughout the night, the headmost British ship carrying lights to guide the fleet. At break of day the Spaniards found the British so close upon them that they had to accept battle. The fleets were off Cape Passaro, near the southeastern corner of Sicily, having sailed along the eastern coast during the night. The Spaniards now tried to save the most vulnerable part of their fleet from the engagement. The galleys and smaller vessels were ordered to separate from the bigger ships, and make for the coast. But Byng detached a squadron of eight ships under Captain

[1] See three letters from Stanhope in Mahon, i. App.

[2] Byng to W. Stanhope, June 20, 1718; Alberoni to W. Stanhope, Escurial, July 15, 1718; W. Stanhope to Byng, July 16, 1718, S.P. 94/86.

[3] Byng to Craggs, July 12 and 25, Aug. 6 (O.S.); Byng to Lede, July 29 (O.S.); Lede to Byng, Aug. 9, 1718 (N.S.), P.R.O.

[4] Cf. Byng's report, "A particular account of the engagement between the Spanish and English fleet off Cape Passaro, July 31, 1718", P.R.O.; further Byng to Stair, Aug. 15, 1718, in Graham, *Annals*, ii. pp. 79-81.

Walton, and sent them in pursuit. It was here that the first shots were fired by the Spanish ships, and the battle was formally begun. On this ground it was subsequently contended by the English that the responsibility for it lay with the Spaniards, though it was the English who had sought battle; and it is of minor importance which side actually fired the first shot. The eight English warships took some of the Spanish ships, ran ashore and burned others, and only the galleys got away.

Only gradually did the battle between the main British fleet and the bigger Spanish warships develop. It has been disputed by Admiral Mahan [1] whether the engagement which ensued can be called a battle. The fleets were not in line, as the Spaniards still always tried to break away but were pursued by the English—a running action ensued in which the two fleets were soon intermixed. Byng had sent his best sailers after the headmost Spanish ships, but as the battle developed, he was hardly in a position to direct it. It resolved itself into a number of single combats, each captain attacking the ship which was nearest to his own. The British fleet, superior in number and skill, won an easy victory. Many Spanish warships were captured, others were destroyed, and less than half escaped. The Spanish Admiral himself was taken prisoner. The sea power of Spain was annihilated.

The battle off Cape Passaro set a term to the Spanish dreams of conquest and to the hopes of Alberoni. The British fleet wintered off southern Italy and put a stop to all further Spanish expeditions. A war against the Quadruple Alliance offered no chance to Philip V, and the more he persisted, the more marked became their superiority and the downfall of Spain. Even Alberoni's last hope, that the Austrian armies would be detained by the Turkish war, was shattered. On July 21, 1718, peace between Austria and Turkey was signed at Passarovitz.

---

[1] A. T. Mahan, *The Influence of Sea Power upon History*, 1660–1783 (1894), p. 236.

CHAPTER XIII

BRITISH MEDIATION IN THE TURKISH WAR

At the close of long and exhausting wars nations turn pacifist and are willing to put up with evils and renounce cherished hopes rather than face the danger of new conflicts. In such times hardly anything can earn greater popularity for a Government than honest work in the interests of peace; and it is foremost on the victorious Powers that falls the task of building up a new system for peaceful co-operation between nations. The British Government honestly worked for it at the close of the War of the Spanish Succession, and Stanhope's mediation extended even to the Austro-Turkish War.

The old struggle between the two Powers had changed its nature since the defeat of the Turks before Vienna, in 1683. Austria's mission to act as barrier against the advance of Islam into Central Europe had been accomplished, and she was now engaged in the reconquest of the parts of Hungary still under Turkish occupation. The ultimate expulsion of the Turks from Europe henceforth entered within the realm of political speculation, and the future of her subject races became a standing problem in European politics.

At Carlovitz, in 1699, after sixteen years of war, the Emperor Leopold concluded peace with Turkey through the mediation of the Maritime Powers, and especially of England. It was the first time that the Turks accepted the official mediation of neutral Powers. The achievements of Ludwig of Baden and of Prince Eugene of Savoy— the conquest of Hungary and Transylvania—were secured in the Treaty. But it was neither peace for its own sake, nor concern for Turkey, such as was present in later times, which caused England to interpose. William III had to reckon with the danger of a European war on the death of Carlos II, and was trying to secure allies in advance: Austria could not have intervened in such a struggle with all her strength unless peace with Turkey was re-established.

Similar reasons led to the mediation of the Maritime Powers in 1716. A term had to be set to the Turkish War for the sake of the Quadruple Alliance and with a view to checking the Spanish plans; for Alberoni counted on Austria being engaged in war with Turkey and being therefore unable to protect her Italian possessions. Great Britain, preponderant in Europe, seemed specially called upon to mediate in this war. In the Treaty of Utrecht she had gained possession of Gibraltar and Minorca, important stations for her Mediterranean Fleet, which enabled her actively to intervene in Turkish affairs; her sphere of interest now extended to the Balkans and no great decisions in the Eastern Question were henceforth to be made without her.

The Venetian Republic had been at war with Turkey since December 1714, and the conquests of Morosini were lost in the course of a few months. The Turks conquered Morea, attacked the Venetian possessions in Dalmatia, and threatened Venice itself. By the Treaty of Carlovitz the Emperor was to help Venice against a Turkish attack, and Prince Eugene pointed to the dangers which a decisive defeat of Venice would involve for Hungary, and even for the German provinces of Austria; the Emperor, in his own interest, was bound to declare war against Turkey.

But peace with Spain had not been concluded, nor a Barrier Treaty with Holland; Victor Amadeus threatened trouble in Italy, and the Northern War continued. It seemed therefore desirable that the Emperor should retain a free hand. Prince Eugene headed the war party at the Vienna Court, and the motive ascribed to him, not without reason, by his opponents was that a war against Turkey would render him indispensable. The Spanish Ministers of Charles VI favoured peace, as the reconquest of Spain was their sole concern. Also some of the German Ministers were opposed to war with Turkey —Count Sinzendorff said to the British *chargé d'affaires*, Luke Schaub, that they thought Italian affairs were more important for the Emperor than anything which could be gained in Hungary.[1]

Nor did the British Government wish for such a war; Schaub, when reporting to his Government on the policy of the Spanish Ministers and of their adherents, added that "the Spanish Ministers might be helpful in an attempt to prevent it".[2] He was in fact instructed to encourage the peace party at Vienna. But it was in

[1] Schaub to Townshend, Dec. 11, 1715, S.P. 80/32.
[2] Same to same, Sept. 14, 1715, *ibid.*

vain; for though some of the Austrian Ministers sincerely wished for peace, they all finished by agreeing that war was inevitable. None the less, England continued to work for peace and the British Ambassador in Constantinople, Sir Robert Sutton, was instructed "to give the Turks such a formidable idea of the affairs of Europe, as to move them to lay aside the thoughts of wars, and seek peace with the Emperor".[1] But to the Venetian Envoy, Grimani, Schaub indicated that the Republic had best seek peace with the Turks, and that all the victories of the Emperor would not regain for them Morea—a prophecy which proved accurate.[2]

The Austrian Court suffered England to continue her well-meant endeavours; even Prince Eugene and Starhemberg, however keen on war, realized the importance of not alienating England. Nor did they need to fear lest peace might be preserved. Turkey was pushing on preparations for war, and a break became inevitable when in May 1716 the Imperial Resident, Franz von Fleischmann, was imprisoned, contrary to international law.

Prince Eugene declared to the British *chargé d'affaires* that King George could not have obliged the Emperor more than he had by the action of his Ambassador at Constantinople, and that it was desirable for negotiations with Turkey to be continued through British mediation.[3] But when this was formally offered by Schaub, Prince Eugene, in the Ministerial Conference, declared strongly against acceptance. In his report to the Emperor[4] he said that they must not let themselves be any longer "amused and delayed by such uncertain and unreliable negotiations", and that the Emperor must make his strength felt; "with a view, however, to maintaining a good concert with the British Crown and in order to be able to resort to its mediation in the future, it was considered advisable to thank the King for the offer of his good offices with regard to Turkey, and to add that these would always be welcome to your Imperial Majesty". This was the sense of the reply to Schaub. He was to be in a position to undertake the mediation; but nothing was to be done for the present.[5]

As soon as a British mediation was mentioned, the States General desired to participate in it, as they had done at Carlovitz. The Dutch

[1] Townshend to Schaub, Dec. 20, 1715, O.S., S.P. 104/42.
[2] Schaub to Townshend, May 6, 1716, S.P. 80/33.
[3] Same to same, June 10, 1716, *ibid.*
[4] *Feldzüge des Prinzen Eugen*, ii. Section 7, pp. 37-8.
[5] Schaub to Townshend, June 27, 1716, S.P. 80/33.

Minister, Hamel Bruynin, explained in Vienna that their High Mightinesses would not be excluded if an occasion arose for mediation with the Turks;[1] and he received the desired assurances.

In spite of these courteous, but non-committal replies, war broke out and on August 5, 1716, Prince Eugene defeated and annihilated a numerically superior army at Peterwardein. The Grand Vizier himself was killed, and there was joy throughout Europe over the "victory of the glorious and blessed Christendom over the dark sign of the Crescent". Temesvar, the only Hungarian fortress left in Turkish possession, was captured, and the fortress of Belgrade, at the junction of the Danube and Save, now became the objective of the Imperial armies. In 1717, Prince Eugene crossed the Danube and established his camp south of the town. Two pontoon bridges across the Danube and Save secured communications with Hungary. The siege of "the Holy House of War", as the Turks called Belgrade, was in full swing, when a Turkish army of 15,000 men came up to relieve the hard-pressed garrison, and lay siege to the besieging army. A fortnight later Eugene decided on action. A thick fog favoured the attack, and at the critical juncture Prince Eugene himself is said to have led a cavalry charge against the Turks. The victory was decisive, and the Turkish army dissolved in flight, leaving behind their cannon and baggage. The fortress of Belgrade surrendered on August 18, its garrison being granted free departure.

On receipt of the news Charles VI wrote a letter to the Prince, full of joy and gratitude,[2] but expressing the wish that peace might be concluded in the course of the year; ten days after the battle of Belgrade, the Spaniards landed in Sardinia. Still, the Emperor's letter shows what unpleasant memories lingered in Vienna of the mediation of the Maritime Powers at Carlovitz, and the more recent British endeavours. "Even to-day I need but briefly remind your Serene Highness", wrote the Emperor, "that you should lose no opportunity of concluding peace with the enemy, as you know best that a mediation is undesirable and that it is best to treat *sub armis*." The Prince fully shared this view, and for a short time there was hope of his succeeding.[3]

But Britain had already offered her mediation to the Sultan, and the Turkish Government was therefore no longer prepared to con-

---

[1] Schaub to Townshend, July 8 and Aug. 12, 1716, *ibid.*

[2] *Feldzüge des Prinzen Eugen*, ii. S. 8, pp. 412-3.

[3] *Ibid.* pp. 193-5.

clude immediately. In view of the European situation the Emperor dared not endanger his good relations with Great Britain; even Holland could not be excluded from the negotiations, which had to be left to a Congress to be summoned the following year. None the less, extensive preparations were made for a possible continuation of the war. In the next campaign Prince Eugene intended to direct his operations against the fortresses of Nish and Viddin, south of Serbia proper, and against Bihatch in Bosnia. But he himself sincerely wished for peace.

Passarovitz, on the right bank of the Morava, near its junction with the Danube, was chosen by him for the Congress; but as at Carlovitz, its meetings were to be held not in the village but on an adjoining hill. The Imperial Plenipotentiaries were Count Virmond and von Talman, a member of the War Council who had taken part in the Carlovitz negotiations.[1] Turkey was represented by Silihdar Ibrahim and Mehemed Effendi, Inspector of the Artillery, with John Maurocordato, Prince of Vallachia, acting as Dragoman; he played an important part in the discussions about territorial cessions in Vallachia. At Prince Eugene's suggestion the Republic of Venice was invited to the Congress; their Plenipotentiary, Ruzzini, who had been present at Carlovitz, was well acquainted with Turkish affairs.

The Emperor, having to accept the mediation of the Maritime Powers, wished at least to see Plenipotentiaries agreeable to him entrusted with the task. Of all the possible British representatives Wortley Montagu would have been least welcome to the Vienna Court, who had obtained his recall from Constantinople at the end of 1717. After Schaub's fruitless attempts in 1716, he had insistently pressed his mediation on the Emperor and the Prince, who desired to go on with the war, till it seemed as if he sponsored Turkish interests and tried to check the Austrian advance; when Prince Eugene was about to attack Belgrade, Wortley Montagu proposed peace on the basis of a return of Temesvar to the Turks.[2] After his recall, he wrote to Prince Eugene asking for his interest with a view to being employed in the negotiations, but received the cool reply that the Emperor had to leave it to His Britannic Majesty how he chose to employ his Ministers.

Stanyan, hitherto Ambassador in Vienna, was appointed Wortley's

---

[1] Their instructions are printed in *Feldzüge*, vol. ii. S. 8, pp. 440 ff.

[2] *Feldzüge*, vol. ii. S. 8, pp. 4-5.

successor at Constantinople; and, in accordance with his own wish,[1] he received general instructions for the peace mediation.[2] But Sir Robert Sutton, late Ambassador at Constantinople, was the chief British Plenipotentiary at the Congress, and transacted practically all the business, while Stanyan was kept away from Passarovitz, and remained in attendance on the Grand Vizier.

Count Colyer, Dutch Ambassador at Constantinople, was their Plenipotentiary, a choice hardly pleasing to the Austrian Government.[3] He was known to entertain relations with Russia, which rendered him highly suspect to the English also. The British Plenipotentiaries, Sutton and Stanyan, were repeatedly enjoined, besides trying to re-establish peace between Austria and Turkey, to provoke, if possible, a conflict between Turkey and Russia—she seemed at that time to threaten the German possessions of King George.

When Stanyan was informed about his intended mission to Turkey, the question occurred to him whether British mediation had been offered to Venice; it would have been advisable for him, before leaving Vienna, to speak about it with Grimani, but he could not risk doing so on his own initiative. He searched the Embassy archives in vain, and neither St. Saphorin nor Hamel Bruynin was able to enlighten him on this point, while Schaub was at that time in London. Only from a letter of Lord Sunderland's he learnt that British mediation had in fact been offered to the Republic in 1716, and that "His Majesty does not think it amiss that you should acquaint the Venetian Ambassador with it", and assure him that the King "continues in the same sentiments and will undertake the mediation as well for the Venetians as for the Emperor".[4]

Early in May 1718, the various Plenipotentiaries, with their retinues, servants, and body-guards, met near Passarovitz. The Imperial and Venetian Ambassadors were assigned quarters in the village; for the Turks and the "Mediation Ministers" encampments were provided outside. The Turks were at first dissatisfied with that offered to them, and here the first occasion arose for Sir Robert Sutton to employ his offices.

Before the opening of the Congress the full-powers had to be

---

[1] Stanyan to Sunderland, Aug. 21, 1717, Private; Oct. 3, 1717, S.P. 80/35.

[2] Sunderland to Stanyan, Oct. 1 and 15, 1717, O.S., S.P. 104/42.

[3] See *Feldzüge*, vol. ii. S. 8, p. 343.

[4] Stanyan to Sunderland, Nov. 3, S.P. 80/34; Sunderland to Stanyan, Nov. 8/19, 1717, S.P. 104/42.

exchanged, and these were based on both sides on the *status possidendi*. But it was found that the Turks were not authorized to conclude peace with the Venetians, who were, moreover, referred to in unbecoming terms. The Imperial Plenipotentiaries declared their inability to enter negotiations under these conditions.[1] Several weeks elapsed in mutual suspicious observation, and in waiting for news which from every part of Europe was coming to the small Serbian village—about the armaments and policy of Sweden and Russia, the Spanish expeditions, and the conclusion of the Quadruple Alliance. At last, on May 31, the Turkish Ambassador received his new powers instructing him to negotiate with the Envoys of the Emperor and of Venice on the basis of the *uti possidetis*. Thus the formal side was settled, and preparations for the opening of the Congress were pressed forward. The Austrians and the Turks alike wished on that occasion to give emphatic expression to the high dignity of their respective masters, and Sir Robert Sutton had no easy task in trying to satisfy both sides; he had to spend several days almost continually on horseback, passing from the Austrians to the Turks, and from the Turks to the Austrians.[2]

On Whitsunday morning, June 5, two elaborate processions moved from the villages of Passarovitz and Costelliza towards the tents prepared for the Conference in an open field; the retinue and guards on each side amounting to 700-800 men.[3] At the invitation of the mediating Envoys, Sutton and Colyer, the Imperial and Turkish Plenipotentiaries came into the tent; they entered it simultaneously from opposite directions, walking at a measured pace; and silence was preserved till Sir Robert Sutton, in the name of the Mediating Powers, opened the Conference.[4]

Although the most important points had been settled beforehand, the course of the Congress was neither as easy nor as favourable as Sutton had expected. Moved by lurking suspicions, the Imperial Envoys had not fully informed him of their intentions, and now advanced new demands, while by their proud demeanour they made the Turks feel that they were the victors. The first conference started with the fixing of the *uti possidetis*. Only with regard to Venice, the

---

[1] Sutton to St. Saphorin, May 16, 1717, Han. Arch. Further see *Feldzüge*, vol. ii. S. 8, pp. 349-51, and Hammer, vii. p. 230.

[2] Sutton to St. Saphorin, June 2, 1718.

[3] *Theatrum Europaeum*, 1718.

[4] *Theatrum Europaeum;* Hammer, *Geschichte des Osmanischen Reiches.*

Austrians would not accept it, demanding just reparation for her. After a long dispute, the Turks gave in. Now, to the astonishment of the neutrals and the Turks, the Austrians demanded that the Sultan should extradite the Hungarian revolutionary leader, Rakoczi, and his followers. Even on this point the Turks gave way, so far as it was possible without loss of honour to their master.[1] But when the Turks proposed an armistice for the duration of the Congress, the Austrians refused off-hand—what use was an armistice when they were about to conclude peace? On the Turks repeating their demand, the Imperial Envoys rose, and persuasion was required to make them resume their seats. No general armistice was concluded, and only a narrow district round Passarovitz was marked off as neutral ground.[2]

In the second sitting, on June 7, it was found how difficult an understanding was even on the apparently clear basis of the *uti possidetis*. Belgrade having been taken, the Austrians demanded its entire province, *i.e.* the ancient kingdom of Serbia, including even the fortresses of Nish and Viddin, which were still in Turkish hands. But the Turks neither would, nor could, surrender these towns, as even their religious law forbade them voluntarily to cede fortified places which contained mosques. Nor could anyone, either in the Turkish or the Austrian delegation, clearly define the frontiers of Old Serbia, though this was not meant to denote the Empire of Stephen Dushan. It would have been simpler to enquire which was ethnic Serb territory—but such ideas were not current at the beginning of the eighteenth century.

When the Grand Vizier heard what had happened, he wanted immediately to resume military operations. How could the Emperor on the basis of the *uti possidetis* demand territory not in his possession? The Turks would much rather suffer defeats for ten years on end than cede an inch of territory not conquered by their enemies.[3] For a few days Sir Robert Sutton was wellnigh in despair. The Austrians now added a demand for the cession of Vallachia, though only the district west of the Aluta was in their possession. Sutton wrote to St. Saphorin to make the Vienna Court moderate their demands; and so did Prince Eugene, who had arrived at Belgrade to watch both over the negotiations and the campaign.

The intervention was successful. The Imperial Plenipotentiaries

---

[1] See *Feldzüge*, vol. ii. S. 8, p. 372.   [2] *Ibid.* pp. 348-9.

[3] Stanyan to St. Saphorin and to Prince Eugene, Philippopolis, June 16, 1718, Han. Arch.

had in fact gone further than was desired by the Emperor, to whom at that time peace was more important than two Turkish fortresses. Prince Eugene set things right. At the military review on June 15, he had a private talk with the Imperial Envoys and settled with them the demands to be made on the Turks.[1] Not even Sutton learnt anything about the details of that conversation.[2]

The next meeting of the conference, arranged by the mediators for June 17,[3] was opened by Virmond and Talman with a declaration on behalf of the Prince that the Imperial army was ready to resume operations; and that they desired to know whether it was war or peace. They called on the Turkish representatives to declare whether, without applying for new instructions, they were empowered to concede the demands which could be made on the basis of the *uti possidetis*, as understood by them. This had been conceded by the Turks long ago, and it was only the arbitrary interpretation put upon it by the Austrians that had caused the difficulties. But these were manœuvres to cover up the Austrian retreat. The Turks did not at first see through them, and, suspicious of the Austrians, asked for a clear statement of their demands. Besides what the Turks had previously conceded, the Austrians demanded the Bosnian fortresses of Novi and Bihatch, both still in Turkish possession; but dropped the demand on meeting with a firm refusal from the Turks. Next, the Austrians advanced the equally futile demand for the whole of Vallachia and Moldavia; again the Turks refused—these provinces had long been theirs. The Austrians acquiesced, but now insisted on the cession of the territory west of the Aluta, called Little Vallachia. Although this was in possession of the Emperor, and therefore due to him on the basis of the *uti possidetis*, the Turks resisted for some time, and finished by demanding two days for consideration. They yielded in the conference of June 19. The limit was now reached of Turkish concessions. Sir Robert Sutton, who had supported the Austrians in their last demand (and had encountered many difficulties in settling various minor problems), thought this the crisis of the negotiations:

[1] Prince Eugene's report to the Emperor, Belgrade, June 20, 1718, *Feldzüge*, vol. ii. S. 8, Suppl. No. 209.

[2] Sutton in his letter to St. Saphorin, on June 17, 1718 (Han. Arch.), merely reports that the conversation had taken place; while his report of the meeting on June 17 shows that he was as little prepared for the opening chosen by the Imperial Envoys as were the Turks, though the Envoys acted in the manner agreed upon with Prince Eugene; cf. *Feldzüge*, vol. ii. S. 8, pp. 364-5.

[3] Sutton to St. Saphorin, June 17, 1718, Han. Arch.; *Feldzüge*, p. 365.

"I have pulled the rope so hard that I have very nearly strangled them and my strength is exhausted".[1] Everything depended on the Emperor; the Turks could not be expected to go any further—"for by now we have got the bowels and soul out of their body".

But Virmond and Talman were able to declare themselves satisfied with the Turkish concessions, for the points set out as indispensable by Prince Eugene had been secured. His conquests now remained to the Emperor: Temesvar and Belgrade—the key of the Balkans—Serbia and Little Vallachia, and the line of the Save. The territorial gains made by Charles VI in his first Turkish War could compare with those of the War of the Spanish Succession.

No serious difficulties arose in the further conferences, though on one occasion the Turks, having received fresh instructions, tried to go back on some of the concessions which they had made with regard to Bosnia. But Prince Eugene, who was in the neighbourhood, made his influence felt, and the mediating Powers also declared that concessions once made could not be withdrawn.[2]

Meantime, on June 16, Sir Robert Sutton had opened the Peace Conference[3] between Venice and Turkey, and in a short time managed to bring it to a conclusion acceptable to the Republic. Morea remained in the possession of the Sultan; and though the Grand Vizier would not hear of compensations for the despised Venetians—only of small favours[4]—in the end they received lenient treatment.[5] It was no mere boast on the part of the Turks when they declared that nothing but regard for the Emperor had made them negotiate with the Venetians. Stanyan, who was with the Grand Vizier at Sofia, preferred not to repeat the terms in which the latter spoke of that ancient republic. "They should kiss the hands and feet of the Emperor", he wrote to St. Saphorin, "for having been admitted to the peace negotiations. Otherwise they would have been destroyed by the Turks."

The two peace treaties were signed on July 21, 1718. As at the opening of the Congress, the Plenipotentiaries proceeded to the conference tent in splendid array, and entered it simultaneously. The

[1] Sutton to St. Saphorin, June 20, 1718, Han. Arch.
[2] Hammer, *Geschichte*, vii. p. 233; *Feldzüge*, ii. S. 8, p. 369; Sutton to St. Saphorin, July 11, 1718, Han. Arch.
[3] Same to same, June 17, 1718.
[4] Stanyan to St. Saphorin, Sofia, July 1, 1718, Han. Arch.
[5] Cf. *Feldzüge*, ii. S. 8, pp. 377-8.

Venetian Envoy now accompanied the Imperial Plenipotentiaries. After all had signed, "the Plenipotentiaries embraced one another tenderly, and kissed as a sign of peace". A banquet with speeches was held in the afternoon, and an ox was roasted for the crowd, while a fountain "estimated at 25 buckets" supplied red and white wine. Six days later a commercial treaty was signed near Passarovitz between Austria and Turkey, the first between them; but it was thought that the Maritime Powers would grudge the Emperor the advantages of such a treaty, and it was negotiated with the Turks direct.

Besides Prince Eugene, who had directed the Imperial diplomats at the Congress, Sir Robert Sutton had the chief merit of the success; he had done his work to the satisfaction of all the parties. The Dutch Envoy, who had for some time been prevented by illness from assisting in the negotiations, had played a very subordinate part. Sutton would not share the *kudos* even with his colleague Stanyan, who was not popular at Vienna, and was slow and clumsy in transacting business. Even with the Grand Vizier he had done little to promote the negotiations, however much he afterwards endeavoured to place his achievements in the most favourable light; Sutton had done his best to keep him away from Passarovitz. Stanyan repeatedly complained about it to St. Saphorin, but received the reply that whoever is successful is considered to have been in the right. Finally, he was not even given the satisfaction of being mentioned in the Treaty as a mediator, together with Sutton and Colyer. But what pained him most was that on the conclusion of the Treaty Sir Robert received from the Sultan, the Emperor, and the Republic of Venice, the customary rewards in money and gifts, while he received nothing; and he seems to have failed to obtain a division of the presents.[1]

The Emperor had no reason to complain of the British mediation; his anxiety and suspicions had proved unjustified. The terms of the Treaty fully answered the results of the campaign and the frontiers of the Habsburg Empire now extended into the Balkan peninsula. Had Austria later on proved equally successful in war, she might have solved the Eastern Question on her own, and driven out the Turks from Europe; for as yet Russia's influence was insignificant in those regions. It seemed the mission of the House of Austria to

[1] Stanyan to St. Saphorin, July 1, 31, Sept. 27, Nov. 30, 1718; Stanyan to Craggs, n.d. (about beginning of September); St. Saphorin to Stanyan, Aug. 3, Sept. 3, 1718, Han. Arch., *Feldzüge*, ii. S. 8, pp. 338-9.

liberate the Christian nations of the Balkans, to spread Western civilization, and organize the economic forces of those countries, impoverished by Turkish misrule. Such an extension of Austrian power would have been of first-rate importance for Germany. But no general like Prince Eugene commanded the Austrian armies in later years, and most of the conquests of 1717 were lost in the next war against Turkey.

In 1718 the Emperor would have been less inclined to peace with Turkey had it not been for the Spanish attack—early that year several regiments had been recalled from Hungary for service in Italy; [1] and after the peace of Passarovitz Charles VI wrote to Prince Eugene: "Thank God that this peace has been concluded, and has freed our hands; this will enable us to give the proper reply to those who provoke us".[2] As for Great Britain, the aims of the Quadruple Alliance, and not the acquisition of some Turkish fortresses for Austria, were her concern: the Spanish plans of conquest must be foiled and Alberoni's hopes frustrated. To prevent the conclusion of the peace, the Spanish Ambassador at Constantinople had promised rich subsidies and a close alliance between Spain and Turkey. Now Alberoni had to face the formidable, united forces of the Quadruple Alliance.

Within a few weeks Great Britain had scored three signal successes: the Turkish war was concluded, the Quadruple Alliance formed, and a naval victory won off Passaro. She was at the head of a peace league, the mediator between contending nations. At that moment George I attained the zenith of his power.

[1] *Feldzüge*, ii. S. 8, p. 284.   [2] *Ibid.* p. 385.

APPENDIX

In the letters reproduced below the spelling has been modernized and misspellings of names have been corrected.

No. 1

THE BRITISH CIVIL LIST AND THE GERMAN COURT IN LONDON

Bothmer to Goertz. (Stowe MSS. 227, f. 393)

Extrait de ma lettre à Mr A. B. de Goertz, Londres, $\dfrac{\text{le 27. août}}{\text{7. sept.}}$ 1714

Je vous supplie de ne pas songer à mettre le payement de vos tables ou aucune autre dépense pour la cour que vous amenez, sur la liste civile d'ici, cela serait indirectement contre la loi qui exclut les étrangers des charges et émoluments d'ici, et bien loin d'espérer pour l'avenir un adoucissement à cette loi, une telle prétention aigrirait les esprits et ferait naître la pensée de la rendre encore plus forte, voyant que nous prétendons l'éluder comme la France élude ses traités.

Si le roi paye de ses finances d'Hanovre toute sa cour qu'il en amène, cela lui fera un bien infini dans l'esprit et dans le cœur de la nation, cela montrera son désintéressement, sa générosité, sa droiture et son bon ordre en toute chose. La seule proposition de mettre cette dépense sur la liste civile lui ôterait non seulement cet avantage et donnerait de lui une idée tout à fait opposée, mais causerait encore de grandes difficultés auprès du Parlement prochain, pour l'augmentation de cette liste civile, que sans un tel contretemps on a lieu d'espérer aussi bien que l'adoucissement de la loi dont je viens de parler. On peut être assuré outre cela, que cette prétention d'entretenir ici aux dépens de l'Angleterre notre cour d'Hanovre ne sera point accordée, et au lieu d'attribuer alors à la générosité du Roi, qu'il fait cette dépense de ses finances électorales, on l'attribuera uniquement au refus d'ici. Comme vous répondez vous-même à l'argument tiré des coûtumes de la cour de France, je n'ai plus rien à dire là-dessus, vous jugerez bien aussi qu'on ne serait pas bien venu auprès des Anglais de leur alléguer un exemple français pour l'imiter.

Je me flatte que vous trouverez mes raisons si bonnes, qu'on ne parlera jamais de cette proposition.

No. 2

BONET'S DESCRIPTION OF THE BRITISH COURT AFTER THE ACCESSION OF GEORGE I

A Londres ce vendredi $\frac{24.\ déc.\ 1714}{4.\ jan.\ 1715}$

Comme j'ai tâché de ne rien omettre dans mes relations de ce qui peut influer sur les affaires d'État, j'apporterai à présent la même attention pour satisfaire à l'ordre qui m'a été donné de marquer le petit détail de cette nouvelle cour.

On ne peut dire qu'elle soit fertile en intrigues, sauf celles qui regardent les charges, et qui ont été assoupies dès qu'elles ont été conférées, les Torys en ayant pour ainsi dire été exclus dès le commencement, les brigues à la cour ont été l'occupation des Whigs, comme elles ont été la tâche des Torys dans les provinces pour les élections, afin de faire le dernier effort en parlement pour renverser tout le ministère, et tout le plan que Sa Majesté a formé.

On est tombé dans un écueil à l'égard de l'un et l'autre parti. On a trop affecté d'éloignement pour les Torys, et on n'a pas fait à tous égards un assez grand choix des Whigs. L'alliage de ces deux partis est effectivement difficile, mais bien des gens ont été surpris de ce qu'on a refusé au chevalier baronnet Thomas Hanmer, époux de la duchesse douairière de Grafton, la place d'un des lords de la chambre du lit du roi qu'il recherchait, sous couleur que ces places n'ont jamais été données qu'à des lords, mais comme il est de meilleure famille que plusieurs d'entre eux, qu'il a un air revenant, poli, qu'il est bel esprit, et grand orateur, et qu'il a surtout un grand parti parmi les Torys, tous ceux-ci ont participé à son mécontentement, et ont jugé que la cour avait peu de confiance en eux, puisqu'elle rebutait un homme de ce rang. Ce préjugé s'est beacoup fortifié par la manière dont on a usé envers le duc d'Ormond: Il est vrai que sa grande naissance, et un certain port noble fait son plus bel apanage, mais il est populaire, très considéré par l'université d'Oxford dont il est chancelier, et l'homme qui entend le mieux à faire les honneurs d'une cour; cependant, sans réfléchir sur ces choses on l'a dépouillé généralement de tous ses emplois pour en revêtir le duc de Marlborough qui est estimé, mais non aimé; et par là la cour s'est attiré à dos les Torys, le peuple qui aime le premier de ces ducs, cette formidable université, et par-dessus tout le clergé, qui est un corps composé de gens plus attachés en bonne partie à l'épiscopat et à l'écorce de la religion qu'à la religion même, et qui par cette raison ne se faisait pas un épouvantail du prétendant. Cette corruption leur donne un penchant pour l'église romaine, et un éloignement pour les églises gouvernées par presbytères, en tant qu'ils regardent celle-là comme une église régie par des évêques, qu'ils disent être successeurs des apôtres, et les presbytériens comme des laïques, qui n'ont aucune légitime mission que celle qu'eux et leurs prédécesseurs se sont arrogée; d'où vient que les outrés d'entr'eux ne les croyaient pas en droit d'administrer les sacrements, ni ne croient celui qu'ils administrent valide. Selon leur système quiconque n'est pas batisé par un ministre ordiné par un évêque n'est pas chrétien, ce qui a porté un ministre rigide de l'église anglicane de dire, que si c'était de son département d'officier dans la chapelle royale, il ne savait s'il pourrait donner la communion au roi.

. . . Si les Torys trouvent que le roi a peu gardé de ménagements pour eux, qui sont plus considérables en fonds de terre que les Whigs, ceux-ci n'applaudissent pas non plus en tout au choix que Sa Majesté a fait de ses officiers. Et on ne peut disconvenir que, les grandes charges exceptées, la brigue n'ait eu plus de part que le mérite dans la distribution qu'on en a faite; on en a gratifié des gens de médiocres talents, tandis qu'on en a laissé qui leur sont fort supérieurs, et qui avaient rendu des services réels à la succession.

On excuse cependant assez facilement cette conduite, parce que le roi ne pouvait connaître toutes ces personnes par lui-même, et qu'il y a bien des considérations qui ballancent souvent la différence du mérite de l'un à un autre. Mais on taxe de faiblesse cette multitude de charges conférées à une seule personne, ou à une seule famille qui prive Sa Majesté de se faire beaucoup de créatures, qui donne de la jalousie, et qui ouvre la porte à ceux d'un ordre inférieur de former de pareilles prétentions ou de faire les mécontents. Celui qui a été le plus ardent à en accumuler est le duc de Marlborough, qui n'a que son mérite personnel, et peu de crédit dans le pays à cause de son insatiable avarice, qui rend ses richesses, et même son amitié et ses bons offices inutiles à la société, parce que les premières sont ensevelies, et qu'il ne donne l'autre qu'à prix d'argent. Le roi voyant qu'il lui était impossible d'assouvir son avidité lui en fit un reproche adroit; Sa Majesté lui demanda un jour, si l'archevêque de Cantorbéry n'avait point de parents. Le duc répondit qu'il en avait. Je m'en étonne, reprit le roi, il a passé deux heures avec moi, sans me rien demander pour aucun. Le duc sentit cela, et devint plus modéré et plus retenu; en effet ce prélat qui, comme un bon Siméon attendait la délivrance de son église, en a soutenu les droits avec une fermeté exemplaire; et quoiqu'il soit le primat du royaume, qu'en ce poste il ait été en état de rendre de grands services, il a montré qu'il servait par devoir, pour le bien de la cause et non par intérêt.

On est aussi enclin à croire que le roi a manqué de prévoyance quand il conféra d'abord toutes les grandes charges aux premières têtes des Whigs, non que ce choix n'ait un bon côté, mais de ce que leur capacité est si supérieure que Sa Majesté s'est mise dans une dépendance d'eux, et qu'il ne connaît les choses que par eux; au lieu que s'il avait conféré quelques unes des charges en chef aux Torys, il aurait été mieux éclairé des affaires, et il aurait tenu en respect les uns par les autres.

La ressource qui reste au roi est celle de pouvoir passer d'un parti à un autre, mais ce serait un fâcheux expédient, qui lui serait autant pernicieux que déshonorable, surtout dans les commencements et vu l'âge mûr de Sa Majesté.

.   .   .   .   .

Sans contredit le roi serait plus maître, s'il possédait mieux les affaires de ce pays, et s'il en entendait la langue. Mais le défaut de connaissance de l'un et de l'autre contribuent encore à le rendre dépendant. Il ne peut conférer qu'avec ceux qui parlent français, et il y a d'excellentes têtes, comme celles du grand-chancelier, du baron de Somers, du grand juge Parker, du S^r. Walpole etc. qui ne l'entendent point, ce dont d'autres profitent.

C'est jusqu'à présent un secret que la première connaissance de toutes les affaires vient aux ministres d'État de Bernstorff et de Bothmer, mais il est incertain jusqu'où on s'en accommodera dans la suite, quand le fait sera connu: sans s'en embarrasser tous les soirs le duc de Marlborough et milord Townshend se rendent, à la faveur de la nuit, chez le dernier, et ce quadrumvirat règle tout. Le baron de Goertz, quoique voisin, n'y est jamais admis; ces deux ministres allemands ne confèrent aussi jamais avec lui sur les affaires du nord, parce qu'il est très-contraire au plan projeté sur ce sujet. L'opposition entr'eux va plus loin, tous les Torys recherchent son amitié, et tous les Whigs le regardent comme suspect, et s'attachent aux deux autres pour qui on a généralement plus de considération et d'estime.

Cette ignorance de la langue et des affaires, qui donne lieu à ces conférences nocturnes, n'a pas permis au roi d'abolir un conseil que l'ignorance des affaires dans le chef a introduit sous le règne précédent. Je veux parler du comité du conseil du cabinet, composé des principaux officiers, qui s'assemblent en l'absence du roi, et qui minutent toutes choses, pour rendre compte ensuite du résultat à Sa Majesté en conseil. Cette nécessité où Sa Majesté est de continuer ce conseil le prive d'une infinité de lumières, ne lui fait voir que l'écorce de plusieurs affaires, et confère un grand pouvoir à ses ministres.

Le comte de Nottingham se trouve d'ailleurs fort embarrassé par cette ignorance de la langue, en ce qu'il est obligé par sa charge de président de conseil de rendre à Sa Majesté compte des matières qui s'y agitent, et qu'il est très difficile de trouver toujours sur le champ des termes propres pour expliquer chaque chose, ou les lois du pays qui en sont la règle. Cela fait que Sa Majesté donne souvent son consentement à des choses qu'il n'entend pas bien, et dont il ne comprend pas toutes les raisons.

Il y a encore d'autres inconvénients qui naissent de cette ignorance de la langue. Celui de ne pouvoir converser avec ses sujets des provinces dans l'occasion, point essentiel pour se faire aimer. Celui de se servir de ses ministres pour entendre les requêtes de ses sujets et pour leur répondre. Celui de devoir se servir de la bouche du grand chancelier pour s'expliquer à sa nation assemblée en parlement. Celui de ne pouvoir lire dans leur original les lois qui comprennent les constitutions du royaume, ni les livres et les histoires qui par des exemples et des préceptes enseignent l'art de règner.

Nonobstant cette ignorance de l'anglais, on assujettit le roi à ne fréquenter que sa chapelle anglaise. Sa Majesté s'y rend tous les dimanches matin, mais sans pouvoir entendre que très-peu de la liturgie, et beaucoup moins du sermon. Le comte de Nottingham, homme dévot, attaché à sa religion, voulait bien que le roi se conformât en toutes choses aux rites de l'église anglicane, mais qu'il se servît de ministres allemands ou français, qui seraient ordinés par des évêques, et qui suivissent exactement l'usage établi par les canons, mais son sentiment n'a pas prévalu.

La maxime des rois d'Angleterre a été d'être en exemple de piété; d'avoir les prières soir et matin faites par un chapelain, de faire bénir les viandes aussi par un chapelain, d'aller tous les dimanches et toutes les grandes fêtes à l'église, de communier tous les mois; la feue reine observait fort régulièrement tous ces devoirs, cela lui attirait le respect de ses sujets, et le roi Charles deux qui n'était rien moins que bigot, faisait par politique ce que d'autres faisaient par piété; mais les rigides Anglais se plaignent de ce que le roi se contente d'assister une fois par semaine au service divin; de ce que ses chapelains sont sans fonction, de ce que le prince de Galles ne pousse pas plus loin la dévotion; mais ils se louent de la princesse qui se rend régulièrement tous les matins à la chapelle à l'heure de la prière, quoiqu'elle s'en absente le soir.

C'est aussi celle des trois qui gagne le plus dans l'esprit du peuple par le soin qu'elle a de parler sa langue, quoiqu'elle ne la parle pas fort correctement, cependant, comme elle n'en est pas fort maîtresse, non plus que le roi et le prince, le théâtre commence à changer de nature. Pour divertir Sa Majesté et Leurs Altesses Royales, on néglige les pièces ingénieuses pour donner dans le spectacle, dans les machines, dans les dances, les décorations, les farces, et autres choses qui récréent plus les sens que l'esprit.

Mais si le roi a le malheur de ne pas parler l'anglais, on l'excuse sur son âge, et sur ses affaires, et son bon esprit rectifie bien des choses. D'ailleurs il se familiarise d'une autre manière par la coutume qu'il a d'aller presque tous les soirs sans bruit ou à l'opéra, ou à la comédie, ou en quelque maison particulière où sont quelques dames, dont madame de Kielmannsegge est toujours du nombre, et quelques hommes. Là il joue à petit jeu à l'hombre, il y soupe, et il s'y comporte avec une douceur, une affabilité, et une grâce qui ne gêne personne, et par ce moyen Sa Majesté apprend bien des choses, Elle se récrée, et Elle se fait des amis, mais cela l'a aussi engagé à accorder des charges à des gens qu'on n'en croit pas les plus dignes.

Tandis que le roi va d'un côté, le prince va d'un autre pour y jouer et y souper, mais jamais avec Sa Majesté. La princesse qui reste seule, tient cercle lorsqu'elle ne va pas à l'opéra ou à la comédie, et reçoit très-obligeamment le monde à sa cour. Elle ne joue à la bassette que par complaisance, et dès qu'elle a mis une compagnie en train, elle la quitte pour aller jouer au piquet dans une autre chambre: et si le roi et le prince ne sont pas de quelques soupers particuliers, ils se rendent pour une demie heure, ou une heure au cercle de madame la princesse, mais sans s'y asseoir, ni y jouer. Une chose en quoi elle ne consultait pas le génie de la nation, et qu'elle s'éloignait de sa bonté naturelle, est que trouvant sa cour mêlée de dames de tout ordre, elle voulait n'y recevoir que les dames titrées, mais le roi s'y est opposé, parce que ce serait offenser toute la chambre basse, et toute la petite noblesse du pays qui fait le gros de la nation, et qui souvent ne le cède pas en antiquité à celle qui est titrée.

La vivacité de madame la princesse plait aux dames, et est bien reçue des hommes; mais celle du prince ne quadre pas assez avec le phlegme anglais, pour avoir le même applaudissement. On voudrait aussi qu'il s'attachât plus à l'anglais et aux affaires qu'il ne fait; d'ailleurs on rend justice à ses autres bonnes qualités, surtout à l'attachement qu'il a pour la princesse son épouse, à une certaine franchise et liberté d'esprit avec laquelle il s'exprime, et à la bonté qu'il a de tenir cour tous les jours pendant une demie heure avant dîner.

Le prince et la princesse ont ainsi leurs jours de cour réglés, mais le roi n'en a encore aucun. On ne le voit ni à son lever, ni à son dîner, ni à son souper, ni à son coucher. Seulement pendant quelques minutes à son retour de la chapelle, et cela en s'arrêtant dans un passage de chambre bordé de part et d'autre d'une double haie de courtisans qui le touchent de tous côtés, en sorte qu'il n'y a pas dix personnes de qui il remarque les visages, et à qui il peut parler. Au lieu que sous les règnes précédents, le roi ou reine se rendaient vers la cheminée, là on faisait un grand demi-cercle devant eux, qui donnait lieu à ces princes d'être vus et de voir beaucoup plus de monde.

Comme Sa Majesté ne paraît point en public, on ne lui parle point d'affaires que dans une audience formelle, après y avoir préparé le secrétaire d'État, et avoir fait avertir le maître des cérémonies. Et cette retraite que la nature des affaires présentes fait tolérer, ne serait pas bien prise dans un autre temps.

La coutume que le roi a constamment observé de manger seul avec ses deux Turcs, sans se faire servir à genoux par les lords de la Chambre du lit, et de manger dans la même Chambre ou il couche, et d'aller toujours sans le prince partout où il va, de ne se parler presque jamais, du moins en public, même de se placer à la comédie dans une loge différente de celle de Leurs Altesses Royales, fait soupçonner s'il n'y a point quelque froideur entre le père et le fils.

Mais ce qui choque plus que tout, ce sont les grandes familiarités que la duchesse de Shrewsbury, dame italienne et dont la réputation n'est pas des mieux établie, affecte de prendre avec le roi en public et en particulier. Comme cette dame est sur le retour, on ne la taxe pas de galanterie, mais tout le monde observe qu'elle ne veut manger que ce que le roi touche, ou que des plats dont on le sert; qu'elle lui parle avec plus de hardiesse que de respect; et on ne fut pas peu surpris qu'elle fit venir un soir à la comédie dans sa loge, où était le roi, la chanteuse Sanclos, en ses habits de théâtre, et lui mettant la main sur le sein, lui dit devant bien des témoins, voilà, Sire, une belle gorge. Les familiarités de cette duchesse donnent beaucoup à penser, mais on ne s'explique pas davantage.

Il y a encore à remarquer que le roi a des maximes toutes différentes de ses prédécesseurs, et même du roi Guillaume qui était étranger comme Sa Majesté. Elle a choisi ses officiers d'entre les Anglais, chacun se rend à la cour, quand il est de semaine, mais pas un n'en fait les fonctions, comme s'ils n'étaient nommés que pour la forme, et pour avoir des appointements. Il ne se fait servir que par ses officiers allemands, et surtout ses deux Turcs, à l'habit desquels on est si peu accoutumé que le peuple les croit encore mahométans, et s'offense de les voir à la cour. Il est vrai qu'aucun des Allemands n'est sur l'état de la Grande-Bretagne, que ce sont les Anglais seuls, mais s'il se confiait entièrement en ceux-ci, et s'il ne se servait que d'eux, la liaison serait plus grande entre le chef et les membres. Le prince en use à peu près de même, mais madame la princesse se sert des femmes de chambre anglaises, ce qui la fait aimer.

Sa Majesté a sa maison et celle de Leurs Altesses Royales fort remplie d'officiers, mais Elle n'a point voulu avoir de premier lord de la chambre du lit, afin que la grande assiduité de cet officier ne lui fût pas un espion incommode. Et Elle n'a point non plus nommé de trésorier de la bourse-privée, où il entre 26,000 £ par an, afin qu'on n'entrât pas si aisément dans ses secrètes dépenses ou épargnes; le baron de Bothmer en fait secrètement la charge.

Tout le monde convient que le roi est un prince d'ordre et fort économe. Cependant il paye le logement, et il donne une subsistance à tous ses officiers allemands, et cela d'une manière convenable à leurs postes, et à la cherté de ce pays, ce qui va assez loin toutes les semaines.

La dépense de la maison de Sa Majesté est à quelques égards du triple plus forte que celle de la feue reine. Elle ne dépensait par exemple que 6 à 7 £ par jour en bougie, et on en dépense à présent pour vingt livres. Les tables de la reine revenaient à 26 et 27 £ par jour sans le vin, celles du roi vont à 82 et 83 aussi sans le vin. Il en sera bientôt de même de la dépense des écuries. Enfin la dépense va si loin que, le comte de Halifax a compté que celle de cette année, y compris les frais du deuil, de l'enterrement de la feue reine, et du couronnement du roi, ira à 900,000 £ et cependant les revenus qui lui sont assignés pour soutenir le gouvernement civil, sont les mêmes que ceux de cette princesse, et ces

2 B

revenus n'ont monté pendant les 10 premières années de son règne qu'à 590,999. 6. 4 sterling par an, et les trois dernières années qu'à 549,215. 10. 9, une année portant l'autre. Elle n'avait point d'apanage à donner, et cependant Elle s'était endettée de 5 à 600,000 £ pour l'acquit desquelles on a fait une lotterie, mais pour le paiement de laquelle il faut lever annuellement 35,000 £ des plus clairs revenus de cet état civil. Il est encore vrai qu'il y a sur cet état pour 130,000 £ sterling par an de pensions, sur lesquelles le roi ne s'est pas encore expliqué.

No. 3

BONET'S REPORT ABOUT GEORGE I AND HIS COURT

Written in the summer of 1716. (Prussian State Archives)

[The following, very outspoken, account was probably written at the express request of the King and Queen of Prussia, who expected shortly to meet George I on the Continent. Ultimately, for political reasons, the meeting did not take place.]

A Londres ce mardi $\frac{17.}{28.}$ juillet 1716

Réflexions diverses sur le roi et la maison royale

Sire,

Je vois par le rescrit de Votre Majesté du 7e de ce mois que ceux-là ont fort grossi les objets qui ont prétendu que le prince de Galles s'était entièrement jeté dans le parti des Torys et qu'il se détachait des Whigs. Ceux-là n'ont pas même considéré qu'il n'a ni la liberté ni la disposition d'esprit à cela.

Il n'en a pas la liberté, parce qu'il doit être soumis au roi et rapporter tout à lui comme au centre: qu'on étudie de plus près sa conduite que celle d'un sujet d'un rang inférieur: Et s'il ne peut avoir pas même un valet de pied que de l'agrément de S. Maj.; on lui permettrait bien moins de prendre un parti contraire aux mesures du roi.

Mais S. A. R. n'est pas portée de cet esprit, je ne lui ai jamais ouï parler des affaires d'État, ce qui est arrivé fort souvent, qu'avec la déférence due. Elle est assez éclairée sur les sentiments des Torys rigides, pour savoir que la mortification de n'avoir pas les emplois les a jeté dans le mécontentement, dans le murmure, dans la rébellion. Ces rigides ne pardonnent pas au prince sa vivacité, ni ce qu'ils appellent emportement en lui, ils l'aiment, disent-ils, bien moins que le roi; et ils sont irrités de ce qu'en parlant des Whigs, il dit nos amis, ce qu'ils regardent comme une réflexion contre eux-mêmes, et ce qu'ils ne croyent pas convenir à un prince de son rang.

Il est vrai qu'il y a une froideur manifeste entre le roi et le prince;

ils ne se parlent pas l'un à l'autre; ils ne se sont jamais rendu dans les appartements l'un de l'autre; ils n'ont jamais mangé ensemble; ils n'ont jamais été ensemble ni dans des maisons royales ou particulières, ni dans des promenades, ni à la chasse, mais seulement au conseil, à la chapelle, et le soir au cercle de madame la princesse, sans se parler: Mais il faut que cette froideur soit antérieure à leur arrivée en ce royaume, n'étant rien survenu ici qui ait pu les causer.

.   .   .   .   .   .

Ce qui les a fortifiés dans ce préjugé est le genre de vie que le roi a mené pendant les 22 mois qu'il a été ici, différent de celui des rois ses prédécesseurs, et de celui qu'il menait lui-même à Hanovre.

Renfermé dans son palais de St. James, ou pour mieux dire dans une chambre et un cabinet, les autres appartements étant pour les courtisans, S. M. n'en est point sortie pour aller à Kensington, à Hampton Court, ou à Windsor, qui sont spatieux, plus commodes, et qui ont un air plus royal. Dans cette chambre Elle couchait et Elle mangeait, et dans le cabinet voisin Elle donnait des audiences. Elle ne s'est fait point de plan pour destiner certains jours aux affaires, et d'autres à la récréation, et à l'examen de ce qu'on lui représentait dans ces audiences.

Elle avait établi des seigneurs pour gentilhommes de la chambre du lit, qui auraient dû la servir à table, et d'autres gentilhommes inférieurs pour l'habiller, mais Elle n'a voulu recevoir ces services ni des uns ni des autres, et Elle n'a voulu les recevoir que de ses Turcs, et de ses valets de chambre allemands.

Elle restait seule tous les matins dans cette chambre jusqu'à midi qu'elle passait dans le cabinet pour y donner des audiences à ses ministres d'État des deux nations jusqu'à deux heures, qu'Elle se mettait à table pour dîner; après le dîner Elle se promenait seule dans le jardin de St. James, où Elle se rendait chez la duchesse de Munster, et le soir au cercle de madame la princesse, jusqu'à minuit, ou bien à l'opéra où Elle se rendait dans une chaise de louage incognito dans une loge particulière; ou chez madame de Kielmansegge, ou bien Elle soupait avec le grand maréchal, l'abbé Conti etc. et il arrivait très-rarement que ses ministres d'État lui parlassent les après-dîners.

Pendant un temps S. M. a soupé chez quelques seigneurs anglais, Elle s'y rendait toujours dans une chaise de louage, mais ceux qu'Elle honorait de Sa présence songeaient plus à obliger leurs amis, qu'à chercher une compagnie agréable à S. M., et rarement ils La laissaient sortir sans en avoir obtenu quelque grâce.

Les affaires dont ses ministres anglais l'entretenaient dans les audiences journalières roulaient sur des disputes de parti, sur leurs intérêts ou ceux de leurs amis, sur la rébellion, sur des lois et coutumes, ou sur des personnes inconnues à Sa Maj., ce qui leur a donné l'occasion d'exercer une grande autorité, sans être beaucoup contrôlés, parce que le roi se confiait en eux. Dans la distribution qu'ils ont faite des emplois, ils ont apporté une particulière attention à avancer leurs proches, leurs amis, ceux de leur parti, et lorsque ces avancements se sont trouvés en opposition avec ceux que le roi leur recommandait, ils ont trouvé moyen d'éluder les prétentions de ceux qui voulaient parvenir aux emplois par un autre canal que le leur.

. . . . . .

Ce qui a encore fait penser que le roi avait plus d'affection pour son électorat que pour son royaume, est le soin qu'il prend que le prince Frédéric, qu'on souhaiterait fort ici, soit élevé à Hanovre pour y attacher son coeur et ses inclinations dès sa jeunesse, et qu'on n'a songé d'envoyer quelqu'un pour lui apprendre l'anglais qu'à présent. Ce qui a fait dire à quelques uns qu'ils seront toujours sous la domination d'étrangers, qui ne parleront jamais bien leur langue, et qui ne connaîtront jamais la constitution du royaume.

. . . . . .

Ils font une autre plainte, ils disent qu'il manque à la cour une certaine gravité et majesté, ou un certain caractère de grandeur et de supériorité qui fait révérer les puissances souveraines. Ils approuvent la douceur et la grâce répandues dans les manières du roi, du prince et de la princesse, mais ils voudraient qu'elles fussent tempérées d'une certaine reserve. Ils trouvent par exemple que le roi Guillaume savait mieux inspirer du respect et garder son rang que le roi George; et les dames disent qu'elles se trouvaient plus honorées d'un mot que leur disait la reine Anne avec son air de grandeur, que de tous les longs et affables discours que leur tient madame la princesse.

Une chose, ajoutent ces mêmes Anglais, ramenerait bien des gens, c'est si le roi entreprenait quelque chose de populaire, qu'il fît par exemple quelque bâtiment public pour sa propre commodité à St. James's et qu'il laissât quelque monument pour montrer qu'il aime et nous et notre pays: qu'il se communiquât à ses sujets: qu'il mangeât en public: qu'il voyageât dans les provinces: et qu'il se conformât à notre génie, qui est d'amasser de l'argent pour le dépenser. On connaîtrait par là, disent-ils, le caractère du roi, bien mieux que par les alliances et les affaires que ses ministres traitent avec les cours étrangères. . . . Telle est la liberté avec laquelle on s'explique par deçà.

No. 4

TWO LETTERS FROM CRAGGS TO BYNG, WITH ORDERS TO DESTROY THE SPANISH FLEET

Enclosed in French translation in Pendtenriedter's report of August 9, 1718. (Vienna Archives)

1. WHITEHALL, 2/13. July 1718.

. . . Pour cet effet, vous ne perdrez aucune occasion de trouver les Espagnols, de vous jeter parmi eux et les joindre, afin de prévenir, autant qu'il sera possible, qu'ils ne commettent aucunes hostilités, qu'ils ne fassent aucune descente ou n'entreprennent aucune chose qui puisse donner atteinte au repos public et rendre les bonnes intentions de S. M., pour accommoder les affaires, impraticables et sans effet. Vous suivrez de près et à la vigueur vos instructions et observerez soigneusement les moyens qui y sont prescrits pour tenir en bride les Espagnols et les détourner d'aucune entreprise qui doit naturellement engager le reste de l'Europe dans une guerre.

2. WHITEHALL, 14/25. July 1718.

... si vous receviez les instructions d'attaquer la flotte espagnole, vous ne vous amuserez pas à commencer à prendre quelques vaisseaux simplement, mais, le premier coup que vous frapperez, vous tâcherez de détruire toute leur flotte, puisque la conséquence ne sera qu'égale à notre commerce à présent, et si on peut tout à fait supprimer leurs forces maritimes, les conséquences en seraient très avantageuses pour l'avenir, car il est très-évident, que s'ils augmentent leurs forces maritimes, notre commerce dans ces quartiers-là se perdra tout à fait avec le temps, aussi bien qu'en temps de guerre. (. . . noch einmal, falls er zu Feindseligkeiten schreite): vous tâcherez au premier coup que vous frapperez de détruire tout à la fois toute leur flotte.

GENERAL INDEX

ABERDEEN, accession rabble at, 59

Act of Attainder, against the Pretender, 4; against Ormonde and Bolingbroke, 129

Act for Encouraging Loyalty in Scotland, 155

Act for Enforcing the Laws against Papists, 214

Act giving land to those who refused to join the Jacobite Rising, 156

Act of Precedence, 12-13

Act of Regency, 4, 5, 9, 10, 28, 57

Act of Settlement, 2 *sqq.*, 57-8, 69; a suggested evasion of, 38, the Pretender's attitude to, 39; aliens debarred by, from place at Court, 103; infringements of, 106, 284-5, 287, 291; on the King's leaving the country, clause repealed, 220; on pardon after impeachment, 211; on the Regency Council, 53

Addison, Joseph, 59, 331

Ahlden, 80

Aislabie, John, 127

Alberoni, Cardinal Giulio, dominance of, in Spain, 269 *sqq.*, 275, 276, 278; British mistake regarding, 282-3, 339, 340; policy of, for Spain, 337, 352, and the attack on Sardinia, 338; difficulties with, 342; wrath of, at the Treaty of Quadruple Alliance, 353; and Stanhope, 356; hopes of, from the Austro-Turkish War, 358, 360

An Inquiry into the Miscarriages of the Four Last Years' Reign, Whig pamphlet, 116

Anglesea, Arthur (Annesley), Earl of, 57; on the peace (1714), 25-6; in George I's Privy Council, 101; on the effect of the impeachments, 130; loyal speech of, 145

Anglo-Austrian alliance, negotiation for a Treaty of, 235, 247-8, 254 *sqq.*; effect of, on Spain, 281; Holland's accession to, 326, why essential, 339; the vital words in, 256, 257, 258, 259; signature of, 259-60; ratification of, 237, 261, 313; English obligations under, how far acted upon, 338-9

Anglo-Dutch alliance, 116

Anglo-French alliance, Treaty of, desired by the French, 166, 203; delays in negotiations for, 321 *sqq.*; affairs in the North as affecting, 320 *sqq.*; Dutch accession to, 326; advantages of, to Britain, and to the Regent, 326-7, 332; "the true key" to, 333; Austrian view of, 332-3, 338

Anglo-French relations, 201, 204, 263

Anglo-Prussian negotiations (1714), 286; a Treaty of Guarantee proposed, 300-301

Anglo-Spanish Commercial Treaty, 22-3, 44, 45, 48; effect of, in France and Austria, 252, 279; history of, 266 *sqq.*; principal articles in, 277-8

Anglo-Spanish relations (*see also* Alberoni), 263 *sqq.*

Anglo-Swedish friendship in 1714, 286

Anjou, Duke of, *see* Philip V of Spain

Anne, Princess, daughter of George II, 87

Anne, Queen, 38, 102, 125, 126, 154; and the Protestant succession, 2 *sqq.*, 71; and her Hanoverian relations, 6, 8-9, 11, 13, 19, 30, 31, 33, 36, 41, her letters to them published, 47; and Marlborough, 10, 11; last years of, 11 *sqq.*, 20 *sqq.*; inclination of, towards the Pretender, 18, 19, 37, 38, 39, 45; appearance of, in 1713, 19; on the Treaty of Peace and Commerce with Spain and on the Succession, 22-3; Address to, asking for a Proclamation against the Pretender, 26, and her reply, 27; and her pension, 32; reply of, to George Lewis's memorandum, 35-6; letters to, from the Pretender,

383

INDEX TO APPENDIX

THE END